The Remembered and Forgotten Jewish World

The Remembered and Forgotten Jewish World

*Jewish Heritage in Europe
and the United States*

Daniel J. Walkowitz

RUTGERS UNIVERSITY PRESS
NEW BRUNSWICK, CAMDEN, AND NEWARK,
NEW JERSEY, AND LONDON

Library of Congress Cataloging-in-Publication Data

Names: Walkowitz, Daniel J., author.
Title: The remembered and forgotten Jewish world : Jewish heritage in Europe
 and the United States / Daniel J. Walkowitz.
Description: New Brunswick : Rutgers University Press, [2018] |
 Includes bibliographical references and index.
Identifiers: LCCN 2017059101| ISBN 9780813596075 (cloth : alk. paper) |
 ISBN 9780813596068 (pbk. : alk. paper)
Subjects: LCSH: Jews—Europe—History. | Jews—United States—History. |
 Jews—Travel—Europe. | Jews—Travel—United States. | Jewish socialists—History.
 | Public spaces—Europe. | Public spaces—United States. | Europe—Description
 and travel. | United States—Description and travel.
Classification: LCC DS135.E83 W35 2018 | DDC 940/.04924—dc23
LC record available at https://lccn.loc.gov/2017059101

A British Cataloging-in-Publication record for this book is available from the British Library.

♾ The paper used in this publication meets the requirements of the American National Standard for Information Sciences—Permanence of Paper for Printed Library Materials, ANSI Z39.48-1992.

www.rutgersuniversitypress.org

Manufactured in the United States of America

From the past for the future.

*For my grandmothers, Marian Tarnofsky Margel Bakker and
Chaia Lubertofsky Walkowitz*

—To my granddaughter, Lucy Turner-Walkowitz

Contents

Preface

Research often takes unexpected twists and turns. A project begins with one set of questions, but dead ends; unexpected paradoxes, and accidental discoveries take the research into unexpected places, often substantially refining the project. Such was the case with this book.

About a decade ago I attended a seminar at the Center for the Cold War at New York University's Tamiment Library to discuss a paper on postwar "Red" summer youth camps. The room was unusually crowded; the subject had attracted many old-timers—gray-haired men and women "of a certain age"—eager to revisit their youth. Although they looked old to me, they were my peers. Like me, they had attended legendary left-wing summer camps such as Camp Kinderland in Hopewell Junction, New York, and Wo-chi-ca (an abbreviation for Workers Children's Camp) in Port Murray, New Jersey, that had been organized by the International Workers Order (IWO), an adjunct of the Communist Party. Anticommunist political pressures forced Wo-chi-ca to close in 1951, and it merged with Camp Wyandot, a similarly interracial, coeducational camp based in Mt. Tremper in the Catskill Mountains. In 1952 and 1953 I was a camper at Wyandot for two memorable weeks each summer, until it also closed after an outbreak of polio.

The Tamiment seminar was reminiscence as well as analysis; one person after another spoke of how meaningful as a child it was to participate in a like-minded community for those weeks. Although organized by the Jewish order of the IWO, the interracial character of the two camps distinguished them—from one estimate 30 percent of the campers were either African American or Puerto Rican but most campers were Jewish and from communist or communist-leaning homes like mine.

Most of the seminar participants were white and Jewish. They grew up in New York City or in Jewish New York suburbs among many other Jews. This was not my experience. I was the only Jewish student in my high school graduating class of over 300. Yet all of us at the seminar remembered the camp as a safe space where we could "be ourselves," speak our mind, sing songs of peace and brotherhood, and in general, freely express the social views we heard at home. Indeed, if there were any constraints, it would have been from departing from camp values. But that was not my problem as a ten- or eleven-year-old. I dissembled in public and in school; at camp I remembered feeling I could speak freely.

After the Tamiment seminar, an increasing number of young scholars of the Cold War asked if I would share my experiences of camp, but also about what it was like to grow up in a communist household in a conservative suburban Republican town in North Jersey. Reflecting on this past, I began to envision an embryonic version of this project as The Secret Life of a Red Diaper Baby.

Initially, I set out to reconstruct what Irving Howe in his 1976 best seller called the World of Our Fathers [and mothers!—although I only much later came to appreciate the significance of that amendment], which I thought shaped my childhood. The memories of a few relatives who still lived provided some sketchy anecdotes and details of life before the twentieth century. Their accounts told me very little about my grandparents' generation or of their predecessors. What were the array of possibilities available to my grandparents, and to their parents and grandparents? How were decisions made about whom they married? What occupational and political choices could they have made; what led my paternal grandparents, Ida (Chaia) and Alexander (Zishe) Walkowitz, to become secular Jewish socialists and communists, but led my maternal grandparents, Marian and Kunie Mayer (Max) Margel, to think of themselves as apolitical? And what of their siblings and Orthodox ancestors: how did the world shape the choices they made or had made for them by others; what options did they have; what paths did they take?

During the next months, which stretched into years, I engaged in the highly popular pastime of family history. I began doing extensive genealogical research to identify the places where my ancestors had lived. Translation from one language to another complicated tracing the family. Walkowitz was probably Wolkowicz, and various relatives took on permutations of those spellings. In the late twentieth century, at least one American daughter simply became "Walker." But using online genealogical information I was able to trace over a thousand relatives scattered over eight generations back to the mid-eighteenth century in a series of central Polish and Galician villages and cities. Genealogical records, though, often did little more than hint at places from which they might have earlier come. For instance, Ida's family, the Lubertofskys, probably came from the Polish town of Lubartów. But over time, generations shortened or modified the name to Libert or Lubert. My maternal grandmother Marian Tarnofsky's family may well have come from Tarnów.

Frustrated by the limits of genealogical information, I flipped the project. Rather than a memoir, I decided to look for the remaining traces of lives that could be heard and seen in the present. What began as a personal quest became a larger interrogation of Jewish heritage tourism as remembered and forgotten. Relying on skill sets developed as a historian—albeit without expertise in Central and Eastern European history—I moved into ethnographic and library research. Gleaning what I could from local histories, I began to do tourism-related research that surveyed Jewish heritage tourism. The visits brought me back to a long-standing set of concerns I had with memory and history connected to public history and representations of the past in public spaces.[1] The research in several cities relied on interviews, advice, and path-breaking work done by former students, colleagues, and friends in Jewish public history sites and programs. In my analyses, I have strived to be transparent about my relationship to each of them.

I began with sites in present-day Poland and Ukraine personally connected to my immediate families' pre-emigrant past, hoping to get a sense of place, of signs of their lives in the urban environment. I then followed the paths of their immigration to London and New York, and continued my journey to a range of major heritage sites linked to varied postsocialist national histories and museum cultures of central and eastern European cities. In the end I sampled Jewish heritage tourism in eleven cities and two towns (small cities or towns that evoked images of *shtetlekh*) in eight countries.

Over the seven years I traveled, I continued to research the lives of my family using genealogical archives and public oral history collections. Near the end of my writing I rediscovered extensive oral interviews with an uncle and aunt that had been conducted in the 1980s and 1990s (ironically, by two of my own doctoral students) and some newer interviews with them I had not known. These interviews challenged the heroic images I had preserved about my communist paternal grandparents, Chaia and Zishe Walkowitz, whom I had thought of as models for "my secret life." The research and interviews raised important questions for me about the role of the Jewish family in radical politics and the heritage project. Sometimes research confirmed what I "knew"; sometimes, though, it challenged telling preconceptions I had brought to sites. The voyages of discovery thus took place at home, but also at new museums, such as POLIN Museum of the History of Polish Jews in Warsaw that opened its core exhibit in late October 2014. Weaving this personal history as "interludes" into each chapter, the book suggests the kinds of stories tourists bring to sites and then describes what I experienced and learned.

Writing can be a lonely enterprise, but it is done with the remarkable support of a collective of friends, scholars, and accidental visitors one meets along the way, some of whom I am sure to have neglected to thank. All, however, made this project possible and much the better. Many helped in ways small, many in ways profound. And many offered advice I gratefully took. Shortcomings of course remain mine alone.

The two outside readers for the press were exceptionally helpful. One, Barbara Kirshenblatt-Gimblett, identified herself to me and generously provided a remarkably candid, comprehensive, and full set of comments, suggestions, and advisories. I have striven to meet the high standard of her work in addressing them. But as an Americanist by training I was also especially dependent on readings and advice from a large and varied group of historians that included colleagues and friends: Molly Nolan, David Feldman, Daniel Soyer, Daniel Stone, Olga Linkiewicz, Hasia Diner, Frank Mechlenburg, Antony Polansky, David Shneer, Natan Meir, Ruth Ellen Gruber, Samuel D. Kassow, Barbara Mann, Vladyslava Moskalets, Jack Sasson, Kenneth Moss, Larry Wolff, Mariana Net, Thomas Bender, Ares Kalandides, Reinhard Bernbeck, Gábor Gyani, Miklós Konrád, Milan Ristovic, Olga Manojlovic Pintar, Gordana Ristic, Łucja Piekarska Duraj, Andrzej Dyczak, Katarzyna Szuszkiewicz, Michele Barrett, Alisse Waterston, Rayna Rapp, Melissa Fisher, Harvey Molotch, Yanni Kotsonis, Alona Zinder, James Deutsch, Marcin Wodziński, Anastasia Riabchuk, Eszter Gantner, Teresa Meade, Andor Skotnes, Betts Brown, Donna Haverty-Stacke, Aaron Welt, Van Gosse, and Deborah Holmes.

The research took me to libraries, archives, and museums in all the cities I discuss, where the staff were unfailingly welcoming and helpful. They include Stephanie Diorio, Jewish Historical Society of North Jersey; Anna Przybyszewska Drozd, Jewish Geological & Family History Center, Warsaw; staff at the YIVO Institute for Jewish Research, the Ackman & Ziff Family Genealogical Institute, and the Center for Jewish History, New York; Daniel Wagner, Stanley Diamond and Mark Halpern at JewishGen; Aneta Papis, Łódź-Centrum; Marek Szukalak, Jewish Łódź Cemetery archives; Paweł Śpiewak, Emanuel Ringelblum Jewish Historical Institute, Warsaw; Pécsi Katalin, former Curator, Budapest Holocaust Museum; Chana Schütz, Centrum Judiacum Neue Synagogue, Berlin; Cilly Kugelmann, Jewish Museum Berlin: Sofia Dyak and Iryna Matsevko, Center for Urban History for East Central Europe, Lviv; Anna Gulińska, Jewish Community Center, Kraków; Jakub Nowakowski, Galician Jewish Museum; and the staff at the Tamiment and Bobst Libraries at New York University, British Library, and New York Public Library.

This project also relied on the cooperation of many guides, museum directors, and curators. I want to thank Alex Denisenko (Lviv/Mostysko); David Rosenberg (London), Stephen Burstin (London guide); Elizabeth Selby (Jewish Museum London), Esther Brumberg (Museum of Jewish Heritage: A Living Memorial to the Holocaust), Jacek Dobrowolski (Poland); Mykhailo Borisovich Kalnytskyi (Kiev), Helise Lieberman (Warsaw); Cristina Losif and Alexandru Dumitru (Bucharest); Grzegorz Olędzki (Warsaw); Barbara Kirshenblatt-Gimblett

(Warsaw, The Museum of the History of Polish Jews); Seth Kamil (Big Onion Tours); and Olga Papash (Kiev).

I wrote an early draft of this manuscript at the National Humanities Center (NHC) in 2015–2016. The NHC creates a wonderfully collegial environment and is particularly distinguished by its library services and the wondrous librarians, Brooke Andrade and Sarah Harris. My year there was productive, with director Robert Newman, IT specialist Joel Elliot, copyeditor Karen Carroll, and the rest of the staff unfailingly helpful. They and the other fellows were also memorably supportive when I went through some harrowing medical problems. I thank all, but a special shout-out goes to Jack Sasson, Laura Lieber, Nancy Cott, Jane Newman, Anthony Kaye, John Smith, Bill Schwarz, Colleen Lye, Owen Flanagan, Paul Otto, Janice Radway, April Masten, and Judith Walkowitz.

For translations, I thank Sheva Zucker, Elizabeth Weber, Alona Zinder, and Jack Sasson. Many cousins lovingly provided family photographs and shared memories with me—Karen Zelermyer, Tami Gold, Charlotte Berzin Tambor, Judy Walker, Ruthie Lubert Sacks, Howard Leiner, Joe Margel (UK), Tony Margel (UK), Alex Berzin (Berlin), Beverly Conner, Rachel Margel Steinhouse, Bob Shamis, Paula Gringer (Denmark and Swedan), Paul Libert, Sy Lichtenstein, Gabriel Wolkowicz (Buenos Aires), Adam Saks (Berlin), and Howard Leiner.

Finally, a few special thanks. Micah Kleit, the director of Rutgers University Press, embraced the project. He placed me in the capable hands of the editor for Jewish Studies, Elisabeth Maselli. Her confidence, enthusiasm, editing, and responsiveness regularly settled an anxious author. Irina Burns and Angela Piliouras, in turn, provided careful copyediting and publication services. Various people provided individual photographs for the book, but I am especially indebted to my former NYU colleague, country dance friend, and IT guru, Jeffrey Bary, for generously editing them for publication. Many people advised, read, and offered support along the way, but three were especially important to helping me see the project through. Daniel Stone, the Canadian historian of Polish Jewish history (and also a terrific Morris dancer), knew my earlier book on the country dance revivals, and read draft chapters at an early stage. The German historical archeologist, Reinhard Bernbeck, provided close readings, remarkably done in his second language, that were consistently careful, thoughtful, and meticulous. An extraordinarily generous scholar, person, and friend, he read for me while taking time from work on his own book as a fellow at the NHC on the remnants and memory of concentration camps in Germany. The third person was my NYU colleague, the distinguished historian of American Jewry, Hasia Diner. Hasia gave me careful readings, but she also regularly checked in with me on things medical and historical as I moved the book toward publication. She was a model friend and colleague.

Lastly, and appropriately given the personal dimension of this project, there are family, and especially women to thank. The narrative conceit looks back to prior generations and singles out the quest for stories of my Jewish socialist paternal grandmother. But the book, like my life, draws on the love, support, and advice of three contemporary generations: my wife, Judith; my daughter, Rebecca; and my granddaughter, Lucy. The first two are accomplished scholars in their own right, and advised, cajoled, and nurtured the project and author. Looking back to past generations, the project offers a legacy of activist strong women to my Lucy to carry forward.

Daniel J. Walkowitz,
October 2017

Note on Text

First, the cities in Poland and Ukraine have had different names under different rulers. Most contemporary tourists know the capital cities of Poland and Ukraine as Warsaw and Kiev and I have chosen to refer to them as such. Rather than use the German or Russian names for other places, I use the Ukrainian and Polish spellings for the cities of Mostyska and Lviv in Ukraine, and Mszczonów, Bałuty, Łódź, and Kraków in Poland.

Second, the discussion of socialism in the text does not mean to refer to the Socialist parties or its adherents, but to the larger world of left-wing activism and political culture that includes many and sometimes conflicting affiliations across the long twentieth century (since 1870) with socialism, communism, and anarcho-syndicalism, some Marxist, some non-Marxist, and some anti-Marxist.

Third, curators and directors with whom I conducted oral histories are identified with their permission. In the case of walking tours that I joined anonymously, guides are given pseudonyms in the text and noted accordingly.

The Remembered and
Forgotten Jewish World

Introduction

Since the 1970s, tourism has rapidly become a major civic and development project in older industrial cities, an engine for new jobs and income in a service
economy. Heritage tourism in particular has emerged as a major cultural and
commercial enterprise of this service economy. And Jewish tourists seeking to
discover their heritage—as well as non-Jews drawn to that history and to the
Holocaust—have constituted major consumers of that enterprise in cities around
the world where Jewish communities once and, in some cases, still thrive.

In Eastern Europe, the breakup of the Soviet Union after 1989 enabled Jewish tourism to expand to former places of major Jewish settlement. As former
state socialist countries rushed to embrace capitalism, Jewish heritage tourism
offered a promising consumer market: for the first time in a generation, Jewish
tourists born in Eastern Europe could visit family homelands in towns and cities in countries that had long been closed and unwelcoming. Many of these
tourists, as we shall see, retained an abiding interest in Holocaust tourism, in
"witnessing" the sites of collective trauma. But in the post-1989 era the aging
generation who escaped the Holocaust became a diminishing market overshadowed by later generations of grandchildren born in the diaspora. These younger
tourists arrived with stories they had heard, as a "postmemory," to quote Marianne Hirsch, and focused less singularly on the Holocaust.[1]

A visit to Eastern European cities that had been the former home to millions
of Jews also appealed to tourists like myself whose parents emigrated several
decades before The Shoah. I went to cities such as Warsaw, Kraków, Łódź, and
Lviv seeking insight into an earlier era and signs of a Jewish political culture
informed by the Yiddish world of social and political socialist culture inhabited
by my parents and grandparents. I hoped to see sites of prewar Jewish culture—
theater, concert halls, shuls, salons, and newspapers—as well as sites of political
agitation, exhibits of vernacular Jewish life and working conditions.

National and local politicians, developers, and museum curators recognized the possibilities of a widened heritage tourism for travelers like myself, and the increased tourism dollars, pounds, and euros that would result. They oversaw a host of institutions and activities that engaged contemporary Jewish heritage tourists: Jewish museums, substantial Holocaust memorials, sites of remembrance, monuments large and small to Jewish leaders and events, and a remarkable array of Jewish-themed walking tours. However, different stakeholders also brought their own vision and priorities to the sites. Developers and politicians made financial and political investments in a commodified past to attract national and international visitors, win their favor, and boost civic pride. By way of contrast, others with claims to professional expertise—curators, directors, tour guides, docents, and historians—tended to privilege historical accuracy over entertainment.

Even as developers, politicians, and curators might contest interpretations, seismic world-historical events often overdetermined the historical reconstruction of the Jewish past as Holocaust tourism. First, the Six Day War in 1967 quickened a renewed focus on the Holocaust as a compelling justification for support of Israel; at the same time, Soviet bloc states distanced themselves from a Jewish history they believed to be tied to Zionism.[2] Second, the postcommunist aftermath complicated how Jewish history, and Jewish socialist history in particular, could be remembered. The fall of the Berlin Wall in 1989 and the breakup of the Soviet Union in 1991 motivated new national (and often nationalist) regimes to repudiate socialist or communist pasts. State actors concerned with advancing a positive national identity could and, in some cases, did pressure curators, tour guides, and museum officials to whitewash thorny problems of local anti-Semitism. Moreover, former Soviet bloc states, and states within the USSR such as Ukraine were often anxious to distance themselves from any association with communist and socialist movements integral to significant sectors of the Jewish community since the last quarter of the nineteenth century. Politicians and local citizens in many states, for instance, sought to make symbols of such a past disappear by destroying monuments to socialist leaders.[3] For their part, many Jews were anxious to distance their own past from the history of state socialism. In capitalist places like the United States, the Cold War made association with left social movements unrespectable, while in Eastern Europe, Jews (and non-Jews) living there sought legitimacy by distancing themselves from any association with "Commie Jews" in the Soviet bureaucracy. I experienced contemporary Jewish heritage tourism in this context.

The Dominant Narrative

The Remembered and Forgotten Jewish World argues that the Holocaust narrative, a story that focuses overwhelmingly on synagogues, cemeteries and

Holocaust memorials, dominates Jewish heritage tourism. It is a narrative emphasizing Jewish identity as a religious identity and underscoring the Holocaust as the lesson from the past for the future. For many, Jewish educators and memorialists alike embrace Holocaust tourism as a political project to "Never Forget" the genocide, to memorialize the martyred millions, and to justify the need for a safe Jewish homeland. A large swath of Jewish tourists shared these views, leading them to view the national sites they visit in Central and Eastern Europe as wholly anti-Semitic spaces.

I understood the hostility many Jews brought—and still bring—to places they dismiss as historically and unremittingly anti-Semitic. It is a view I regularly encountered during years of research in the United States among Jewish friends who wondered what in the world I was doing going back to "those places." It was because I sought a different story. I hoped to hear and see stories that would speak to the lives of women like my paternal grandmother, my Bubbe Chaia or Ida Walkowitz, a secular Jew whose activism in the labor socialist Bund—an abbreviation of Algemeyner Yidisher Arbeter Bund in Lite, Poylyn un Rusland; "General Jewish Workers Union in Lithuania, Poland, and Russia"—I imagined as a model for my own political involvements.

The Remembered and Forgotten Jewish World provides a unique critical and timely analysis of the flourishing heritage industry, highlighting the state of tourism in eleven cities across Europe and the United States. It juxtaposes the rich historical scholarship that historians have excavated of Jewish life to the history told and untold at heritage sites. Although the Holocaust narrative remains dominant, along the way we discover a New Jewish History and identify projects that attempt to tell the story in new, diverse, and inclusive ways.

My focus is Jewish heritage, but this book more broadly analyzes the relationship between history and memory that has so engaged critical readers and scholars in the last few decades. Indeed, efforts to forget or to "disappear" a past is integral to what is privileged as "remembered," and as the title *The Remembered and Forgotten Jewish World* suggests, the relationship between the two frames this book. My quest builds on the redemptive inquiry into the "politics of memory" that the Jewish historian Jonathan Boyarin engaged fifteen years ago to remember and honor the history of immigrant Jewish radicals.[4] This book extends his memory work into the public sphere, not to substitute Jewish socialism for something else, but to ask how a history that includes that part of the story changes the whole story. Traditional heritage narratives, like much history writing, focus on "winners," on political and economic leaders as benefactors and "makers," whereas giving voice to the perspective of the putative "losers" makes all Jews active agents in the heritage story. In fact, such voices are always present, but muted. For remembering and forgetting work together as what Freud termed psychic disavowal. What is forgotten is always revealed, even if it is marginalized in the presentation. But recovering and giving voice to the

Jewish socialist past does not merely add to the story; more importantly, it changes it, integrating and centering a major element in the making of modern Jewish identity into the dominant narrative. I see that as a project for public venues of heritage tourism.

I do not try to uncover and present the hidden history of the many social, political, and cultural expressions of Jewish socialism in this book. For cities like New York, such an assignment would be relatively easy; in war-ravaged cities of Eastern Europe, finding extant artifacts of such a past would be more daunting, though I am confident I could have found guides up for the task. But I deliberately chose not to seek experts who might construct such a tour for me. Rather, I investigated the history publicly available to a broad set of visitors. The focus was also a reaction to my having led a secret life. The repressive Cold War political climate had silenced me as a child in the 1950s and I have ever since chafed at allowing silencing in the public sphere to go unexamined and unchallenged. This volume is at once an extended essay on the politics of history and memory, and a study of how the history of Jews, and in particular, of Jewish socialism cast broadly, is being remembered, forgotten, imagined, and lost in the public sphere.

But where to begin? Early generations of my family lived and died in various towns and cities across what is now Poland and Ukraine; too many perished in the Holocaust, and a fair number emigrated in search of a better life elsewhere. The majority came to the United States, but migration patterns of the others ultimately traced the path and reach of the international Jewish diaspora, a trek that took Jews to virtually every part of the globe—from Germany, France, and England and to Siberia, Australia, China, Cuba, Argentina, Israel, South Africa, and other ports. Each of these places would be a plausible site for a significant Jewish heritage tour.

But choices had to be made. I began with visits to small towns where my paternal grandmother and maternal grandfather were born and to the nearby cities to which I had evidence they had migrated: Łódź and Lviv, respectably. I then included London and New York as cities to which they and their landsmen had immigrated. Subsequently learning that post-1989 Jewish heritage tourists had oriented themselves back toward Central and East European cities from which their ancestors had emigrated, the second half of the book focuses on such places. I visited major sites of Jewish settlement and robust heritage tourism such as Berlin, London, Kraków, and Warsaw; other cities, such as Belgrade, Budapest, Kiev, and Bucharest I visited as a result of fortuitous happenstance when I had invitations to speak there. What began as accidental tourism, however, proved to provide substantive examples of how different national and civic cultures of Central and Eastern European cities could create a range of possibilities and challenges for Jewish heritage tourism. The sites also reflect the uneven state of commercial and public Jewish heritage tourism. Cities such as New York and London have had robust programs for nearly fifty years; cities such as Berlin, Warsaw, Budapest, and Kraków have well developed tourist industries. Lviv, Kiev, Belgrade, Bucharest, and Łódź have programs in varied but relatively early stages of development. Given my hope to engage, renew, and open a conversation about Jewish heritage, I invite others to join the discussion and examine additional major Jewish sites, both older ones such as Budapest, Vienna, Odessa, and Vilnius, and relatively newer settlements such as Buenos Aires, Moscow, Johannesburg, Cape Town, and Jerusalem.

―――――

The narrative strategy of the book that follows intercuts site-specific chapters with inserted interludes that draw on my own family history. Although these interludes are personal, they highlight key aspects of Jewish heritage, such as the history of secular radical Jews, like my paternal grandmother, Bubbe Chaia, the Bundist Ida Lubertosfsky Walkowitz, that are thinly referenced or missing in conventional heritage tourism. Using the conceit of a quest to hear and see stories of my grandparents—or paradigmatic versions of stories of people like them—the interludes give a personal and human dimension to abstract historical data. They also give a sense of the questions and expectations travelers bring to heritage tourism.

I began in Poland. For while everybody talks about his or her Bubbe, I sought echoes of her life where she grew up, as Chaia Lubertofsky in the Polish village of Mszczonów (Amshinov in Yiddish), and after her marriage in 1909, as Ida Walkowitz in Łódź.[5] I saw and heard virtually nothing of Ida's life in Poland, and frustratingly, I learned little of the lives of other radical Jews like her. So I broadened my search to include the history of my maternal grandfather Max. He was raised in Mostyska (Mościska in Polish), a village forty-one miles west of Lviv. A few tantalizing hints of the lives of people like Bubbe or Max appeared in the most unlikely places—in statues or memorial plaques to the Yiddish writer Sholem Aleichem in Kiev and Lviv such as that on the cover of the book— but I was more often disappointed to find little about their past or about ordinary people like them as historical actors in any of these places, and even less about the history of Jewish socialism.

Moving on, like my relatives, I followed the trails of Ida, Max, and the relatives out of Central and Eastern Europe westward to the new immigrants' "promised lands" of London and New York (see chapters 4 and 5). I thought I would have better luck there. London's East End and New York's Lower East Side both hold special places in Jewish collective memory as foundational sites of Jewish settlement. Once more, I would hear fragments of stories of people like Ida and Max and get some poignant glimpses into such lives. But I would also learn that Jewish heritage tourism had moved eastward since the 1980s to cities in Central and Eastern Europe, so following the Jewish heritage tourists, in the second half of this book, I return with them to major sites of Jewish heritage in Eastern Europe.

Berlin (chapter 6), a city with a rich museum culture and home to one of the more famous Jewish museums, was the first stop. Berlin also documents how Germany depicts the genocidal policies in its Nazi past, and how its Jewish sites locate the history of the Holocaust within the longer history of Jews in Germany. But Ida's and Max's history in Eastern Europe predates the Holocaust, so I turned south and eastward to see how Bubbe's story—or a paradigmatic version of the Jewish socialist—appeared elsewhere. The places to which my travels had taken me up to this point reflected the dominant role of Ashkenazi Jews in Central and Eastern European cities; moving southward, in chapter 7 I look at Jewish heritage tourism in three cities with larger Sephardic populations and influences from the Ottoman Empire: Budapest, Bucharest, and Belgrade. A couple of references in Berlin, however, reframed my heritage tourism to these cities. Exhibit topics in sites within the former East Berlin hinted that a legacy of Soviet-era socialism may have provided receptive openings (or romanticizing) of the Jewish socialist past and made me curious to see how that past played out in these cities. Naturally, I was also curious to see how each of these cities— like Łódź, Lviv and Kiev—would bear the marks of new post-1989 and post-communist nationalisms.

The final stops in my travels (chapter 8) brought me back to Poland to look, arguably, at two of the most robust and developed sites of Jewish heritage tourism today—Kraków and Warsaw. Yet what Jewish tourists such as myself see and hear in these places has been framed by the relationship between history and contested memories, the growth of heritage tourism as part of urban development, and ongoing debates about Jewish identity. Before taking readers to sites of Jewish heritage, the book begins with a chapter that provides an overview of these matters.

Prelude

My paternal grandmother, Bubbe Chaia (Ida Lubertofsky Walkowitz), spoke only Yiddish. Alas, I resisted several efforts by my family to get me to learn the language at Sunday morning Jewish School, and Bubbe and I spoke very little. Yet as an icon she loomed large in my sense of self and in my relation to my parents and their friends' struggles in the labor, peace, and civil rights movements.

I grew up in a communist family living in and around Paterson, New Jersey, an industrial city eleven miles west of New York City. As a "red diaper baby," a child of communists, I took secret pride in the fact that as the head of the Young Pioneers my father had spoken at the famous 1926 Passaic textile strike (at the age of eleven). To celebrate May Day, 1934, he and a comrade had also secretly hoisted the red flag atop the Paterson Public Library, an exploit that had made it into the *New York Times*. Slogans demanding unemployment relief and opposition to fascism adorned the flag and were painted on sidewalks outside the library.[1] My mother had been a socialist, and in the opening presented by the Popular Front I suppose my father deigned to talk to her—and soon after they married. Growing up in the 1950s in a New Jersey suburban town, this communist lineage remained my secret life, not values or associations I would talk about in school. With my parents' support, I demonstrated for nuclear disarmament and civil rights, but in public we spoke in codes of "social justice," "progressives," or "peaceful coexistence." Beyond this, I knew to keep silent about my family life.

Struggles coded as "social justice" were a family tradition with which I proudly identified, and in the context of McCarthyism, hid in fear. In 1962 I participated in CORE's Route 40 Project, the Chestertown, Maryland, "Freedom Riders" campaign to integrate restaurants and diners on the Maryland Eastern Shore, a road frequented by UN diplomats. In 1967 I was one of about two dozen graduate students briefly suspended (and consequently subject to the

Figure 1. The Walkowitz Family, ca. 1923. Zishe has his youngest son, Joseph, on his lap. My father, Sol, sits to his left, the younger daughter, Rose, is seated in the middle. Bubbe Chaia stands behind Zishe on his left, daughter Belle to his left. The others are Uncle Joe and Tante Neche Katz and their daughters and my Tante Baila. Neche and Baila are Bubbe's sisters and Joe Katz sponsored and paid for the Walkowitz family's immigration from Denmark. Courtesy of Ruthie Lubert Sacks.

draft until faculty and student protest compelled the university president to reduce the penalty to probation) for a sit-in against Dow Chemical Company recruiters (the company that produced Napalm). I also implicitly imagined my civil rights and antiwar activism as an expression of social commitments rooted in my Jewish cultural upbringing. Like the merging of culture and politics in Yiddishkeit, we marched and walked picket lines by day, and then sang songs of "the people" at night. Many of these songs, like "Go Down Moses," were nineteenth-century African American spirituals sung by slaves seeking freedom. The song's story of the Jews' escape from Egypt illustrated its interwoven hybrid meanings as radical Jewish cultural expressions. Jews sang the song at Passover Seders with its cultural rendering of the story of the Jews' escape from the tyranny of the Egyptian pharaoh.[2]

In my experience Jewishness was embedded in this radical political culture. My parents shared these values and never questioned any of my political actions, nor did we address the cultural appropriation of such songs, or their meanings after 1968 when the historic alliance of American Jews and African

Americans in the United States fell apart in the wake of the Six Day War and conflict over the Ocean Hill-Brownsville teachers' strike. Rather, my parents always supported my activism and its cultural expressions as right, proper—and in the family tradition. From family lore I understood the root of that tradition to be Bubbe.

As I mentioned earlier, I knew rather little about Bubbe. One anecdote that sticks in my mind involved her participation in the Emma Lazarus Club, which I somehow knew to be a radical organization. As an adult I learned the club was organized in 1944 by leftist, mostly Yiddish-speaking women in the Women's Division of the Jewish People's Order of the International Workers Order to provide relief to wartime victims and to fight anti-Semitism and racism. In 1951, after the New York Attorney General attacked the organization as subversive, the group changed its name to the Emma Lazarus Federation of Jewish Women's Clubs (ELF). According to Joyce Antler, ELF's name change represented an effort to resist McCarthy-era stigmatizing of Jewish radicals as un-American communists, and to affirm Jewish identity "by promoting a progressive, secular Jewish heritage."[3] In this sense, Bubbe's activism resonated with my sense of my family's radical tradition.

I knew even less about Zishe (Alexander), Ida's husband and my Zayde. I knew my father looked like him, and I look like my father. He was, so I was told, larger than life. A tailor and a secular Jewish communist, he ran Friday evening soirées at home for the Party faithful—Fridays to compete with Shabbat—with Yiddish poetry reading and song. I always saw my own involvement with Jewish theater at the YMHA as an extension of my family's engagement with Jewish culture. I played Bontche Schweig in skits from *The World of Sholem Aleichem*, and remember to this day lines from *The Dybbuk*, the play by S. Ansky, in which I had the role of Khanan, the poor Yeshiva student who as the *dybbuk* (a malicious spirit of a deceased person) possesses a young woman who has become betrothed to another.[4] But Zayde died when I was an infant, so his history mattered, but in the abstract; Bubbe, a laughing, smiling but enigmatic presence, was flesh and blood.

Of course, I romanticize. After a stroke, Ida was for the better part of the last decade of her life in a wheelchair at the Daughters of Miriam, a Jewish home for the aged in Clifton, New Jersey. But I "knew" she had been a member of the Bund in Poland, and the delicious family story told to summarize her character, and typically laughed about, depicted her as doubly transgressive: she was always getting arrested in Paterson, angering her husband (a traditional patriarch with a notorious temper) because she was not home to make dinner. She was, then both a socialist and a strong woman. As the 1950s morphed into the 1960s, Bubbe Chaia/Ida Walkowitz was the activist model for my own nongendered activism. Like many men in those years, I was tone deaf to the gender part of the story.

Of the politics of the left—sans gender—I heard much. There were few family conversations about the relationship of the Bund to the communists, and the cut off for stories seemed to be after arrival in America. Stories of fights within the left in Paterson were the stuff of dinnertime jokes. My family only laughed about those older divisions and the tensions between factions. I understood myself to be growing up in a communist household reared in a modern form of Bund culture—immersed in Yiddishkeit and strongly secular, prounion, and communist. My parents were Communist Party members and, I—too young to understand or make such a commitment—was, I suppose, a communist, that is, someone who identified with the antiracist, egalitarian, anticapitalist ideas I associated with the Party. My family never belonged to a synagogue—I never set foot in one save for a childhood friend's bar mitzvah or to play on a basketball team—but I was taught Jewish history and the history of the Jewish religion as a historical creation at Sunday shul. I was never a bar mitzvah boy, though my parents did hold a thirteenth birthday party for me as a coming-of-age marker. On Jewish holidays, my parents often kept me out of school so that other kids would not stigmatize me as irreligious, which of course I was. I never spoke of my antipathy toward organized religion, for it was quite enough to keep quiet about issues of class or race in school. By the 1970s I felt comfortable letting my guard down. When my parents died, I wanted to acknowledge them as brave and just people. At their funerals, I had the service end with a recording of the legendary African American radical, activist performer Paul Robeson singing "Zog Nit Keynmol." The song was written by an inmate in the Vilna Ghetto, Hirsch Glick, inspired by the news of the resistance of the Warsaw Ghetto Uprising of 1943, and it was embraced by Jewish partisan groups operating in Eastern Europe. In the postwar era, the song came to have special meaning to a left community beleaguered under the threat of McCarthyism. Defiantly optimistic, the song opens,

> Never say that you are walking the final road
> Though leaden skies obscure blue days
> The hour we have been longing for is still to come,
> When our steps shall thunder out—We are here!

With these memories and stories, I set out to see what more I could learn in commercial mass Jewish heritage tourism—the public history of Jewish life—about a radical Jewish communist, or more broadly socialist heritage and the role of women like Ida Walkowitz in it. But a cache of new material came to my attention in the spring of 2017 that compelled me to once again rethink what I thought I knew.

Seeking some additional recollections from older cousins, I reached out to them. One, Judy Walker, off-handily mentioned that she had deposited some memorabilia from her father, my uncle Joe Walkowitz, at the Jewish Historical

Society of North Jersey. Judy also remembered that she had also deposited a local study, *Voices from the Paterson Silk Mills*, containing oral history excerpts from, among others, her father and his sister, my aunt Belle Bernstein.[5] In the volume and in archived oral histories, Joe and Belle spoke eloquently of the Paterson Jewish chorus, of women in the Communist Party, and most especially of Zishe and Chaia. Extensive and revealing, the interviews richly detailed what I increasingly came to accept, following the writer Vivian Gornick, as my romance with American Communism.[6] Although their accounts confirmed some foundational family legends, they also challenged my heroic narrative. Both Joe and Belle made clear, as we shall hear, that both Zishe's and Chaia's stories were more complicated than I had been led to believe. Zishe was at once an accomplished and revered Yiddishist and an imposing patriarch and regular child beater. Depicted in the family story as a woman who allowed her political commitments to get in the way of her family responsibilities, the accounts portray Chaia instead as a woman who quietly worked a double day as both home carer and worker, labored tirelessly in relief and benefit causes, and stood up to inquisitors from the House Un-American Activities Committee in the mid-1950s. These accounts, unfolding to me contemporaneously with my heritage tourism, led me to realize that my channeling of Bubbe Chaia and women like her was especially fortuitous as a point of entry into Jewish heritage. The world of Jewish socialism of which she was a part, was also a history in which gender—that of patriarchs and activist women—defined Jewish socialist experiences.

CHAPTER 1

The Jewish Heritage Business

Yiddishkeit, socialism, and Jewish labor have been displaced by the new centrality of the Holocaust, Israel, and new forms of Jewish particularity.
—Kenneth Waltzer (1999)

The history of secular—and for our purposes, socialist—Jews in contemporary heritage tourism is not easy to find. In his widely celebrated, award-winning 1976 book *World of Our Fathers*, Irving Howe gave a central role to *Yiddishkeit* (Jewishness), Jewish socialism, and labor in the experience of immigrant Jews on the Lower East Side.[1] The publication coincided with the popularity of the *Roots* miniseries on African American slave origins. It also coincided with a rapid uptick in heritage tourism. However, by the mid-1970s the past that Howe celebrated had begun to lose its potency for large parts of the Jewish community. The 1967 Six Day War raised anxieties for many about Israel/Jewish security. Also, the 1968 Ocean Hill-Brownsville, Brooklyn, teachers' strike challenged historic ties between blacks and Jews in America and further worried many Jews. Advocating local "community control" of jobs and curriculum, African American residents contested the authority of the Jewish-dominated Teachers Union. For many Jews, especially second- and third-generation American Jews who celebrated their social mobility "out of the Lower East Side" to new middle-class suburban enclaves, the contest initiated a shifting focus from fights for social justice to struggles on behalf of Israel. Twenty years later, when the critic Kenneth Waltzer noted that Howe's story had disappeared from Jewish memory, he was identifying a shift that had roots, ironically, at the very moment in which Howe wrote.

The events of the mid- and late 1960s created a climate conducive to the nostalgic celebration of pre-Holocaust Jewish life thought to be irrevocably lost. Although a carefully crafted social and cultural history, Howe's book contributed to the nostalgia. It partially accounts for the popularity enjoyed by the acclaimed 1964 Broadway musical *Fiddler on the Roof*. In 2007, *Fiddler* still ranked as the seventh most frequently produced musical by U.S. high schools. Drawn from Sholem Aleichem's heartfelt tales of shtetl life at the turn of the century, the show depicts how Tevya the dairyman and his daughters struggle to maintain their religious and cultural traditions in the face of anti-Semitism and the lures of modernity in the Pale of Settlement. To be sure, the play and its 1971 filmic adaptation had its Jewish critics. Phillip Roth, writing in the *New Yorker*, dismissed it as "shtetl kitsch"[2] while recent scholarship by the historian Yohanen Petrovsky-Shtern finds the shtetl in its nineteenth-century "golden age" to have been "economically vigorous, financially beneficial, and culturally influential."[3] Yet, despite these critics, the musical and film versions of *Fiddler* shaped popular postwar understandings of Eastern European Jewish life around the world and Jewish heritage tourism.[4]

This world of popular Jewish culture set the stage for the rise of Jewish heritage tourism in the late twentieth century. As big business, it also coincided with the ascendancy of mass tourism as a major growth sector of the postindustrial economy. To remake old industrial cities as tourist destinations businessmen, entrepreneurs, and politicians incorporated traditional advertising concerns with marketing to brand a saleable past into their projects. Reflecting the politics of urban deindustrialization, development revitalization, and the rising place of tourism in service economies, the stories told by guides and museums had to meet expectations of visitors and satisfy or reconcile with the profit demands of the burgeoning corporate enterprise.

The growth figures in the travel industry were astounding. In 1960, 25 million tourists traveled to foreign countries; in 1970, the number traveling increased to 250 million; in 1995 the number reached 536 million; and in 2012, over 1 billion people traveled abroad. In 1993, tourism produced over 6 percent of the world's gross national product ($3.2 trillion). By 2012, it had become the largest global business in the world, employing an estimated one in twelve people and generating $6.5 trillion of the world's economy.[5]

The increase in American tourism, the largest share of the world's industry, reflected the upsurge. In 2013, the *New York Times* travel section interviewed Brenda S. Sprague, the deputy assistant secretary for U.S. passport services, who noted that the number of Americans with passports had grown from 7 million to 113 million from 1989 to 2013, an extraordinary sixteen-fold increase in the number of American passports in a quarter of a century. Equally telling, Sprague added that travelers were "no longer sticking to the London-Paris-Rome circuit."[6] Heritage tourism partially accounts for this tremendous increase. It is what the folklorist Barbara Kirshenblatt-Gimblett describes as "destination culture."[7]

Jewish Heritage Tourism

History

Jewish heritage tourism constituted a major set of destinations for this growth industry in the latter third of the twentieth century, but there were earlier precedents. German Jews who settled in America and England in the nineteenth century undoubtedly joined non-Jewish bourgeois Germans returning to their former homeland. Wealthy German-Jewish families like the Guggenheims, Loebs, Sachs, and Schiffs likely also participated in the Grand Tour culture graphically depicted in Edith Wharton's novels.[8] In the interwar years, the social base of Jewish tourism broadened. For example, Gustave Eisner, a journalist from Łódź, set himself up as a travel agent in New York in 1926 and advertised in the communist daily *Freiheit* (Freedom). Starting in 1936, the Federation of Polish Jews in America organized annual trips back to Poland, while, according to historian Daniel Soyer, "thousands" of well-heeled Jews took "pilgrimages" to the Soviet Union or back to Poland during the interwar period. A fictionalized autobiography by Jacob Glatstein, for example, traces the Yiddish writer's trip to visit his dying mother in Lublin in 1934. Visiting a Polish resort sanatorium and Kazimierz, which he casts as a Jewish tourist attraction, Glatstein's traveling companions include a Jewish prizefighter, a Dutch Jew returning from a three-week visit to America, a Jewish dentist traveling to the Soviet Union to study Soviet hygiene, a young Jewish student-pianist, and a "well bred" seventy-year-old Jewish gentleman.[9]

Prior to the middle of the twentieth century, international tourism of this sort remained not only limited but also informally organized. Eisner's case provides an example of the fledging Jewish industry in the first half of the century. Such travel agents put out commercial advertising for *landsmanshaft* (societies of immigrant Jews from the same town) business right after World War I. On-site locals also offered services: in 1937, for instance, historian Daniel Stone's parents were approached by a "runner" at the Warsaw railroad station who offered to give them a tour of the Jewish section.[10] By the 1930s, a rising middle class of immigrant American Jews from Eastern Europe had begun to visit cities in the United States in search of their past. As these Jews began to "move up" and out of the Lower East Side to places like the Grand Concourse in the Bronx, they engaged in a tourist return to roots in America. (In England, a similar process brought Jews from the North London suburb of Golders Green back to the East End.) Historians Suzanne Wasserman and Hasia Diner have described the romantic reengagements on New York's Lower East Side of second- and third-generation American Jews. Visiting places that their immigrant forbearers had fled, they returned to dine on palatable memories of knishes, pickles, and pushcart fare and then safely return at the end of the day to their comfortable suburban homes (which in the 1930s might be in the Bronx!).[11] Thus, Jewish heritage tourism has long roots and always reflected the invention of tradition and selective memory.[12]

In the postwar aftermath of the Holocaust, leaders of the Jewish community sought to rescue remnants of the Central and Eastern European past from the wrecking ball. Historian Michael Meng has described in detail how local municipal leaders, urban planners, and historic preservationists in both communist Poland and divided Germany rebuilt cities and expunged "traces of the Jewish past" in service to aesthetics of urban modernism and Soviet realism. Rabbis concerned with preservation concentrated on salvaging synagogues and cemeteries. Their interests would receive a major boost from the U.S. government two decades later: in 1990, Congress funded a United States Commission for the Preservation of America's Heritage Abroad, a project initiated in 1979 by a Brooklyn rabbi and Holocaust survivor. Although the Commission's mandate was cast in universal terms, the project produced major work in preservation of Jewish sites, the large majority of which were synagogues and cemeteries.[13] And in marking and monumentalizing what they deemed significant, the rabbis' preoccupations shaped heritage trails.

There was, of course, logic to this preservation focus. For many Jews these sites were central to Jewish religion and heritage. Citing the *Encyclopedia Judaica* entry for cemetery, the Commission's Report cites the Talmud: "Jewish gravestones are fairer than royal palaces (Sanh 96b; cf. Matt. 23:39)," and notes that in "normal circumstances the entire Jewish community shares the protection and repair of the cemeteries willingly."[14] When Nazis and anti-Semites tried to exterminate the Jewish people, in attacking the synagogues and cemeteries they sought to destroy symbols of the Jewish religion. In city after city, the Nazi invaders targeted synagogues for destruction, and those that they left standing were kept primarily for use as storage for the military machine. Cemeteries fared no better. With no one left to maintain them, cemeteries fell into disrepair or disappeared altogether. Often, they were desecrated and destroyed, and in some cases, gravestones were reused as paving blocks for road construction. Cemeteries that survived were obliterated by communist regimes. Communist officials also often expropriated Jewish religious sites. After the war, Soviet law, which various Soviet bloc states used as a model, declared that any land unused for twenty-five years could freely be developed for other purposes, such as housing. Nonetheless, in 2005, the Commission successfully identified over 1,500 sites of Jewish cemeteries, synagogues, and mass burial sites in Ukraine.

Religiously observant Jews, especially the Hasidim, felt a particularly deep responsibility for the recovery and upkeep of the cemeteries. Hasidic Jews, the Report goes on to say, increasingly make "religious pilgrimages" to these sites to honor rebbes. For these people, Jewish identity is a religious identity that easily translates into their privileging cemeteries in Jewish heritage tourism. But religious Jews represented only one of several groups invested in heritage tourism. The Report also notes that Jewish genealogists doing family research also particularly valued the cemetery sites. The Report concludes that the growing numbers of pilgrimages from Israel and North America in particular express "a quest for an emotional connection to the destruction of Jewish life."[15]

Coincident with this focus on synagogue and cemetery preservation, Jewish heritage tourism expanded during the 1970s in Central and Eastern Europe. Jewish ruins, Meng writes, triggered "interest, curiosity, nostalgia, recollection, and melancholy" and attracted local, national, and even international attention. Following the rise of the independent labor protest movement, Solidarity (Solidarność), the Polish state rebuilt the only surviving Warsaw synagogue in 1983, and East Germany restored Berlin's bombed out "new" synagogue on its side of the Wall in 1988.[16]

The collapse of communism and the fall of the Berlin Wall in 1989 opened Jewish tourist floodgates to Poland and cities such as Berlin. Virtually every major city with a Jewish past or present opened a Jewish history museum. Most of these institutions were dedicated to the Holocaust. The Holocaust Memorial Museum opened in Washington, DC in 1981, and similar institutions were opened, renovated, or consolidated afterward in New York, Frankfurt, London, Budapest, Berlin, Warsaw, Moscow, and elsewhere. Some, like the Moscow Jewish Museum, opened only in 2013; while planning for the Museum of the Polish Jews began more than two decades ago, the core exhibit opened, after many delays, only in late October 2014.[17]

Like all heritage tourism sites, these museums operate in local, national, and international politicized contexts. Many sites were established in cities that looked to tourism as the leading sector of a new economy that could replace declining manufacturing and industrial sectors. Local and national politicians, Jewish communities (both local and foreign), developers, and tourists all invested in how the tourist industry would represent the city's past. And they did not always agree. Older, now vacant industrial buildings presented planners and entrepreneurs with local development opportunities while the same structures provided interpretative challenges to others. Developers and politicians could laud modern reconstructions as comfortable and attractive, but critics worried that such development projects risked being wedded to a commodified past cleansed of labor struggles, a "Disneyland" version of history for comfortable Whiggish national and urban narratives. This has meant that the diverse stakeholders in both capitalist and postsocialist countries often found themselves enmeshed in "culture wars" where museum staffs' loyalties were tested and divided.

The Master Narrative—Holocaust Tourism

A cataclysmic and world-changing event, the Holocaust cast a dark shadow over both the history of the Jewish people and the history of Eastern and Central Europe. Before the war about 60 percent of the world's Jewry, an estimated 9.5 million people, lived in Europe. Nazi genocide exterminated approximately 6 million Jews; in 1945, 3.5 million survived. It is not surprising then that many Jews and non-Jews, compelled by the beacon cry, Never Again! traveled to bear witness to this catastrophe (the Hebrew term is Shoah). For many, the tour offered opportunities to atone, reflect, recuperate, or memorialize the Holocaust. Some tourists made "birthright" visits to Israel whereas others increasingly concentrated on the sites of the Holocaust, and many did both.[18]

Hasia Diner has documented the postwar attention of American Jews to the Holocaust, and Peter Novack has raised provocative questions about the increased political capital invested in its memorialization after 1967. According to Novack, the 1962 trial of Adolf Eichmann, the Frankfurt Auschwitz trials of 1963–1967, and the Six Day War in Israel in 1967 converged to increase self-conscious commitments to "witness" the Holocaust, to memorialize a Jewish past that Jews saw threatened in the present. According to Novack, Jews invocated the Holocaust and the Six Day War to justify unqualified support for Israel, a position seconded by Western politicians who sought to curry favor with Jewish Americans.[19]

Jewish scholars emphasize the emerging Jewish attachment to a nationalist redemptive Holocaust narrative in heritage tourism. Ethnographer Erica Lehrer in her seminal 2013 study of Polish tourism and Kazimierz sharply observes that Poland "has been treated by the Jewish establishment as ritually desecrated; it has become a symbol of condensed evil that overrides meanings or history other than 'the Holocaust.'"[20] Historian Jackie Feldman and anthropologist Jack Kugelmass further elaborate Lehrer's critique. They document how the long shadow of the Holocaust made tourism to Poland a religious experience. Although their critique applied to Jewish heritage visitors broadly, they specifically addressed travel by Israelis and Americans: visits had become "a ritual of memory and mourning, testimony and victory." Kugelmass acknowledges that after the Six Day War, the Holocaust had become incorporated "into the ritual life of American Judaism," part of a commitment to "honoring an irretrievable past." But ultimately, he sees the trips as performances "to affirm a mythic past and not-so-mythic future." Feldman is even more explicit about the nationalist agenda of Israeli student tours. Some Israeli students reacted with compassion toward Poles on the trips, but the abiding message of the Israeli state-sponsored visits was that "Poland is a Jewish cemetery and an anti-Semitic hostile country, and that continuation of Diaspora Jewish life is in Israel."[21]

The Shadow of the Long Cold War

The postcommunist political context profoundly shaped the national and local political environment in which heritage creators, whether they were museum directors, curators, or tour guides, functioned. Claims to patriotism could impel heritage interpreters to accept or reject ethnic perspectives. Surges of nationalist xenophobia led various European states to distance their history from any association with a communist or socialist past.

The actual or presumed relationship of Jews to socialism and communism in the postwar and Cold War eras complicated the history of Jewish heritage sites and post-1989 tourism. As we shall see, socialism inspired many Jews who were confronting harsh industrial regimes in the second half of the nineteenth century. They joined a panoply of socialist and communist organizations engaged in social movements, cultural clubs, and political struggles. The Bund and socialist Zionist groups were two such affiliations, but there were many others. Jewish socialists were divided about Russia. Some idealized it and the Soviet Union as models of a brave, new, and just socialist society. For example, the Warsaw Jewish revolutionary Maksymilian Horwitz (pseudonym Henryk Walecki) served on the Executive Committee of the Comintern during the 1930s.[22] While hardly typical of Jews, Horwitz's devotion to the Soviet Union resonated with many socialist-inclined Jews who had been exploited in rapidly industrializing cities and were repeatedly threatened by nationalist pogroms. USSR policy remained actively opposed to anti-Semitism during the interwar era, and Soviets may have even given Jews preferential treatment during the 1920s as a group opposed to the Whites. The Soviets supported Yiddish as an antibourgeois and antireligious marker and allowed a Jewish Section of the Party to set policy and carry it out.[23] During the interwar years, some Soviets institutionalized a particular version of Jewish Studies, which emphasized Jewish internationalist culture and social justice. The Soviet version of Jewish Studies was also part of the fight against nationalism. In 1924, for example, the Belorussian Academy of Sciences established a Jewish research center; in 1929, the Ukrainian Academy of Sciences in Kiev organized and then tasked the Institute of Proletarian Jewish Culture with a "struggle with bourgeois Jewish nationalist ideology and science." Yiddish writers and an All-Ukrainian Jewish State Theatre also flourished.[24]

The relation of Jews to communism changed dramatically in the postwar era, thanks to the onset of anticommunism during the Cold War in the West, and the emergence of active anti-Semitism in the USSR and Soviet bloc nations. The shift did not occur overnight, however, and the legacy of past Jewish imaginings of a Soviet ideal persisted. Alternatively, after the 1939 Hitler-Stalin Pact many such Jews rejected the Soviet Union and any affiliation with the Communist Party. However, in Nazi-controlled lands, many Jews welcomed the Soviet

Army (which had many Jewish officers) as liberators while others took the opportunity to escape to the West. But some of those who stayed continue to idealize Russia as a model socialist country. Jews had felt excluded from power by local nationalists in prewar cities and villages; many had also seen local nationals collaborating with the Nazis. In these contexts, a few of the relatively small number of Jews who survived the war did take positions in the Soviet bureaucracy. Maks Horwitz was one example of a Jew who ascended in the bureaucracy (until his execution). Again, most Jews did not take such positions, and the typical bureaucrat was not Jewish. In any case, the tolerance of Jews by the Party in the 1920s and early 1930s evaporated by 1936/37. In the end, hundreds of thousands of Jews, especially "bourgeois" business figures and religious leaders, were exiled to Siberia, and Stalin executed any Bundist leaders he thought politically suspect. Nonetheless, in Soviet bloc nations, local nationalists identified Jews as pro-Russian officials of the communist state.

Although a few Jews in some states attained positions in the local bureaucracy, the postwar era was notably inhospitable to Jews. For example, 1968 student revolutions in Eastern Europe focused on social inequalities, imperialism, bureaucracy, and cultural transformation. But in Poland and much of the Soviet Union, authorities crushed that protest and further discredited it by associating it with Zionism. The USSR severed diplomatic relations with Israel following the Six Day War. Shortly afterward, it unleashed an anti-Zionist attack on the March 1968 protest, an attack in which "Zionism" easily became an anti-Semitic code for "Jews." In Poland, Mieczysław Moczar, the minister of Internal Affairs (the Secret Police) after 1964, invoked anti-Semitism in a failed effort to replace the Władysław Gomułka as head of the Polish state. Within a year, an estimated 20,000 Polish Jews immigrated to Israel, the United States, and elsewhere. In 1980, the independent trade union Solidarity arose at the Gdansk shipyards and became the first union in a Soviet pact country outside the control of the Communist Party. Within a year it had become the vanguard for a popular workers' movement with 10 million members. Years of struggle and political repression followed, but by the end of the decade, a Solidarity-led coalition was elected to form a government. With the ascendance of the popular dissident workers' movement, in 1988 the anti-Solidarity Polish government acknowledged and apologized for its anti-Semitic history. It also took some steps to initiate relationships with Jewish cultural institutions and to allow Jewish studies programs to open in its universities. But these gains were a modest and recent deviation from a longer story in which Jews in postwar Eastern Europe suffered either way they turned: by identification as radicals with Russia or as subjects of Soviet anti-Zionist policy that operated as a cover for anti-Semitism.

The history of the Jewish relationship to communism and to anticommunism profoundly shaped the emerging Jewish heritage industry of the post-1990 era. The Cold War made any association with communism suspect, and nowhere more so than in the United States. Americans undertook destination travel to cities once part of the Soviet bloc after perestroika (openness, the policy of communist reform associated with Mikhail Gorbachev in the late 1980s), when anticommunism had begun to lose some of its credibility and ideological power but the legacy of the Cold War still cast a long shadow. State and institutional leaders would keep their communist/socialists history, if acknowledged at all, romanticized and safely in the past.

As cultural consumers, Jewish tourists confronted the often-fraught interpretive world abroad created by modern cultural producers. To begin with, Stalin had relegitimized Soviet nationalism during World War II and privileged it after the war. And in the decades leading up to 1989, Soviet celebration of internationalism against nationalism shaped the sites presented to tourists. In war memorials, Soviet Man was comfortably identified as a victim of Nazis. Twenty-million Soviets died in the war, but memorials to the homogenized Man blurred discussions of *which* men (and women!) were killed. Six million Jews might—might—be counted, but other marginal groups such as gypsies, homosexuals, and disabled victims, were significantly left out of the story altogether.

The attitudes of the postwar Soviet bloc toward religion and its policy on unoccupied and untended land and buildings adversely affected Jewish sites. In the decade that followed World War II Soviet bloc governments closed some houses of worship, gave them over to other enterprises, and declaring cemetery land vacant, used it for other purposes, such as housing blocks for the millions of Russians displaced by the war. New political imperatives also compelled states of the former Soviet Union to distance themselves from any association with communism, and from any studied consideration of the communist past and the place of Jews within it. The easy association of Jews with communists in the stereotype of the "Commie Jew" or "Bolshevik Jew" (*zydokomuna*) made Soviet bloc politicians, Jewish tourists, or local curators all reluctant to incorporate the long history of Jewish radicalism into the heritage story.[25]

In sum, post-1989 events—resurgent nationalism, a surge of development projects, and a backlash against anything associated with the prior communist regimes—helped shape the master narrative of Central and Eastern Europe Jewish heritage. These events did not challenge the dominant Holocaust narrative, but they helped mute or eliminate most traces of the socialist Jewish past in that story. Together these elements played important roles in determining which Jews were incorporated into or written out of that narrative. Western capital from NGOs and Jewish funders flowed into Eastern Europe after the collapse of the Soviet Union in 1989 to help support the design and erection of new Jewish and Holocaust museums. Local and regional state agencies and national governments, like Germany and Poland, committed funds to "atone" for their past; others allotted monies to nurture a national and nonsocialist identity; some were motivated by both goals. Regime change could and did change views and commitments of governments, but whatever their motives, local, national, and historically contingent politics shaped how the history of Jews was remembered, forgotten, disremembered, or ignored at these sites.[26]

Openings

As cultural critic Stuart Hall often pointed out, hegemony is damn hard work; in the end, cracks in the master narrative allow other stories to seep through.[27] Even in the face of dominant redemptive Holocaust narratives, a stream of Jewish tourists traveled back to Eastern Europe with other agendas and with other stories in mind. Recent work by three literary scholars illustrates a wider range: Daniel Mendelsohn travels the world looking for prewar and wartime traces of six of his relatives; Marianne Hirsch and Leo Spitzer return with her parents to Czernowitz to revisit memories of the town they had fled before the war; and the Yiddish writer David G. Roskies's memoir, *Yiddishlands*, focuses on his mother, born in Vilna in 1905, as part of a tour of a vibrant, resonant twentieth-century Yiddish culture that takes readers from Vilna to Montreal and to New York.[28] Two recent cultural texts also re-create the Jewish world of the Łódź and the Bund mobilization during the opening decade of the twentieth century. Israel Joshua Singer's grand epic novel *The Brothers Ashkenazi* details Łódź's Jewish life, both its proletarian and entrepreneurial sides, through a contested family story, while *The Promised Land*, by contemporary Polish filmmaker Andrzej Wajda, dramatizes the origins of the 1905 Revolution in a story of resistance to the rapacious capitalism of Łódź textile manufacturers.[29]

Site Challenges and Opportunities

Counter-narratives could seep through openings—in between spaces—in the master narrative. "Museum discourse," anthropologist Tamar Katriel observes, "is unabashedly saturated with ideological assumptions." Museums are "open texts," she notes, but tour guides "perform" ideology. As "cultural brokers," they are ventriloquists, who privilege objects and make walls and streets "speak."[30] Chaim Noy adds that tourists also perform for locals and for themselves to produce a collective identity as "testifiers taking what they imagine to be a ritual or transcendent voyage.[31] So while guides and tourists self-consciously perform in settings "open" to interpretation, their performances are also constrained by the spaces and material objects that curators, city planners, and guides have marked and privileged. Memorials, for example, are cast in stone and commemorate one moment, one event, or one era in time. In assigning monumental meaning to an event, memorials do memory work for the viewer.[32] By selecting some material objects for public display, cultural brokers privilege some artifacts and leave them open to being fetishized. In addition, in their privileged status, material objects and physical sites claim "authenticity" for experiences that visitors associate with them.[33]

Oral history, however, illustrates how the privileging of certain voices can legitimize the erasure of others. Embraced in the 1970s as a way to empower perspectives "from below" often ignored in top-down accounts, oral histories reflect the voices of survivors alive to recall events. But their stories, like all memories, are not uncomplicated: respondents tell the stories they recall at a particular moment. They are inclined to censure unflattering or uncomfortable details. Curators then edit the stories for use in kiosks. The repeated accounts then lend a privileged choral affect to testimonies and obscure their constructed quality. At the same time, these utterances tend to mute dissonant voices of individuals who might have been less heroic, compelling, or oppositional.[34]

A New Jewish History

Thanks to a new historical practice that has gained recognition, especially after the opening of the Warsaw Jewish museum POLIN's core exhibit in late October 2014, cracks in the dominant narrative are appearing in some Jewish heritage sites. A "New Jewish History" ascendant during the seven years of my travel challenges the dominant redemptive Holocaust narrative by diversifying agents, voices, and the chronology of the remembered past. It has found a receptive audience among many curators and the scholars who advise them. Revisionist curatorial and scholarly teams now articulate a critical museology that problematizes the ideological apparatus sustaining the dominant narrative and its silences. Let me be clear though: this is a promising and emerging development but it is not by any means prevailing.

The new generation of scholars pioneering the New Jewish History, such as Erica Lehrer, Michael Meng, and Scott Ury in European studies, stand on the shoulders of veteran ethnographers such as Kirshenblatt-Gimblett.[35] The work also builds on the New Social History that transformed historical scholarship in the late 1960s and 1970s and in the new millennium produced comparable work by Tony Michels and Daniel Katz in the United States. Howe's *World of Our Fathers* and new institutions such as New York's Tenement Museum further reflected the influence of that history in American and European Jewish history. In its twenty-first century articulation the New Jewish History has adapted and developed this venerable tradition in social history to provide a new polyphonic heritage story in Central and Eastern Europe as well. It tries to convey multiple voices speaking from contending points of view that are driven by local and even extra-local transnational imperatives (such as the cause of Israel in the Holocaust narrative).[36] Equally important, it identifies some players as having greater access to authority than others. Against an omniscient Voice of God narrator or guide who speaks with unquestioned authority, a new generation of scholars and curators emphasize the importance of mounting exhibitions that encourage self-reflection about their own assumptions, representations of the past they see and, importantly, perspectives they miss.[37]

The New Jewish History is, however, more than a rethinking of narrative complexities; rather, it is a new way of thinking and writing the Jewish past. For example, Ury's urban history of Warsaw during and after the 1905 Revolution, *Barricades and Banners*, offers a new paradigm for Jewish history, especially for that of the last two centuries. In a powerful analysis of conventional Jewish historiography, Ury centers the history of Jewish socialism as part of the foundational story of Jewish modernism. He critiques historians of the Jewish past for having focused too heavily on intellectual and political history that emphasizes the roles of Great (i.e., wealthy) Men—Orthodox rabbis, intellectual "giants" such as Moses Mendelsohn, banking and manufacturing leaders, and political institutions. Their wives might occasionally (and only occasionally) appear, but principally as "benefactors," not unlike the Lady Bountifuls described among comparable Protestant elite women of the time. By contrast, Ury embraces social history, with its attention to social movements, class structure, and political culture. His claim for the recuperative work of social history also helps explain the place of ethnography and folklore in this New Jewish History.

Significantly, the move into social (and cultural) history revises the master narrative in fundamental ways. First, against accounts of relentless victimization, Jews are agents of their own history. By shifting from the Great Man in history to the people of the streets, the theatre, and the workshop, Ury's paradigm offers a much broader range of agents as well. His model also elaborates a more ambiguous history: all Jews did not see Poles as anti-Semites, and all Poles did not see Jews as Judeo-Commies. Second, multiple identities in the social history of Jewish life provide a complex model of the Jewish self that cannot be reduced to an essential checklist or easily dismissed as assimilated or secular. Third, the Holocaust is one part of a longer history, not a teleological endpoint in the making of the Jewish modern identity. Perhaps most important, Ury highlights the emergence of a new specifically "Jewish public sphere" with a "modern political movement," the Bund, a movement using the Yiddish vernacular spoken by two-thirds of Jews in Eastern Europe.

The Bund

The Bund was a labor socialist trade union and political movement. It was a transnational movement that Tony Michels sees beginning in New York among Russian immigrants in the 1880s and being transported back to Europe.[38] The Bund arose as a formal political organization in Vilnius in 1897 in the face of the pogroms of 1881, the regime of state repression that followed, and dislocations from industrial capitalism. These developments compelled many Eastern European Jews to seek alternatives to the *Haskalah* (the Jewish Enlightenment) and rationalist institutions and thought, while still appropriating secular values from them.[39] Recent scholarship sees the Bund and Yiddishkeit as primarily forms of cultural nationalism in reaction to rising tides of anti-Semitism in Eastern Europe.[40] In this context, both Bundism (and its socialist precursors) and Zionism arose as the two modern Jewish political movements of the last century, the former advocating "Jewish cultural autonomy based on Yiddish" and the latter offering the promise of a national homeland.[41] The two movements sometimes overlapped and spawned a range of political parties and sects—the Zionist Socialist Party, Seimists (Jewish Socialists Workers' Party), and Poale-Zion (Labor-Zionists).

Historians have elaborated the central role of the Bund and Bund political culture in Jewish history. According to Zvi Gitelman, it contributed to "the democratization and modernization of Jewish political life, perhaps more than Zionism." Gitelman and others state that the Bund lies at the heart of a "dialectics of Jewish modernity" among the urban proletariat, Jewish working class, and socialist culture in cities in the years after the 1905 Revolution. The Bund flourished in the first decades of the twentieth century in various Polish, Lithuanian, and Belorussian industrial cities. Bundists also established a few centers in Ukraine. Historian Jack Jacobs documents how over the next three decades, the Bund and other left-wing political groups would become the leading voices of the Jewish street and the burgeoning interwar Jewish culture sphere.[42] Although the Bund as a political party had little or no formal organization outside of Europe, immigrant Jews who identify as Bundists left a legacy on the political and cultural life in cities of the Jewish diaspora as far flung as Buenos Aires, London, and New York.[43]

The centrality of the Bund (with Zionism) in the making of modern Jewish identity was a personal revelation that brought my research and personal stories together. Jews like Chaia and Zishe Walkowitz embraced the Bund. As they migrated to industrial cities for work and subsequently immigrated westward, they brought the Bund's political culture of literature, folk song, theater, and plays with them. Bundists were steeped in Yiddishkeit, a word that came to have very particular meaning for radical Jews. It literally means "Jewishness" or "Jewish way of life." While Orthodox Jews spoke Yiddish in daily life and could easily identify with the term, as advanced by Jewish socialists, Yiddishkeit came to encompass what anthropologist Karen Brodkin describes as "a synergistic mixture of religious and secular emphases on social justice" with "a strong anti-capitalist streak."[44] In New York, immigrant Jews endowed Bundism and Yiddishkeit with an American inflection; as David Feldman has observed, in contrast to Eastern Europe, in the United States, Yiddishkeit and the Bund were more informed by the experience of being an immigrant than by the "national question."

Embracing Yiddish as the language of working-class Jews, U.S. Bundists created vibrant Yiddish literature, music, theater, and journalism in the hope of building a progressive class-conscious Jewish proletariat and socialist labor movement.[45] Łódź, the second largest city in Poland, from which my paternal grandparents emigrated in 1913–1914 to Denmark (and six years later, after the war, to America), was a major center of the Bund.[46]

Gender analysis was a second interpretative contribution of the New Jewish History, although, again, it rested on the important work of feminist social and cultural Jewish historians such as Marion Kaplan for Germany and Hasia Diner for the United States done decades earlier.[47] This analytic focus, especially vivid in the work by Michels and Katz on New York's Jewish socialists, addresses the experience of women like my grandmother in the history of Jewish socialism. As Gitelman has observed, women "formed a substantial segment of both the intelligentsia and the kase-organizing working force" and women's emancipation "shook the very foundation of Jewish life."[48] In juggling factory jobs, part-time work out of the home, raising politically engaged immigrant children to advance in the new world, defending the family before congressional inquisitors, and managing an ambitious and headstrong unpredictable husband, activist women like Chaia/Ida Walkowitz played central roles in Jewish modernization.[49]

Unfortunately for museum directors, tour guides and local tourism officials, the complexities and paradoxes of the New Jewish History do not always conform to audience expectations. New paradigms do not necessarily provide welcome narratives. Tourists—often much like myself—come to hear (preferably flattering) stories of their ancestors. Along the way, they do not want to be bored by historical details shorn of lively anecdotes; they want to be amused and have their past as they imagine it confirmed. Both Jews and non-Jews, for instance, may have little tolerance with uncomfortable historical narratives that feature communists, criminals, or exploiters.

The troubled past of the Holocaust and questions of complicity by national actors place a special burden on Jewish Heritage purveyors who try to introduce complicated and detailed accounts. In the case of the Holocaust, Jews may expect to hear about local collaborators with the Nazis, while locals may prefer stories of local resistance fighters who try to save Jews. And nowhere are these issues more vexing than in countries that were occupied by the Nazis. The case of Poland is illustrative, though similar stories could be heard in accounts of Vichy France, Hungary, Ukraine, and elsewhere. Traditional Polish national narratives of heroic resistance to the Nazis as memorialized in Warsaw's Rising Museum dedicated to the 1944 Warsaw Uprising contrast with the traditional Jewish picture of unrelenting anti-Semitism. Historian Jan T. Gross's compelling, controversial 2001 account of Polish complicity in the murder of perhaps as many as 1,600 Jewish residents of Jedwabne in 1941 reflects a prevalent Jewish view of Polish collaboration. In Neighbors, Gross indicts everyday Poles for their agency in the Holocaust.[50] But others, like the Polish filmmaker Pawel

Pawlikowski, dramatize a more complex picture. In his 2013 film *Ida,* a father and son divide over the personal costs and advantages to helping protect Jews and, ultimately, what each is prepared to do.[51] Some non-Jews helped Jews; in Israel, Yad Vashem recognizes them as the "Righteous among the Nations." Some non-Jews also suffered at the hands of the Nazis and others who collaborated with them. Yet many more Poles quietly eked out a fragile and fraught existence enmeshed in their own struggles with poverty and occupiers. At the end of a tour, however, the guide or museum director, concerned that tourists need to be sufficiently pleased to recommend the experience to others, has to negotiate the slippery boundaries and sometimes contradictory perspectives, between challenging or accommodating expectations, and between history, memory, entertainment, and politics.

JEWISH IDENTITY AND HERITAGE-MAKING

The search for an inclusive history of Jewish heritage is especially meaningful in light of my interest in stories of people like my radical grandmother, and against the fraught and contested politics of Jewish identity happening today. Judaism is matrilineal—if the mother is Jewish, the child is Jewish—and accordingly Jewish identity rests primarily on the mother's roots and, secondarily, on religious association; by contrast, ethnic claims have no legal standing. Moreover, in Israel, ultra-Orthodox rabbis control marriage and conversions and have the sole authority to determine Jewish identity.

Social scientists, however, have documented a complicated picture of how Jews represent themselves, a picture at considerable remove from rabbinical dicta. The Pew Foundation's Research on Religion and Public Life Project claims that 93 percent of Jews born between 1914 and 1927 identified as Jews by religion. Historians, though, query that view. They note the absence of a category in the Pew data for ethno-cultural identity undoubtedly framed responses. By contrast, historian Annie Polland finds a secular identity to be prevalent among Jews in turn-of-the-century New York: "religious authority had diminished in importance for most eastern European Jews." A sizeable number of Jews living on New York's Lower East Side identified as "secular" or only "High Holy Day Jews."

Letters in the socialist *Forverts (The Jewish Daily Forward)* draw an even more complicated picture. In practice there was no "stark division" between the "secular" and "the pious": correspondents spoke of religious socialists, a religious Yiddish culture, and even religious Bundists.[52] Pew surveys, catching up with the increased secularity of Jews over the course of the twentieth century, note in 2013 that 22 percent of Jews claimed no religion, and the percentage rose to 32 among those born after 1980. Equally significant, when asked if Jewish identity involved culture and ancestry rather than religion, 55 percent of those who identified by religion also answered ancestry/culture. The rate for those claiming no religion was a whopping 83 percent.

Recent scholarship also notes the permeability of secular and religious boundaries, concluding that it is neither "productive nor resonant to separate the political/social/cultural and religious worlds and identities."[53] Indeed, many people live their lives in a gray liminal area between these terms. Some Jews disavow religion entirely; for many others, the "High Holy Day Jews," observance is lax or casual. In pastimes, the former included Bundists, who typically were militantly secular and distanced themselves from any institutional religion and rejected any notion of a Supreme Being. But as David Feldman (and the New Jewish History generally) reminds us, such a position raises the question about multiple identities for radicals as well as for their critics: in privileging their political identity, do such activists cease to be Jewish? For some, an alternative identity, whether it be a national identity (e.g., British, Polish, Hungarian) or a political identity (e.g., a communist), or an occupational identity (e.g., a banker, a worker) was a choice, albeit a choice constrained by time and place. Recent scholarship disputes the idea of a stable normative Jewish family or, by extension, of Jewish identity. Rather, as Jonathan Boyarin notes, there are "infinite ways of being both Jewish and Other." Jewishness is constantly invented.[54]

Some radicals, like the Bundists, rooted their political principles in a tradition of Jewish social justice immersed in a culture of Yiddishkeit, and taught it in their Jewish schools.[55] Still, again, the boundaries could be blurred: the Bund tradition was born in the Vilna Rabbinical Seminary, a government institution that trained young men to be official "state rabbis" and "produced a number of famous revolutionary figures." One graduate of the Seminary, Aaron Lieberman, founded the first Jewish socialist society, the Union of Hebrew Socialists, in London in 1876.[56] More than a half century later, Raphael Samuel, a red diaper baby in London, recalls that family Passover began with Hebrew prayers to satisfy his Orthodox grandmother but ended with Soviet songs.[57]

Finally, the equivocal response of many Jews identifying as secular suggests the elasticity of the category. For a different project I surveyed respondents about their religious affiliation. I knew many of these individuals identified culturally as Jewish, but in the survey, a majority both checked off "none" and added a comment that they were "spiritual."[58] This last designation has particularly gained currency in modern America. Many individuals reject institutional religion in favor of a freethinking spirit. Such claims may be religion by another name; or faced with conservative criticism of atheism as immoral godlessness, it may simply be an assertion that one is moral, ethical, and sensitive to others.

A relatively recent book on Jewish heritage in Poland illustrates the complexity of narrating the story of Jewish heritage. Joanna Olczak-Ronikier's *In the Garden of Memory,* is a history of the author's Warsaw Polish-Jewish family. The book also raises larger questions of Jewish identity, including of who is a Jew and who should be included in the stories told.[59]

Olczak-Ronikier's personal account highlights the ever changing, fleeting, and at times tangential nature of Jewish identity, especially among secular Jews like her parents and grandparents who try to negotiate parallel national identities. In her memoir "assimilated Jews" participate in the Jewish story, even as they tried to privilege their Polish identity over their Jewish roots. Her grandparents ran the Mortkowicz publishing house and bookstore. They were part of a young secular Jewish intelligentsia committed to the fight for Polish independence. The birth and marriage documents of her grandparents and mother listed their Jewish origins, but while "they never hid their ethnic origins, they were reluctant to talk about [them]." Activists in the Young Poland artistic movement, these individuals were proud of their Polishness and "preferred not to emphasize what a short distance separated them from the Jewish world they had run away from." Her great uncle, Maks Horwitz, mentioned earlier, expressed another variant of Jewish modernity. He was more active in radical political and educational actions. Throughout his life, he supported the Polska Partia Socjalistyczna (Polish Socialist Party). In Zurich in 1916, he held "endless political discussions" with Lenin; he joined the Central Committee of the Polish Workers' Communist Party in 1918. In 1927, now known as Henryk Walecki, he moved his family to Moscow where he continued to work "within the Comintern leadership."[60]

The author's parents' history provides a contrasting set of complexities for the story of Jewish identity. Her father was the only non-Jew to marry into the family and her mother subsequently converted to his faith. But in 1939, her mother and grandmother (the grandfather had committed suicide after bankruptcy in 1931) put on armbands with a Jewish star "because they did not want to tempt fate."[61] When Jews were told to move to the ghetto, they quietly refused and went into hiding. The daughter, Joanna, was hidden with a dozen Jewish girls in a convent school. Meanwhile, the mother and grandmother moved surreptitiously during the next five years to seven hiding places. They hid in the last place for fourteen months. Squeezed into a small, windowless back room of a building, they survived with the help of a caretaker. They never looked outside, yet like many of the Polish-Jewish intelligentsia at the time, they found it hard to understand or accept a hyphenated identity. While effectively incarcerated as Jews, they remained committed to their Polish identity. In a will written while in hiding, her mother asked her Polish friends to tell their daughter about her mother's and grandmother's "activities and work for Polish culture and the Polish national identity."[62]

Reflecting on these paradoxes and contradictions, Olczak-Ronikier offers a concluding appraisal about the complicated but expansive boundaries of Jewish heritage. Her family occupied an elite niche of educated, bourgeois, and bohemian Jews who spoke Polish and German, not Yiddish.[63] While the Horwitz clan and its descendants claimed no obvious Jewish spiritual and ritual traditions, their lives illustrate the ephemeral, and blurry lines of Jewish identity, an identity self-fashioned, imagined by others, embedded in their psyche, and historically contingent.[64] A half-century after her mother and grandmother, reiterating their identity as Poles, penned their will, Joanna's daughter, Katarzyna, worked on the curatorial staff of Kraków's Schindler Museum and published a book on the fate of Kraków's Jews between 1939 and 1945. Her daughter, Maria, became Orthodox (now as Miriam) and married a Polish Jew who is as of 2017 a rabbi in Łódź.[65]

The "Assimilated Jew" and the "Secular Jew"

The Assimilated Jew and the Secular Jew are fuzzy, problematic category descriptors, but they remain category markers increasingly in discussions of Jewish identity. Those critical of nonreligious Jews deploy them to normalize "plain and simple" religious Jewishness. Religious identity in this framing becomes the core and bona fide Jewish identity; the Secular Jew remains liminal and the Assimilated Jew, no longer Jewish. Boyarin notes that Jewish assimilation "assumes a fixed and approachable non-Jewish culture" that Jews can join "if they have the will and are given the chance."[66] Thus, some curators and museum directors with whom I spoke explained the absence or invisibility of those Jews who embraced local national cultures and politics by categorizing them as no longer Jewish.[67] By way of example, let me mention a conversation I had one morning in Kazimierz with another American tourist from Brooklyn. Hearing our common accents, we exchanged greetings and he asked what I was doing in Kraków. I playfully explained I was studying Jewish tourism and tourists like himself. I did not explicitly identify him as Jewish, but he took that meaning, telling me he was not Jewish. He explained that he had converted to Christianity two years earlier. Now a Baptist, he assumed Jewishness lay only in his religion and that in exiting the religion he had effectively left his culture, his heritage, behind, too. The experience of the Horwitz clan, and most poignantly, the fate of Olczak-Ronikier's mother and grandmother demonstrate the limitations of such thinking.

What is conventionally discussed as Jewish assimilation arose in the middle of the nineteenth century when the *maskilim* (Jewish followers of the Haskalah) "modernized" ritual practices—that is, use of an organ, conducting services in Polish or German—and began to work more actively within the local culture. However, the idea of assimilation as the wholesale rejection of Jewish culture and religion, has been overly universalized and un-nuanced. Feldman prefers to think about this process as acculturation, a less complete process that sees Jewish culture and the Jewish community as changing rather than degenerating.

Historian Marcin Wodziński insists that the Jews labeled as assimilationists were subjected to a rhetorical device "conjured up by their adversaries" to denigrate their Jewishness, if not dismiss it entirely. In his path-breaking study of "assimilationists" in Warsaw, Wodziński also offers an alternative category for them as "integrationists." He notes that modernizing Jews did not speak with one voice. While some "radicals" explicitly rejected their Jewishness, this group was small. Another small group of Hebrew-Germans rejected Polonization. The majority occupying a "moderate" middle position were "integrationists." These people were not maskilim at all. Retaining a strong identity as Jews by religion and Poles in the culture, they were "Poles of the Mosaic faith."[68]

Scholars of Jewish assimilation, such as Feldman and Wodziński, thus challenge the conventional division of Jews into two clear camps—the "real" observant Jew and the Assimilated Jew. Borrowing from the writing of E. P. Thompson and Michel Foucault on power and culture, Feldman assesses identities as evolving, ever-changing, hybrid formations. Moreover, they both make the case that assimilation is not a useful historical category; it is a political term. In this framework, Jewish identity is formed in time and place and as struggles between contested cultures. Such Jews are acculturating integrationists operating inside the Jewish community.

The debate over assimilation bears directly on the history of Jewish socialism and the inclusion of secular Jews in the heritage narrative. Following Wodziński, it is possible to interpret the dismissal or marginalization of socialist and secular Jews from Jewish heritage as an ahistorical and hostile political project. Rather, Jewish heritage should encompass secular and radical Jews as well as other complexities and contradictions that have historically riddled Jewish identity. Such an inclusive cultural representation would narrate Jewish heritage as a turbulent story of the religious and secular, the wealthy and the poor, peddlers and merchants, capitalist entrepreneurs and idealist communards, Zionists and internationalists.

To tell such a wide-ranging and diverse history, researchers, curators, and guides must represent both those they deem admirable and suspect. One examination of a formal curriculum for guides suggests they are rarely trained to do so, and the pressure on them to make tourists feel good with stories they want to hear, disinclines them to learn, value, and give a counter-narrative.[69] Even though scholars have worked to develop a broadened and inclusive conception and narrative, much Jewish heritage still remains wedded to a Holocaust narrative and an exclusive sense of Jewish identity.

Reinventions of Jewishness

Since 1989, the revival of Jewish heritage in cities such as Berlin, Warsaw, Lviv, Budapest, and Kraków have illustrated the potential and possible pitfalls for incorporating a capacious notion of Jewish identity in heritage tourism. In 2002,

Ruth Ellen Gruber described this reinvention of Jewish life in cities where few Jews now live as "virtual Jewishness." The reconstruction of Jewish Poland has entailed conceptions of Jewishness imagined by Jews and non-Jews. Building on Gruber, ethnographer Erica Lehrer details the complexities of the Jewish past in this revival. In the new heritage industry that sprang up in the 1990s, curators, politicians, developers, shopkeepers, residents, tourists worked—sometimes in alliance, and sometimes in opposition—to reimagine the district as an urban development project. In her richly layered ethnography of Kazimierz, the Jewish quarter outside Kraków, Leher unpacks Jewishness in Kazimierz through discussion of the annual weeklong Jewish cultural festivals held there and how the district functions as a site for destination tourism.[70]

Lehrer finds few traces of the prewar history in museum exhibitions. New historical sites, like the Schindler Museum and new monuments and memorials, draw attention to the Holocaust. Guides discuss anti-Semitic policies of the Polish Communist Party in 1968, but make no mention of prewar Jewish communist activism. Lehrer does find a postwar reinvention of Jewish life on the streets of Kazimierz though. By 2011, the area had become a "hip, bustling youthful quarter," with "general commercial hubbub." In the heritage experience of Kazimierz, Holocaust redemption coexists with commodified Jewishness, most famously seen in the annual weeklong Festival of Jewish Culture where film, klezmer, food, and contemporary political discussions attract crowds of both Jews and non-Jews.

Other analysts both confirm and challenge Lehrer's account.[71] However, unlike critics who condemn Kazimierz as Disneyfied shlock-development, Lehrer draws a more optimistic conclusion.[72] The question of nostalgia, she notes, raises a major theme of recent anthropological work that sees the practice taking many forms. According to this literature, the past and "heritage" are constantly invented, not unchanging and "essential." Some may interpret a depiction as a rose-tinted reversion to an idealized past, while others view the same representation as ironic, perhaps even invested with more positive meanings about the present's relationship to the past.[73] Of course, tourists visiting such heritage sites do not necessarily see them through the eyes of anthropology texts. It remains to be seen if they can distinguish the range of meanings produced by artists and artisans from what appears to some observers simply to be kitsch.

Lehrer's concluding discussion of Kraków's progressive, ecumenical Jewish Community Center (JCC), offers a second perspective on the renewal of Jewish life. Her question about the development and role of the JCC in contemporary Kazimierz also returns her story to my quest for broadened and inclusive Jewish heritage tourism. "There is," she writes, "a growing schism in the Jewish world between those whose own narrative of victimhood trumps all other concerns and those whose commitment to inclusive liberalism is forcing them to reconsider pillars of contemporary Jewish belonging (particularly Zionism) whose dominant forms increasingly conflict with more universal values." In that regard, the JCC, she notes with significance, is not a synagogue and its leader has an "expansive view of the Jewish ecosystem," welcoming anyone "Jewish-identified." Thus, Lehrer finds the JCC and the Kazimierz neighborhood a "surprisingly vital" source of Jewish renewal in Poland. At the same time, in acknowledging the liminal social space occupied by the JCC in the town, she summons up big questions haunting Jewish heritage tourism. Whose narratives are being privileged in Poland? Who will count as a Jew when the "Polish rabbinate is affected by decisions of the Israeli (Orthodox) establishment?" Who will speak for the Jewish community? What will be the fate of the secular voice?[74]

—————

In sum, the politics of the present frames how guides, curators, and other commercial and public cultural producers tell stories of the past. The world of Jewish socialism, Yiddishkeit, and civic culture may be elided in popular memory, but as Howe's voluminous study demonstrates, it has a long and vital history. Not all historians have consigned that past to oblivion. In 1992, almost a decade before Waltzer's sentinel warning of the lost Jewish socialist world, Jonathan Boyarin wrote of the need to "construct a memory" for immigrant Jewish socialists on the Lower East Side. In the decade following Waltzer's review essay, a notable spate of serious books were published on Jewish socialism, the legacy of the Bund, and what Roskies called "Yiddishland."[75] Moreover, the contemporary interest in Yiddishkeit to Jews in social movements suggests that a contemporary market/audience for an inclusive, critical heritage tourism that engages with social history exists. Whether or not there is an audience for Yiddishkeit and the political culture of Jewish socialism, however, may be moot; the question at hand is whether that part of Jewish life is being told in public history venues at all.[76]

The telling, however, depends on whom storytellers understand to be a Jew and what life experiences they deem memorable—or to be remembered. What do heritage tour guides and sites of memory and history tell us? Which stories do they tell; which do they forget; which do they privilege? And then, how do guides and curators negotiate among the many stories? How do they deal with the variety of expectations of foreign Jewish tourists and local non-Jewish visitors? Finally, and most basically, how do they understand heritage and identity? Jewishness is both a religious and an ethnic identity, but in practice these were not simple binary opposites. As detailed above, Jews expressed their identity along a continuum of possible meanings with many gray areas. A Jewish socialist actively engaged in labor struggles in Łódź. Jews, such as Ida Lubertofsky Walkowitz, my Bubbe Chaia, was at once a Jew, a socialist, a woman, a proletarian, a secularist, a wife, and a young adult. Identities would change over time; they were not static categories. The story then and in its retelling was and is complex and layered, and messy in its richness.

So I set out to hear Bubbe's secular story and the history of Yiddishkeit in the parts of Poland where she spent her early life. It was a logical starting point for a broad historical and personal family quest: the area that was the Russian-controlled Kingdom of Poland until 1918 and the Pale of Settlement to its east and south were major sites of Jewish habitation. Since 2000, Poland is also estimated to be the second largest destination for Jewish tourism after Israel.[77] Jews had a long, complex history in the region, but the final question, of course, would be what, if any, of this rich but messy story would I hear.

Interlude

I am not sure what it meant to me in my early teens to be growing up in a communist household, much less in a Jewish communist one. That we were Jewish and communists were given "facts." Jewishness was spoken of, and often, as a cultural identity; we were secular. The family never spoke much of communism, but my father liked the fact that I volunteered in my senior year of high school to defend socialism against capitalism in a social studies debate, and he helped me prepare for it. Neither the teacher nor popular culture at the time (and generally since) distinguished socialism from communism, and as a rule, the "lost world" encompassed both. In any case, my father advised I simply concede at the outset that totalitarianism is bad and shift the debate to one of economic systems. (My father's advice served me well and the teacher felt the need to intervene on my opponents' behalf.) The weight of a hidden past came at a price though: before she died my mother told me how remarkable it was that I always seemed to know who we were, what we believed, and what I could and could not say in public. Years later, in a therapy group, I began to appreciate the psychic burden of internalizing such momentous views and feelings. But I believed my parents were at risk and I had to do my part to protect them with silence. Like most Communist Party (CP) households, I knew the Rosenberg case. We had the volume of their prison letters at home, which I read several times, perhaps imagining how that story might repeat itself in my family. I had also seen a picture of a family friend, Al Shadowitz, a physicist who was also part of a regular bridge foursome with my dad, on the front page of the *New York Times*. Shadowitz had been called before the McCarthy Committee and advised by Albert Einstein to plead the First Amendment, not the usual Fifth. I was proud to know him, but also knew the publicity would (and did) cost Shadowitz his job. My father believed himself to be too undistinguished to be targeted by McCarthy. I learned years later that my father provided the liaison for

Martha Stone Asher with her son when the New Jersey CP leader was underground during the McCarthy era. But my father was only a shopkeeper and was convinced that "naming" him would have little payoff for McCarthy.

There were periodic reminders of my family's vulnerability. On one occasion, for instance, home alone, I answered a phone call from California from someone wanting to speak to my dad. The caller wanted to know who was "ratting" to the FBI. In retrospect, I wonder if the caller spoke to me out of pure fear or somehow knew I would understand. I have no idea. I do remember FBI agents coming to our front door. I also have a vivid memory of the FBI stopping my father one Saturday afternoon while we drove around Paterson in his truck collecting money. (It was one of those tragic ironies that my father, who sold cheap furniture, linoleum, rugs, and mattresses to poor Patersonians, engaged in the most exploitative end of capitalist shopkeeping. He charged people based on what he thought they could pay in weekly—if he was lucky—installments of one to maybe five dollars.) In both encounters with the FBI that I witnessed, my father quietly and firmly just told the agents he had nothing to say to them and turned away.

Where did being Jewish fit into this experience? Were we Jewish communists, or were we communists who happened to be Jewish? Like Bubbe/Ida, people have many identities: they can be Jewish, a woman, middle-aged, Polish, American, and so forth. Circumstances call on us to summon up one or a combination of the alternatives. At times, an identity can be attenuated; at other times, it can intense. The boundaries of an identity like Jewishness can also be porous, contested, and challenging. Both Jewish and communist identities were classic examples of such contested identities with a range of meanings held and ascribed. In this context, I "knew" most Jews were not communists, and that most communists were not Jewish. Most of my family's friends I "knew" to be Jewish and communists. And, thinking back, I believe they identified as such. More to the point, I was growing up in a world of Yiddishkeit that (even in translation) I saw as integral to a Jewish communist labor movement. I never formally associated our politics and social activism with the voluntarism of kehillah social services or Jewish communalism. Rather, I understood our social engagements as an activist commitment to "social justice" within a Jewish tradition nurtured by Bund socialism/communism and its cultural expressions. And recent work on Minsk Jews in the interwar and postwar eras illustrates how Jews carried the customs, sentiments, and political culture of the Bund forward with an "entangled loyalty to [both] Bundism and Bolshevism."[1]

My grandfather Zishe, for example, had a passion for the theater that Yiddishkeit nurtured. He always regretted he could not be an actor. In Copenhagen he took an active role in the Jewish theater and soon after his arrival in Paterson in 1921, joined the vibrant Jewish theater there. He also sponsored dramatic and poetry readings at his home. In Paterson, Zishe became a leading member of the Freiheit Gesang Ferein (later, the Paterson Jewish Folk Chorus).[2] Singing mostly in Yiddish—by the 1950s the repertoire mixed in English verses or songs—the chorus was affiliated with the CP and sang songs in support of its struggles.[3] The chorus was also a Walkowitz family institution. My aunt Belle and uncle Joe, my father's siblings, both sang with the chorus and took turns as president from 1940 until the chorus's demise in the mid-1970s. My aunt Lillian Katz Heller also sang with the chorus. But her father (who was my grandmother's brother-in-law), Joe Katz, was a socialist and a bitter enemy of the communists. While I suspect he also identified with the Bund, he saw Lillian's involvement with the communist chorus as a traitorous act. The profound disagreement between Katz and his brother-in-law Zishe extended to their families.

Differences between the two families are lost in history, but undoubtedly mirrored sectarian disputes and divisions that famously divided the Left in the wake of Lenin's rise to power. Some Left-wing militants formed the Communist Party and aligned with the Soviet Union as a model for moving forward; "moderates" opposed what they saw as abridged civil liberties of communist centralism and supported instead democratic socialism.[4] A socialist labor activist, Katz considered the strategies, policies, and what he saw as the dogmatism of the communists to be rigid and anathema. By extension, joining the CP-affiliated chorus was a despicable act of complicity. Of course, growing up I only thought of the chorus as singing songs in support of the "good fight."

The difference between the families and how it was bridged, though, illustrates what I have since come to understand as the complexity and vitality of Jewish radicalism and family life. Disagreements between Jewish socialists and communists, like other divisions familiar to students of political movements, created bitter family arguments among landsmen. They had fought alongside one another in Łódź and shared opposition to the hated capitalists, but they could barely tolerate being in the same room with one another when discussions turned to politics. Socialists and communists each insisted they were the real radicals and that the others were "soft" or "reckless." Katz's granddaughter, Ruthie Lubert, remembers being told how angry her grandfather was that Zishe had his boys, Joe and Solly (my dad), stand on street corners handing out communist propaganda. In turn, I recall my father regularly regaling me with a song, sung with an accented Jewish-immigrant English, that ridiculed the socialist Clothing Workers Union: "the cloakmakers' union vas a no-gooter Union, a company union of the boss." There were two Jewish community centers. Socialist youth like Ruthie went to the Arbiter Ring (Workman's Circle) schools to learn Yiddish and in the summer to Camp Kinder Ring on Sylvan Lake, sixty miles north of New York City. Communist youth like the Walkowitzes went to communist-affiliated folk shule on Sunday and to a camp organized by the International Workers' Order across the lake from Camp Kinder

Ring, Camp Kinderland. Bitter enemies, the two camps never socialized. My father, I was told, and it may be apocryphal, helped "organize the waiters" at Kinderland. When I came of age, I was sent to what we later affectionately called "commie camp"—Wyandot, the camp in the Catskill Mountains that had an earlier existence in North Jersey as Wo-Chi-Ca.[5]

As I discuss later on in the book, Joe Katz played an important and supportive role in my family's history and, ultimately, to maintain a relationship, the Katzes and Walkowitzes agreed not to discuss politics. Through the 1950s, the two clans, the families of the two Lubertofsky sisters, Bubbe Chaia and my Tante Neche, met regularly in a "family circle."[6] Rather than an association of people from the same village or city—landsmenshaftn—family circles or cousin clubs brought together family members for emotional and financial support. I remember several meetings at our home. I have no idea what was discussed, though such gatherings in the early years may have considered mutual aid for family in the Paterson area and those elsewhere in the Jewish diaspora—Łódź, Copenhagen, Buenos Aires, and California. Every summer the families also gathered one Sunday at Penners, a park in nearby Spring Valley, New York, for a grand picnic, swimming, horseshoes, talk (lots of talk), and camaraderie. It was a radical family, both divided and together. By the late 1950s, as the family grew and married, I heard grumbling among the self-identified radicals of, horror of horrors, conservative newcomers. Division among radicals was one thing; conservative antiradicals stretched the bonds of family. Thus, the history of Jewish radicalism in my family, a history I hope to learn more about, uncover, and hear, was not monolithic. Like Jewish history generally, it was vibrant, contested, complex, and multivocal.

My travel, however, began in a town my grandparents called, in Yiddish, Amshenov (now Mszczonów) with simplified versions of this family story echoing in my head. I had few expectations of what I would find there, and little more for Łódź, where they lived before emigrating. I had been there forty years earlier to speak at a conference and saw then that their neighborhood had been destroyed in the war. Still, like most tourists, and especially those "returning" to a one-time family home, I brought an agenda with me. I wondered what of the Jewish socialist past and political agitation that had animated my grandparents—and ultimately forced them to flee the city—would I see and hear?

PART I

Looking for Bubbe

CHAPTER 2

Mszczonów and Łódź

HERITAGE ENTREPRENEURSHIP

Mszczonów

In October 2011 I drove to the village of Mszczonów from Łódź accompanied by my cousin Alex Berzin, a Buddhist scholar and linguist living in Berlin. His mother Rose was my father's younger sister and Bubbe Chaia was also his grandmother. The city was an unlikely place to begin a study of Jewish heritage tourism. Despite containing one of the largest settlements of Jews in prewar Europe, the city was a case of underdeveloped tourism. I engaged a translator-guide from Warsaw, Jacek Dobrowolski, who some American friends had recommended to lead us. Mszczonów, the town my grandparents knew as Amshenov in Yiddish, was located 29.8 miles southwest of Warsaw and 54.2 miles northeast of Łódź. It had a population of 6,231 people in 2006.

History

Jews settled in the town at least as early as the eighteenth century and were granted civil rights in a 1778 agreement between the Kehillah (the organization representing the Jewish community) and the Christian townspeople. The terms of settlement allowed Jews to trade and build houses, although it restricted them to two plots of land. It provided them with an ordered and contained citizenship with a measure of tolerance. The security of the Jewish community evaporated, however, as Polish merchants grew anxious over competition with Jewish traders and Jews became unsettled by news of the pogroms in 1881–1882 in the Pale of Settlement to the east that followed the assassination of Czar Alexander II.[1] In 1897, at about the time my ancestors might have left there, Mszczonów's population peaked at almost 4,900, of which 49.9 percent (2,437) were Jews. Like my grandparents, many sought opportunities in cities like Łódź in the next decades, but in 1939, an estimated 2,200 Jews still lived there.

Immigrants from Amshenov recorded their memories of the vital and con-tested world of the turn-of-the-century town in the twenty-fifth anniversary book of the Amschenover Independent Benevolent Society published in New York in 1941. The book carries the names of five Liberts, one of the American-ized variants of Chaia's maiden name. It describes tensions and divisions between traditionalists and modernists in the Jewish community that resem-ble the accounts of many comparable communities. The anniversary book's history describes a "home-town . . . divided into two distinct classes. The store-keeper and merchant considered themselves the superior element. To them belonged the choice seats in the eastern section of the synagogue and other hon-ors. And they regarded the artisan and wage-earner as the humblest element [who] . . . merely performed routine work." These social divisions, it goes on to state, were exacerbated by profound religious differences. The town was the home of the renowned Hasidic dynasty founded by an Amshinover rebbe, Reb Yaakov Dovid; by the turn of the century, however, the Hasidim were at war with *Misnagdim* (opponents) and both of them were at odds with increasing numbers of more secular Jews.[2]

Whether Chaia still lived in Amshinov or her family had moved on to Łódź, essays in the Yizkor (memorial) Book draw a picture of the active political and cultural world that she would have inhabited as a twenty-year-old in 1905 Amshe-nov (or, as we shall see, in Łódź). Manufacturers, Jews included, generally did not employ Jews in the area's factories. They may not have wanted Jewish employees because they would not labor on the Sabbath, but also because gentile workers were less likely to support trade unions and assert worker rights.[3] By contrast, some Jews, engaging modernity, mobilized trade unions, and Jews there held twelve of the twenty-four city council seats.[4] The town also had its share of famous artists, a "well-organized Peretz Library," and a range of political par-ties, including the Poale Zion (Workers of Zion Party). A former socialist resi-dent, Harry Koyfman, remembers the "stormy revolutionary years just before the 'Fifth Year' [1905], and the part the Jewish working youth of Zyrardow [a vil-lage seven kilometers NNW of Amshinov] played in the struggle against the Rus-sian czarism of the time." He recounts how they organized trade unions "for the improvement of workers in all occupations" that "assisted the Amshinov people in their work." When czarist police planted spies in the Polish Socialist Party, Koyfman hid in Amshinov.

Arriving in 2011, I came with imbedded expectations as to what I might still be able to see of a lively combative past. Would there be historical markers of cemeteries, synagogues, workshops, the Peretz library, and strike agitation as in the United States and UK? Would there still be buildings where organizers met or hid? At the least, I thought that in walking the streets, I might inhale the spirit of a place where my grandmother forged an identity that continued to inform my own life.[5]

∼ Interlude ∼

Ida Lubertofsky was born in Amshenov in 1885 to Josek and Ruchla (née Weicner) Lubertofsky. She was the youngest of three sisters and two brothers would follow. She lived among many relatives as well; local birth and death records dating back to 1815 list three earlier generations of Lubertofskys in the town.

Fewer records have yet to be found for the origins of the Walkowitzes. Alexander, or Zishe as he was called, was four years Ida's junior. He was born on February 8, 1889 in Amshinov to Jankel and Chana Sheindel (née Klapersak) Walkowitz.[6] Zishe was the third of five brothers and had a younger and older sister. The earliest extant record in Amshenov of a Walkowitz is the marriage record for Jankel Wolkowicz and Chana Klapersak there on June 15, 1876. In contrast to generations of the Klapersak and Lubertofsky clans listed in birth, death, and marriage records, I could find no mention of Jankel or any other Wolkowicz (or Walkowitz) in Amshinov. Jankel is only listed as a soldier on leave. His parents had died and he may have come from Błonie, for the marriage record notes that local officials had to obtain permission from officials there for the union to take place. A town about 17.5 miles west of Warsaw and 16.2 miles north of Amshinov, Błonie was one of many small market towns Jews migrated to in search of opportunities: in 1857, the town's 88 Jews constituted only 7.7 percent of the population; by 1897, one-third of its 3,000 inhabitants were Jewish.[7]

Jankel's marriage to Ida was most likely an arranged marriage, and in initially reading the record I wondered if they were Orthodox, or if the religious ceremony was to please their parents? Five years after my visit I rediscovered oral histories completed with my aunt and uncle in the 1980s that answered some of my questions, even as they raised new ones. My great grandparents, they said, had in fact been Orthodox. Rabbi Dovid Kalish, the head of the Amshinover dynasty performed a marriage in the Hasidic tradition far removed from the secularism of my grandparents. The rejection of religion had occurred in my grandparents' generation. The move to a secular identity occurred when my grandparents came of age in Łódź amid the social, political turmoil and cultural transformation of the early twentieth century. Socialism seems to have offered them an alternative to a religion they rejected.

Only a few details of my paternal grandparents Zishe Walkowitz and Chaia Lubertofsky's years in Łódź emerge from these oral histories and records. They married there in 1909. She was twenty-four years old; he was twenty. She worked as a handloom weaver and he was a trained tailor who worked both at home and in textile shops. Like other Jewish workers, they must have endured harsh working and living conditions: residents drew water from wells, relied on oil lamps and wood for heat and cooking, and the family—men, women, and children—worked long hours in basements or homes on out-of-date wooden

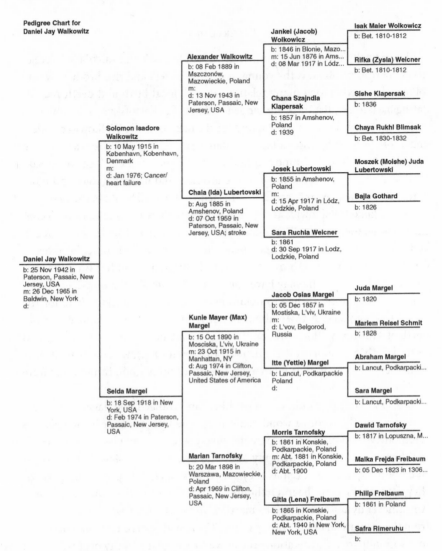

Figure 2. Walkowitz Family Tree: five generations of the immediate family.

looms. Work and wages were "sweated," dependent on exploitative and unreliable patriarchs—fathers who disciplined family labor and middlemen who fronted for manufacturers, or perhaps, fathers of other workers. By 1920, 20 percent of the Jewish workers in Łódź had joined the Bund, and in the uprising of June 1905, they revolted. Weavers and citywide textile workers united to work "seven to seven" and be paid in a timely and fair way. The 1906 American Jewish Yearbook reports that 341 Łódź Jews lost their lives in the Revolution; scores more were wounded.[8]

The Walkowitz family seems to have cut its political teeth in these struggles. They were inspired by Chaia's brother-in-law Joe Katz, who had married Neche Lubertofsky, Chaia's older sister. Twelve years Zishe's senior, Katz, a weaver by trade, was a Bund firebrand blacklisted for his role in the protest. The Jewish underground subsequently helped Joe Katz flee Łódź to continue his political work abroad.[9] Leaving the "Manchester of Poland," by 1910 he had taken up residence in the "Lyon of America," the silk city of Paterson, New Jersey. After Zishe's early death in 1943, Joe would go on to live for almost another quarter of a century, and I vividly remember the love and respect my father bore for him when we made periodic visits to Joe in the mid-1960s.

Political, social, and cultural manifestations of the Bund continued to inspire Łódź radicals like Zishe and Chaia who remained in Łódź. In the wake of the Revolution, Polish democrats and the Yiddish section of the Polish Krzewiena Oświaty (Association for the Dissemination of Enlightenment) sponsored regular lectures, amateur theater, and a choir. A Bund initiative in the spring of 1908 would have especially resonated with Zishe; in 1908, Bund members played a leading role in the establishment in Łódź of a Society for Music, Singing and Drama. In the recollection of one socialist activist, the organization was "the main activity of the Jewish workers' parties in Łódź."[10]

The ultimate objective for Jewish Bundists such as Zishe continued, however, to be the organization of the Jewish working class. Following in his brother-in-law's footsteps, he soon also faced the wrath of manufacturers. By 1912, he too had fled Łódź. His family situation did not permit him to transport his wife and daughter to the distant shores of Paterson though: his wife was pregnant, and his daughter, Belle, but one-year old. Leaving Chaia behind to give birth while in the care of her mother-in-law, Chana Klapersak, Zishe traveled to Copenhagen where his two sisters and a brother had already settled. Even though the Bund did not exist as a political organization in Copenhagen, Zishe remained inspired by it. By the time he fled Łódź, Zishe had become a committed Bundist, a political radical who wielded poetry, song, and his particular passion, theater, in service to the building of a revolutionary working-class. A tailor by trade, Zishe was in his heart a cultural worker for whom Yiddish culture was a vehicle through which to reach the Jewish proletariat.

Zishe and Chaia might have entered the century as children of the Orthodox; in Revolutionary Łódź they had come of age as secular radicals within a socialist Yiddishkeit culture. I knew only the bare outlines of this past as I entered Mszczonów and Łódź, but it nonetheless framed my expectations.

∽

Heritage Tourism in Mszczonów

The drive from Łódź to Mszczonów took nearly two hours, but road construction delays added at least an extra half hour to the trip. In preparation for cohosting the European Cup with Ukraine during the summer of 2012, Poland was busy building four-lane highways. One of them, connecting Kraków to Warsaw, passed through the outskirts of Mszczonów. As noted above, the village is considerably closer to Warsaw, a fact I had never realized; I had imagined the family's move to Łódź as a journey to the nearest city. It was not. Rather, with its burgeoning textile industry, Łódź became the destination with the best job prospects.

The road took us though a flat, monotonous landscape. Our guide Jacek remarked that the terrain had constituted a sort of "German highway" for the easy and rapid movement of tanks and armies as the Nazis rolled through Poland. Alex and I could only imagine what it was like making such a trip to Łódź at the turn of the last century. As the nearest rail service would have required schlepping to Warsaw and then taking the train to Łódź, villagers may well have chosen to travel directly by horse and cart. It was not an expedition easily made and the return trip by members of the Walkowitz family would not have been casual or incidental.

It was a magical moment when I saw the town signposted from the highway. From the new highway, it was a half a kilometer down a single lane road into town. Interwar accounts in the Yitzkor book describe the town as remarkably unchanged from a half-century earlier. In 2011, almost three-quarters of a century later, it still felt like a sleepy village. The town was quiet with little pedestrian or motor traffic. There was little commercial activity. A rebuilt central square housed the local town administration. Otherwise, single family houses and one and two story-shops predominated. Development had passed Amshinov by. As for the Jewish past, it quickly became readily apparent that the town's Jewish history shared the dismal fate of Jewish *shtetlekh* in Galicia surveyed by historian Omer Bartov and anthropologist Jonathan Webber a few years earlier. Jews had been doubly erased—liquidated in the Holocaust while any material remembrance of them was equally obliterated in the physical town.[11] Well, maybe not quite. Seeing one or two weather-beaten, modest old cottages on lanes around the town, one could imagine Bubbe in the window or tending a garden or chickens. One marked artifact of the Jewish past remained: the Jewish cemetery. Although there was no signage pointing the way to it, a local fireman directed us to a small road out of town. We drove down a lane that our GPS map identified as Poniatowska Street; I imagined this might have been Jewish quarter (this was later confirmed by the Virtual Shtetl website, https://sztetl.org .pl/en/towns/m/585-mszczonow), but there was no historical marker, signage or town brochure to direct us there. In fact, a later visitor posted on-line an image of a residence on Poniatowska Street, noting that it was once a *mikveh* built on the former site of the ritual chicken slaughterhouse and synagogue. Going past it, we were not aware of its sedimented history. Simple cottages lined the street, which was only now being paved. We drove as far as we could—perhaps, 200 meters, where the road stopped at a construction yard. Across the highway one could see the Star of David on the cemetery gate. Cemeteries were customarily established at a distance from residences, but the new highway endowed this one with an especially stark physical isolation. What was once accessible and connected to the Jewish community now appeared dead-ended. Accessing the cemetery required trying to cross the busy expressway by foot or finding some back road to it out of town.

The cemetery appeared behind some junk and dustbins near a very low-end auto repair shop. It occupied about eighty square yards and was now enclosed with a brick wall surrounded by a black wrought-iron fence. The Star of David adorned the top of an arched gateway of red brick, and signage to the front left noted the cemetery's provenance and benefactors. On the left side, gravestones remained visible but their markings largely illegible. Most of them were broken, half-buried, or badly deteriorated. There could have been 150 of these stones, silent sentinels to a long forgotten past. Graves were barely visible on the right side, as the plots had become covered with ankle-height weeds.

There seems to have been some restoration of the site in the last decade, presumably by Jews from Israel and the United States, most of them Orthodox. This was not surprising. In the town's "culture wars" at the end of the nineteenth century between secular and Orthodox Jews, the winners turned out to be the religious, a group I subsequently learned included my great grandparents. The town had been and would continue to be the center of the Amshinover rabbinical tradition. A one-room brick mausoleum-prayer house that stood in the front of the Cemetery memorialized that tradition. The building was perhaps fifteen feet square. Inside were a couple of prayer books; additionally, visitors could take down and read from prayer sheets in Hebrew that hung in protective plastic on the wall. The interior wall acknowledged the town's rabbinate. The building also contained a wood railing behind which stood a tomb for the Amshinover rebbe. Whatever conflicts shaped the past, in the present the tomb privileged the memory of the rebbe.

There were no visible signs of Bubbe or her likeness here; maybe I would find something of her life in Łódź.

ŁÓDŹ

Knowing in advance that Jewish heritage tourism in Łódź was underdeveloped, my expectations resembled those most other tourists brought to the city. I knew that the Jewish quarter had been largely destroyed and that tourists typically gravitated toward extant remains. Even in the absence of material traces, I still hoped to find a trail that marked out physical sites of a Jewish socialist past, cultural and political. In the end, thinking of New York's Tenement Museum, I was disappointed that I did not find exhibits or guideposts that evoked the living and working conditions that animated Jewish socialism and the world of Yiddishkeit more generally.

I had visited Łódź almost thirty years earlier in 1982, to speak at a conference on industrial architecture. Putting on my headset at the opening of the conference for the English translation, I heard myself invited to assume an honorary chairmanship of the conference "because I was returning to my homeland." Knowing my grandparents had fled Poland made it hard for me to imagine Poland as my homeland. But the next day I was quite moved when some Polish colleagues in the Solidarity trade union took me on a surprise lunchtime visit to 10 Zgierska Street, my grandparents' last address before emigrating. The buildings on the site had been destroyed in the war and the address was now the site of a drab postwar state socialist housing block. My visit thirty years later would find little changed. But we get ahead of ourselves.

Zgierska Street was in the middle of the Litzmannstadt Ghetto, historically the center of a poor Jewish district, the Bałuty, a quarter vividly captured in I. J. Singer's epic 1936 Yiddish novel, *The Brothers Ashkenazi*. In the novel, Bałuty Jews struggle and survive the ravages of frontier capitalism in a city that grows almost overnight into a major textile center. Singer depicts a history full of conflict—between bosses and workers, Jews and anti-Semites, Russians and Poles, rabbis and secular radicals. The narrative is organized around a family story of two brothers. One, becomes the leading textile manufacture in the city, and is a stand-in for Izrael Poznański, the Jewish owner of the city's major textile mill complex; the other is his more proletarian rival, both in love and politics. Alas, walking on Zgierska Street in 2011, nothing in the gray, drab pre and postwar buildings of the poor area spoke to the city's vibrant Jewish past. Łódź's modest modernization schemes left this area untouched; returning in 2015, a major development project focused on the downtown business district but still ignored the Bałuty.

History

The history of Łódź published in 1976 by Yad Vashem as part of its Yizkor memorial book project offers a view of the vibrant Jewish past that provides an alternative framework for imagining the content of a Jewish heritage tour. "There is no mention of a Jewish presence in L[ódź] before the 18th century," it begins, but notes the national census counts 58 Jews in 1808 (13.4% of the population). By 1820, the number of Jews had grown to 259 as Jewish merchants and craftsmen helped transform the city from an agricultural hamlet to an industrial and commercial town.[12] Over the next forty years, the number of Jews expanded twenty-two fold to 5,633 in 1863 when they constituted a third of Łódź's population. The Russian state severely restricted Jewish migration and settlement in the Pale, however the Kingdom of Poland, the westernmost part of the empire, still preserved an amount of separateness in legal regulations and was more open to Jews. Here opportunities for work in the fledgling textile mills led many to enter the city without permission. Others found a way to pay the entry fee—between 9,000 and 20,000 zloty—required by the Russian state. Except for two "Europeanized" Jewish families, Jews settled in the Jewish quarter, the only area open to them.

The restrictive settlement policy shaped the evolution of the Bałuty. Overcrowding and high demand for housing allowed landlords to exact high rents in Łódź, while rendering the neighboring village of Bałuty where they were "free of all the legal and administrative restrictions" an attractive alternative for poor Jews. By 1910, the Bałuty had 100,000 inhabitants but was hardly Edenic: it remained a separate village, administratively under the charge of the village of Radogoszcz, which was unwilling or ill prepared to invest in it. Fearful that its "potentially revolutionary" proletariat would incite the rest of the population, the Congress Kingdom of Poland refused to incorporate Bałuty into Łódź. The streets remained dark and unpaved. Sewers remained nonexistent.[13]

The tsar's decree of 1862 removed guild and housing restrictions on Jews and set in motion the city's transformation into the "Manchester of Poland," complete with a "potentially revolutionary" proletariat. Large textile mills developed as early as the 1860s. Skilled German weavers kept Jews out of their guild and the mills. But Jews played a major role as industrialists; between 1881 and 1909, Jewish manufacturers established 141 of the 358 new factories (39.4%). Izrael Poznański, the most prominent among them, employed thousands of German and Polish workers—but not Jews—and made his mark as a leading philanthropist. In 1888, he founded a new Jewish hospital, gave generously to the new cemetery, and founded and headed the Jewish religious school, Dobroczynność, a self-help institution that focused on welfare—aid to the needy, a soup kitchen, interest-free loans, a maternity home, a reading room.[14]

Even though its political consciousness was forged in the sweatshop conditions of homework shops, the Jewish proletariat supported strikes among the non-Jews in the textile mills. Of the approximately 75,000 textile mill workers in Łódź, only an estimated 2,000 were Jewish. However, three or four times that number worked as handloom weavers in home production, and thousands more were underemployed or unemployed. Women like Ida Lubertofsky typically did such homework under the supervision of a skilled male tailor or cutter, who could have been their husband. And as the term sweatshop evokes, the work was arduous. They, too, faced harsh working conditions and fragile living conditions that challenged the role of benign philanthropist Poznański cultivated. The chronicler sums their situation up in stark language: "All in all, the condition of the worker at home in 'good' times was hard, and in times of crisis—tragic."[15]

Poverty and exploitative work and living conditions for Jewish and Gentile labor created fertile ground for political organizing, but also provoked familiar anti-Semitism. In May 1892, for instance, the *New York Times* reported that class antagonism (allegedly abetted by the Russian secret police) manifested itself in anti-Jewish violence: by May 10, Łódź was "in a state of siege" as 30,000 workers on strike since May Day had turned to "violent attacks on the Jewish quarter."[16] In the next decade, Jewish socialists determined that if they were to build a social democratic society and state they would have to educate the Polish and Russian peasantry and the new industrial proletariat, teach them the lessons of Marxism, and mobilize them. Yiddish, the language of the Jewish street, was the means to do so. And the Bund was their political vehicle. Soon after a small group of organizers established the Bund in Vilna in 1897, it spread to Warsaw, Minsk, Bialystok, and Łódź. In Łódź, Jewish socialist workers joined textile strikes as early as 1895. Most famously, the Bund played a leading role in solidarity with non-Jewish socialist textile workers in street battles during the 1905 Łódź Insurrection, or the June Days, and in the more general revolutionary Polish protest of 1905–1907 against the Russian empire.[17] One can imagine ideals of social justice forged in the passions, commitments, and fraternity/sorority of these heady Bund actions between a tailor such as Alexander (Zishe) Walkowitz and a weaver such as Ida (Chaia) Lubertofsky, the woman who was to become his wife.

Bund mobilization expanded into and generated an extraordinary modern secular cultural enterprise. Yiddishkeit played a central but not singular role in this project. Chaia and Zishe would bring this Yiddish culture with them to Paterson and would use it to organize on behalf of the working class. At its core it inspired them and their comrades to create a social justice movement, complete with a Yiddish secular school system, where academic courses mixed with drama programs, literature, and poetry. In Łódź, Bund printing presses made popular dissemination of the culture possible; choral societies sang songs in Yiddish of solidarity and social significance; Bund athletic clubs advanced socialist physical culture.[18]

Of course competing religious and political claims on Jewish identity and "appropriate" behavior challenged the Łódź Bund. A range of other political and social organizations—secular and religious—competed with the Bund to meet the challenges of the new modern industrial world. Individuals in Poale Labor Zion, for example, were Jewish socialists too, but with a vision of Jewish state in Palestine, not in Łódź. The major division lay between secular and religious communities, although such divisions had fuzzy edges. As many as twenty other small Zionist groups, some drawing from the educated classes, some from workers, also organized their own Tarbut school system, summer camps, youth clubs, club houses, kibbutzim, and so on. The Orthodox Jews and Hasidim, each also with its own schools and social networks, bitterly opposed both the Zionists and the secular socialists.[19]

Heritage

The complexity, richness, and drama of Łódź's Jewish history suggest a set of possibilities for a heritage narrative that describes daily struggles with harsh living and working conditions, different political and religious alternatives, and a network of social and cultural institutions. The historical accounts also provide a benchmark against which to measure Jewish heritage tourism in Łódź today.

The substantial Jewish population of Łódź (230,000 Jews prior to World War II) constituted one of the largest Jewish settlements in the world and the second largest in Poland. In this age of global tourism, the sheer number from the city, who settle in the Jewish diaspora, represent an enormous potential for Jewish heritage in the city. Visitors to Łódź today, however, find one of the least developed Jewish heritage tourist industries in a major city. Since 2002, the city has held an annual week-long Festival of Four Cultures that includes Jewish culture as part of the celebration of its multiethnic history of the city. A tourist might be lucky enough to visit that week. I was not, and saw no advertising for the Festival during my visits. The conventional alternative typically available on any day was a walking tour.

Walking Łódź. Four companies advertised to provide Jewish heritage tours online; one tour atypically offered a local (presumably "Jewish"-run) tour. A four-hour tour was $70. All promised visits to the same four sites: The Jewish cemetery, the former Litzmannstadt ghetto, Poznański's Palace, and *Manufaktura Centre*, the conversion of the Poznański factory complex that also housed the Museum of the Factory.[20]

Despite its large potential audience, Łódź's heritage tourism is a backwater, and insiders within the industry point to limited tourist demands to explain the framing of tours in the city. In an interview, Paulina Zatorska, a Łódź guide who provides Jewish heritage tours for well-known Warsaw-based Polish tour companies, suggests that tours' foci on cemeteries and former family home addresses reflect the expectations of Jewish tourists with family roots in Łódź. A native of Łódź, Zatorska studied philology at the University of Warsaw but parlayed her connections to tour companies like StayPoland and RealPoland into employment as a tour guide in her hometown. Building on her love of the city and research interest in genealogy, she self-studied the history of the city. The groups sent are on day trips, and are typically two to eight people, all Jewish and mostly elderly. Not unusually, they consist of a family with an elderly grandparent with family roots in Łódź. Most are Americans, some Australians. In the first half of 2014 she led four groups; in prior years, there were a few more. Łódź, clearly, has not made it to the beaten tourist path.

Zatorska's tour is a formulaic visit based on tourists' conventional assumptions of facts. It takes four hours. The tourists, she notes sadly, are "remarkably ignorant" about Łódź; they think it is a small town. Most of them want to see the house in the Jewish quarter (the Bałuty) where they or their ancestors lived—or as likely, its site—and then the Jewish cemetery. After that, Zatorska takes them to other places she imagines they might want to see: the one synagogue that survived the war, the ghetto, the Poznański factory (Manufaktura); if time permits, she adds non-Jewish industrial complexes in Łódź. On a rare occasion, someone asks to see the Jewish community center in contemporary Łódź. No one sees examples of prewar worker housing that might evoke a sense of their relatives' past life; nor do they visit sites of the revolutionary protest or of the Yiddish theatre and schools. Rather, Zatorska, a bright, engaging, and open-minded presence, relies on what she knows and what she imagines these tourists expect—a chance to witness a family's past presence, and then its synagogues, cemeteries, and Holocaust memorializing. Poznański's factory complex hints at an industrial history, but as we shall see, it figures as a site of "famous" Jews, not as part of vibrant, contested political or social history, if it is mentioned at all. There is no story of the Bund.[21]

For tourists who travel to Łódź on their own, the principal guidebook they find at their hotel is Łódź *In Your Pocket*, the local edition of a corporate guide produced by a European tourism company with branches across the continent. Each volume has an interchangeable city format. Published three times a year and available online, the eighty-two-page booklet advertises restaurants, hotels, and tourist activities and mixes in historic sites. The Łódź edition offers a detailed walking tour of the Litzmannstadt ghetto as the centerpiece of the city's heritage experience. Four additional pages offer readers an introduction to the history of Jewish Łódź and another walking tour that marks the cemetery, the new community center, and two synagogues "Of Jewish Interest." The primary walking tour takes visitors to the Radegast train station from which Jews were herded to concentration and extermination camps, the Jewish cemetery, and various other ghetto sites and memorials: the Gypsy Camp, the Children's Memorial, and so forth. The trail is a poignant story of victims, punctuated by the limited echoes of an imagined past that synagogues and cemeteries can tell. The text includes a lengthy paragraph summary of the 1905 Insurrection that highlights the role of workers and the Socialist Party. But the paragraph is a sidebar, symbolically marginal to the main tourist event—the ghetto walk—and it makes no mention of Jews or the Bund. It treats the event as a Polish political action. *In Your Pocket* positions the history of Jews in Łódź primarily in the context of the wartime experience and the ghetto. In brief, it mentions the postwar migration of Łódź Jews to Israel and the approximately 5,000 Jews who remain in the city.[22]

My visit in October 2011 (again with cousin Alex and our guide Jacek) provided me with an inside view of the sites of the protean past, and I had some hope that we might hear Bubbe's story. We returned to 10 Zgierska Street, where

Figure 3. "London" Photographic Studio, Łódź, postcard of baby Belle, ca. 1912–1923.
Courtesy of Michael Bernstein.

she had lived before the war. Walking along a tramway in the street, the building seemed unchanged from how I remembered it from my 1982 visit. Although
the tenement at 10 Zgierska was erected in the postwar Soviet era, it felt old,
neglected, and superannuated. It was as if time in the neighborhood had stood
still in the century since Bubbe had left.

This section of Zgierská Street was quite narrow. Number ten on the north
left hand side was a postwar structure, but the building to its immediate north,
like much else in the neighborhood, seemed to date from earlier in the century.
We entered a courtyard bounded by the building and its adjacent structures at
the back from the street. The window frames were new, but the housing resembled tenement housing in the Lower East Side of New York from the same
period: paint was peeling, litter and garbage was omnipresent, and apartments
were without indoor plumbing or hot water. It was easy to envision an impoverished daily life in the Bałuty.

While drafting this chapter, I found a photo that suggested how easy it was
to romanticize the poverty. In December 2014 my cousin Michael uncovered
and forwarded a photograph from Łódź of his mother, my aunt Belle, found

among his mother's papers. It was a photo of a baby no more than a year or two old, reproduced on a postcard by a private studio on Middle Street in Łódź. Bubbe had mailed the postcard to her sister, my Tante Neche, in Paterson, New Jersey. The image of the smartly attired baby, sitting upright, depicted a family of modest means that saw itself as proud, self-possessed, and modern, with access to and able to take advantage of the new urban consumer service. The studio's promotional card on the reverse with its name, "London," offered the cachet of a cosmopolitan site abroad.

There was no way to see inside the apartments in 2011. But this area was untouched by the contemporary Renaissance that, according to our guidebooks, Poland was undergoing. The Bałuty and its Jews had been neglected a century ago, and the area seemed little changed except for the ethnicity of the current residents. It was now the home of poor, working-class Poles with reportedly high crime rates and poverty—and vestiges of long-standing anti-Semitism (now without resident Jews). Graffiti on the walls urged support for the local football team, which echoing the racism in European football culture, locals derisively called "the Jews."

The main heritage trail took visitors through the Liztmannstadt ghetto in the Bałuty. I had visited Auschwitz, which is three hours south of the city, thirty years earlier, and felt no need to walk the trail. Besides, Chaia and Zishe had emigrated well before this dark history. Instead, in the convention of heritage tourism, we went off to the Jewish cemetery to look for relatives.

The Jewish Cemetery. Cmentarz Żydowski, founded in 1892, was the second Jewish cemetery in Łódź (housing has been built over the first). It is the largest Jewish cemetery in Europe and it contains the remains of 180,000 bodies; 45,000 of them died in the Holocaust and are located in an adjacent ghetto field. It also houses the biggest Jewish mausoleum in the world—it is dedicated to Izrael Poznański, the leading Jewish manufacturer.

We found the cemetery about one-third of a mile down an off-hand dirt road barely visible from the main thoroughfare. We simply parked on the side next to the single other car there and walked inside the gate. A sign pointed us to a very modest stone building where one could buy an entry ticket. Entry was, however, free to anyone visiting graves of relatives and their guide. Alex and Jacek picked up flimsy skullcaps (*yarmulkas*) to wear, which they affixed (poorly) with bobby pins. My bush hat served as my yarmulke.

The condition of the cemetery—enormous but in terrible disrepair—dwarfed our Amshinov experience. It was enclosed in a brick wall about ten feet high. Outside and across from the entrance was a substantial unmarked building that may have served as a synagogue for services before interment. We entered the cemetery and proceeded up the central alley. About sixty feet wide, the alley was one of three pathways leading through the ten rows of graves (with about

Figure 4. Poznański Mausoleum in the Old Jewish Cemetery in Łódź. Photo by
Caroline Cormier. Courtesy of Caroline Cormier.

fifteen sections in each row). Massive mausoleums of the rich and powerful
Jewish magnates dominated the first rows and reminded us that class as much
as ethnic culture marked the Jewish history of Łódź. The large Poznański
family mausoleum provided a resting place for Izrael and his immediate family
in a massive Art Nouveau-domed construction on a raised stone platform. The
structure occupied perhaps as much as thirty square feet. Adorned with a
mosaic-tiled ceiling with religious themes, Poznański's grandiose architectural
statement separated itself spatially and by scale from the masses whose labor
gilded his life.

The mausoleum contrasted sharply with the modest graves of the Jewish proletariat. The graves of my great grandparents, Yankel Wolkowicz and Josek and

Figure 5. Grave of Sara Ruchla Lubertofsky. Łódź Jewish Cemetery, ca. October 1917.
Family photo in the author's possession.

Sara Ruchla Lubertofsky, are cases in point. When my grandparents abandoned
Łódź before the war, they left two elderly patriarchs and a matriarch behind with
Zishe's youngest brother, Schlome, who would be murdered in the Holocaust.
All three elders died a few years later: Jankel on March 7, 1917, at the age of
seventy-one; Josek on April 16, 1917 at the age of sixty-six; Sara Ruchla on September 30, 1917, also at the age of sixty-six. According to the digitized online
index, the men were buried in section 10/4, and Sura Ruchla in 9/9. The family
took a photograph at her grave to share with those who had departed for Denmark and America. It marks the grave of a "righteous woman of upstanding
valor" as a memory to an obviously saddened family.

   When I visited in 2011, the disrepair of the cemetery in these back sections
made it virtually impossible to find any particular name. The cemetery had
transformed into a forest or wood. Row 10, section 4, where my grandparents
were interred, was overgrown and in disarray. Many gravestones were broken
or half buried; limestone decay seriously limited the possibility of reading
inscriptions. It was sad to leave without having found the graves of Yankel or
Sara Ruchla, but I felt as if I had nonetheless walked the spaces of the graves
and paid respects to ancestors my family left behind when they fled in 1913. In
paying my respects to my great grandparents' memory, I had closed a circle.

Visiting the cemetery was a poignant experience, but its disrepair spoke more to the Nazi assault on Jewish institutions and postwar neglect than to a prewar history.

Manufaktura and the Museum of the City of Łódź. If there was a place to re-create and to hear echoes of my grandparents' story, I thought to get beyond formulaic heritage sites like the cemetery by visiting the Poznański mill complex and the Poznański mansion. In truth, I had no reason to believe she worked there; as noted, Poznański made it a practice not to employ Jews. No landsmen's plight could compromise his business objectivity. In 1905, though, if they had already migrated to the city, Zishe and Chaia would have been sixteen and twenty years old respectively. As local witnesses to the strikes, armed violence and brutal police actions, they might well have emerged with a radical consciousness.

In twenty-first century Łódź, the mills and the Poznański mansion have been transformed into a shopping mall and a Museum of the City of Łódź respectively. The French developer Apsys bought the complex in 2000, and opened it in 2003 as "Manufaktura: At the Very Heart of Dreams," a "multifaceted cultural extravaganza." The largest restoration project in Poland since the reconstruction of Warsaw's Old Town in the 1950s, the development project turned Poznański's former textile mill complex into a consumer tourist magnet. In freshly repointed red brick that has been steam-washed, the classic four-story mill buildings mirror the giant textile mills of nineteenth-century Manchester and Lowell. (The Lowell Mills have also been spruced up, but as a National Historic site for the history of the American textile industry and labor movement.) Now spiffy and sparkling, Manufaktura hardly evokes industrial labor conditions. The complex, covering thirty-seven acres, consists of restaurants opening into outdoor cafes in the center square, a multiplex cinema, boutiques, a branch of Citibank, arcades, promenades, and a Museum of the Factory. With the squeaky clean look of the brick buildings, complete with the marble and brick flooring, the mall is now "industrial modern."

The museum is accessed by an elevator that takes visitors to the fourth floor where a panoramic view of the development may well capture something of the pride Poznański must have felt gazing on his dominion. There is a minimal entry fee to the museum, which consists of two small rooms. There is signage with some English alongside the Polish. The first room focused on the workers. Pictures presented most workers as respectable men: the one picture of women was a candid shot of people routinely exiting the mill after work, and in the other, staged photos, non-Jewish men wore their Sunday best suits and ties. On the whole, the exhibit told visitors little about worker living conditions and wages, and nothing of the broader social and political conditions leading to the

Figure 6. Manufaktura. The former Poznański mill complex, Łódź. Photo by the author.

dramatic strikes in 1895 and 1903 and the lockout of 1907 that included the activism of Bund radicals.

The second room introduced visitors to work in the mills. Visiting schoolchildren were being shown the one working loom. They saw how the woof and warp worked, and then, when it was turned on, they heard the din of the machine. A photo on the wall of the mill floor showed the hundreds of looms on the floor and left the cacophony as well as the danger of the work to the imagination. The museum brochure offered a benevolent interpretation of the mills as an "iconic place" that "paid tribute to the entrepreneurial spirit of its industrial past." Poznański spared no money in hiring the best architects and designers to build the mills. The brochure did not acknowledge that it was a Company Town that came with both services and constraints: it had its own church, hospital, and worker housing, and Poznański even built his own railroad to Warsaw to obtain raw materials and market his goods. A visitor might wonder why anyone ever felt aggrieved and what price a complaint would have on continued employment.

The Museum of the City of Łódź, located in Poznański's grand mansion, was a block away from the factory complex. Maja Jakóbczyk, director of Education and Community Relations, spoke with us and she invited a middle-aged man involved with research on the workers to join the conversation. He spoke knowledgably about mill working conditions, the role of the Jews and non-Jews in the mills, and the politics of mill workers that I missed in the exhibits. Yet the exhibition in the Museum of the City also celebrated its former owner, Izrael Poznański, while the director repeated the message presented in the Museum of the Factory. In her words, Poznański was "an example of the long history of Polish entrepreneurship." Although the City Museum was closed when we visited, the director opened the rooms for us to see the splendor in which Poznański lived. The exhibit itself made no mention of the low wages Poznański profited from that allowed such splendor, nor did it speak of the Bund, strikes, and years of protest. For the curator, Poznański's story exemplified his generous charity to Catholic and Jewish houses of worship and Bałuty soup kitchens. He built a "free" hospital, although workers had to contribute to his insurance scheme to fund it—a contradiction that went unmentioned. He also erected housing for his workers. In sum, Poznański's story was one of considerable entrepreneurship and philanthropy but the director articulated no comment on company paternalism in its gendered and political manifestations as a stick as well as a carrot. For instance, the six-story brick tenements that Poznański built for his workers were nearby. They appeared worn and in need of renovation, but they remained in use. Incorporating one of the apartments into the museum exhibit would be an opportunity to call attention to the housing benefit, and also to the dangers of work, the exploitative labor conditions that led workers to protest, and what it was like to live in the company housing. Such exhibits are standard protocols of industrial sites and living museums in the United States and UK and would have allowed the conditions of workers to be seen, their voices heard.

If Jewish heritage tourists or commercial enterprises such as Manufaktura or Łódź city fathers (and they do seem to be men) seek comfortable or redemptive stories, the Łódź heritage narrative fits the bill. The contested prewar Jewish past has been sanitized, if expressed at all. Contested stories of proletarian men and women such as Bubbe Chaia do not conform to the local and national preference for heroic industrial stories. Developers and curators seem reluctant to acknowledge a socialist Jewish past. The Jewish history of Łódź I witnessed was overshadowed by a focus on Holocaust remembrance. To be fair, I suspect social historians and radical Jews who care about the prewar story of a secular radical past have not been consulted in its reconstruction. I further suspect that financial and emotional investments principally emanate from religious Jews from Israel and the United States, including those who have jump-started the Łódź

Jewish Center replete with ritual bath and kosher meals. The center provides a base for tours and offers 150-odd inexpensive beds for visitors, but it is not an institution committed to the history of secular, radical Łódź Jews like my Bubbe.

The underdeveloped state of Jewish heritage tourism in Łódź leaves plenty of room for growth—and it can begin without discarding tours of cemeteries and factories already in place. Still, on my tours neither Chaia nor Zishe's story was to be seen or heard. Would I have more luck, I wondered, pursuing the story of my maternal grandfather, Max Margel, who was born in a town 270 miles southeast of Łódź in Galicia?

CHAPTER 3

Mostyska, Lviv, and Kiev

DOUBLE ERASURES

Lviv, the city my maternal grandfather spoke of as his home city, was situated in Galicia. Unlike Łódź, which was in the Kingdom of Poland and part of the Russian Empire when Chaia and Zishe lived there, Galicia was a notably poor area in the Austro-Hungarian Empire. Encompassing what are now contemporary parts of northwestern Ukraine and southeastern Poland, Galicia stretched from Kraków in the west past Lviv to Ternopil in the east.

Founded by Prince Danylo of Galicia in the thirteenth century, Lviv remained a part of Poland for 500 years and was called Lwów. When Poland was partitioned in 1772, the city became part of the Hapsburg Empire, but its population retained a Polish majority. Its name changed to Lemberg and it became the capital of the Kingdom of Galicia. With the collapse of the Hapsburg Empire after World War I, Lviv became part of Poland again. The Soviet Union occupied the city between 1939 and 1941, and when the Nazis took over after 1941, it was known again as Lemberg. During brief periods of Russian control, it was known as Lvov. After the war, it became the Ukrainian city, Lviv. But at the time of my grandfather's emigration, it was Lviv and part of Galicia.

Jonathan Webber outlines a history of Jews in Galicia that resembles the impoverished world of Poland to its west, minus the strong presence of the Bund. The rapid expansion of the Hasidim in the first half of the nineteenth century was accompanied by the rapid growth of the Jewish population in the second half. The Jewish population in Galicia more than tripled over the course of the nineteenth century, from 250,000 to 822,000.[1] At the same time, while state political and constitutional policies granted "important freedoms for Jews" and new educational opportunities, political and economic constraints narrowed possibilities. Jews made only sporadic efforts to settle on the land as they generally could not enter agriculture. Occupations open to Jews were limited to commerce, intercity transport, professions, and crafts such as butchering,

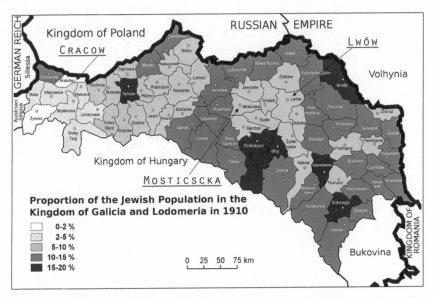

Figure 7. Proportion of the Jewish Population Density in the Kingdom of Galicia and Lodomeria in 1910. Map by Jay Osborn and Daniel Baránek, license: CC BY-SA 4.0, Wikimedia Commons.

tailoring, and shoemaking. Poverty increased. State-sponsored pogroms after 1881 accompanied the rise of modern forms of anti-Semitism. Kiev's Jews lived in daily fear of murderous assault. Less efficient than the Russian Empire in which Kiev to its east was situated, the Austrian state spared Lviv's Jews the worst horrors until 1918 when a local pogrom erupted during the war. Poverty and the constant threat of state violence and repression led to widespread emigration and political responses: notably, socialism and Zionism.[2]

My maternal grandfather, Max Margel, chose the emigration route to America. He left from a village west of Lviv called Mostyska. Although records provide little information about daily life in Mostyska, they do describe stressful economic and political transformations typical of small towns in Galicia.[3] The earliest record of Jews in Mostyska dates from 1567. It was a law forbidding them to live there, though subsequent records assess the law as only "minimally effective."[4] By the mid-nineteenth century, Jews were allowed to settle in the town and by the opening of the twentieth century they represented 55 percent (2,548) of the town's counted 4,633 inhabitants.[5]

Rich genealogical records enabled me to reconstruct Max's lineage and track local migration between neighboring villages. Such records provide little sense of these individuals, however. They do not explain what might have animated someone like Max to pick himself up, perhaps at age twelve, and five years later as a teenager, take a boat to America. In retrospect, I was naive to expect personal visits to Mostyska and Lviv to provide insight on this flight. But tracking down Max's past brought me to Lviv and led me to Kiev, another potential destination for Jewish heritage tourism. In the early modern period Kiev had been within the Polish-Lithuanian Commonwealth, but during the partition period (forward from 1772) was part of the Russian partition, not the Austrian partition that was designated Galicia in which Lviv was located. To the best of my knowledge, Max's travels were limited to Austrian Galicia and he had no contact with the Russian Empire. But modern tourists do not stop at those borders, and nor would I.

Traveling to Lviv and then on to Kiev, I expected I would have more success with Jewish heritage tourism than in Łódź. Jewish Ukraine was not on the main Jewish tourism path, but UNESCO had designated Lviv a World Heritage site and Kiev was the only major Eastern European city besides Budapest to have retained a large postwar Jewish population. But as we shall see, my expectations were only partially met.

∽ INTERLUDE ∽

I knew Max well, or at least I thought I did, until I started this research. He stayed with my family every other weekend and slept in my bedroom until I was about nine years old. After the birth of my sister Karen when I was six-and-a-half years old, my parents sought larger accommodations with separate bedrooms for us. My parents may have been political radicals but they followed many suburban bourgeois conventions of the 1950s: in 1952, they moved from a two-family house in Fair Lawn, New Jersey, a suburb just east of Paterson, to a garden apartment in East Paterson (Elmwood Park today) to save money for a house mortgage. Two years later we moved into a split-level track home on a quarter acre in a new development in Cedar Grove, New Jersey, in which my sister and I each had our own bedroom. In both places, Max was a part-time family resident: in East Paterson he slept on a couch in the living room, and in the larger split-level, he had a bed in the downstairs family room. When Max arrived for the weekend, he spent much of the day in his room ironing the family's clothes. This was his way of trying to help my mother. I suspect I considered ironing to be women's work and never quite understood why this was his task until I saw him listed as a "presser" (a skilled garment finisher in the tailoring trade) on the manifest of the ship that brought him to America.

Max remained a fixture in my life, but he was not a person I particularly esteemed. His position in the house was fraught for both personal and political reasons. Max had, in my mother's words, "a problem with the horses." When she was growing up, he always disappointed her by losing money the family needed to live on at the racetrack. Then one day in the mid-1930s, he simply picked up without a word and left his wife, Marian (née Tarnofsky) and two children. My mother was heartbroken that he left without saying anything to her or providing support. She had been devoted to him. He also left a teenage son, my uncle Phil, six-years junior to my mother. Phil never forgave Max and decades later, when my mother died, I, not Phil, needed to tell Max.

Political differences between Max and my parents positioned him on the margins of the household and kept me from identifying with him even though Max was a rebellious youth, which should have increased his appeal. As the story went, he ran away from home "in Lviv" as a teenager; the story I heard repeatedly was that he fled from a deeply religious home before his bar mitzvah. According to family lore, his father was a mohel, an important religious figure in the town who performed ritual circumcision of newborn boys on the eighth day after their birth. Despite his own extraordinary act of rebellion, Max always chided me and my sister and my parents as "rebels" for our radical political actions. My parents were socialists and communists. I was a firebrand activist in the civil rights and antiwar movements of the 1960s. My sister was a "hippie" who did not wear a bra, to the shock of both Max and my culturally conservative father. (Of course we were happy to be thought of as rebels, just not to be criticized for being so.) A daily emblem of Max's objectionable personal politics and ignominy to my mother was his insistence on bringing "that rag"—the tabloid New York Post—into the house. Finally, sin of sins, Max supported the New York Giants baseball team, while we were fans of "dem Bums"—the Brooklyn Dodgers. The Dodgers were the team that brought Jackie Robinson, the first African American baseball player, into the major leagues, and we cherished the Dodgers as the perennial underdogs, much as we saw ourselves.

So, I loved my grandpa Max, but I did not emulate him. He regularly took me to ball games in New York between the Giants and Dodgers. I also remember playing cards—canasta, pinochle, and gin rummy—with him all the time. He spoke Yiddish well, and though his written English was ungrammatical, he spoke fluently. I knew him as well as a child and young adult might, but never asked him questions then that haunt me now.

What did I "know" of Max? I "knew" that at the end of the nineteenth century he came from Lviv, a city in western Ukraine that was a main urban center of Galicia. What I did not know was that Lviv was also the name of the administrative seat and county in Galicia. He had not been a resident of the city of Lviv proper. My genealogical research on JewishGen uncovered his birth record in the small village of Mostyska (Mościska, in Polish), forty-one miles east of Lviv and less than ten miles from the current Polish border (a moving border with the same changing history of Lviv/Lemberg/Lwów). Sometimes, Mostyska was in Poland, sometimes in Ukraine, sometimes part of the Austro-Hungarian Empire, and later part of the Soviet Union.

These records position Max in a long tradition of Margels. From the microfilmed birth, death, and marriage records of the town preserved by the Mormon

Church I traced this family with over 200 Margels back to the 1780s. Occasionally an individual makes a mark and leaves a trail in other historical documents. Rabbi Moshe Margel (Mościska, Poland, October 13, 1875–Zagreb, Yugoslavia, April 30, 1939), for example, gained fame as the founder of the Margelov Institute in Zagreb, another point in the Austro-Hungarian Empire.[6] More typically the Margels of Mostyska exist in relative anonymity.

In following the Jewish tradition of naming children after recently deceased relatives, the Margels affirmed the family's history in Mostyka. In 1889, a descendant born in 1815, Kunie Mayer Margel, died. The next year descendants honored him by naming their newborn sons after him. On September 20, 1890, Dawid and Chana (née Salik) named their new baby Kunie Mayer after his uncle. This son probably died (the records do not tell us) and less than a month later, on October 15, Margels in the same town gave their baby the same name. Jacob Osias and his wife Yettie (née Margel) Margel (a cousin who had come from Łańcut, a nearby Galician town in what is now southwestern Poland) named their newborn son Kunie Mayer as well, after his deceased great uncle. In America, this second Kunie Mayer became Max. Thus, individuals like Max represented a lineage of Margels. His name represented continuity with a past being brought forward. He was also part of a community and an extended family network of siblings, cousins, aunts, and uncles. An anecdote told by my mother spoke to the caché his name had because of his father's esteemed position as mohel. One day a patient or visitor from Mostyka at the Jewish Barnert Memorial Hospital in Paterson where my mother was a nurse recognized the name Margel on her uniform badge and *kvelled* (beamed with pride), asking, "are you related to the famous mohel?"

During travels throughout his life, Max regularly drew on the Margel network from Mostyska. For Max was a runner: he ran from Mostyska; he ran from his wife; and in a fitting irony, he spent the last years of his working life as a commercial runner, a messenger boy. But apart from knowing he had fled from a religious home, my personal knowledge of Max's past came from anecdotes told about his early life in America. Max and his young family lived in the 1920s in Passaic, New Jersey, the textile city roughly five miles south of Paterson. With a horse and cart, he claimed to be the city's first banana importer. (I learned later from the historian Michael Ebner that his grandfather also claimed to be "the first" banana importer in Passaic.) Max never told me why he went to Passaic, but scrutiny of the 1920 Federal Census holds a clue: he seems to have joined relatives who were already established there. A cousin, a thirty-nine-year-old fruit peddler named Isadore Margel, already lived there with his family.

Max as I knew him in my childhood was single and poor. He left his family in the 1930s and his postwar life was one of downward mobility. He lived in a tiny studio in midtown Manhattan, cooking on a hotplate. He worked as an elderly messenger boy. After walking became difficult for him, he "retired" to a single rented room in Paterson paid for by my parents. I had no sense that religion played any part in his adult life. While Max supposedly had run away from a deeply religious home, I never saw him set foot in a synagogue or celebrate any Jewish holidays. In contrast to Chaia, I thought him relatively modern and assimilated into American life: he spoke English without an accent and read it well. When he saw me with a copy of Thomas Mann's *Buddenbrooks*, he told me he had read it in his youth, presumably in German. Consistent with self-presentation as educated and relatively cosmopolitan, he seemed to know classical music and the theater. Max also lived independently in Manhattan outside the traditional bonds of the Jewish family. Never remarrying, he lived a modern anomic life outside the fold as the wayward boy who forsook traditional male family responsibilities as breadwinner. Late in life Max reentered the Jewish community part time: as noted above, on alternative weekends he visited with the more traditional Walkowitz family; and after retirement, he spent his days at the Paterson YMHA playing pinochle with other single men.

Although Grandpa Max was a secular native Yiddish-speaker like Chaia, he lived outside the boundaries of Yiddishkeit. He had a rebellious background, but not a radical one. The stories Max told me, family anecdotes about him, and Census records spoke little about social life in Mostyska, of the choices a young man might make, of the home life that might impel a young boy to run away before his bar mitzvah, or of why he felt compelled later to bet on horses and abandon his family.

So I began to research Mostyska and plan a visit to see what I could find of Max's story.

~

Mostyska (Mościska)

I visited Mostyska in late October 2011. Vladimir,[7] an English-speaking guide and translator with Travel Ukraine Agency, whom I had found online, drove. Like many tour leaders, Vladimir was a self-taught guide with little formal historical training. Although non-Jewish, he keenly appreciated the tragic history of Ukraine's Jews in the war and had studied with Yad Vashem, the World Holocaust Remembrance (and research) Center in Israel. I still wondered if he would incorporate a discussion of Yiddishkeit and the secular, radical tradition into his tour.

Vladimir estimated the drive would take an hour and twenty minutes. He was spot on. The cobblestone roads of the city and traffic made for a slow and bumpy beginning, but our pace quickened once we passed suburban outer settlements and entered rural Ukraine. The four-lane paved road extended about ten miles out of Lviv and then gave way to a two-lane highway. The land was flat with little woodland; there was a lot of arable land and the occasional grazing cow. The roadside was festooned with half a dozen devotional icons and small chapels, but other than one or two villages, there were few other signs of human habitation. Traffic was sparse and I was surprised to see horses pulling carts dart across the highway. They carried everything from dung to machinery. We would also pass horses and carts driving on the highway—much like the tractors one competes with on rural American roads. A French couple I had spoken with at breakfast in the hotel that morning described the scenes of rural life they had seen on the bus ride from Poland that passed Mostyska en route to Lviv as from a distant era.

Then I saw the road sign announcing Mostyska. Much as in arriving in Amshenov, my excitement surprised me. Max had died thirty-five years earlier, but seeing the sign summoned up vivid, distant memories of him. With a sense that I was entering a hometown of sorts, I asked Vladimir to stop the car and take my picture.

Driving on, I saw spires of churches rise about a cluster of houses. It was a clichéd rural picturesque view, but no less moving for being so. Vladimir told me the town's name in Ukrainian means "little bridges," and then, as on cue, we crossed a small—a very small—bridge. It would have been easy to miss it. Later, driving in and out of town to see the remaining vestiges of a Jewish cemetery, we crossed a similar second bridge.

As with Amshenov, I had little sense of what I would find, but hoped I might acquire a local guidebook or observe historical markers. Alas, Mostyska had no visible tourist trade. It was an important railroad stop with a break of gauge where the railway systems of Poland and Ukraine meet. As a rail junction, it had the feel of a town on the way to somewhere else. For Max, it had been; the train east went directly to Lviv. As of 2001, Mostyska had a population of slightly more than 9,000. But the town's character derived as much from its physical condition as from its size: apart from the main road through town, which was a highway to the Polish border, and a few adjacent streets, its roads remained unpaved. I saw little post-1960 construction. Modest houses and cottages dotted the lanes leading from the town center. We drove into town and easily parked along the town square, now a park, and began to explore.

Vladimir's tour, reflecting his experience with Jewish tourists, kept returning to the town's synagogues and cemetery. During the Soviet era, a complex of three high-rise apartment buildings had been erected over the main Jewish cemetery. Housing was needed, but the Soviet choice of the site reflected its enmity toward religion and the cultivation of ethnic national identities. (I did not see or inquire as to the fate of Christian cemeteries, but of course Christians were present to defend their cemeteries.) We saw nothing of the housing or any signs marking the cemetery site.

Walking about the central area, Vladimir explained that the market square historically bustled with vendors, most of them Jewish. At the outbreak of the war, about one-third of the town was Jewish, but no signs of their descendants were visible now. Moreover, post-1989 development had not come to Mostyska. Behind the square, the gardens were in disrepair. The bus station and post office, also behind the square, bustled with people coming to the historic market town to shop, but stores also looked dated and worn, badly in need of a coat of paint, if not a remake. (Of course, they may have borne that same scruffy look in Max's time, too.) Vladimir's quest was for the site of the former synagogue. He found a plain two-story office or shop front and some locals confirmed the site for him. I understood the synagogue was a major touchstone for Jews in a town such as Mostyska with a strong Orthodox presence. To be sure, nonreligious people, too, can appreciate the majesty of synagogue architecture and interior space. So while the synagogue is not a primary source of Jewish identity for me, in the context of the Holocaust, traces of its former existence could poignantly memorialize Jewish persistence in the face of Nazi genocide. Yet, in Mostyska, there was no way for a Jewish tourist to know of this site and it told me nothing about Max, other than to remind me of the omnipresent Orthodox Jewish past he found so oppressive. As historians of Galicia have suggested, nothing of educational institutions and political alternatives in a town like Mostyska remained. No brochure, historical markers, or guidebooks pointed to them either. The Holocaust forcibly and brutally removed the Jews from these towns, and the erasure of Jews from public memory has been no less callous.[8]

With little of the Jewish past to see, I decided to try to find elderly people who might remember my family, the Margels. It was probably an unreasonable expectation. Most of the town's Jews had been murdered seventy-five years earlier, and I would have had to find ninety-year-olds with memory intact. None of the residents asked knew of any Jews or could identify someone who might recall them. Finally, one old woman with what I imagined to be a classic peasant affect—stooped and wearing a pleasant blouse and babushka—told us about one Jew who had returned after the war and resettled in town. His son now worked at the brick factory, and she pointed "down the road." So off we went.

The brick factory laid about half a mile to the west of the town center. A trailer functioned as the office, and the secretary who worked there immediately identified the individual we wanted to see. He was out on a delivery and she called him. Even if the built environment looked shabby and deteriorated, cell phones had come to Mostyka. Ten minutes later we piled into the cab of an aging dump truck with Eugene Leonovich Fuss, Mostyska's "last" Jew. The office manager gave him leave to take us to see a Jewish site. Her blasé attitude made me wonder if this role as "representative Jew" was a familiar one. His deceased father, Leonid Fuss, had a Jewish father and identified as a Jew; his mother was Ukrainian Orthodox. The "last" Jew's ancestry was in fact one-quarter Jewish.

Eugene Leonovich drove us in his large truck down a series of winding unpaved village roads, past small farms and through wooded areas. No roads

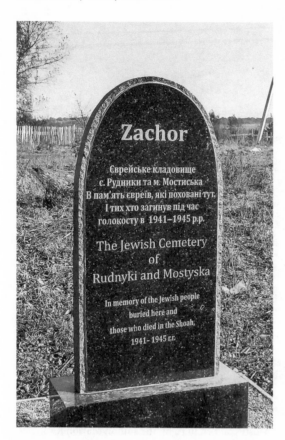

Figure 8. "Zachor" (Remember!), memorial gravestone in front of the cemetery outside Mostyska. Photo by the author.

were marked and we would never have found the way. We arrived after about fifteen minutes at a small farmhouse with ducks congregating at its front gate. Across the road stood a modest wood indicator pointing to a cemetery. At its front, a plaque memorialized the Jews of Mostyska and Rudnyki, a small village a half mile east, who had been buried there as well as those who were slaughtered in the ditch behind the grassy plain during the Shoah. The plaque had been erected scarcely a month earlier by Edgar and Rachelle Hauser, Jewish tourists from the United Kingdom, to honor her relatives from Mostyska who had perished in the Holocaust.[9]

When we arrived at the cemetery, Eugene Leonovich introduced me to a second "last" Jew, Marion Kwatciny, who also had a Jewish father and non-Jewish mother. Marion tends the cemetery, though with little visible effect. The cemetery itself was an open, grassy pasture. The farm's ducks meandered through it and parts of few broken gravestones embedded in the grass were visible. The two men embraced me as a landsmen, a fellow Jew from Mostyska. The age, stoutness, and genial demeanor of the men reminded me of Max as I remembered

Figure 9. The Remaining Jews of Mostyska. Left to right, the author, Marion Kwatciny, and Eugene Leonovich Fuss. Photo by the author.

him in his later years. Of course, I now approached that age. I imagined myself standing in for Max and could only wonder what he would have thought of the photograph of his descendant and the last two Jews of Mostyska smiling for the camera.

I left Mostyska much as I had left Amshenov, failing to find anything specific to my relatives. But I did feel I had a sense of Max's origins: a bustling market town in which half of its approximately 5,000 people were Jewish at the time of the Great War. The dirt roads and small bridges were accompanied by poverty, desolation, and limited opportunity. Ironically, unadorned and still untouched by the commercial dynamics of tourism, I came to realize in retrospect that the lack of a commodified past may have brought me closer to the Jewish world I sought to find than the heritage tours that were marketed in the large tourist cities. Talking to people on the streets and meeting Eugene Leonivich and Marion broke the formula of the organized trip Vladimir had planned, brought me to an otherwise hidden site, and personalized the visit.

The visit also helped me understand the logistics of Max's flight from town. Mostyska was at the edge of two national cultures. Only ten miles from the Polish border, the town had been at different times part of Poland and Austrian Galicia, and the local population had one of the largest ethnic Polish minorities in Ukraine. Mostyska's location at the gauge break of the rails symbolized its liminal status: the depot could bring in visitors, but such a small town could confine an ambitious boy, and its transport system allowed escape. Lviv probably served as the next destination; Kiev was further on. I delighted in having made contact with the past in the bodies on two surviving sons of the imagined shtetl, but I was ready to follow Max and move on to Lviv as well.

Lviv and Kiev: History

My visits to Mszczonów and Mostyska confirmed scholarly critiques of the shtetl as romantic versions of Jewish village life.[10] These visits cured me of any nostalgia for their birthplaces, but vestiges of dilapidated cemeteries offered hints to the folk practices of Yiddish-speaking Jews in such places. I hoped that more sophisticated Jewish heritage tourism in Lviv and Kiev, historically two of Ukraine's largest centers of Jewish life, might tell me more.

There were established histories of Jews in these cities and preserved remnants of that past; it remained to be seen what of this knowledge filtered into tourist sites and tours. The outlines of this history are well known. Jews have resided in the regions of Lviv and Kiev since medieval times. By the mid-nineteenth century there were 600,000 Jews in the area of what is now Ukraine. In the era before World War I, Jews of Kiev and Lviv lived under two different political regimes: Lviv was in the Austro-Hungarian (Hapsburg) Empire; Kiev was in the Russian Empire. Moreover, Galician Jews in Lviv enjoyed greater freedom than their Russian brethren in Kiev. Defeat by France in 1859 in one of the periodic territorial wars compelled the Hapsburg emperor to introduce reforms that lifted basic political restrictions on Jews in Galicia. In 1867, the constitution officially emancipated these Jews, although discrimination against them in employment and property rights persisted. Lviv modeled itself on Vienna in everything from its architecture to its café life, but whereas many Viennese (and Budapest) Jews obtained social mobility, Jews (and non-Jews) in rural parts of Eastern Galicia languished in poverty.[11] Jews in the Austro-Hungarian Empire were spared the pogroms of 1881–1882, but elsewhere in Ukraine they were widespread. The infamous 1881 Kiev pogrom, which soon spread to neighboring villages, coincided with rural economic distress and stimulated Jews in the area to migrate—first to the large cities like Lviv, Odessa and even Kiev, and ultimately to the United States and elsewhere abroad. In the early twentieth century, one-third of the urban population was Jewish, with Lviv and Kiev each counting over 100,000 Jews.[12]

Despite living under different state regimes, Lviv's and Kiev's Jews both experienced diverse and robust religious lives. In the first half of the eighteenth century Israel ben Eliezer (known as Ba'al Shem Tov) became the first charismatic leader of Hasidism in western Ukraine. Initially centered in Podalia, Ukraine's southwestern and central region that bordered on Moldavia, the Hasidic movement spread westward through Galicia and encompassed the area around Mostyska. A century later, impact of the Jewish Enlightenment, the Haskalah, also made itself felt in Lviv, albeit more so in Brody and Tarnopol. Finally, in the twentieth century, secular Jews established active radical socialist movements, including a Bund presence.

Kiev and Lviv also both became centers of a rich Yiddish culture and literature in the early twentieth century. At the turn of the century, an estimated three of every four Jews in these cities spoke Yiddish. Kiev's most famous Yiddish writer, Sholem Aleichem (1859–1916), the pen name of Shalom Rabinovitz, resided there from 1888 until his departure for New York in 1906. (He also spent a few months in Lviv after the 1905 pogrom, and then in 1906.) During the Soviet interwar era, Kiev continued to be notable for its Yiddish culture. The Soviets institutionalized an extensive school system that enrolled thousands of Jewish youth and supported secular Yiddish culture in the Institute of Proletarian Jewish Culture. State-sponsored Yiddish writers flourished alongside the All-Ukrainian Jewish State Theater, and Yiddish in various newspapers, journals, and a children's theater.[13]

Finally, these cities' dynamic social and political histories reflected achievement and division, contentment and protest, within Jewish communities that had tremendous inequalities. In 1910, while 5,000 Jews constituted 42 percent of the merchants in Kiev, the Jewish community there was among the wealthiest and poorest in Russia at the time. One-quarter of the Jewish population lived in poverty and needed to apply for Passover alms that year. University-educated Jews and established merchants in both cities built welfare institutions— hospitals and orphanages—to meet needs of the poor; in Lviv, they also opened a Jewish elementary school and, contrary to the rituals and beliefs of the Orthodox, established a Temple that held bar mitzvahs for girls.[14] But the inequalities also reinforced socialist appeals and initiatives, and while in Kiev and Lviv the Bund never approached the numbers found in Polish cities and places like Vilna, it established active groups in both cities. To capitalize on Lviv's place in the growing movement, the Bund held its seventh convention there in August–September 1906. In 1918, Ukrainian Bundists, who had repeatedly suffered from state persecution and pogroms under the Czar, established the Kombund (Communist Bund). They would divide later over affiliation with the Russian Communist Party and ultimately suffer persecution from the communist government, but their political trajectory demonstrates the significant legacy of a Jewish radical heritage in Ukraine.[15]

Jewish political activism in Ukraine took other forms, too. Zionism was particularly popular in Odessa, where its leaders, such as Leo Pinsker and Vladimir Jabotinsky, were decidedly antisocialist. After the fall of the czar, groups of Jews in Ukraine supported socialist-oriented Zionist parties such as Zeire Zion (Young Zion) and Poale Zion (Workers of Zion). Protest—or even the Russian Revolution—did not result in social equality. Famine and tuberculosis ravaged cities like Kiev after the Great War and with industrialization, poor Jews who had migrated from rural villages became dependent wage laborers. In 1927, one in five trade union members in Kiev (16,690) were Jewish and four of every five of the 3,300 workers in the shoe factory in 1931 were Jewish.[16]

The Jewish history in Lviv and Kiev, then, was conflicted, tumultuous and, rich, but it remained to be seen what tour guides and popular tourist sites would tell of this history. Would I hear stories of the world that animated Max?

Lviv (Lwów, Lemberg, Lvov)

Despite its importance in Jewish history and the designation of its Old Town as a World Heritage site, Lviv has remained largely off the Jewish tourist trail. Like Łódź, at its prewar peak over 200,000 Jews lived in the city. After the Shoah and emigration to America, Israel, and elsewhere, the number dwindled to about 5,000 in the new millennium. The legacy of a city's rich history can be seen, however, in its built environment: it is an extraordinarily beautiful Renaissance city embellished with baroque, Renaissance, and Art Nouveau architecture, domed churches, handsome squares, red-tiled roofs, and cobblestone streets. During my October 2011 visit, the city was preparing to host the European soccer championships in 2012. Many of the downtown streets were torn up and renewed with new cobblestones. Buildings were getting a fresh coat of paint. A new international airport would soon open. Where the renovation was already complete, the elegant buildings and quaint streets were stunning.[17]

My tours of Kiev and Lviv duplicated my experience in Łódź. Without a Jewish tourist industry in place, I had to rely on a private tour that came with disadvantages and advantages. On the minus side, private tours could be relatively expensive, running up to several hundred dollars. Such tours would be prohibitive to visitors on limited budgets, though groups could share costs. On the plus side, a personal tour could be customized. I could ask to visit sites difficult to reach or of personal interest to me. For example, I arranged for Vladimir to take me to Mostyka. Generally, tour leaders tended to follow a set routine based on their assumptions of what visitors wanted to see and/or what local interests wanted them to see. By way of contrast, a personal tour allowed me to break with the routine, improvise, and establish my own priorities, including time to speak with locals on the street and at various Jewish sites.

Walking (and Driving) Lviv

My Jewish heritage tour of Lviv began the day before my trip to Mostyska, when shortly after leaving the airport, Vladimir made a surprising first stop at a church. We parked on a hillside outside the city in front of the Greek Catholic Cathedral of St. George. Vladimir explained that grand eighteenth-century baroque-rococo edifice sat on one of the seven hills of Lviv. Inside many young women and a few men knelt in prayer above a crypt where the bodies of the revered archbishops and various nobles were buried. There was a Jewish connection, he explained. It attached to Metropolitan Andrey Sheptytsky, the head of the Ukrainian Catholic Church. Long a friend of the Jews and horrified by the Nazi brutality, the Metropolitan collaborated "sufficiently" with the Nazis to keep them at bay while he hid Jews in the Church, especially children and, notably, Rabbi David Kahane (later the chief rabbi of the Israeli air force). The stop offered a preview of how narratives to follow turned on stories of heroic Ukrainian resistance to the Nazis.

Vladimir's formal Jewish heritage tour began the afternoon after the visit to Mostyka with a three-hour walk. The Nazis did little damage to the city, other than some preliminary terror bombing in 1941 prior to taking the city. They (and the allies) respected the medieval grandeur of the city, leaving the city fabric largely intact. Jews and the symbols of Jewish religious life were not so lucky. The Nazis immediately destroyed synagogues. Of the approximately forty-five synagogues in Lviv at the outset of the war, only four used by the Nazis for storage or stables survived the war. This made it possible to see all the major Jewish sights of the city in three hours—or rather, the *former* sites of Jewish buildings, synagogues, and cemeteries.

On the tour Vladimir introduced the spatial geography of Jewish social life in the nineteenth and early twentieth centuries. The city, he explained, had a series of four market squares serving the different communities—Armenians, Jews, Ukrainian, Greek Catholics. The main square, Rynok Square, centered on the neoclassical City Hall, functioned as the commercial, political, and cultural heart of patrician Lviv. I observed forty well-preserved buildings in a variety of architectural styles that emphasized—though Vladimir did not speak to it—the ethnic and class divisions in the city and displayed the visible and impressive signs of Ruthenian elite cultural and political capital.

Vladimir briefly summarized the city's early Jewish history. The city was first settled in 1256, and Jews began to move in during the mid-fourteenth century, migrating from Saxony following their persecution and demonization as agents of the Black Plague. By the end of that century, the city rejected new applicants for residence. As a walled city, Lviv had two Jewish settlements, one inside and one outside the wall. Each settlement had its own synagogue and mikveh, but they shared a cemetery.[18]

The Jewish quarter outside the city center possessed a large square, the Old Market Square, near where the city had been founded in the thirteenth century. This square was now an open park, but prior to 1941, a large synagogue, the largest progressive synagogue in the former Galicia, stood on the site. The synagogue was destroyed, along with three others in the immediate area, in 1941. One of those, the former Tempel Synagogue, dated from the seventeenth century. No vestiges of these buildings remain, but Vladimir pointed out historical markers on the side of two buildings. In several instances vandals had scratched out the word "Jewish."

The Nazis turned a third synagogue, two blocks away, into a stable. This modest building now served as the Sholem Aleichem Cultural Center. My visit found it in deplorable shape with paint peeling badly and obvious leaks in the roof and façade. Because of the leaks everything inside the main room was covered in plastic. Two elderly Jews greeted us, spoke a *bissel* Yiddish to me, and related their experiences during and since the war. One, Boris Dorfman, who had been born in 1923 in Cahul, a city in southern Moldavia, told a poignant story of how he escaped the Nazis and hid during the war. They gave me a copy of their recent newsletter, *Shofar*, a twelve-page issue printed in Ukrainian, Russian, and Yiddish. They also briefly provided their insiders' perspective on contemporary Jewish life in Lviv. The men estimated that about 3,000 Jews remained in Lviv, although they acknowledged it depends on how one defined Jewish identity. Their estimate was lower than the 5,000 typically cited in guides, and they also thought many of the estimated 3,000 were quite secular and did not identify as Jewish. I wondered what being identified as Jewish meant considering they were being "counted" as Jewish, but that was a discussion for another time and place. Still, the complexity of counting raised fraught matters of assimilation/integration and Jewish identity and the place of such people in the story of Jewish heritage.

Continuing our walk, we came upon a bas-relief on the side of a building with an image of Sholem Aleichem. Text on it identified the site as the 1906 residence of the great writer in the city. The building itself was undistinguished and told little about the famous man. He had come to Lviv that year, seeking a safe haven from pogroms in the Russian Empire before departing for New York the next year. As we walked, I decided to share something of my particular interests with Vladimir, and he pointed out that a plain-looking building with the yellow stucco facade across the street was the location of the Yiddish press and the Bund headquarters. It would not have been apparent to any one as there were no historical markers on either of these sites. At a lovely café nearby Vladimir and I sat for some cake and cappuccinos and saluted an unmarked hidden heritage.

As we walked around the next blocks Vladimir introduced the place of philanthropy in the Jewish community. He did not include the inequality and poverty that wracked Lviv's Jewish community at the time as part of the story; his commentary dwelt on the accomplishment of the benefactors. But he did hint at tensions between the secular and religious communities. At 6 Rappaport Street stood a massive red brick establishment with an elaborate cupola. Built between 1905 and 1907, it was once the Jewish Hospital. Adorned with a Moorish-style multicolored dome decorated with the Star of David, Jacob Rappaport, a doctor and the richest Jew in Lviv, had funded its erection. A secular man, Rappaport weathered criticism from rabbis and funded the project to serve everyone in the city, Jews and non-Jews. The hospital now functions as a gynecological center. A nearby second site of the Jewish Women's Society had busts of babies on its bas-relief. So in these adornments the tour marked the history of Jewish women and children, but as subjects of beneficence that the guide left unremarked upon. We next entered the walled-in Jewish quarter inside the city. This quarter dated from the fourteenth century and had two sections. An inner section was near the large Market Square. Jewish professionals and artisans settled the area and one street was named after the blacksmiths. Rich Jews built grand four-story mansions in the area in styles with Renaissance, Baroque, and Art Nouveau details to impress others with their wealth and elite status, and the architectural features impressed me now, too. A second smaller market square also served this inner Jewish community.

Two synagogues, one still active, the other destroyed during the Holocaust, were the highlight of Vladimir's tour of the inner quarter. He pointed out that Chabad, the Hasidic movement with a leading role in Judaic outreach in Eastern Europe since 1989, operates the city's main synagogue, Bais Aron V'Yisroel (also known as Tsori Gilead Synagogue). It is a simple, unpretentious yellow stone edifice built in 1924 in Renaissance style and rededicated as an Orthodox synagogue in 2007. It survived because the Nazis had used it as a stable, and was restored thanks to American philanthropic donations. The second synagogue site was that of the former Golden Rose Synagogue, which the Nazis had burned down in 1942. Vladimir left a small donation in lieu of an admission fee to help sustain the site. The Golden Rose Synagogue had not undergone renovations since the war, although a design competition organized by Lviv's Center for Urban History of East Central Europe in 2010 promised future improvements at the Synagogue.[19] A couple of elderly people sat in the kitchen-office. They provided access to the rear of the building and the remnants of the Golden Rose. The single wall remaining served as the back wall of a Jewish-themed restaurant next door.

The area around the synagogue had visible markers of Jewish life. One site housed the Kehile, the center of the organized Jewish community from the mid-nineteenth century to World War II. Other sites had signs literally inscribed on the buildings. Although few Jews now lived in Lviv, numerous buildings bore faint inscriptions in Yiddish or Hebrew on the front. Such inscriptions had

Figure 10. Lviv Commercial decorative signage in Polish and Yiddish advertises "Dairy Products: Milchig [dairy] meals / Coffee, tea / Breads / Butter, cheese / Sour Milk /Buttermilk." Photo by the author.

undoubtedly once been ubiquitous and others had since been painted over. In a couple of cases, shopkeepers painted new signs in Hebrew, Yiddish, and Polish as decorative motifs. The new ones were contemporary kitsch rather than historical remnants, but the additions indicated both a budding appreciation of the past and its potential commercial cachet.

Consistent with the dominant Jewish interest in Holocaust tourism, Vladimir's tour of Lviv's Jewish heritage gave prominence to sites of the Shoah. Thus, on the return trip from Mostyska, Vladimir stopped about fifteen minutes outside the city at the Kleparov railroad station. Here was the location of the transit camp, Janowska, a way station for Jews from the entire region being sent on to the Belzec extermination camp. Only a small sign on the station wall indicated this horrific past. Vladimir showed me a memorial stone that noted as many as 200,000 Jews were "put to death," but then he tried to offset the horror with a heroic story of survival: the story of how Simon Wiesenthal and a friend escaped from the camp in 1943. Wiesenthal, who went on to a distinguished career locating Nazis and holding them responsible for their actions, killed a guard, and then putting on his uniform, pretended to guard the other Jew while they made their escape.

The city's other major Holocaust site memorializes the murdered victims of the ghetto. It is located is a park behind the main town square at the edge of the ghetto and just outside a railroad trestle that confined Jewish worker housing to its far side. A menorah and a large imposing stone figure of a man with one hand stretched up toward heaven and the other in a fist of resistance marks the site.

At the end of my visit to Lviv I tried to make sense of all I had seen. Exhausted, with Vladimir leading, we wended our way back to my hotel, and crossed the main square. This "square" is actually a long rectangle with a park down the center, at the head of which stands the opulent Opera House, dating from the turn of the twenieth century. Facing it, he pointed out on the left the grand four-story mansion of Rabbi Bernard von Lowenstein, rabbi of the Progressive Tempel Synagogue. The building now serves as the home of Lviv's Jewish Community Center. Von Lowenstein was obviously a wealthy man (the "von" reflected his elite pedigree, or was adopted to claim one) and he outfitted the second floor as his own personal temple. Vladimir's tour had passed by vernacular housing and sites of worker cultural, political, and social life, but they were tangential to his narrative of Jewish Lviv. He had focused on synagogues and the homes and establishments of the rich Jews. Indeed, "ordinary" daily life and vernacular architecture can be mundane, unheroic, and less memorable for many tourists. I also suspect that neither Ukrainian political and business leaders (many with nationalist and entrepreneurial agendas) want to sponsor these quotidian stories, nor would Jewish tourists from the United States and Israel with primarily religious identities or interest in the Holocaust necessarily want to hear them.

Museums

Challenges in the commercialized private and politicized public spheres also shape the city's museum culture and historical consciousness. Two institutions exemplify the breadth and depth of this challenge. The first, a commercial enterprise, is an unintended living museum to Jewish food culture: it is a relatively new popular Jewish restaurant, Under the Golden Rose. Part of a chain of fifteen themed bars and cafés, the restaurant is the brainchild of Yurko Nazuruk, a flamboyant young Ukrainian entrepreneur. His restaurants brashly exhibit the marketing of Jewish heritage via kitsch, stereotypes with anti-Semitic resonance, and Ukrainian nationalism. In one restaurant leather-clad waitresses in the bar offer a diet of sadomasochism (whips and chains) with your meal. In another, a basement bar designed to imitate World War II bunkers used by Ukrainians to fight Russian troops (presumably on the side of the Nazis), requires patrons to say the magic words, "Glory to Ukraine," before a burly guard in military attire will admit them. A third establishment makes a nod back to the nineteenth-century heyday of Jews in Lviv and describes itself as a Jewish Galician rather than a Jewish Ukrainian restaurant. Located below the Golden Rose Synagogue site, it has similarly doubtful connotations. In its

"Jewish atmosphere" guests are invited to put on *peyes* (sideburns) and hats while dining on matzo and chopped liver. The restaurant's signature feature, however, is the absence of any prices: invoking mercenary stereotypes, diners are told to haggle with the waiters. One critic, writing in Public Radio International, pointedly asks, "How about some anti-Semitism with that dish?" Tourists and local non-Jews have recorded their pleasure with their visit on TripAdvisor, where the restaurant enjoys a four-star rating (of five).[20]

One blog insists that few local Jews have rushed to patronize Under the Golden Rose, but it thrives and cities such as Łódź and Kraków have similar places.[21] By contrast, local Jews have striven to counter the commodified and stereotyped Jewishness represented by Under the Golden Rose. Take for example, Meylakh Sheykhet, the director of the Union Council of ex-Soviet Jews in Lviv. Sheykhet led opposition to a developer's plan to build a hotel over the ruins of the Golden Rose Synagogue that jeopardized Jewish artifacts. Moreover, and consistent with the identification of cemeteries and synagogues as core elements in the dominant Holocaust heritage narrative, he led fund-raising for archeological work at the synagogue, and more broadly, helped preserve over 150 Jewish cemeteries in Ukraine.[22]

When I returned to Lviv in 2015, I visited a second institutional site that illustrates other challenges and possibilities for the present and future of Jewish heritage in Lviv.[23] It was a small branch of the city's Museum of the History of Religion. The museum's main building, which Vladimir had taken me to see on my first trip, occupies a dilapidated former Dominican monastery on Museyna Square, a block from the main Rynok Square. Its exhibit had not been modernized and was drab, poorly lit, and minimally signed, its Jewish history limited to about fifty artifacts of Judaica. There were a wealth of other artifacts languishing in government storehouses and museums, I was told. For a secular Jew like myself, localizing everything Jewish in a religious museum was troubling. Equally telling, Vladimir left me with the impression no modern museum in Lviv dedicated to the social, cultural, and political history of its former Jewish life existed.

Returning four years later, I learned this was and had not been the case. The Museum of Religion had opened a small museum about three blocks away on Staroyevreyska St. (Old Jewish Street) dedicated to the history of Jews. Websites like TripAdvisor referred to it as the "Jewish Museum." Visiting it in June 2015, the "Jewish Museum" was easy to miss. I walked past the entryway several times because the small sandwich board in front of the door only advertised it in English as the Lviv Museum of the History of Religion.

A woman sitting at the front door desk greeted me and confirmed that I had in fact entered the Jewish Museum. I paid the entry fee (10 hryvnia [less than 50 cents]) and was directed to English-language loose-leaf guidebooks that translated Ukrainian texts posted on the walls of the exhibit. I passed through a small

Figure 11. Sandwich board in front
of the Lviv "Jewish Museum."
Photo by the author.

middle room consisting of a half-dozen illuminated religious artifacts to the
main exhibit. Titled "Those Who Saved the World," the exhibit filled another
small room with artifacts and photos providing a familiar narrative of the Holocaust and Ukrainian heroism. The exhibit began with images and news clip-
pings of the Lviv concentration camp and then moved on to its main tale: a story
I had already heard from Vladimir in his 2011 introduction to Lviv regarding
actions by the Ukrainian Greek-Catholic Church and its Metropolitan Andrey
Sheptytsky to save Jews during World War II. The Jewish Museum was essen-
tially a Holocaust museum that provided an unproblematic account of Ukrainian support for Jews. It offered no discussion of any Ukrainian collaboration
with the Nazis.

Returning to the room I had first entered, however, I discovered a few tantalizing artifacts that evoked an older Jewish presence in the city and its once
vibrant popular culture. A table and a woman's dress suggested the more domestic world. In one cabinet, photos of a 1931 Jewish summer camp, and of two men
identified as part of a left-wing movement gave a hint of a lively political culture
in the interwar years. A second cabinet in the room contained photographs and
documents dedicated to a history of Lviv rabbis and the major synagogues. In
all, the museum provided brief but enticing glimpses into life outside the Shul
that whet my appetite for more.

The potential for more exists in Lviv, a city that has two advantages over a place like Łódź. First, the preservation of Lviv's architectural gems and the designation of the Old City as a World Heritage site attract tourists to the city. Second, Lviv's Center for Urban History in East Central Europe provides intellectual resources and a vision of an inclusive history of Jewish Lviv. With the initiative of the city administration and support of the German Society for International Cooperation and Jewish partner organizations, the Center has taken on the development of major sites of Jewish heritage. The Center has developed a program that incorporates daily life of the prewar community into the heritage narrative by assembling a team of local and international social historians who are engaged with the ideas of the New Jewish History (full disclosure: I was invited to help in that project). The exhibits are planned to be site-specific museums of the street. Titled "Space of Synagogues: Jewish History, Common Heritage and Responsibility," the first phase opened in September 2016 with the conservation of the Golden Rose Synagogue fragments, the installation of a Perpetuation memorial, and the marking of foundation of the Jewish House of Learning Beth Hamidrash. A second phase will commemorate the Great Synagogue that once stood on the site, and provide a place for reflection on the history of Jews in Lviv.

The memorialization, commemoration, and conservation of these synagogues restore a critical part of the city's Jewish past, but also serve as points of entry into the longer narrative of Jewish urban history in the city. For example, the Center describes the Golden Rose as a "site for knowledge and remembrance of the long and rich history of Lviv Jews" and an important step in the renovation of Lviv's Jewish heritage program. Working with local universities, the Center has also initiated a program in public history to train teachers and museum professionals while reclaiming that history in and for the public. While Jewish heritage tourism in Lviv during my 2015 visit remained largely a diet of synagogues, cemeteries, and Holocaust memorials, the Center had begun to chart more ambitious new frontiers for a broadened and inclusive Jewish heritage.[24] Yiddish culture and its engagement with socialism and Zionism would, I had reason to hope, in time be memorialized.

The state of Jewish heritage tourism in Kiev remained to be seen.

KIEV

Most of the 224,000 Jews in Kiev fled the city with the outbreak of World War II. Those who stayed faced brutal incarceration and extermination. By the mid-1950s Jewish survivors had returned and constituted 14 percent (150,000) of the population. Many Jews later immigrated to Israel and the United States after 1990, but an estimated 60,000 Jews remain in Ukraine, 20,000 to 30,000 of them in Kiev.[25]

Despite this substantial Jewish population, Jewish heritage tourism turned out to be even less well developed in Kiev than in Lviv. Kiev was not a World Heritage site, nor did it have the resources of Lviv's Urban History Center. Anastasia Riabchuk, a brilliant young sociologist at the National University of Kiev-Mohyla Academy, had invited me to Kiev to show a documentary film I produced in 1990 on miners in Donetsk during the collapse of the Soviet Union. She and her colleagues in Cultural Studies recruited Mykhailo Borisovich Kalnytskyi, a leading scholar of Jewish Kiev, to give me a tour.[26]

Walking (and Driving) Kiev

Kalnytskyi spoke no English and did not own a car, so two of my hosts from the Academy, Olga Papash and Stasislaw (Stas) Menzelevskyi, accompanied us to translate and drive their car. As in Lviv, this was to be a private tour, but the presence of two non-Jewish locals on the trip created a much richer dialogue en route. My companions added their own perspective as students of history and long-time residents of Kiev. My guide also took us off the beaten path of commercialized Jewish tourism in Kiev, such as it was. Ruth Ellen Gruber's comprehensive guide to Jewish travel in Eastern Europe, *Jewish Heritage Travel*, enumerates the conventional tour sites. She notes three synagogues and a prayer house, monuments to former Israeli prime minister Golda Meir and Sholem Aleichem, and the Babi Yar Memorial.[27] By contrast, Kalnytskyi had my hosts drive to a hospital and an industrial site not advertised in online Jewish heritage tours.

We began our trip on the outskirts of the central city with a visit to a large complex of substantial buildings on tree-lined streets. It was a vast hospital complex built in 1862 as the Jewish Hospital. Funded by the Kiev sugar baron, Izrael Brodsky, the hospital was a charitable project of the wealthy Jewish community. As a model philanthropic institution, the hospital admitted Jews and non-Jews, but its primary mission was devoted to the poor and working-class Jewish community. It was in historian Natan Meir's words, a "civilizing project"—a way of "creating model Jews."[28] The Brodsky family name adorned various Jewish landmarks in the city and KalnytskyI pointed out a dilapidated old building in the complex that had been erected in 1906 by Brodsky's children in honor of their father.

Large urban institutions such as the hospital were often built in unsettled areas where land was cheap, but Meir attributes the hospital's remote location to the desire of elite in the City Council to keep the contagion associated with the poor at a distance. The distant site also meant to mask the presence of the Jewish establishment to avoid provoking anti-Semitic hostility.[29] It appears the desire for invisibility worked: my companions from the Academy, both of whom thought themselves relatively attuned to Kiev's Jewish past, had been to the hospital several times and expressed amazement to learn of its Jewish provenance.

A second stop on the car tour brought us to a main stop on any Jewish heritage tour in Kiev: the ravine on the outskirts of Kiev where SS troops had massacred 34,000 Jews in September 1941—the site of the Babi Yar Memorial. Subsequently, the number killed reached over 100,000. The majority were Jewish, but the victims also included Roma (gypsies), resistance fighters, and Soviet prisoners of war.

Pre-1989 Soviet and post-1989 Ukrainian agendas framed how the site memorialized the past. The Babi Yar monument was a massive heroic Soviet-era sculpture mostly consisting of writhing, male bodies. The statue was erected in 1976 at the height of a public outcry against Israeli "Zionist" assertions over the West Bank in which the Soviet Union identified with Palestinian claims. Dedicated to Soviet Citizens of the War, the monument's inscription makes no mention of Jews (or Roma). In 1991, Ukrainian independence from the Soviet Union unleashed pent up demands from Ukrainians for recognition of them and others at the site. Over the next few years a monument appeared to commemorate the murdered Roma, another to remember concentration camp victims, and two crosses were erected in memory of the murder of 621 Ukrainian nationalists in 1942 and 2 Ukrainian Orthodox priests in 1941. The appearance of another monument to victims of 1961 mudslides illustrated how the site had become generalized as a place of victimhood, distinct from its roots in Jewish slaughter. But eventually, Ukrainian independence allowed for the erection of a specifically Jewish monument. On September 29, 1991, in commemoration of the fiftieth anniversary of the Babi Yar massacre, the newly independent Ukrainian government dedicated a menorah-shaped monument on a large tiered plinth. Unlike the earlier Soviet monument, the Menorah held pride of place at the end of a long pathway through the woods in the actual ravine where the massacre took place—in the "killing fields." A decade later, in 2001, the state erected a more equivocal monument in bronze of broken toys to commemorate the children massacred. Although the victims were mostly Jewish children and not Ukrainian nationalists or Russian soldiers, the sculpture universalized the children but made a sly reference to their Jewishness. The sculptor includes a small reference visual to the astute observer: the young boy wears a yarmulke.

The car tour ended with a visit to the Podol neighborhood, one of two poor areas where Jews were required to live in the nineteenth century. Located in the northern part of the city on the banks of the Dnieper, Meir's history describes it along with the Lybed neighborhood in the upper part of the city as the poorest areas of the city, without sanitation or running water. The guide pointed out shells of the many old factories and mills—flour factories, breweries, brick works, a tannery, and candle factory—where Jews worked. The scene resembled run-down, superannuated, and vacant industrial neighborhoods in many postindustrial American cities. Save for a few Yiddish signs on buildings in Yiddish, there were no markers of the social history of Kiev's working-class Jews.

Kalnytskyi did point out a building he thought to have once housed a Jewish kindergarten or home for the aged, which he attributed to Brodsky philanthropy. He did not, however, take the opportunity to address the gendered system of philanthropy within the wealthy Brodsky, Rozenberg, Ginzburg, and Zaks clans. The wives and daughters of these men and their affluent merchant allies took substantial leadership in welfare initiatives. Along with the missionary or "uplift" perspective toward the poor of these haute bourgeois women and their middle-class allies, Kalnytskyi's commentary could also have included a discussion of labor conditions and protest by the revolutionary Podalia-Zionist Socialists pictured by Meir in his account of turn-of-the-century Kiev.[30]

For the remainder of his Jewish heritage tour, Kalnytskyi had my hosts drive back into downtown Kiev to focus on more conventional heritage sites—synagogues and monuments to the notable, rich, and famous. As in the other cities I visited, accounts of Kiev's synagogues reflected the dominant narrative of Jewish history: built with monies from the wealthy Jews, they had been seriously damaged during the war, used for other purposes during the Soviet era, and renovated and rededicated since 1989. For example, the benefactor of the Central (or Brodsky) Synagogue downtown was "the sugar king's" son, Lazar. Like his father, Izrael, Lazar desired to create model institutions that would win the approval of the entire Russian Empire. His will directed that the synagogue be built near the Bessarabian Market, a high-end indoor market built in 1910–1912. Situated at the head of the most famous street in Kiev, the market displayed the wares of Jewish merchants who made up an estimated 60 percent of the city's merchant class. The building became a puppet theatre during the Soviet era and was rededicated as a community center and synagogue in the mid-1990s. In the new millennium it serves the Orthodox Chabad Lubavitch community. When I visited, Chabad was outside distributing matzos for the coming Passover. The synagogue also houses a Museum of Jewish (Religious) Heritage with religious books, menorahs, and similar religious artifacts.

The Great Choral (or Main, or Podol) Synagogue of the Kiev Jewish community told a similar story of elite patronage. A red brick building in the Moorish style, Choral was an Aesopian synagogue constructed in the Russian empire to disguise a building's religious function (although this was not a story told by my the guide). Financed by the merchants Gabriel Jakob Rozenberg and Vladimir Ginzburg, it was erected in the Podol district in 1894. It was another example of a synagogue that survived the war because Nazis had used it as stable. Unlike other synagogues in the Soviet Union, state authorities allowed the synagogue to function after 1945, making it the longest serving synagogue in Kiev. It operates now as religious center with mikvah, kosher kitchen, and matzo bakery.

Kiev's third historic synagogue, the Moorish style Galytska (Galician) Synagogue (1909–1910), is located in the Evbaz area, a district name that is shorthand for the Evreiskii Bazaar, or Jewish Market. Its history resembles that of other

Figure 12. Sholem Aleichem statue in Kiev. Photo by the author.

Jewish areas of the city: it was heavily destroyed in the war, used for ammunition storage for the next half century, and rededicated after its renovation in 2001. It now serves as educational center for the Jewish Agency for Israel.[31]

Finally, my Jewish heritage tour of Kiev also consisted of a few plaques and one terrific statue. The plaques were to Golda Meir's birthplace and to two houses in which Sholem Aleichem lived briefly in 1905 before moving on to Lviv and New York. The plaque to Meir could easily be missed—literally and figuratively, as it was inconspicuous. More impressive was the welcoming statue of Sholem Aleichem. This statue was about as close as I came to popular history in Kiev's Jewish heritage tour. The distinguished playwright and author of numbskull tales where the self-proclaimed knowledgeable folk are fools and the fools are clever, materializes as an inviting Everyman, tipping his hat to all who pass by.[32]

I enjoyed my visits to both Lviv and Kiev, but the faint echoes of proletarian Jewish voices like those of my grandparents disappointed me. The cities' Jewish heritage sites did not present the social history I knew from historians' accounts. Both cities had once had a large Jewish presence; both cities contain relatively small numbers of Jews in the present, but Jewish communities in each have a growing vitality. In both cities the heritage tourist business remains in its infancy, largely untouched by the rich past. Still, I was left with a sense of a great potential for Jewish heritage in these cities. In particular, Lviv's World Heritage status and its Center for Urban History provide bases on which heritage tourism can build; indeed, I was excited by initiatives already underway there, and by opportunities to participate in them. But I was also wary of how the struggling Ukrainian economy could constrain development. Ukrainian desire to establish a national identity complicated the place of a Jewish heritage in the nation, let alone consideration of a redemptive socialist and communist past. The Bund sites and the statue of Sholem Aleichem referenced a past lived by people much like Max and Chaia, but most of that past remained muted, hidden, or ignored. So, I thought it was time to follow Chaia, Max and their families out of Eastern and Central Europe to places like London and New York. Would Jewish heritage tourism there differ I wondered? And what effect would the rise of Jewish Holocaust tourism in Eastern Europe have on the Jewish heritage industry in the West?

CHAPTER 4

London

HERITAGE TOURISM UNPACKED
IN THE JEWISH DIASPORA

The Walkowitz, Lubertofsky, Margel, and Tarnofsky families were among the 2 million Jews who emigrated from Eastern Europe in the last quarter of the nineteenth and first quarter of the twentieth centuries. These four families dispersed across the globe in the first two decades of the new century, participating in the creation of an international Jewish diaspora. As early as the interwar era, family members resided in virtually every part of the world and established thriving communities in Denmark, Sweden, Argentina, England, Israel, Canada, and across the United States. One of two cities they most identified with new opportunity was London, England. The London metropolis received 7 percent of Polish emigrant Jews, a number estimated as between 120,000 and 150,000. The United Kingdom's Jewish population of 60,000 in 1881 swelled to 300,000 in 1914. Approximately 260,000 people identified as Jews for the 2011 census, making the United Kingdom the fifth-largest Jewish community in the world. The number is an indeterminate undercount, however, that reflects the public confusion and contested nature of Jewish identity: the census only treats Jewish identity as a religious category, and it does not offer the choice of "Jewish" as an ethno-cultural classification. About two-thirds of them lived in the Greater London area, with the rest concentrated in Leeds, Manchester, and Glasgow. Only New York, the subject of the next chapter, would attract a greater number than London.[1]

LONDON: HISTORY

The development of social history in the last third of the twentieth century spawned an extensive and comprehensive historiography of Jews in England.[2] Historians draw a picture of a dynamic and vibrant Jewish community in

London, its history punctuated by struggles and achievements, division and unity. Jews struggled with the host native-born community and among themselves.

Jews have a long history in Britain. The Crusades depleted royal coffers, but decrees making moneylending heretical also removed Jews as a source of royal taxes. The king had no more need for their presence, and in 1290, Edward I expelled roughly 4,000 to 6,000 Jewish merchants and artisans who had settled in England since Roman times. Approximately 350 years later, in 1656, Jews were gradually allowed to resettle in England. They were primarily Sephardim from Spain, Holland, and Portugal. During the mid-nineteenth century, a second migration of Ashkenazi Jews arrived from Germany.

In the nineteenth century, the British Age of Reform ended colonial slavery and expanded rights for Catholics and workers. Jews won political rights as well, and symbolically in 1858 Baron Lionel de Rothschild took a seat in the House of Commons. In the following decades Jews built magisterial synagogues and established a communal support system. By 1881, about 47,000 Jews resided in England and Scotland. Many of them continued to live apart from the dominant majority, but nonetheless Anglicized. Adopting some of the trappings of English culture, they took on a hybrid national-ethnic identity as Anglo-Jews. Wealthy financiers like Sir Moses Montefiore (Queen Victoria had knighted him in 1837), Lionel Louis Cohen, and Rothschild took philanthropic roles, developing and leading communal institutions such as the Jewish Board of Deputies and Jewish Board of Guardians to represent and tend to the needs of their "less fortunate" brethren.[3]

Jewish London life dramatically changed with immigration that followed the Russian pogroms and economic distress in 1881–1882. Poor Jews arriving from rural villages and urban slums increased the social and moral imperatives of Jewish philanthropy. Arriving from the Kingdom of Poland, the Pale of Settlement to its east (the western regions of Imperial Russia), and Galicia, they concentrated in the East End. Yiddish became the lingua franca in many stalls and shops around Spitalfields Market and in Whitechapel where whole families worked to make ends meet, often in subcontracted sweated labor in garment shops.[4]

The harsh conditions of daily life provoked a range of responses, from outright hostility toward the poor to charity benevolence. Historian James Appell quotes one observer stridently bemoaning Polish Jews as "demoralized . . . savages" whose "dirt, stupidity and obstinacy, with scant sentiments of integrity, seem to be the principle feature of their characters."[5] Feldman and other historians have contrasted this stereotyping with the more temperate, but equally anxious perspective of older Anglo-Jewish leaders from the Sephardic and German Ashkenazi communities. Believing the poverty and "degradation" of their Eastern European brethren undermined their own higher status, these elite Jews worked "with a sense of urgency and foreboding." Schools, asylums, poor relief, and institutions to contain delinquency like the Jewish Board of Guardians would Anglicize the "foreign Jews" and teach them the "class appropriate skills/ trades" as a path to Englishness.[6]

A third set of political and cultural responses came from within the East End Jewish community itself. Socialists, communists, trade unionists, Zionists, and social democrats—sometimes in overlapping configurations such as socialist Zionists—competed politically for support; religious and secular Jews vied in competing cultural institutions, in Alderman's words, to shape immigrants' "sense of self."[7]

The Jewish religious presence is visible in handsome synagogues. German Jews erected the Ashkenazi Great Synagogue in 1722 and subsequently enlarged it. The German Blitz destroyed this synagogue in 1941, but the magnificent Sephardic Bevis Marks Synagogue (consecrated in 1702) in the Aldgate district just outside the City of London Gate that borders on the East End, continues to serve the London Jewish community. By the end of the nineteenth century, Reform and Orthodox Jews had established a series of synagogues across the city and its suburbs that still serve their respective constituencies.[8]

Jewish political associations left less visible material remains, but sites of organizations, meetings, and agitation among radicals exist throughout the East End. The radical presence in London was a landmark in Jewish history, and vice versa: Jews played formative roles in London's radical history. Aaron Lieberman, the revolutionary Socialist émigré from the Vilna Rabbinical College, established the Union of Hebrew Socialists in the East End of London in May 1876. In 1884, two other émigrés—Morris Winchevsky and Elijah W. Rabbinowitz— opened the first radical Yiddish newspaper in the world, *Der Poylisher Yidl* (The Polish Jew). The next year Rabbinowitz published the first nonpartisan socialist paper, *Der Arbeter Fraynd* (The Worker's Friend). A subsequent generation of radicals remembered this circle of radicals "considered themselves 'cosmopolitans' and 'revolutionaries.'" Their political work extended to social and cultural radicalism, including the International Workers' Educational Club, a group popularly known as the Berner Street Club. With origins in the Vilna center that nurtured Jewish socialism, in 1897 the Berner Street Club organized as an association of London anarchists and social democrats who propagandized in Yiddish to reach the Jewish masses. Steeped in Yiddish culture and politics, these Jewish East End radicals were the vanguard for Jewish radicals in London and elsewhere. Reflecting in 1967 on that period, an anniversary publication of the British Jewish radical labor movement noted Whitechapel was for "a certain period the 'Jerusalem' of Jewish socialists and anarchists to American radicals; even as [American] socialists and anarchists [and communists] often fought among themselves, they looked to the Jewish revolutionary circles in Britain for guidance, inspiration and leadership."[9]

Revolutionary activity culminated in the 1889 strike of 10,000 garment workers in London for a twelve-hour day and controls on sweated work. But divisions among workers and the vast reservoir of unskilled workers that characterized industrializing cities such as London weakened the subsequent Jewish labor movement, especially in comparison to the widespread and militant strikes among New York garment workers in the early twentieth century. The 1905 Aliens Act further stunted the impact of radicalism, including Bundism, in London. Nonetheless, in 1902, London still counted thirty-two Jewish trade unions, and in 1909, Russian-born Bundists in Stepney organized a socialist society and a political-cultural club. Other Jewish socialists formed a Zionist labor movement, Poale Zion, which continued into the mid-twentieth century and beyond to affiliate with the British Labour Party. Thus did socialism and anarchism shape the radical Jewish milieu in early twentieth-century London.[10]

In the interwar period, while British Jews Anglicized, becoming Englishmen with a difference—Anglo-Jews—Jewish radical political activity nonetheless continued. Twenty-two Bundist clubs existed, and Jews joined the Communist Party in disproportionate numbers.[11] The Jewish place in London's history extended though well beyond this relatively orthodox and male-dominated political account of radical and nonradical Jewish history. Jewish women played major roles in both the domestic and public spheres. Jewish women, mirroring the role played by Jewish financier husbands, took leading roles in philanthropy and reform movements. In doing so, some also challenged Jewish male authority. In October 1913, the New West End Synagogue evicted three members of the Jewish League for Women's Suffrage, including the leading suffragette activist Henrietta (Netta) Franklin, after they spoke out against the opposition to suffrage by two leading congregants, Sir Rufus Isaacs and Herbert Samuel.[12]

Anglo-Jews also played leading roles in the development of British popular and commercial culture. Jewish impresarios ran many of the variety theatres. Popular Jewish-owned food service chains like Tesco's, Lyon's House, and Sainsbury shaped modern British food culture. Jewish women pioneered ready-to-wear in Soho. Peter Sellers was one of many Jewish film producers, actors, painters, writers, and scholars who helped develop twentieth-century British intellectual and cultural life. So while London's Jews were small in number, they played an integral and disproportionately large role in the making of Modern London.[13]

In post–World War II London, Anglo-Jewry "fractured" with the rise on the right of the ultra-Orthodox. Jews remained a vital presence in popular culture and the commercial life of the city, but Jewish socialists, increasingly disenchanted with the Soviet Union, declined in numbers. Many found alternate expression in affluent Jewish left, reform, and secular-minded organizations that supported more inclusive and multi-cultural expressions of Jewishness.[14] David Rosenberg, for example, a leading member of one such organization, the Jewish Socialist Group, makes an appearance later in this chapter as the guide for London's Radical Jewish walking tour. Once again, though, it remains to be seen what of this radical history is remembered, what is forgotten, what is imagined, and what is lost in the public telling of it.[15]

∿ INTERLUDE ∿

Max, the first of my grandparents to set out from home in search of a better world, briefly found himself in England. He never told me where he spent the four years after running away from Mostyska in 1903 at the age of twelve. I have vague memories of his speaking of Lviv and Vienna, but on August 3, 1907, Maier Margel, age sixteen, boarded the ocean liner SS *Blücher* in Hamburg. He was bound for America. According to the ship manifest, he paid for his own ticket, and probably traveled third class. The next day the ship arrived in Southampton, England. A day later it continued to New York.

Other Jewish immigrants arrived in the United Kingdom and stayed, but for the majority, like Max, Southampton or another port such as Liverpool was an intermediary stop. A few greenhorns inevitably thought they had reached America and disembarked. An estimated 80 percent of the emigrants continued on, primarily to America, but others went to South Africa or to other destinations. For some, though, England was a destination, especially if landsmen were there. Leeds, for instance, was settled by large numbers of Litvaks from in and around the town of Kolno.[16] Max's father's cousin from Mostyska, Levi Margel, settled in Liverpool with his family just a few years before Max's own trip. This branch of the Margel family, my distant cousins, in the next decades became the base for an extended Margel family in Leeds.

This scant personal familial attachment to London meant I embarked on my Jewish heritage tourism there with little baggage from the distant past, though I did begin with expectations nurtured from more recent experiences: I had been coming to London with my family regularly for forty-five years. My wife, Judith, is a British historian and I often use the city as a base for research and writing. Over the years, we established a network of radical socialist and feminist colleagues and friends in England. Some of them, as well as some neighbors, were Jewish and told stories of a rich radical Jewish history on the East End. They also spoke of a conflict associated with German Jews and "bourgeois" Jews who had fled the East End for the greener pastures of outer North London boroughs. So, I embarked on my tourism ready for a story of diverse Jews with different perspectives.

∿

HERITAGE

London offers Jewish heritage with a marked difference from the continent. There are no Holocaust or major cemetery sites associated with it. It is also a heritage story unmarked by the collapse of the Soviet Union, except of course that the rise of Jewish heritage alternatives in Central and Eastern European Jewish tourism drew people away from London tours. But that is a subject to which we must return later.

Jewish heritage tourism in London may have declined after 1991, but tourism to London generally did not. The city remained one of the leading tourist destinations in the world. In 2013, 16.8 million visitors spent over £11 billion in London.[17] These tourists cite history, heritage, and culture as the most popular reasons for their visits, and they identify eight of the top ten destinations as museums. Heritage tourism alone generates £20.6 billion of the UK's GDP and provides 466,000 jobs.[18] Jewish heritage, however, is far down on the list of popular tourist interests. Without the Holocaust sites, Jewish heritage tourism in London mostly focuses on its Jewish Museum and walking tours.

The Jewish Museum London

The Jewish Museum London (JML) does not make the list of the top ten museum sites for London tourists. Located on a side street in Camden Town, it occupies a converted historic Victorian-era building that has been combined with an adjacent former piano factory. The area is a north London neighborhood best known for the crush of its weekend Camden Market and its rocker teenage nightlife. The building is one of about 600 "listed" by English Heritage as significant to English history. The JML was formed in 1995 from the merger of two very different earlier museums: the Jewish Museum (founded in 1932) and the London Museum of Jewish Life, founded in 1983 as the Museum of the Jewish East End. The JML has had to negotiate tensions between its two founding institutions' different orientations. The merged institution, which dedicated itself to the preservation of the East End Jewish heritage, was informed by a more democratic understanding of Jewish life than had been the case in the Jewish Museum. Following the merger and years of "planning and fundraising," the JML reopened to the public on March 17, 2010, joining the ranks of new or remodeled Jewish museums that opened in many centers of the Jewish diaspora during the last thirty years.[19] In 2015–2016, the small Jewish Military Museum, which had been located in the outskirts of the city in Hendon, Barnet, moved to the Camden Town museum and fifty of its artifacts were incorporated into the JML exhibit.[20]

I visited the JML several times during annual visits to London. One can cover the museum in a single visit. Among the new breed of Jewish museums with oral histories, video, animated constructions, and interactive modules, it is also one of the smallest. The ground floor consists of a welcome gallery and small shop. The gallery introduces visitors to Jewish London rather than to the exhibition, and only hints at the richness of the museum's collection and its interpretative potential. Ten video projections drawn from the museum's 310 oral histories evocatively illustrate the diversity of the contemporary Jewish community and demonstrate that Jewish life extends well beyond the synagogues. The video collection is a virtual museum on its website, however, not the on-site museum tourists visit.

The main exhibition consists of three rooms upstairs. A prominent sign at the entrance to the core exhibit summarizes the museum's tripartite division of Jewish heritage: "The contemporary Jewish world is shaped by three major events: the migration of Eastern European Jews at the turn of the century, the Holocaust, and the subsequent establishment of the state of Israel." As a condition of the merger the new museum had to agree to keep the Jewish Museum's extraordinary collection of Jewish ceremonial art and artifacts intact and exhibit it. Accordingly, the exhibit in the first room, *Judaism: A Living Faith*, which comprises one-third of the museum, is dedicated to Judaica.[21] In a smallish room of perhaps 225 square feet, visitors are told that that "Judaism is the religion and the way of life of the Jewish people." For a secular Jew like myself, the definition of a Jewish "way of life" as religion without acknowledging Jewish secular cultural identity is troublesome, but the problem is less one of commission than omission. The subject of the artifacts in the room is religious identity rooted in following the Torah and "common practices . . . shared by observant Jews everywhere."

The rest of the museum occupies the next floor and is divided between rooms dedicated to the 1,000-year history of Jews in England since 1066 and the Holocaust. Panels dividing the larger front room create a pathway that winds visitors around a chronological tour of Jews in England. This part of the tour is simply called, *History: A British Story*. We move quickly through time. A map illustrates the many origins of Jews coming to Britain; a panel covers the medieval history of Jews in England, marking their arrival in 1066 and their subsequent 350 years of persecution; graphs provide population data on Jews in England from their exile in 1290 to the present. In a section on nineteenth-century immigrants, "Fitting In," the text references division within the Jewish community, noting that late nineteenth-century Jewish immigrants encountered the hostility of the "existing Jewish community," fearful of "losing its own hard-won status." The text does not break down the members of this existing community by class or national origin or sect (i.e., wealthy Dutch-Spanish Sephardim, German Anglo-Jews). Panels reference poor housing, sanitation, and Yiddish theater, but description is privileged; there is little analysis of causes of these conditions, of the strengths and weakness of responses by Jewish philanthropy, or of the role of the state, all subjects on which historians have written powerfully.[22]

One visually engaging section on labor and trades complicates the traditional heroic narrative that dominates the museum's exhibit. A handsome poster of the "Great Strike of London Tailors" in 1889 accompanies the large TV projection of a tailor shop. Superimposed on the image of the shop, three actors' voices bring three people to life, each articulating different social perspectives: a young female stitcher, proud of her skill, sees opportunity in work; a male ironer and trade-union organizer, describes exploitative working conditions; a "boss" of the shop floor counters trade unionists with descriptions of competition he faces and reform opportunities. In this one display, visitors hear of class and gender differences that shape and reshape the Jewish community in struggles to win, sustain, and eke out a fragile existence. I wished for additional examples with multiple Jewish perspectives that further animated Jews' efforts to validate— individually and collectively—desires for a better life. Unfortunately, visitors learn little more of Jewish workers' and employers' values and ideologies or of the cultural productions that framed them.

The main exhibit on Jewish history in London continues into the twentieth century with panels dedicated to Jews in World War I service, Zionism in Britain, the move to the suburbs, the coming of Nazis, the 1938–1939 Kindertransport, and post–World War II immigration to England from Eastern Europe. Again, the exhibition offers relatively little commentary, and there is scant documentation of the British government's limited (and for it, politically uncomfortable) support of Jews in the 1930s; anti-Semitism, highlighted earlier in the exhibit in its portrayal of early Jewish life in England, largely disappears as a subject of twentieth-century Britain. Jewish involvements with socialism, communism, or anarchism are similarly muted or invisible. Neither Marx (or even his daughter Eleanor, who was a major Anglo-Jewish labor activist) nor Freud, who spent his last years in North London and whose own museum is a short bus ride away, makes an appearance.

Although British Jews escaped the Holocaust, the back room on the museum's second floor commemorates that history with a moving account of a British Holocaust survivor, Leon Greenman, who had been trapped in Europe when the war broke out. Greenman's story depicts the history of brutality, but balances it with an uplifting message of Jewish survival. Born in the East End, Greenman married a Dutch woman, and they had moved to Holland in the 1930s to take care of her parents. Although Greenman was subsequently transported through six different concentration camps, including Auschwitz, he survived to tell his story.

The third floor houses a temporary exhibit space. During one of my visits it contained a traveling exhibit from the Berlin Jewish Museum, on R. B. Kitaj, a draughtsman who turned to figurative art in the 1960s. Ironically, the exhibit on this American-born artist, *R. B. Kitaj: Obsession. The Art of Identity,* presented the complicated aspects of Jewish identity that I associated with my grandmother's life and missed in the core exhibit. Raised in a secular left-wing intellectual home in America, Kitaj's maternal grandmother was, like my grandmother, a Bundist. Kitaj, a panel explains, connects with his ("a" [sic])

Jewish identity, which unfolds as rather more complicated and changing. He becomes deeply religious and paints to recover what the accompanying text cryptically describes as the "meaning of Jewish identity in a modern age." Remarrying after having moved to England, he weds the America painter Sandra Fisher in an Orthodox ceremony at London's Bevis Marks Synagogue in 1983.

I left the exhibit feeling the Jewish Museum London was a work in progress. Like good appetizers, various exhibits whet my appetite. Subsequent comments from the curator gave a further sense of the museum's challenges. She would like to see visitors "surprised or challenged in their assumptions." She acknowledged that while the museum takes "a very broad view" of how Jews might self-identify, such questions are "not raised explicitly."[23] To be fair, the JML is relatively small, has to honor its different collections, and has to meet diverse viewer interests. The section on labor and trade, which brilliantly depicts how different players have unequal sources of power and authority, is a model exhibit. But divisions within the Jewish community and from outside it are otherwise underdeveloped. Secular Jews challenged both the older Jewish community and British status quo, playing a disproportionate and major role in the making of British social democracy. The JML gives these radical and secular traditions short shrift, especially in comparison to the room dedicated to the religious life. Chaia Walkowitz's and Max Margel's London working-class brethren remain a spectral presence. They hover meaningfully in places, but are consigned to the cultural margins. The dominant story, one that will surprise or challenge few visitors, remains that of a hard won and triumphant assimilation into Britain.

Several aspects of the museum suggest a brighter future, however. To begin, the largely vacant area to the right of the main history exhibit affords the museum room to expand its interpretative exhibit. Moreover, it has the archival material and interpretative skills to do so. The museum's website has two rich online exhibits: one tells the story of *Jewish Britain* through fifty of the museum's "most treasured objects." Each object is fitted into one of six themes: sport and leisure, family and home life, migration and settlement, charity and welfare, religious life and London's East End. The online text is also revealing and promising. Analysis accompanying objects reveal nuances, contradictions, and values that would enrich the museum's exhibit.

A second online exhibit, *The Yiddish Theatre in London*, is an equally wonderful resource. Online one can hear the 310 oral histories of women and men, the secular and religious, workers and tradesmen, employers and professionals that are drawn upon in the welcome gallery. Moreover, readers can access a database of nearly 500 objects and documents in the museum's collection. The website exhibits provide only virtual heritage tours, and it is only accessible to those who have the means, information, and inclination to seek it out on the Web. Yet these materials and analyses can give greater shape to the exhibit that tourists visit, and provide the curatorial staff with artifacts on which to build interpretation and document quotidian experiences. The use of the oral histories in the entryway and the multiple social perspectives presented in the interactive video on the sweatshop labor and protest entice and provide ample evidence of what the museum can do.

Finally, the Kitaj exhibit demonstrates how the museum utilizes its temporary exhibits to enlarge upon its story. Nineteen temporary exhibits mounted from 2010 through 2015 similarly displayed a rich tapestry of Jewish London's social and cultural history. One of the longest running of the exhibits, *Entertaining the Nation: Stars of Music, Stage and Screen*, was open for seven months. It told the story of British entertainers from vaudeville through the present. Another exhibit, *Four Four Jew* analyzed the experience of Jews in soccer. And, although the core permanent exhibit emphasizes the dominant role of men—rabbis, benefactors, politicians, and moguls—two temporary exhibits foreground stories of gender relations. During the May 2015 election season, the museum exhibited "Blackguards and Bonnets," the dramatic story of Jewish suffragettes. Then, in 2016, the museum schedule included an exhibit on queer Jews. Sex radicals thus, had a voice at the museum, albeit a "temporary" one not afforded to Jewish labor radicals or socialists. The permanent or core exhibit remained the master narrative in two ways: as "core" it was definitive and it privileged the voice of the master, not the mistress, never seriously engaging the issue of patriarchy in Judaism or Jewish culture. In the "in-between" spaces of temporary exhibits, stories that might complicate the master narrative could be heard, but they would be at the margins and be "temporary."

Walking London

A daunting array of walking tours competed for London tourists' pound notes, but few addressed the Jewish past. I took three that did, and they provided an opportunity to witness and appreciate differing tour guide experiences and trainings. One tour, by London Walks, the largest company offering walking tours, promised to deliver what its website called a "classic" Jewish London walking tour. The second was a Jewish East London tour led by Stephen Burstin, who specializes in Jewish London walking tours. David Rosenberg, who leads tours that focus on Radical Jewish London history, conducted the third walk. Each charged between £8 and £10 for a tour that lasted from ninety minutes to two hours. Typically, seniors and children paid a reduced fee. To hear the supplementary lecture from the local Bevis Marks Synagogue guide required an additional £4 (£3 for seniors).

The "classic" London Walks tour required no reservation. Twenty-four tourists joined the walk; most of them were British, about half came from outside London. The rest included a couple of Americans, two from South Africa, and an Italian. Half the group consisted of seniors; no one was under twenty-one. Most had previously taken one or two walking tours; for some, it was their first such trip. About half identified themselves as Jewish. But all saw the tour as a chance to learn about a quintessential Jewish area they had heard about in school or from family.

Burstin and Rosenberg required reservations for their tours. While their Jewish tours typically sold out, the days I went they were not. Burstin had fifteen on his tour. Most were Americans, including a family of four now living in Israel, and he described the preponderance of Americans as atypical. Rosenberg's tour had eleven participants, mostly Brits. Again, half were seniors. The distinguishing characteristic of Rosenberg's group, however, seemed to be its identification with a radical tradition. A majority identified as Jewish, but, tellingly, two middle-aged women described themselves as "secular Muslims."

These tours testified to the ways that guide training and the expectations of both the tour companies and tourists shaped the London Jewish heritage tour experience. London Walks believed that it provided the experience that Jewish heritage tourists expected and could most readily find accessible. Its website hails *Fodor's Great Britain's* description of it as "the first—and . . . best—of the walking tour firms" in London.[24] In the fall of 2014 the company offered 124 weekly walks, most of them lasting about two hours. The majority of the walks took visitors to neighborhoods associated with quaint London, including a melodramatic tour of London by Gaslight. According to London Walks' brochure, each "guide . . . brings the place to life with the judicious use of gossip, scandal, offbeat detail and general oddity." Walkers could visit fashionable or historic neighborhoods such as Mayfair and Greenwich. Or they could walk through "Darkest Victorian London," go on a "West End Ghost Walk," or imbibe on the "Rock 'n' Roll Pub Walk" or "Old Hampstead Village Pub Walk." To meet demand, one popular walk, "Jack the Ripper Haunts" (with a variant called the "Jack the Ripper Tour"), was offered every evening, and twice on Saturday. On Friday the Ripper tour was offered in Spanish: "Jack el Destripador."

In contrast to the daily walks to visit "Jack," London Walks offered its Jewish-themed tour, "The Old Jewish Quarter: A Shtetl Called Whitechapel," only three times each week, on Wednesday, Friday, and Sunday mornings. Different guides lead each tour. One guide is Judy, "winner of the London Tourist Board's prestigious *Guide of the Year award*" and a "qualified *Blue Badge* and *City of London Guide*." Blue Badge guides are part of the Guild of Registered Tourist Guides that formed in 1950 to train a cadre of guides for the 1951 Festival of London. They number 1,800 (in 2014) and operate throughout England. London-based guides, who complete two years of classes often at local universities or colleges of further education, comprise the largest number. The Guild describes the course work as a combination of practical training in leading tours and a core curriculum in "the history, architecture and social development of the country."[25] The social history, however, often consists largely of factoids and anecdotes about famous buildings and their masters (and less the ladies of the house)—one hears little about vernacular architecture or the lives of the workers who built and staffed the grand estates. A friend who had trained as a Blue Badge guide described her skill set and it suggested the limited nature of the social history: she emphasized how they learned to describe a building with their back to it.[26]

London Walk's other Jewish London Tour guide—and the one who led the tour I took—was Mike,[27] described in the company brochure as London Walks' *"fizziest* guide." He is "an accomplished actor, a playwright, a song writer, a musician . . . *and* the father of twin lads!" Although not formally trained, his background was typical of those leading tours.[28] He was an autodidact. He read and loved history, and learned much of the nuts and bolts of guiding on the job. He had led tours for twenty years. For training, London Walks sent him on a tour or two conducted by some of their other guides, and to learn the "path." He then developed his own version and shtick. He did not come from the East End; nor could he draw on a Jewish family history; he did cite as relevant the fact that he had lived in Stoke Newington, a once-Jewish north London neighborhood that had gentrified in the last twenty years. But Mike's background in the theatre was his preeminent skill: he was an engaging, welcoming leader, and regaled us with information about buildings and people that he embedded in anecdotes, stories, and amusing factoids.

Burstin was another self-taught historian. After an earlier career as a journalist, he worked with his father in a hotel and tour operation. Around 2008, having gained some experience as a Jewish tour guide in Rome, he started research for Jewish London tours. Born in the East End, his website describes his eclectic research, how he listened to stories from family and old-timers, went on research trips to the British Library, and did lots of reading. Burstin brought engaging audio-visual trappings to his tour: he used a remote microphone and carried a red loose-leaf folder with embossed photos and newspaper excerpts to read. He also began by playing some klezmer music on his smartphone "to set the atmosphere." Consumers rewarded his efforts: TripAdvisor awarded him its Certificate of Excellence in 2013 and 2014.

Rosenberg was also self-taught and had immersed himself in the scholarly world of Jewish and East End history. Another East End native, Rosenberg's Jewish grandparents arrived there in the early 1900s, and he used their story as a paradigmatic point of entry to his tour. Unlike the other guides, tours are not his main source of income: when not leading them he divides his time between teaching primary school children, adult education, and freelance writing. He regularly attends lectures by leading scholars on Jewish London (admission: he recognized my name and noted he had attended lectures by my wife), researches in local history collections, and is the author of *Battle for the East End: Jewish Responses to Fascism in the 1930s* (Five Leaves Publications, 2011). Like Burstin, his tour also included a thick folder of images illustrating the Jewish past.

The three tours covered much of the same ground, but dramatically illustrated different strengths and weaknesses in the London Jewish heritage walking tour business. London Walks' tour departed from the Tower Hill Tube; the other two tours began a little further east outside the Aldgate East station. The London Walks and Burstin's itineraries were both geared to present a comprehensive history of Jews in London's East End and visited the same sites. Rosenberg's more detailed focus on Radical Jewish history meant that he went to fewer sites but spent about twice as long at each than the other two.

London Walks' and Burstin's main advantage over Rosenberg's tour was their historical scope and breadth. They included sites that marked the eighteenth- and early nineteenth-century role of Sephardic Jews in London, such as the fountain dedicated to Sephardic financier, David Mocatta, and Jewry Street.[29] In addition, London Walks' and Burstin's tours covered religious sites and other non-radical aspects of the British Jewish experience, such as the Bevis Marks Synagogue. These tours spent almost a quarter of the time in the Synagogue. As tourists gazed at its resplendent Queen Anne furnishings, the Synagogue manager regaled those who had paid the additional fee with stories of Moses Montefiore's beneficence and Benjamin Disraeli's prominence in British politics.[30] Breaking with a tradition of speaking exclusively about places with existing structures, London Walks also noted the former site of the Great Synagogue built in 1691.

In a gesture to the appeal of Holocaust tourism the London Walks and Burstin tours commemorate the heroic story of the Kindertransport. Both tours include stops at the statue in front of the Liverpool Street train station that honors the 10,000 unaccompanied Jewish children who arrived at the station between 1938 and 1939 to escape persecution in Germany and Austria. In keeping with the political blandness of most public accounts, neither the monument plaque nor the guides raised any potentially difficult questions about the British government's reception of Jews before and afterward.

The centerpiece of all tours was Whitechapel, and in this neighborhood all three tours covered the same spaces. Yet each told a very different story. The London Walks and Burstin tours played to the nostalgia of those returning to an area their parents or grandparents had left. The tales told by the guides stressed the upward social mobility of immigrants and exploited the voyeurism of visitors curious about an exotic past. These tours emphasized quaint sites peopled by Jewish rogues, prostitutes, street vendors, and philanthropists, each adorned with a memorable anecdote or what the London Walk guide called "fun facts." For example, both Burstin and Mike remembered the Shooting Star Pub as the former site of the prominent social welfare institution, Jewish Care, the forerunner of the Jewish Board of Guardians that philanthropists funded to aid and "uplift" poor Eastern European Jews. Similarly, these guides described how the sculpted reliefs of bakers on the facade at 12 Widegate Street recall Levy Bros, the matzo makers whose bakery was once the oldest shop in London. The

Burger King on Whitechapel Street is noted as the former site of Bloom's Deli, an Anglo-Jewish East End institution that closed in 1996. On Gunthorpe Street the guides pointed visitors to the home of Daniel Mendoza, renowned Jewish bare-knuckled boxer. Mendoza, Burstin notes, was the great grandfather of the actor Peter Sellers. The present Jewish "Cat Walk" on Heneage Street is the occasion for a melodramatic story of white slavery for Jewish girls. And the Jack the Ripper murder site on Petticoat Lane becomes a tale of "Jacob," the Jewish Ripper. Oh, those wonderful Jewish rogues!

Rosenberg's sites in Whitechapel often replicated those on the other tours. All three tours, for instance, visited the stalls of Petticoat Lane, the Soup Kitchen for the Jewish Poor from 1902 on Brune Street, and the homes of the Yiddish theater and Miriam Moses, the reformer and first Jewish female mayor in 1931–1932, on Princelet Street. All three tours also ended at the Jamme Masjid Mosque on Brick Lane with a paean to British multiculturalism and historical changes and gentrification in the East End. In earlier incarnations the building served the changing local immigrant population. Established in 1743 as a Huguenot Protestant Church, it became a Methodist church in the nineteenth century and, in 1898, the Spitalfields Great Synagogue. In the new millennium, the mosque reflected Brick Lane's new character as a South and East Asian neighborhood.[31]

To be sure, Rosenberg's tour differed in its narrower chronological focus. His tour sites focused on the experiences of the great migration of the Eastern European generation at the turn of the century. Still, some of the sites Rosenberg visited were unique to his tour. His was the only tour to visit Angel Alley where a plaque and an anarchist bookstore spoke to the historic presence of Jewish (and non-Jewish) anarchists in London. On Gunthorpe Street, Rosenberg forsook the romance of the Jewish boxer to look at Toynbee Hall, the pioneering Christian settlement that catered to the Jewish immigrant poor. And nearby, he took his tour to Brune Housing, the pioneering East End social housing project that served immigrant Jews.

Rosenberg's additional sites provided perspectives on the life of ordinary Jews missing in the other tours, but as important, his story differed in fundamental ways from that heard on the other tours. In Rosenberg's account immigrant Jews were not the stuff of melodrama, nor were they passive victims of poverty or enlightened benefactors; rather, working-class East End Jews became agents of their own lives who struggled among themselves and with others, both non-Jews and elite Jews. Rosenberg also typically complicated each site's history. In his discussion of Brune Housing, for example, he noted how the housing both provided decent accommodation and served as a base for community organizing.

Rosenberg's tour was additionally distinguished by his use of a group of related stops that addressed social welfare. Rather than a list of disconnected stops, Rosenberg wove together a series of stops that spoke to one another. And, more than the usual repertoire of anecdote and description, Rosenberg consistently offered analysis by way of raising questions. He integrated discussions of East End poverty with those of politics—both the views and actions of immigrant East Enders and those of more affluent outsiders. Petticoat Lane, for example, became a place to speak at some length about sweatshops, unions, and poverty, and importantly, the conflicts that arose between German Jewish bosses and their Eastern European brethren.

REFLECTIONS ON WALKING THE TALK

The main difference between all three tours was in the story they told and I want to suggest six analytic points that mark these differences. The focus is on London, but the tours raise questions that echo in Jewish heritage tourism elsewhere.

1. *The Power of Place.* The general inclusion of the Great Synagogue, despite the absence of physical remains, powerfully countered the justification offered by many guides for the omission of certain subjects because of the lack of existing artifacts. Physical remains help people connect with a past, but the judicious use of photos and the sense of a place can mobilize interpretative and emotional meanings. This strategy would be especially important in cities that suffered extensive bombing or destruction.[32]

2. *Problematizing Identity.* The two general tours' presentation of Disraeli's Anglicanism missed the opportunity to raise the question of Jewish identity as both religious and cultural heritage. Disraeli's inclusion was driven by his political prominence and described as a celebratory testimony to Jewish success. Both are important subjects, but the discussion could have both problematized Jewish identity and engaged questions about paths to success and inequality within and outside the Jewish community.

3. *The Politics of Philanthropy.* The general London Jewish tours detailed the beneficence of wealthy philanthropists such as Montefiore and Rothschild, but did not invite visitors to reflect on the objectives and philosophy animating charity, or the benefactors' perspectives of its recipients. Rosenberg's Radical Tour demonstrated the analytic and pedagogical power of these and other questions. The difference was most apparent when all three tours stopped in front of the Rothschild Building at Flower and Dean Walk. At a prior stop at Toynbee Hall, Rosenberg had asked his group to think about the possible alternative meanings of charity in self-help and paternalism; he returned to the topic at Flower and Dean Walk. His presentation elaborated the contradictions and paradoxes of this history: wealthy Sephardic and German Ashkenazi Jews, fearing "the undeserving" Jewish poor, led efforts to repatriate thousands of them back to Eastern Europe; for the "deserving" poor, they offered "modern" plumbing at "four percent" (rather than eight). The arrangement was a financial and political bargain. Their lives would be improved and, along the way, they

Figure 13. London "Radical Tour" before the entrance to Flower and Dean Walk.
Archway Gates, "Erected by the Four Percent Industrial Dwellings Company, 1886."
Photo by the author.

would learn the lessons of investment philanthropy and develop "responsible" habits of paying rent—at a discount. For the philanthropists, the arrangement had unintended consequences, however: the new residents included radical
Bundists who established an Arbiter's Ring (Workman's Circle) as a community
center at the housing complex with a library, conference room, legal aid, and
school. Using the facility, resident workers organized on their own behalf, and
ironically, against the wealthy they saw exploiting them. Rosenberg was able to
hold his audience with the multiple perspectives of his complicated account,
and more than the other guides, he provoked lively questions and interactions.

4. *The Ironies of Inclusive History*. The chronological inclusiveness of the
more general tours masked their profound interpretative exclusiveness. These
tours included the long history of Jews in London from the in-migration of
Sephardim in the seventeenth century, continued on to the experiences of German Jews in nineteenth century London, and extended the story into the mid-
twentieth century with the Holocaust and postwar eras. They also recognized
leaders of the Jewish community and major philanthropic institutions. But the

guides' presentations at Petticoat Market, a major site of Eastern European Jewish life in the first third of the twentieth century, highlighted interpretative limits to the general tours. Eastern European Jews were certainly crucial to these general tours, but in the presentation they were more acted upon rather than actors themselves. Instead, Petticoat Market became a shopping opportunity and the general tours did not use the occasion as an opening to invoke the range of competing Jewish voices of garment workers and bosses heard at the Jewish Museum. Moreover, these tours silenced other voices that divided the Jewish community: those of Jewish socialists and anarchists, the Orthodox and the secular Yiddishkeit community, and Jewish wives and children who, as in my own family, had to deal with their patriarchal husbands in sweated labor. Ironically, Rosenberg's Radical tour was more inclusive than the others: it presented a multitude of Jewish voices on various issues, not just those of the Sephardic and German Jews, of men, or of the rich and powerful. It also asked visitors to reflect on each individual or group's perspective and the social and political power or cultural capital each had to advance its interests.

5. *Whiggish Anglophilism.* Everywhere guides walk a tightrope when they attempt to address shameful parts of the historical record that may offend visitors or ruffle local political feathers. The subject of British anti-Semitism (like that of Ukrainian or Polish anti-Semitism) is a case in point. Tour leaders comfortably discussed British anti-Jewish attitudes and policies in earlier centuries, but as they moved toward the Holocaust, they waffled. Thus, at the Kindertransport Statue, guides paid scant attention to British hostility toward nineteenth- and twentieth-century Jewish immigrants and to Jewish refugees to Great Britain or Palestine before 1938. Burstin, wearing his British loyalties on his sleeve, lauded Winston Churchill as pro-Zionist, and chose not to speak of the hostility of wealthy Jews to poor Jewish refugees or of the reluctant British state.

6. *The Power of Melodrama.* Typical tours spoke of the "unrespectable poor," albeit in ways that reified that category. Historical complexity and accuracy was sacrificed for melodramatic narratives and depictions of Jews as victims. All the East End tours make a point of walking to the site of one of the Jack the Ripper murders, but the "typical" tours made this an opportunity for salacious stories about "Jake the Ripper" and white slavery, both subjects historians have traced more as imagined fears than social reality.[33]

So, if historians find issues such as white slavery problematic, why do they make such a dramatic appearance in these conventional walking tours? Most important is audience demand. People take tours as much to be entertained as instructed. And the companies and the guides promise them as much. People delight in hearing of Jewish criminals or of the life of a Jewish world champion boxer. There is a visceral pleasure, maybe even a vicarious thrill, in learning about Jewish prostitutes.

Ultimately, however, class and gender biases dictate the stories told and not told. The biases were implicit in the more typical and general walks. They celebrated *machers* (big shots): male captains of industry, financial giants, politicians; members of the organized and unorganized working class were reduced to anecdote or melodrama. Take, for example, an anecdote told by Burstin to illustrate Churchill's importance to Jewish history. Two or three "criminals" had bungled a jewelry heist on the East End that resulted in the deaths of three policemen. The thieves were found hiding at 100 Sidney Street in Stepney. The men were thought to be anarchists (and recent research seems to bear that out). Two hundred policemen surrounded the building and the anarchist "criminals" were killed. In the telling, Burstin makes no mention of what might have attracted Jews to socialism, anarchism, or trade unionism or even animated the theft. His account presumed there was no need for a jury trial. Rather, the punch line for the story was that the thirty-one-year-old police chief (the person was actually home secretary) was Churchill. We are not told that he stood by in his fur coat and watched.

Rosenberg's tour had class and gender biases as well. His class bias was explicit, however, not hidden behind anecdote or a veil of presumed objectivity. He privileged the voices of radicals and gave short shrift to the achievements of the rich and powerful. Wealthy Jews were present in his story as an integral part of the entire Jewish community, but generally not in flattering ways.

Rosenberg's account also remained within a largely orthodox political history. He discussed worker housing, but said little of the social and cultural life of women activists, entertainers, and consumers heard and seen in the oral histories and temporary exhibits at the Jewish Museum of London. Some of his foci and explanations I expect would have disappointed those who chose other tours; I found them a refreshing change. Other tours provided meaningful material on the achievements of wealthy Jews, Jewish politicians, and religious life, but they came off as sanitized accounts devoid of "power" in the history—of who held it and exercised it. For the most part, in the more conventional commercial tours working-class Jewish immigrants were victims, scamps, or the poor. Perhaps because he had embedded himself in the world of working historians himself, Rosenberg avoided simple explanations and melodramatic caricatures. He also made no effort to avoid controversy. He eschewed history as factoid and anecdote; in his account, the past was contested and made. I left only wishing he would develop one of the "typical" tours as well. He saw his radical tour as about radical Jews in London rather than a radical telling of Jewish history in London. Nonetheless, I heard echoes of Bubbe Chaia in his radical tour, albeit more as socialist than an activist woman.

Reflecting on my London tours, one disquieting note from the walks stayed with me. It arose from a comment I heard from Steve, my London Walks guide. Observing the relative paucity of Jewish tours offered by London Walks, he noted that in past years there were many more Americans on the Jewish tour. Now they were going elsewhere. Many, I suspect were taking the Jack the Ripper Haunt. I suspected others were going to the newly opened museums and sites in Eastern and Central Europe. I was curious to see if Jewish heritage tourism in New York would confirm or revise this suspicion. I took pleasure in hearing through Rosenberg the echoes of my grandmother's experience, but wondered if it might be too late to hear such echoes in New York. I hoped my heritage tours there would tell me otherwise.

CHAPTER 5

New York

IMMIGRANT HERITAGE IN THE JEWISH DIASPORA

Absent the Holocaust on American soil, Jews have a relatively continuous and robust past and present in New York. The small Jewish communities at the end of the twentieth century in Łódź, Lviv, and Kiev, and the less than 200,000 Jews in London, paled in comparison to the New York Jewish community. In 2012, the New York Metropolitan area counted almost 2.1 million people identifying as Jews. Only Tel Aviv, with 3.2 million, had more, and Haifa's 708,000 left it a distant third. Manhattan and Brooklyn were home to the overwhelming majority of the city's 1.1 million Jews, but many lived outside the city in Westchester and Nassau counties to the north and east of the city, and in northern New Jersey and southern Connecticut suburbs. Many of those concentrated in particular suburban towns, such as the "Golden Ghettos" of Great Neck and the Five Towns on Long Island and Scarsdale in Westchester.[1]

Jews first settled in New York and its environs in the mid-seventeenth century, but immigrant families from Eastern Europe like the Margels and Walkowitzes shaped American history after 1880 and made the modern American Jewish community. The Walkowitz family joined the Paterson Jewish community in 1920 just before Congress closed the Golden Door with restrictive immigration laws in 1921 and 1924. Max and the woman who would be his bride, Marian Tarnofsky, arrived in 1907 and 1906 respectively, during the heyday of Jewish immigration. Together both families joined approximately 2 million Jews and 20 million immigrants who arrived between 1880 and the end of the war. Many, if not a majority, settled on the Lower East Side and other neighborhoods in New York or in nearby cities like Paterson, ten miles to its west.

Eastern European Jewish immigrants who entered New York between 1880 and 1919 competed for jobs, housing, and social services with generations of other immigrants and migrants to the city. Three million Italians arrived then too, and both Jewish and Italian newcomers had to make their fortune amid descendants of earlier generations of Irish and German immigrants already established in the city. The increased presence of a second group in northern cities such as New York further complicated immigrant lives: a half million African Americans had migrated north from the Jim Crow South. Race riots that erupted across more than thirty American cities in the summer of 1919—though not in New York—illustrated how racism and the social and economic premium on "whiteness" further marked the immigrants' experience.[2]

A third group already present in New York also gave particular shape to the experience of the Jewish newcomers: Eastern European Jews found themselves in a city with older Sephardic and well-established German Jewish communities led by families with great wealth, power, and status. Some old-timers felt a responsibility toward their poorer brethren and provided financial and moral support to them; others, fearing the "strange" habits and behaviors of the newcomers would jeopardize this status, wanted to distance themselves from them. Often poor and desperate for work, many of the newcomers were Orthodox who dressed differently. Many workers also unionized in shops owned by the old-timers. And children scavenging for food raised the specter of Jewish juvenile delinquency. This was the turbulent, conflicted, and exciting World of our Fathers that Irving Howe described and the immigrant Margels and Walkowitzes entered.

More has been written about Jews in America, and specifically in New York, than in any other place.[3] Howe's monumental study, though criticized for its relative inattention to gender and religion, was notable for its effort to place the history of Jewish socialism at the center of the story. Earlier studies placed socialism and labor in the context of Judaism, Jewish social mobility, and achievement of great men.[4] Howe, in a "bottom up" account of Jewish life, embedded Jewish socialism in a culture of Yiddishkeitt. Many subsequent historians moved the story back and forward in time, and they provide a remarkably full historical account of the New York Jewish community. Jews arrive and settle, at times confronting challenges from American society; at times drawing upon diverse identities, resources, and interests, they challenge one another. Fine women historians have gendered the story. Still others have produced solid histories of Jewish communal institutions, and social and political institutions such as landsmanshaftn, B'nai B'rith, and the Workmen's Circle in New York. And in the decade after Waltzer's 1999 review bemoaned the disappearance of the world of socialism, major new books by Tony Michel and Daniel Katz restored Jewish socialism and the strong role of women to the center of the New York Jewish heritage narrative, at least in its scholarship.[5] All these historians may debate among themselves the meaning of this history, but collectively they have produced a vivid account on which heritage tourism can draw.[6]

NEW YORK: HISTORY

The history of Jews in New York begins in 1654 with the arrival of twenty-three Sephardic Jewish refugees from Brazil. In the mid-nineteenth century more than 50,000 Ashkenazi Jews from Germany, the Prussian partition, and Alsace arrived and came to dominate Jewish New York life. Within two generations a core group, generally aggregated as "German-Jews," drew on transatlantic family banking connections to establish prominent Jewish banking houses such as Kuhn, Loeb Co., Lazard Frères, J.W. Seligman Co., and Goldman, Sachs & Co. Others became directors of new consumer palaces such as Macy's, Gimbels, and Abraham & Strauss. And still others, joined by many Eastern European Jews, became the owners of as many as 90 percent of New York's garment factories where they employed many thousands of the turn-of-the-century immigrant daughters of the shtetl. As elsewhere, these wealthy Jews led philanthropic efforts to ameliorate immigrants by "uplifting" them from the harsher conditions of urban life in institutions such as the United Hebrew Charities (1874), the Hebrew Benevolent and Orphan Asylum (1859), the Jewish hospital (1856), which in 1872 would become Mount Sinai Hospital, and the Jewish Board of Guardians (JBG, 1907). JBG would become a pillar of the Federation of Jewish Philanthropies when it organized in 1917.[7]

The history of the responses of the working-class Eastern European Jews to institutions created by their affluent German-Jewish and wealthier Eastern European-Jewish brethren reflected class as well as ethnic divisions within the Jewish community. It is a well-documented story different from elsewhere only in its degree of worker opposition: New York's immigrant community had more robust movements of Jewish labor and radicalism than in London, for example.[8] Between 1890 and the anticommunist purge of left-wing unions in 1950, Jewish socialists and communists played major roles in struggles on behalf of New York workers. The role of Jewish radicals was notably vivid in garment and department store workplaces dominated by Jewish workers and owners, although the struggles were not limited to these sites or to Jewish leadership. Jewish radicals led unionization efforts at Federation of Jewish Philanthropy unions, for instance, and non-Jews such as Michael Quill, the communist leader of the Transit Workers Union, played critical roles as well.

Jewish labor struggles had a fundamental class dimension that resembled the conflicts in industrial cities such as Łódź, and drew on that legacy. In Eastern Europe, Bund workers led the revolutionary upsurge in 1905–1907 at the same time as Jewish women on the Lower East Side led a kosher food riot and pressed for tenant rights to decent housing. Scarcely two years later, in 1909, the International Ladies Garment Workers' Union in New York, spearheaded by Eastern European Bund organizers, led the shirtwaist makers' "Uprising of the 20,000." The next year, the "Great Revolt" of 60,000 cloak makers erupted. And in 1911, the famous fire at the New York Triangle Shirtwaist Factory dramatically demonstrated both the vitality of the socialist Jewish labor movement, and how the lives of the wealthy and poor Jews were implicated with one another. Owners had locked the doors to the Triangle Factory on the eighth and ninth floors of the Asch Building, a ten-story edifice located a block east of Washington Square Park so that workers would not take work breaks. In the inferno, management on the tenth floor simply walked to safety. When the ladders on the fire trucks could not reach the eighth floor, 146 young immigrant Jewish and Italian women workers, mostly daughters of the Lower East Side, burned in the inferno or jumped to their death. City residents would not see such a horrific sight of falling bodies for another ninety years, until 9/11. At the subsequent trial, the defense convinced a jury that the two Eastern European Jewish owners, Max Blanck and Isaac Harris, did not know the doors were locked, and they were acquitted. An insurance company reimbursed the owners about $60,000 for their loss, more than five times the amount a civil suit required them to pay the victims' families: $75.[9]

The funeral march and political agitation in protest of the fire reflected how the Jewish community was at times united and at times divided. The fire, in its horror and in the inequities it put on display, galvanized the immigrant Lower East Side community to action. Jewish women, schooled in their rights by the Bund and experienced in protest, led the fight against Blanck and Harris.[10] The horror also won the working women wealthy allies. Some wives of uptown Jewish German financiers and Eastern European professionals and manufacturers joined the protesting workers in a cross-class alliance that worked to win protective legislation specifically for women workers and child laborers, and the implementation of fire codes. Wealthy German Jewish men also organized on behalf of their Eastern European brethren, especially after New York City police commissioner Theodore Bingham attributed the problem of urban crime to Jewish delinquency. But while the provision of benevolent services in an expanded range of philanthropic organizations such as the Educational Alliance and the Jewish Board of Guardians was sincerely felt and offered, their help was the carrot to the strikebreaker's stick. Wealthy Jews, typically bankers or owners of department stores or factories, sat on the Board of Directors of Federation of Jewish Philanthropies, the umbrella organization of the various Jewish agencies that provided aid to children, families, the aged, and the poor. They consistently opposed unions in the agencies or their shops, but were equally concerned that profligate benefits not encourage bad (i.e., union) attitudes. Such views compromised work relations within the Jewish community, providing a chilling effect on staff and clients who worried that support might end if their demands came too close to home.[11]

To be sure, some children remembered the support from institutions such as settlement houses and the Educational Alliance as transformative, but others resented the condescension of the "uptown" Jews. There were also limits to German Jewish tolerance for "downtown" Jewish workers who organized protests by left-wing Jewish labor and political groups during the Great Depression. When Jewish socialists and communists organized rent strikes and radical unions in the department stores and Jewish relief agencies, uptown German Jews fought relentlessly to crush the unions, eventually voting almost unanimously to expel left-wing unions during the McCarthy era.[12]

Yiddishkeit as deployed by New York Bundists early in the century expressed a triad of language (Yiddish), identity (Jewishness), and social justice that fueled their political actions. Yiddishkeit tied the language to secular socialist political culture that could be seen daily in plays on the Jewish Rialto on Second Avenue, in socialist newspapers, and in proletarian literature. The Bund had relatively little organizational presence in New York, but "Bund sentiment"—the ideas of community and justice as embedded in Yiddishkeit—permeated radical Jewish political culture. Anarchists, socialists, and communists in the Jewish immigrant community passionately disagreed with one another, much as my grandfather Zishe Walkowitz and his brother-in-law Joe Katz did. But whether secular or religiously inclined, they expressed this "sentiment" in supportive family and community associations, and in the recreational, educational, and political life of Bund organizations in the Workmen's Circle and Jewish Socialist Federation of the Socialist Party.[13]

The place of socialism and Yiddishkeit is, however, but one strand of New York's Jewish heritage. Significant attachments to religion, Zionism and, especially in the postwar era, to refugees from the Holocaust and post-1989 Eastern Europe, to conservative politics, and to the increasing place of the ultra-Orthodox within the New York Jewish community, among other issues, fill out the story. My above emphases mean to make two points. One, the complex and rich history of Jews in New York includes profound divisions of class, politics, and religious commitment. Two, socialism and communism, for both their advocates and detractors, are deeply embedded in this story. They were central in my family, although as new evidence came to light, in some surprising and ambiguous ways.

~ INTERLUDE ~

The Margel-Tarnofsky Family

The SS *Blücher* departed Southampton on August 4, 1907 on the final leg of its trip to New York. Five hundred and fifty feet long and sixty-two feet wide, the ship carried 2,102 passengers. One thousand and five hundred traveled third class, four decks below. The ship manifest listed one of them as a sixteen-year-old journeyman baker named Meier Margel—Grandpa Max.

Max was part of the peak immigration that brought millions of Southern and Eastern Europeans to the United States. Records give fragmented hints of an extraordinarily fragile, adventurous, and fraught early life. While personal family strains may have driven Max to emigrate, I found myself falling back on macro explanations for Jewish migration. The 1882 May Laws that followed the pogroms in 1881–1882 intensified rural distress already evident in the 1870s and 1880s. Jewish immigrants such as Max from the villages and small towns of Eastern Europe had reason to look to go elsewhere. Many first moved to industrializing cities like Łódź in search of work; others set out with hopes of a better life in cities abroad. Max's immigration, while couched in tales of flight from a rigid deeply religious family, likely took place after word from relatives who had preceded him abroad trickled back to Galician villages. They had not found riches, but could attest to the opportunity for a fresh start in the New World.

Max's life in the years after his arrival at Ellis Island illustrated the extensive kinship network that typically sustained immigrants. Max was one of eight children. His father, Jacob Osias, was one of nine children. As noted earlier, Max's mother, Yettie Margel, was Jacob's distant cousin. The marriage of cousins, which was not unusual at the time, further reflected the complex and extensive Margel family bonds on which a young Max could draw after leaving Mostyska. It may also explain his decision to leave New York soon after his arrival to try his luck in Toronto, Canada. Somewhere there may have been a relative, family friend, or neighbor to whom a sixteen-year-old lad could turn. Years later, divorced, and perhaps needing contacts, his World War II draft registration lists him working and living in Connecticut during the war, possibly to be near a brother—Abe. Although his relationship with Abe is as much speculation as fact, it further illustrates the fraternal bonds that wed immigrant communities of diaspora Jews.

Max's travels during the five years after his arrival at Ellis Island also illustrated the diverse paths and multiple moves these immigrants took in New York to settle and establish themselves. Max's travels began soon after his arrival when the teenager set out for Toronto to find a job. He had $7.15 to his name. Canadian immigration records suggest that from August 1907 until April 1912 Max lived in the middle of Toronto's Jewish working-class immigrant neighborhood at 19 Kensington Avenue. The 1911 Census enumerated a couple from Galicia, a furrier, Benny Shapiro, and his wife Rebecca, as living there. There is no listing for Max. Benny and Rebecca resided with their two young children and two lodgers. The single male lodger is listed as a "rag picker in the lanes." The age of the two parents suggests a reason for Max to have gone straight to Toronto after arriving at Ellis Island. Both Benny and Rebecca were listed as twenty-three year olds, which makes Rebecca about the age of Max's sister, Reisel, born the year before him in 1888.

Max's almost five years in Toronto evidently satisfied neither his financial nor his emotional needs and he returned to New York. New York, though, was no more rewarding and, in early January 1913, he set out to return to Toronto. On his reentry application, Max lists "no address" in New York, noting that he had gone to "seek work." Self-described as a presser (tailor), but without a visible means of support or a job, Canadian immigration rejected his application on January 8 and he was not allowed to reenter the country. On January 24, he applied again at the Port of Niagara Falls and was "debarred" once more.

Two and a half years later, on October 23, 1915, now residing at 219 East 4th Street on New York's Lower East Side, Max married Marian Tarnofsky, a young woman who lived a block east of him at 274 East 4th. Max, son of the mohel, married Marian in a civil ceremony. Marian had arrived in New York from Warsaw as a seven-year-old girl in 1906, a year before Max. She was accompanied by Leib, her seventeen-year-old brother, a saddler by trade. They joined their widowed mother, Lena (née Freibaum), a dressmaker. Lena, her ten-year-old son Moishe and her twelve-year-old daughter Esther, preceded Marian and Max by a year and set up household at 400 Grand Street on the Lower East Side. Ironically in the context of my Paterson birth, Lena and her children had initially gone to Paterson where her mother-in-law lived. Together, these newcomers were part of the "flood" of Jewish immigrants to the Promised Land.

Max's daughter-in-law, my aunt Gertrude Margel, vaguely remembered almost a century after the fact hearing that Marian and Max's marriage had been arranged. Marian's widowed mother had reason to marry her young daughter off, and her daughter was a strikingly beautiful young woman. Max was nine years her senior and had found good employment. On the marriage certificate, he listed himself as "Manager Cloaks." The marriage license lists the bride as nineteen years old, six years Max's junior. She was, in fact, sixteen, and quite possibly pregnant. When my mother, Selda, was born in 1918, the birth certificate notes she is Marian's second child. (The first must have been stillborn or have died in infancy. Although the certificate kindled a faint memory of having heard this from my mother or uncle at some point in the distant past, in fact, I now remember nothing of it.) The early pregnancy suggests perhaps a shotgun wedding, rather than an arranged marriage.[14]

The marriage lasted twenty years, and my memories of Marian were from years later, after she had remarried. Bubbe Chaia is the protagonist of my personal account, whereas Marian was the grandmother with an active presence in my life. Her phone number, for instance, was the one I knew to call if my parents were unavailable. Forty-five years after her death, her phone number remains one of two I remember (the other is the number at my father's store).

Marian's life with her second husband, Richard Bakker ("Uncle Dick") exemplified modern mid-century secular America. She was fully integrated into

American culture. She spoke without an accent, and in an era when few Jews married outside the faith, she wed a non-Jew. Chanukah and Christmas and Passover and Easter were acknowledged with meals and a Christmas tree my sister would help decorate. There never was a menorah. There were no religious observances. It was a secular and nonpolitical home in which Jewish culture was nominally expressed in Marian's cooking and remarkable baking. Uncle Dick's job as an auto mechanic with an oil delivery business provided a comfortable lower middle-class life in Clifton, New Jersey, a suburban town midway between Passaic and Paterson. Their three-bedroom ranch-style development house had a spacious and especially memorable designed garden complete with a goldfish pond. My sister periodically slept over and I drove there for dinner when my parents took a rare vacation.

Marian was a warm, comfortable presence in my life, but not one with which I identified. She was, in truth, a psychologically injured woman who could erupt in rage and become quite mean. I never experienced this temper, but my parents had. They cited, for instance, their experience with her shortly after Max had left. Marian and her teenage son Phillip moved in with them, but my father, exhausted with her complaints and snide attacks on their communist activism, threw her out of their house a year later. Marian, my parents recalled, stood on the sidewalk, berating them as communists and yelling she would call the police to arrest them. My parents raised my Uncle Phil until he was eighteen, at which point, to prove his metal, he snuck off and in 1943 enlisted in the Marines.

So, when Max left Marian after twenty years of marriage, in truth, he as much fled as ran from her. She was a child bride who had lost her firstborn. Traumas in her early life had also left her deeply scarred. Her father had died when she was a baby; when she was six, her mother left to set up the family in the United States, leaving her behind in Warsaw; a year later, seven-year-old Marian had traveled across the Atlantic accompanied only by an older teenage brother to join her mother. Life in New York for the young girl came with trauma, too: a man climbed through a sky light of their apartment and raped her. The experience haunted her the rest of her life, and my mother explained it was why Marian refused to leave her house unaccompanied in the last decade of her life.

The Walkowitz-Lubertofsky Family

The Walkowitz-Lubertofsky immigration story reflected in Chaia Walkowitz's arrival to America provides an exemplary Jewish variant to the Margel experience. The Walkowitz family was driven at least as much by its socialist political vision as by the quest for economic opportunity. As detailed earlier, urban poverty and harsh working conditions in Łódź's increasingly competitive industrial environment led people like the Walkowitzes to radical protest. The repression that followed militant strikes compelled some like my great uncle Joe Katz to emigrate. State persecution of radicals and further pogroms in 1905 across the Pale pushed more to leave. And for others, the rampant rumors of the impending war that would, in fact, shortly engulf all of Europe, was the proverbial last straw. Zishe had briefly been in the army, but had been discharged, supposedly because he was emaciated.[15]

In 1913, Zishe left for Denmark, accompanied by his two-year-old daughter, Belle. He joined two brothers who had preceded him to Denmark and encouraged him to come. His wife, pregnant with her second child, stayed behind where her parents and other relatives could care for her through the birth. Her loneliness was increased by the absence of her older sister, Neche. Neche and her husband, Joe Katz, had already immigrated to Paterson a few years earlier. As a young boy, maybe around 1950, my father took me to visit Uncle Joe in Paterson (he was my father's uncle; my father's brother, also Joe was "my" Uncle Joe), and I remember a kindly, smiling bald man sitting in a bare, simple kitchen. But he had been a radical firebrand in Łódź, blacklisted for his political activities. According to his granddaughter Ruthie Lubert (Lubertofsky) Sacks, "he was literally chased out of the country by the Cossacks for being a revolutionary and made his way to England." Historians suggest "Cossacks" was less a specific threat at the time than Jewish shorthand for anti-Semites and the oppressive, antiunion Russian authorities, but the hostility, especially in the wake of the 1905 revolts, was no less real. In truth, Katz had been blacklisted for his union activities.

Joe Katz left Łódź for Paterson, a city with a comparable textile industry with lots of work for an enterprising weaver. One can imagine the city's strong labor movement also attracted him. Like Zishe a few years later, Katz also left behind a pregnant wife; Neche gave birth a month after her husband's flight and his family joined him only two years later.[16] With Zishe in Copenhagen and her sister in Paterson, Bubbe wrote poignantly to Neche of her loneliness. Zishe, she assured her sister, was sending money from Denmark and pressed her to join them soon, but she would be sad to leave her elderly parents and family behind. What did life in Paterson promise, she wondered?

Paterson textile workers had their own share of troubles. Neche arrived in 1911 to find her husband embroiled in a major textile strike, the famous Paterson silk strike led by the radical Industrial Workers of the World. As a militant and activist socialist, the strike left Joe blacklisted once again. According to his granddaughter, in a bitter irony, he was forced to go into business, first opening a deli and then a grocery. He "hated being a 'capitalist,'" she noted, refusing to "take out insurance, pay taxes, or take advantage of any business deals that might show a profit." Remembered as never making much money, he nonetheless established himself well enough to be able to pay the transatlantic fares for the Walkowitz clan and to welcome them to America.[17]

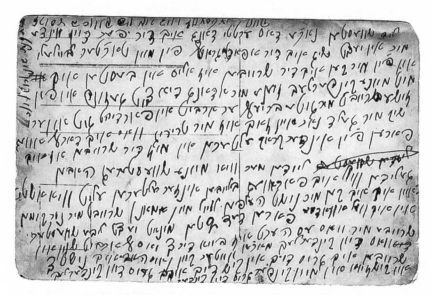

Figure 14. Bubbe's letter from Łódź, ca. 1913 to "My Dear Sister Neche," in Paterson, NJ. It reads, in part, "First I thank you for your wishes to me . . . Of myself I can write that everything is in the best order . . . Zishe writes me good letters; he is working and earning nicely and he sends me money. But one thing is sad for me because I must leave our parents and I must write that I am suffering more over this than my sisters because when I leave our parents will remain as lonely as a stone but I can't do anything about it because my husband keeps writing me to come." Courtesy of Michael Bernstein.

War interceded in 1914. Zishe and Chaia were marooned in Denmark for the war's duration. Living in a three-room apartment, they mostly worked out of their home, Zishe sewing on a large table in the center of one room. Jobs were hard to come by during the war, but Zishe nonetheless refused to sew German uniforms because of that country's treatment of its Jewish conscripts. Destitute, "we were down to our last day of food. . . . My mother was doing odd jobs, whenever possible, if she could find them," recalls his daughter Belle. Destitute, Zishe relented and despaired. Belle remembers seeing "the disappointment in his eyes. I will never forget the look in those eyes: pain filled them to the rim."[18]

The "highlight" of their time in Copenhagen, however, was remarkable: they met and got to know Sholem Aleichem personally. Sholem Aleichem arrived in Copenhagen in the fall of 1914 before traveling on to New York in late November. In the city, Zishe, always passionate about the theater, joined with compatriots to organize a drama club that regularly put on plays by all the great Yiddish playwrights—Peretz, Asch, Sholem Aleichem, and others. My aunt

Belle recounts the family's visit to see the great author off to America. Belle was only four at the time. Her mother was pregnant with my father: "Oh, Mrs. Walkowitz," said Sholem Aleichem, "It's so nice of you to come here but you shouldn't. After all, you're so big with child."[19] This became a celebrated family story, often heard.

On August 7, 1920, Chaia, Zishe, and their four children finally reached New York, landing at Ellis Island on board the *Hellig Olav*. In America, chain migration, in which emigrants typically traveled to places where family members and neighbors had already settled, characterized the Jewish migration from Łódź. Such kinship ties shaped the lives of the Walkowitz family, too, much as it framed Max's moves. As noted, Ida's sister Neche and her husband Joe Katz paid the fare—and not steerage—for the six members of the Walkowitz family and welcomed them into their home. The Walkowitzes also found themselves part of an extensive support network of familiar refugees from Łódź that included friends, neighbors, and relatives—siblings, aunts, uncles, and cousins. Chaia settled in Paterson near her two sisters. One, Neche, had three daughters who lived and raised their families there, too. Chaia's one brother, Morris, had seven children, mostly scattered across Canada and the United States.

Zishe, one of seven siblings, also had an extensive family network on which to draw. All had immigrated to Denmark, except Shlomo, the eldest who remained in Łódź with his aged parents and ultimately died in the Holocaust. In Copenhagen, a substantial extended Walkowitz family clan was established, though over time they too dispersed into the international Jewish diaspora. Walkowitz sisters, Laja and Serel, married brothers, Moschek and Mordica Gringer, whose families had also emigrated from Poland, and the couples had seven and five children respectively. A brother, Riven Wolkowitch, married another Jewish émigré and they with their seven children settled in Denmark. During this research, I connected with many of their descendants—my second cousins—in New York, Miami, Buenos Aires, Copenhagen, and Berlin.

The migration paths of the other three Walkowitz brothers traced more familiar Jewish diasporic trails. Zishe's brother Hershel followed him to the United States, settling with his family in Connecticut. The third bother, Welwel, tried to join them there in 1918, but at the last minute did not board the boat. Two years later, he and his wife moved to Buenos Aires, where he had work and could rely on his wife's family for support.

A Radical Jewish Life in Paterson

In the spring of 2017, the discovery of oral histories with my aunt Belle and uncle Joe challenged some of the romance I had of this past. Their accounts provided surprising personal and social details of life in Paterson for immigrant radical families such as the Walkowitzes. Upon arrival, the six Walkowitzes moved in with the five Katzes for the first few months. They crowded into a three-room cold water flat with no electricity, and a toilet in the hall. One room was a kitchen for cooking and eating; the five Katzs shared the bedroom; the six Walkowitzes slept on the couch and three folding beds in the living room. After a few months, the Katzes moved out into a flat above their new grocery store, but the Walkowitz home, always a refuge for visiting writers, poets, and actors or arriving relatives, remained crowded. In his oral history, my uncle Joe recalled never knowing whom he would wake up next to in bed.[20]

Working conditions were equally stressful. Tailors and sewers worked long hours for low wages out of the home or in small shops. They were easily exploited by what they called "cockroach shops," small shops run by nefarious middlemen. The workers' response was to organize, and strikes erupted every year or two with crippling frequency.[21]

The oral accounts regularly iterate how Yiddish culture was a source for organizing the working-class Jewish community. It was also a welcome respite from the daily drudgery. Zishe put on a coat and tie to go to Chorus rehearsal, waxing, "when I go to rehearsal, it's a holiday for me." But it was not a vacation from the labor struggles. Rather, the Chorus, along with literary clubs, concerts, poetry readings and theatre, was a weapon in a robust cultural arsenal which radical Jews mobilized on behalf of the Paterson workers' struggles for dignity and rights. They sang for solidarity, pleasure, and mobilization. They sang revolutionary lyrics:

Lift up your eyes and see the wonderful things that have been created,
And none of it is yours.
Don't ask me where the grass is growing and the birds sing.
But seek me where my people are in chains.

And they sang at comrade's funerals, like this excerpt from "The Scarlet Banner":

Dear friend, when I die, bring to my coffin our flag
Sprinkled with blood from the working man.[22]

Belle's and Joe's oral histories also confirmed Zishe's larger-than-life quality and prominence in Paterson's Yiddish urban culture. He was storyteller, singer, poet, and actor. Friday night he would gather family to a secular version of Oneg Shabbat he hosted for the community at the Walkowitz house or at the International Workers Order hall. The evening always began with performances by "father's diamonds"—his four children—but everyone attending would read a poem, sing a song, tell a story, or relate an experience. Zishe, both Joe and Belle remembered, would read a poem brilliantly and then perform a one-act play he had written based upon it. Summarizing, Belle waxed about Zishe: he "had quite good taste and a natural courtesy and decorum as well as high intelligence." In the house, cousin Ruthie recalled, Zishe had "quite a presence." While "impressive," she added a warning note I soon learned was an integral part of his character: "he appeared to rule his family, including Tante [Bubbe] Chaia."[23]

I had always heard that Zishe had a dark side, a "terrible temper," but never appreciated its extent. In fact, my wife now tells me she had heard something of this from my aunt Belle before; I had not—they were women' stories kept in private. In her 1980 interview, Belle describes Zishe's extensive history of whipping his children, my father Sol in particular. Rooting his violence in his unfulfilled "fanaticism for the stage," she concludes, Zishe was "a stern disciplinarian . . . [who] believed in whipping his children to keep them in order." She explains his violence as rooted in his greater expectations from Sol, his eldest son. "Sol and Zishe had the same vision, but they seemed to approach it quite differently. . . . When Sol didn't do what Zishe wanted him to do or thought he should do, he would whip Sol. A few times my mother would have to stop Zishe; his whippings could last a long time." Joe also got whippings, "but nothing like the ones that Sol got."[24]

Zishe's austere patriarchal role and self-image demanded a submissive and/ or tough wife. Chaia, I learned, was both. Cousin Ruthie, my oldest cousin, who as a child lived next door to my grandparents, does not remember Chaia as the laughing, smiling Bubbe of my imaginings. Rather, she was "not really pleasant. She spoke little, complained, and her demeanor was somewhat sour." But the picture that emerges from interviews with Joe and Belle is of a piece with both my and Ruthie's memories. Chaia was serious about political commitments and took responsibility for the home. She did the conventional double day, active in the public sphere by day and tending to the home afterward. I had always heard of her being regularly arrested and her husband complaining she was not home to cook. In Belle's and Joe's accounts she remains doubly transgressive as a woman and socialist, but she does not appear as shirking home duties. With these new pieces of information as frames, the family "line" now speaks to me of Zishe's paternalism and the ways in which Jewish family life could sustain and impede solidarities. Belle remembers Chaia's "endless strength and patience," a woman who was quiet, sympathetic, gentle, and always ready to help people. Laid off around 1922 from a job in a Paterson jute mill, for example, she worked part-time in a restaurant, and to supplement the family, with the help of her eleven-year-old daughter, cooked, prepared, and sold dinners to twenty textile workers each day.[25]

For the next thirty years in Paterson, Chaia, like many women in support of community actions, did fundraising and support work for union struggles, Yiddish shuln, and the Folk Chorus, and made a welcome home for the constant stream of visitors who brought Yiddish and radical culture to the city. Moreover, as an anecdote Joe related well illuminates, spunk, principles, and toughness animated this woman. The "Un-American Affairs Committee" (probably the House Un-American Activities Committee [HUAC]) had subpoenaed

Ida Walkowitz to meet with them in Newark. It was the mid-1950s. Joe notes she had "had two strokes, and walked in dragging one leg. Her mouth was distorted, pulled over to one side of her face." Joe was there to translate; Belle and my dad, who were both more prominent in the Party, had reason not to want to risk showing their faces. Uncle Joe was a great storyteller, however, and his story has double layers of translation—both of his mother, where one can only imagine how his version of what she said masked her sarcasm, and his likely embroidering of the encounter fifty years later. The substance of his account nonetheless reveals a strong woman of principle and gumption.

The committee members asked her questions in English and she answered in Yiddish.

> They asked her, "What publications do you read?"
>
> She said, "I can't read." [But of course she wrote the postcard above in Yiddish, so she was dissembling or presuming they meant in English. She read the communist daily, *Morgan Freiheit*, too. My cousin remembers her father saying she "pretended" not to speak any English.]
>
> They rephrased the question, "What publications do you subscribe to?"
>
> She said to me, "What kind of a stupid person do these people think I am, to pay money to subscribe to magazines I can't read?"
>
> At the end of the interview she said to me, "Tell these gentlemen that they can go home and sleep peacefully. They don't have to worry. I'm not going to throw any bombs."[26]

Cousins described Ida, my Bubbe Chaia, as "quiet," and "a homebody." Confronted by state inquisitors from HUAC, however, she showed the inadequacy of such characterizations. In a very public setting, she was a woman of great resolve; she was unbreakable and principled. Moreover, the person described in my aunt's and uncle's oral accounts also resonates with those in the new histories of New York's Jewish socialists, Yiddish political culture, and the role of strong women in that world. Chaia's and Zishe's lives demonstrate that domestic relations and responsibilities within the Jewish family are integral parts of the socialist story. As a historian in and of New York who is familiar with the city's sophisticated social and public history, I looked forward to seeing how heritage sites incorporated experiences such as those of my grandparents into their narratives.

～

HERITAGE

New York City's living Jewish heritage is old, new, and ever changing. Jews have been an active part of the city's history for nearly 350 years. In the twentieth century, however, they permeated the city's social, cultural, and political life.

New York politicians knew a balanced ticket included representatives for office from the three "Is"—Italy, Ireland, and Israel. Jewish-inflected food culture was ubiquitous. Major sports venues offered bagels, knishes, and kosher franks. In 2012, at a time most places in Europe highlighted the one or two kosher restaurants tourists could visit, New York City by one count had 504 of them.[27] And American culture has been infused with Jewish sensibilities. English is peppered with Yiddishisms such as shlep, schtick, kibbitz, mensch, kvetch, chutzpah, nosh, and so forth.[28] Jewish writers, filmmakers, entertainers, publishers, actors and producers have infused American culture with depictions of American-Jewish life. Culture-makers such as the novelist Philip Roth (i.e., *Portnoy's Complaint*), the beat poet Allen Ginsburg (i.e., his poem, "Kaddish"), and Woody Allen, in films like *Manhattan*, imbed Jewish culture, including its paternalism and misogyny, in characterization and plot. Allen's film *Broadway Danny Rose*, set in a classic New York Jewish deli, illustrates the influence of Jewish vaudeville traditions on American culture. Rooted in the Second Avenue Jewish Rialto, Jewish-American comedy, from the Marx Brothers and Jack Benny to Sid Caesar, Mort Sahl, Mel Brooks, and Neil Simon, to name but a few, was honed in Borsht Belt summer resorts in the Catskill Mountains north of the city. Such Jewish humor has served in postwar film, theater, and television as a core sensibility for American humor. And New York City has been the cradle of the Jewish experience in America.

The large numbers of Jews and non-Jews (one long-term guide estimates about one-third of participants were non-Jews) who sought organized tours of New York's Jewish heritage in the new millennium found relatively few options.[29] Like in places such as Łódź, Kiev, and Lviv—and unlike in other major Eastern and Central European cities—few tour companies in New York offered specifically Jewish heritage itineraries, and those that did, suffered to find an audience. Rather, Jews who returned to the New York they knew or imagined they knew, for the most part, took nostalgic, personal, family trips, perhaps with a grandparent or two in tow. Increasingly, many were third and fourth generation Jewish Americans for whom, in the words of historian Jeffrey Shandler and anthropologist Jack Kugelmass, New York "became the new Old World," another way of "Going Home." They came to the city armed with inherited and constructed memories, a fanciful mix of memory, history, and nostalgia.[30]

They found much new to see. By the end of the twentieth century, Chinatown had expanded dramatically through the Lower East Side. It dominated the former Jewish neighborhoods, while Little Italy had contracted into only a couple of blocks. Nonetheless, New York was awash in Jewish heritage sites, both to be seen and in the commercial culture, consumed. Seventy years after the war, many of the Jewish shops had moved out. A working-class neighborhood with many crowded tenements had been displaced by high-end condominiums housing a well-heeled urban gentry of professionals, entrepreneurs, financiers, and corporate executives. Some of the gentry were Jews moving back to the city. But the shops and Jewish institutions that remained—or the sites of former institutions—had become iconic destinations. One could, for instance, walk to dine on a sentimental version of Jewish heritage. At 137 East Houston Street Yonah Schimmel's Knish Bakery offered the prelude to a full menu of delights one could find at Russ and Daughters, down the street. A self-described "appetizing store," Russ and Daughters has offered Jewish culinary delights since early in the twentieth century. From there, one could walk further east to Katz's Delicatessen, made famous in *When Harry Met Sally*. Turning south, while Streit's Matzo Factory was gone from 148–154 Rivington Street, Kossar's Bialy's (367 Grand Street), and the Pickle Guys store (49 Essex Street) made famous in *Crossing Delancey* could sate most Jewish cravings. If not, one could call for some "two cents plain" (seltzer) and a digestive.[31]

Museums

Those seeking Jewish heritage could stuff their memory box with much more than food. The Lower East Side home of the Jewish food culture would remain the repository of a lived memory, but Jewish heritage was also on offer at three other Jewish institutions with origins in postwar New York.

The Jewish Museum. The Jewish Museum on Fifth Avenue at 92nd Street presents the Jewish experience through art. Dedicated to Jewish visual culture, its collection bears evidence of its 1904 roots at the Jewish Theological Seminary. The historical strength of the collection, which now has over 46,000 objects, is its ceremonial art. The museum also regularly presents the work of modern and contemporary artists whose work, like that of the photographer Alfred Stieglitz, depicts prewar Jewish life. In 1947, the museum opened to the public in its present home in the former mansion of the prominent financier and philanthropist Felix M. Warburg. The museum's innovative and celebrated 1966 exhibit "Portal to America: the Lower East Side, 1870–1925," curated by Allon Schoener, was based primarily on photography but drew as well on its collection of fine art, Judaica, folk art, and ceremonial artifacts to depict Jewish culture and identity during the era.[32] Its permanent exhibit, *Culture and Continuity: The Jewish Journey*, now draws on its extended interest in contemporary art, which is best highlighted in its rotating special exhibits. The museum displays the work of Jewish artists, some with passing relevance to New York, and some that speak to vernacular Jewish culture. Exhibits have focused on the lives and work of Modigliani, Pollack, Chagall, and Houdini, for example, but not on New York's Jewish folk chorus, Jewish humor, or Yiddish theater. In the fall of 2014 the museum mounted a notable exhibit of the Jewish fashion entrepreneur and icon, Helena Rubenstein. Born in Kraków, Rubenstein was a cosmopolitan woman with many homes, but the focus on a secular woman illustrated the inclusive vision of the curators on both gender and Jewish identity.[33]

The Center for Jewish History. A second museum destination, the Center for Jewish History, is on West 16th Street, only a mile or so north of the Lower East Side. The Center is a collection of five Jewish societies dedicated to Jewish history: the American Jewish Historical Society, the American Sephardi Federation, the Leo Baeck Institute, the Yeshiva University Museum, and the YIVO Institute for Jewish Research. The Center also houses the Family History Center, which has particular expertise in Jewish genealogical research. The Center is, however, less a museum than a major site for historical research. Its exhibit spaces tend to draw more on the German and Polish historical archives of the institutions than on records for the history of Jews in New York. Exhibits hosted by the American Jewish Historical Society, often in conjunction with another Center institution like Yeshiva's Museum, are the exception. The three exhibits mounted in 2014 illustrate the varied programming a visitor might encounter at any time. They also reflect a consistent uplifting theme of "contribution history." The year opened with *Contributors to the Cause,* billed as "an overview of Jewish philanthropy in the United States" from the 1700s to the late twentieth century. As the title suggests, the exhibit emphasized the contributions of benefactors more than it asked any questions about philanthropy, charity, and uplift ideology. The second exhibit, *The Dawn's Early Light: Jewish Contributions to American Culture from the Nation's Founding to the Civil War,* sustained the museum's uncritical perspective. Finally, although its presentation was cutting edge and modern, the third exhibit continued this tone with a dated model of immigration history as uncomplicated contribution history of Jews. Titled simply *October 7, 1944,* this exhibit integrated photography with digital media to commemorate and introduce visitors to the bravery of four young women who resisted at Auschwitz on that date.[34]

The Center also offers modest but insightful exhibits that take visitors beyond the Holocaust, outside the contribution and uplift paradigms, and into the world of the Bund and protest against the status quo. Both the Leo Baeck's rich German archival sources and YIVO's collection of materials on the Bund periodically provide poignant accounts of a pre-New York heritage of vernacular culture and popular protest. In 2001, YIVO mounted an exhibit on one of the most famous actors of the Yiddish theater in Poland and New York, *Ida Kaminsky, Grande Dame of the Yiddish Theater.* In 2009, it exhibited *Stars, Strikes and the Yiddish Stage: The Story of the Hebrew Actors' Union.*[35]

The Museum of Jewish Heritage—A Living Memorial to the Holocaust. The newest of New York's three Jewish museums, the Museum of Jewish Heritage, opened in 1997. Despite its impressive structure and large exhibit space, this museum has struggled to turn a profit and attract the crowds that visit the uptown Jewish Museum and the Lower East Side's Tenement Museum discussed below. Its 41,000 walk-up visitors per year is one-quarter the number who visit the Tenement Museum and the Jewish Museum.[36] In 2015, in an effort to build an audience, the museum welcomed the famous National Yiddish Theater Folksbiene to take up residence. The impact of its presence remains to be seen, but making Yiddish theater a centerpiece of its programming contrasts with the focus of the permanent exhibit.

Despite the broad purview of its title as a Museum of Heritage, its subtitle, A Living Memorial to the Holocaust, reflects its narrower focus. The museum's three floors divide its core exhibit into three sections, one for each floor. However, the museum dedicates the entire second floor to a Holocaust exhibition, titled *The War against the Jews,* and it dominates the core exhibit; the first and third floor themes each have half the space. On the first floor, *Jewish Life: A Century Ago,* focuses on the period of Eastern European migration between 1880 and 1930, largely ignoring the more than two centuries of prior Jewish settlement by the Spanish-Portuguese and German Jews. New York's Jewish history is compressed, while viewers are pushed forward to the main show—the Holocaust—so that we, in the words advertised as one of the main lessons, "Never Forget!" When asked about what she saw as the main lesson she hoped visitors would take away with them, Esther Brumberg, the curator of collections responsible for the permanent exhibit, eloquently spoke of her desire that they see that not all Jews are the same and that different Jews see the world differently. At its best, the exhibit succeeded in this simple but important mission. Religious Jews and secular Jews, Orthodoxy and Reform, businessmen and trade unionists, Zionists and socialists, even Bundists appeared. Thinking about my paternal grandmother, I asked Brumberg about the inclusion of material on Jewish communists, Bundists, socialists. "We love that stuff," she replied with gusto. But one had to look fast for it. A substantial part of the first floor is dedicated to Jewish traditions, heritage, family life, and ceremonial and communal life. The story of Jewish trade unionism, a vibrant part of that era, was buried in six artifacts; the Bund appeared in one diorama. Differences within the Jewish community were apparent, but were seen in brief snatches arrayed in dizzying order. Other organizations with long roots in Jewish history, such as Rabbinic Judaism, or those more in line with mainstream Jewish currents in the present like the Zionists, received pride of place and extended coverage.[37] In any case, the museum's focus is on the second floor Holocaust exhibit. The section makes extensive use of first person oral testimonies from survivors who came to New York and they envelop visitors in the horrors and poignancy of the accounts. No effort is made to explore the construction of memory, narrative conventions, or stories not told; the object is to stir emotions to the horror, and it succeeds.

Half of the third floor is dedicated to meeting spaces and temporary rotating exhibits. The first half of the floor resumes the heritage story in the postwar era with *Jewish Revival*. The focus, however, is split between the story of Israel and American Jews' relationship to it, and changes in Jewish life in New York and America more widely. Ironically, one wall on this floor backtracks to outline the history of Jews in the United States in the two centuries prior to the immigrant story on the first floor. The latter part of the exhibit demonstrated the inclusive vision Brumberg expressed. It also opened up the story of Jewish identity in ways that included people such as Chaia and Max. The narrative did not privilege secular or religious Jews, the ultra-Orthodox, feminist Jews, or any other group. Rather, it emphasized "struggles [of American Jews] to maintain their identity" and noted challenges raised by both growing numbers of the Orthodox and secular.

The final stop was a television monitor with a series of chairs on which visitors could see the mosaic of diverse American Jews, many from the secular world of New York Jewish culture—Man Ray, Woody Allen, Barbra Streisand, Meredith Monk, Allen Ginsburg, Isaac Stern, Beverly Sills, Mike Nichols, and others. Economically and socially "diverse" they were not, though I appreciated the inclusion of the popular culture icons.

The Lower East Side

For those seeking Jewish heritage in New York, the above museums are an appetizer. One is an art museum, one has limited temporary galleries of varied quality and relevance, and one, in 2017, remains a Holocaust museum framed by historical snippets. For the main course, heritage seekers go to the Lower East Side (LES). For American Jews, New York's LES in particular came to have a special meaning as early as the 1930s, in the historian Beth Wenger's words, as "the most popular locus of American Jewish memory."[38] There was a material base for this memory: in 1892, at the onset of the great in-migration of Eastern European Jews, an estimated three-quarters of New York Jews lived on the Lower East Side. In the next three decades when the vast majority of Jewish immigrants disembarked at Ellis Island, many settled on the LES. Many stayed, but many more moved on to places with higher status, such as the Grand Concourse in the Bronx, or sought out opportunities to fulfill their American Dream in cities across the country. In post–World War II America, many would move into suburban split-levels, ranch houses, or McMansions. By 1950, less than one-quarter of the New York Jews resided on the LES. The movement out, however, did little to diminish the real and imagined place of the Lower East Side; rather, it fostered a heightened sense of the area's symbolic meaning as the cradle of Jewish-American culture.

As early as the 1930s, American Jews began to take pilgrimages to see for themselves or show their children the hallowed LES. Historian Suzanne

Wasserman notes how merchants "came to depend on the visits of ex-Lower East Siders as much as ex-East Siders came to depend on these visits for a hit of *gemultlichkeit*."[39] But, as the neighborhood declined in depression-era New York, its imagined meaning as symbolic testimony to the ability of Jews to survive and succeed rose. This LES narrative, the story of how it was to be remembered, or invented—conformed, in Hasia Diner's words, to a "classic Jewish formulation" with "a distinctly American tenor"—a Jewish Horatio Alger story of pluck, luck, and hard work leading from rags to riches. But as the critic Paul Berman notes, the area "was simultaneously abandoned and sacralized."[40] Thus, while the LES became a metonym for the American Jewish experience, it was a formative experience remembered as much as a home as for one's ability in having succeeded in leaving it. Even as Jews dispersed across the land, they returned to the LES in postwar America as a home where they could dine on the "good old times" with "authentic" Jewish foods and celebrate their successful move from "the bad old times" to the affluent suburbs. So Jewish heritage tourism in mid-century New York became a tale of poverty, piety, and progress told with a mixture of *schmaltz* (literally chicken fat, figuratively, nostalgia) and *tsuris* (woe). Melodrama was the governing narrative genre.

In the second decade of the twenty-first century, the Lower East Side remained the cradle of Jewish American history. Two institutions, the Museum at Eldridge Street (in the old Eldridge Street Synagogue) and the Lower East Side Tenement Museum (TM) anchored visits to the area. The renovated Synagogue opened to visitors in 2007 on the 120th anniversary of its founding and its museum offered regular tours of its architectural splendor and of local Jewish sites. Nearby on Orchard Street, the TM, chartered in 1988 to "promote tolerance and historical perspective," offered itself as a "living history" experience of the immigrant Lower East Side. The experience of Jews was one of several immigrant groups depicted, but the site has remained a beacon for those drawn to the LES for Jewish heritage.[41]

These two institutions, both rich visually and in the experience they offer, also reflect the limits of New York's Jewish heritage history for tourists. Ironically, the Eldridge Street Synagogue, while centrally located on the LES, privileges the work of the exceptional—the wealthiest within the Eastern European community—and the relative minority of deeply religious Jews. Moreover, the splendid synagogue building aestheticizes the experience of working-class Jews who lived most of their lives in the vernacular architectural confines of sweatshops and tenements.

The Tenement Museum. By contrast, the Tenement Museum brings visitors into the more proletarian immigrant world, but with a focus on the immigrant experience rather than on Jewish history. This focus has advantages and disadvantages. Embedding the turn-of-the-century Eastern European experience on the Lower East Side into a story of immigration has the advantage of decentering the Holocaust narrative that dominates and over-determines East and Central European heritage tourism. In addition, the TM dramatizes the immigration story well and puts the social history of everyday life and of the "average" person, not that of philanthropists and uptown Jews, at the center of its story. With its separate rooms dedicated to telling the story of different immigrant groups in past eras, the TM centers domestic life, including that of women and children, in the heritage story. This is a unique and powerful antidote to top-down, male-oriented exhibits. The privileging of domesticity may not extend to the place of socialism and patriarchy in the family, but the engagement with the vernacular architecture and the focus on quotidian life and the home establishes a base for such stories.

To some scholars, however, the TM narrative comes, albeit perhaps unintentionally, with conceptual baggage. The cosmopolitan diversity of a multiethnic immigrant history carries, Kugelmass notes, a Whiggish subtext where poverty gives way to social mobility and progress. The three Ps that dominate traditional Jewish heritage tourism—poverty, piety, and progress—become a comfortable base from which suburban, exurban, and gentrified urban tourists justify a bourgeois present. In this regard, the "Living History" in the six immigrant families' rooms reconstructed at the TM dramatize poverty and squalor but risk conflating a too easily romanticized history with lived experiences. The immigration celebration of diversity and social mobility may resonate with many visitors whose relatives "escaped" the LES, but it risks failing to complicate the story of mobility often denied, for example, to African Americans and many Hispanic migrants to the city.[42] An additional argument by Kugelmass hits close to home: tours that recapture a history of labor radicalism or liberalism as safely in the past may have the ironic effect of discrediting that past for the present. Remembering a heroic radical past of grandparents—like Bubbe!—"can also be seen be a nostalgia maintained."[43]

To its credit, TM staff is well trained to minimize the danger: docents have been schooled in ethnic history and in the presentation of the past to diverse publics; the cofounder, Ruth Abram, had such a background herself (full disclosure, she was a student in my graduate history seminar at NYU), and Dr. Morris J. Vogel, museum president from 2008 to the summer of 2017, came to the position after a thirty-five year career in the history department at Temple University in Philadelphia.[44] Still, as Kugelmass has observed, challenges in the conception of the immigrant story can undermine even the best curatorial intentions.

Walking New York

Heritage tourists seeking stories of the Jewish past in the new millennium typically have gone out of these LES museums into neighborhood streets on walking tours. According to Seth Kamil, whose company, Big Onion Tours, has been a leading provider of historic walking tours in New York since 1992, walking tours of the LES remained the major destination of heritage seekers. In 2000, the LES had "the highest concentration of walking tours of any ethnic neighborhood" in New York, and "quite possibly, the nation."[45]

Tours exclusively of Jewish heritage existed in the new millennium, but such tours were increasingly a dying breed. Phillip Schoenberg's example was illustrative. Schoenberg opened a walking tour business, NYCWalks, in the late 1990s specifically geared toward Jewish heritage. He had the right credentials for the business: he had a PhD in history from New York University, a certificate in Museum Studies from Hofstra University, and an internship leading walking tours at the Queens Historical Society. What he lacked was an audience. His website advertises bus tours, public lectures, walking tours, and lists seventeen imaginatively themed Jewish tours on subjects such as Jewish gangsters, the Yiddish theater, Jewish food, colonial Jews, and the more conventional Lower East Side Jewish tour. In the first years, he had four Jewish tours weekly, but the numbers steadily declined and in 2009, he stopped giving all walking tours except for his Ghost Tours, in which Jews did not appear.[46]

One group, the Chassidic Discovery Center in Brooklyn, offers tours of its specific Jewish New York experience. Daily, except on the Sabbath, Rabbi Beryl Epstein takes a busload through the community of Crown Height to see and learn of the Hasidic community there. Offering an insider's perspective on a way of life foreign to many outsiders, the tour is a window into a narrow slice of mostly postwar Jewish life that is more ethnological than historical.[47]

Several Jewish organizations offer Jewish tours, some of which are on the LES. The Eldridge Street Synagogue, for example, offers regular tours of its beautifully restored building and its museum offers other tours as well. Reflecting the growth of Food Studies, these often have a food theme. But rather than examining the conditions and peoples who grow, harvest, prepare, serve, and consume food both at home and in restaurants, these tours tend to dine on history-lite. A typical one, advertised as a "tasty trip back in time," seeks to entice visitors with a "journey into the kishkes of the Jewish Lower East Side." The Jewish 92nd Street Y, perhaps targeting its educated local audience, presents tours more as education than entertainment, but again the tours are few and infrequent. The Y advertises a couple of bus tours of Brooklyn neighborhoods and a dozen "City Walks" of Manhattan neighborhoods. Two are the ever-popular Ghost tours. The Y's 2013 program also advertised three tours run by the Lower East Side Jewish Conservancy of Jewish Harlem, the Jewish Upper West Side, and the Jewish Lower East Side.[48] The Conservancy, based on the LES, regularly provides the few tours that take the Jewish story outside the LES. It advertises a roster of nine different tours, such as the ones noted above, as well as a Jewish Gangs walk, Tenement Chic (an architectural tour), a LES Synagogue Tour (of the Bialystocker Synagogue and Beth Hamedrash Hagadol, the nation's oldest Orthodox Russian congregation), a tour of Colonial Jewish New York, and a New Williamsburg Walking Tour (where secular Jewish gentrifiers live cheek-to-jowl with the Orthodox). During the eight months between April and November 2016, however, they advertise public walking tours on only eleven days, so a tourist has to hope to be present on one of the few days they are offered. Two are "new" tours, a pre-Passover Nosh and Walk, and a special Mother's Day tour, Great Ladies of the Lower East Side: Heroines, Balabustas, and Yiddisha Mommas! The latter tour was the one walk to focus on the history of Jewish socialists, albeit only on prominent women such as Lillian Wald, Emma Goldman, Belle Moskowitz, and Clara Lemlich. Other Jewish radicals pop up in political activist David Kaynor's book of radical walking tours, but they are embedded in a history of radicalism, not Jewish radicalism. For a professionally guided Jewish socialist heritage tour a tourist had to contract for a private tour and take a chance on the guide's expertise, or arrive on Mother's Day. On most other days, Jewish socialist New York remains a lost world.[49]

Four tour companies illustrate the decline of exclusively Jewish heritage walking tours in the new millennium that Phillip Schoenberg experienced. Joyce Gold has offered walking tours for about forty years. Described by CNN as the "doyenne of walking tours in New York," Gold typically offers about twenty public walking tours each year, only one of which (on Jewish Colonial Manhattan) is Jewish. Her website lists another forty-seven private tour possibilities. One offering is on Jewish Harlem, another on the Jewish Lower East Side, and several imbed Jewish culture in broader explorations of food or cultural diversity. The vast majority focus on the architecture, moguls, scamps, artists, and lore that characterize every part of Manhattan and the other boroughs.[50]

Big Onion Walking Tours, with a professional staff of trained historians, can legitimately claim to be "New York City's premiere walking-tour company." President Kamil believes his walking tour company is the second largest in the world. The company led 1,800 tours in 2017 for about 32,000 customers, many of whom took multiple trips. Kamil studied Yiddish and Jewish history before entering a doctoral program in American History at Columbia University. He stopped just short of finishing his doctorate in history and founded the company in 1991. In 2014, his website listed some thirty-seven guides, all with advanced degrees in American History or an allied field from seven research Universities in the New York area. His guides have classroom experience; Kamil sees his task as helping them learn how to speak to a public audience on the street. Still, he provides each with extensive written material and runs training tours exclusively for guides before setting them off to personalize their own variant. He encourages guides to develop their own point of view, much as they would as practicing historians. On average, a guide stays with the company about six years and most leave for college teaching posts. In regard to historical content, I have seen no company better positioned to give a sophisticated history tour.

Big Onion offers a "rotating roster of thirty history-based neighborhood tours." A few include Jewish history sites, but only one, "Jewish Lower East Side," has Jewish heritage as a focus. When Kamil began giving tours, clients wanted to learn about Yiddishkeit and the life of the Lower East Side; twenty years later, this history has been eclipsed by interest in the Holocaust, about which the Lower East Side has little to say. Big Onion's Jewish tour business has been reduced to about fifteen tours a year, 20 percent of what it had once been. Kamil's Jewish heritage tours, two-hour walks at $20 per person, once capped at thirty, now attract less than twenty people. The decline of his annual Christmas Day Jewish walking tour was symptomatic for Kamil. In past years, the tour had 500 sign up to walk with some thirty guides; in 2012, 180 appeared, and half were "international tourists who did not realize New York shut down on Christmas day." As of 2013, the "Original" Big Onion Walking Tour, "Immigrant New York," had once again become the bread and butter of Kamil's business.[51]

Much newer to the tour scene, and more committed to the entertainment side of tourism, is Levy's Unique New York, a company formed by the father and son team of Mark and Matt Levy. Lest anyone not recognize them as "authentic" Jews, the company logo replicates the script of Levy's famous Jewish Rye bread. But in fact only one of its twenty-two advertised Manhattan-based tours are on Jewish heritage, and its subtitle, "Immigrants and Noshes," reflects its focus on food and entertainment. The tour mixes in food with stops at Jewish heritage sites, but also serves as a broader immigrant tour with stops to sample food in Chinatown and Little Italy. In contrast to the scholarly Schoenberg and professional demeanor of Gold, Levy's advertises its tours as both educational and entertaining. The guides, many Levy family members, are mostly self-taught, enthusiastic "history buffs," who build on their love of the city. As credentials, Mark notes he has lived and worked in the city, retiring from a long career administering low-cost housing; Matt cites his university training in performance art and love of street art. Levy's website encapsulates what it offers, its headline proudly announcing its claim to fame: "Named 'New York's Wackiest Tour Guides' by the Travel Channel." Amusement does not come cheaply: two-hour tours cost upwards of $250; a family of eight pays $800.[52]

[Re]-imagining the Lower East Side Walking Tour: Immigrant New York. The typical Lower East Side walking tour was, like that foreshadowed in the Levy's tour and in the Tenement Museum, a tour of the immigrant experience. In the last decade I took several such tours with Big Onion guides. Most began in Kleindeutschland, the one-time German immigrant area, and moved on to Little Italy,

Chinatown, and then northward to the Jewish Rialto on Second Avenue. Others reversed the order and began at the northern end of the area near Astor Place. Either start allowed guides to reference the earlier history of the Irish and German immigrants with stops at the site of the notorious Five Points Irish slum Dickens visited or the Astor Place Riots of 1849. The Italian, German, Irish, Chinese, and other immigrant sites were interspersed with old Jewish sites, including that of the socialist newspaper, the *Daily Forward*, the Educational Alliance, the Yiddish theater, and the Henry Street and University Settlements. Many renowned Jewish food destinations were added attractions. These tours often referenced newer establishments of Hispanic immigrants and the gentrifiers who characterized the part of the LES neighborhood that realtors had rebranded as the East Village after the 1960s.

Necessary limits of time and space structure walking tours such as the typical LES immigrant tour, and they can focus at most on immigrant Jews of one neighborhood and one era. More problematically, as fundamentally immigrant tours, these LES walks share with the Tenement Museum the strengths and weaknesses that attend the immigrant paradigm. To understand the place of social division within the Jewish community and outside it, divisions that racked daily life on the Lower East Side, guides have to move outside the immigrant paradigm. Fortunately, several sites on the traditional LES tour make it possible to introduce discussions of Jewish socialism, trade unionism, and bourgeois benevolence. The Tenement House and Big Onion tours, within the limitations of the immigrant tour, typically did so. These tours visited the Educational Alliance, the Henry Street Settlement, and the Jarmulowsky Bank building, the monument to immigrant capitalism which is within site of the Forward Building.

But the history of Jews in New York also necessitates that guides move outside the LES. This is not easy to do in a two-hour tour and requires some planning. The most famous site of the City's German Jewish elite, Temple Emanu-El, is at 65th Street and Fifth Avenue, about three miles north of the LES. The Temple, a Romanesque structure with Moorish influences, draws on its high aesthetic, opulence, and grandeur to announce the political and social clout of its German Jewish members. It is also the largest Jewish house of worship in the world and seats 2,500. The Temple's origins were on the Lower East Side however, both as its congregants' first home and as a counter-site, a poor neighborhood with which they did not wish to be associated! In 1868, congregants established the temple at East 43rd Street and Fifth Avenue, to be at a respectable address removed from LES immigrant Eastern European Jews.[53] Temple Emanu-El would be physically out of reach of LES tours, but its existence reflected the imaginative "Othering" of the LES Jew by their brethren.

Other prominent sites on the LES's periphery could, however, be incorporated into a LES walk. Several such sites would materialize the impact of

German Jews on Eastern European Jews and speak to pre-1880 Jewish life in New York. For instance, vestiges of the earliest Jews to come to the city, the Spanish-Portuguese Sephardim, were and are evident in the remains of three cemeteries of Congregation Shearith Israel. The twenty-first-century congregation prays in a synagogue on the Upper West Side in Manhattan on Central Park West at 70th Street, but its first cemetery is on most immigrant tours. In use from 1682 to 1828, the cemetery lays at 55 St. James Street, the site of present-day Chinatown. The second, on 11th Street just east of Sixth Avenue in Greenwich Village, and the third, just west of Sixth Avenue at 21st Street, require a slight detour.[54]

Three sites at the periphery of the LES that were not typically on the tour reconfigure the immigrant achievement paradigm in productive ways and offer an alternative set of questions for tourists to ponder. Each could easily be incorporated into a tour (and I have seen some guides in the area do so). These sites expand the New York Jewish heritage tour beyond the Eastern European immigrants, and beyond the LES area in which many others settled. They also dramatize Jewish history as a story with multiple voices, each with different sources of authority and power.

First, the northern edge of the Lower East Side provides easy access to Union Square, a site of May Day marches and labor rallies for better wages since the 1880s. Socialist and communist Jewish workers employed in department stores and garment factories regularly met in the Square to organize and protest during strikes from the 1890s to the 1930s. Union Square was also adjacent to the Ladies Mile, blocks of new palaces of consumption that arose northward along Broadway and Sixth Avenue after 1880. The stores—emporiums such as B(enjamin) Altman, (Henry) Siegel Cooper, Bergdorf (Edwin) Goodman, R. H. Macys, Gimbels, Bloomingdales, Abraham and Strauss—highlight how the interaction of Jews with different resources shaped Jewish history. Some Jews owned stores in which other Jews, young aspirant immigrant women, worked as clerks, unionized, and fought for a living wage. Working wives also shopped for themselves and their families, both alongside their middle-class "betters" and as customers to white-collar clerks. Such history opens a window to a complex world of Jewish women as workers, customers, wives, and activists that challenges tropes of their piety and poverty.[55]

Second, walking a couple blocks west of Astor Place and one block east of Washington Square Park would bring a tour to the site of the Triangle Shirtwaist Factory fire. As discussed above, the tragedy dramatically demonstrated the entwined lives of the wealthy and poor Jews, of women workers and male bosses, and the integral place of socialism in the lives of the community.

Third, moving west in Lower Manhattan to the Wall Street area, a tour would see business sites of the German-Jewish "aristocracy" implicated in the labor struggles. Less than one percent of American bankers in the prewar era were

Jewish, but Jewish bankers, businessmen and philanthropists such as Jacob Schiff led the investment firm of (Abraham) Kuhn, (Solomon) Loeb, and Co. Felix Warburg, whose mansion is the present home of the Jewish Museum, joined the firm. They and other industrialist-banker-financiers, men such as the Lehman brothers (Mayer, Harry, and Emanuel), August Belmont, J. W. Seligman, and others, created an influential uptown Jewish interlocking directorate with substantial social and economic capital through intermarriages and social ties. Drawing on their connections to prominent Jewish European financial houses like that of the Rothschilds, these families played a major role in capital formation in the United States. Their impact on the immigrant Jewish community was profound. Many of these families became founders, trustees and directors of Jewish communal organizations, returning some of their profits—some, ironically, from the labor of immigrant Jewish men and women—as charity to aid and "uplift" the poor.[56]

Thus, sites important to the history of Jewish socialism—and the critical role of women in it—are easily available for an LES tour. Some, like the *Daily Forward* and Lillian Wald's Henry Street Settlement from which the Great Ladies tour departs, are regularly included. Other sites that hint at the rich and robust Jewish socialist history make rare appearances: they include the cooperative Amalgamated Dwellings on Grand Street pioneered by the Amalgamated Workers Union; the Great Hall at Cooper Union where the International Ladies Garment Workers rallied in 1911; the Jewish Rialto on Second Avenue; the streets of the LES as walked by the beat poet Allen Ginsburg, author of "Kaddish"; Broadway, where musicals like *Pins and Needles* (1937–1940), created by the long-time editor of the Garment Workers' Union newspaper, told the story of Jewish labor in the Great Depression, and so forth. In truth, while some of these sites make it into many ethnic tours and the occasional Jewish tour, the engagement with the range of these sites as a coherent narrative remains a lost world.

Where Are Jewish Heritage Seekers Going?

Tourists joining Big Onion Jewish tours two decades ago learned of the socialist and protean lives of people such as Chaia and Max. Such tours, according to Kamil, have withered since then. Various groups' Lower East Side tours integrate Jewish heritage into their story of immigrant diversity, but the socialist part of that history receives minimal attention. Brooklyn's Chassidic tour, which can be welcoming, proselytizing, or both, provides a specific and limited view of Jewish heritage and tells nothing about its socialist past. Commercial agencies in which the fun factor (mis)shapes any history tend to construct specialized Jewish tours with an "angle" like food. Again, Jewish socialism plays a limited role in such tours. Conservancy tours take visitors outside the LES, but its tours inside the neighborhood emphasize architecture and synagogue history. Its roster of different tours expands its market, but these tours parse

Jewish history into discrete pieces, privileging "noncontroversial" versions of the past in which the story of Jewish socialism typically disappears.

So how does one account for the decline of Jewish heritage tours in and of New York? Where are the tourists seeking such information going? For starters, the decline does not come from a lack of guide enthusiasm. Seth Kamil shares both my professional and personal interests in wanting to see these Jewish heritage tours in and of New York thrive. In addition to his advanced education in the social history of New York and Jewish history, he was raised with a background in socialist Zionism. Kamil also shares the desire to have robust, complicated narratives of both secular and religious Jews, rich and poor, entrepreneurs and labor radicals incorporated into Jewish heritage tourism.

Kamil roots New York's declining Jewish heritage tourism in the changing profile of the New York Jewish heritage seeker. Before 2000, increasing numbers of second, third, and fourth generation Jewish Americans came looking for a past previously denied to them. Visitors in the new millennium seeking Jewish heritage, if they come to New York for such tours at all, come with a different agenda. Increasingly more conservative than their ancestors, and generations removed from the hardscrabble world and political passions that animated their grandparents and great grandparents, they arrive for New York tours with inherited postmemories that focus on a different time and place. Their imaginings and expectations are increasingly shaped by postwar concerns with Jewish identity, Israel's contested survival, and the long shadow of the Holocaust.[57]

Fueled by memories that time and culture have shaped and misshaped, Kamil found that in 2014, his tourists were more inclined to seek stories of an exoticized Jewish past of gangsters and prostitutes than one of working people, socialists and trade unionists. In contrast to "dangerous radicals" easily stereotyped as "commie Jews," the gangsters are colorful rogues. The tourists appreciate that such rogues do not typify Jews, but their existence demonstrates that Jews, too, can be "fun." Kamil contrasts the appeal of these light-hearted subjects with his difficulties explaining Jewish socialist and communist radicals and intelligentsia such as Isaac Bashevis Singer and Leo Trotsky socializing and organizing in the Garden Cafeteria on East Broadway. Walking in the long postwar shadows of anticommunism, such a history does not conform to the stories tourists come to hear or want to hear about their heritage. Many visitors simply do not want to think of this background as integral and popular to important segments of the LES Jewish community. To be heard, Kamil carefully and defensively has to work to historicize Jewish prewar communism and its appeal to Jews, trying to get visitors to step back from their simple equation of communism with Stalinism.[58]

The need the heritage business feels to entertain while educating overlays the legacy of American anticommunism. The popular appeal of melodramatic narratives also helps explain Kamil's need to delicately force-feed unpalatable accounts of Jewish communists and socialists. Popular conventions that reduce the past to Manichean struggles and elide the ironies and complexity of everyday life and the diversity of Jewish life frame these new visitors' imaginings, much as melodrama did in the past. Kamil, for instance, describes his tourists as more inclined to romance than social history; typically well-educated and affluent professionals, they want the fantasy of a life on the edge, from which they can safely return to their condominium or suburban McMansion.[59]

Levy's Unique New York tours' emphasis on entertaining the heritage tourist plays into the fantasy. It also exemplifies an impulse that is hard to resist for organizations dependent on tourist dollars. The Tenement Museum, which regularly hosts programs on subjects such as Meyer London, Emma Goldman, Anzia Yezierska, and the Triangle Fire, has generally resisted such temptations. But constant pressures to attract more visitors and raise money risks compromising programming integrity. In November 2014, for instance, the TM brought together food, fantasy, consumption, and heritage in a new set of evening programs: "Live!" Designed to bring groups to the museum (though individuals were welcome, too), "Live!" invites guests to become reporters in 1900 and interview three staff members dressed up to portray former residents in the tenement. Following one of a dozen different tours of rooms in the building, each emphasizing a difference ethnic heritage and era, guests dine on local foods from area restaurants. For $50, $65, or $75 per person, guests choose from a menu of "Little Noshes," "Big Noshes," and "Sweet Noshes."[60]

While bemoaning the decline in Big Onion's Jewish tours, Kamil notes the commodification of commercial Jewish heritage tourism in New York and forecasts that its decline masks its increased presence in truncated forms in books of walking tours and developing online resources. Books of walking tours and apps that allow visitors to organize their own walks have cut into his business. Big Onion itself published several excellent guidebooks of its company tours after 9/11 dramatically reduced tourism in New York and especially in downtown Manhattan neighborhoods. Other authors have published still more.[61] Online tours are also available for almost any city from companies such as GPSmyCitywalks, and many offer a Jewish tour. Typically they list six to eight sites, offer a paragraph description of each, and allow clients to download walking directions between sites for an upgrade fee. Little historical information is given on the app, but online sources can fill out the story before or after the walk. The Museum of Jewish Heritage in New York, for example, offers a free app for a walking tour of sites related to the life of Emma Lazarus, the young Sephardic Jewish woman who wrote the poem that adorns the Statue of Liberty.[62]

––––––––

Ultimately, Kamil traces the decline of Jewish heritage tourism in New York to the opening up of tourism in Eastern and Central Europe. Third and fourth generation American Jews identify with the Holocaust, not the Lower East Side, as the core Jewish heritage experience. As Kugelmass noted in a 1993 landmark YIVO collection, "Memory culture has typically conflated time into the few short years of the Holocaust for post-1990 Jews," and places the past "into a few principle camps of extermination."[63] Such a perspective finds increasing numbers "going back" to homelands in which grandparents and great grandparents perished or from which they fled. A common request from Kamil's tourists, for example, is to meet Holocaust survivors in the neighborhood. While measuring his words carefully, Kamil playfully echoes this view, observing that the Holocaust as imagined and remembered is now the driving force for Jewish heritage tourism. "If the Germans had invaded Brooklyn and established a concentration camp there," he adds, "I'd be making a fortune." The opening of tourism in European cities of the Pale of Settlement, Galicia, and Poland, combined with the relative affluence of successful American Jews, now makes Central and Eastern Europe and Israel preferred destinations for Jewish heritage tourism. As the history of Jewish socialism recedes in New York tours, it seems that is where I need to return as well.

PART II

Going Back

CHAPTER 6

Berlin

A HOLOCAUST CITYSCAPE

Berlin's highly developed museum culture made it an appropriate place to begin my look back to Europe. A complex of five world-class museums known as Museum Island sits on the north end of Spree Island in the city center. A UNESCO World Heritage site, Museum Island attracts visitors from around the world. In addition, in September 2001, after more than a decade of planning and construction, the Berlin Jewish Museum opened in the Kreuzberg section of Berlin on Lindenstrasse. Designed by the architect Daniel Libeskind, the building's modernist zinc-lined exterior scarred with intersecting diagonal lines signaled the disruptions in German-Jewish history to international visitors and Jews from around the world. It quickly became a recognized landmark of destination culture.

In October 2011, I moved to Berlin for a five-week research fellowship and returned for a second fellowship in March 2013. Once home to the largest community of German Jews, the city was also a convenient base for Jewish heritage tourism in Central and Eastern Europe. I was partially surprised by what I found in Berlin: Holocaust tourism was plentiful; Jewish heritage tourism, not so much.

Touring the city and speaking with some of its curators, guides, and visitors, I began to understand the distinctive character of Berlin's Jewish past and its tourism business. Upward of 160,000 Jews had lived in Berlin in 1933. But unlike New York, I did not experience contemporary Berlin as a Jewish city. Only 8,000 Jews, many of whom had survived by hiding or through marriage to non-Jews, remained there at the end of the war. In 2012, Berlin's official Jewish population had swelled to 11,000, but locals believed 20,000–30,000 to be a more accurate figure. Half were thought to be Israeli ex-pats who arrived to partake of Berlin's lively cosmopolitan scene. Others included Russian Jews who arrived after the fall of the Soviet Union, or secular Jews whom the official count missed. Yet the signs of a vibrant Jewish past were ever present, though some were embedded in communist history. Holocaust memorials were ubiquitous, but street signs were also named after famous Jews in Berlin's history such as Moses Mendelssohn and Baruch Spinoza. Rosa Luxemburg had a street named for her as well in the former German Democratic Republic (GDR) as a legacy of her communist past.[1] Still, it remained to be seen what of Jewish Berlin's history I would see and hear as I embarked on my tours, and what the impact, if any, would be of what I had been led to expect would be a focus on Holocaust tourism.

Any one of the many German concentration camps was typically a de rigueur stop (and often starting point) on a Jewish heritage tour. The Sachsenhausen Concentration Camp, which was principally used for political prisoners, can be reached directly with a thirty-minute local train from Berlin. I had dutifully visited the Oświęcim (Auschwitz in German) extermination camp in 1982. I remember the experience as both moving and surreal. It was both a visceral engagement with remnants of a terrible past and a boring museum walk past inanimate piles of artifacts. The feeling of museum voyeurism I remember as at once dulling the senses and disengaging. Nearly a quarter of a century later, I did not think a return visit to a camp would add to my story. My quest now especially sought remnants of the earlier history of a living culture that had animated Jews such as Chaia and Max.

My research base was New York University's Berlin campus in the Kultur-Brauerei, a converted former brewery in Prenzlauer Berg. Located in the former East Berlin, Prenzlauer Berg had become a byword for Berlin gentrification. In the two decades following the fall of the Berlin Wall, developers had transformed the district into a lively, vibrant neighborhood chockablock with trendy restaurants, boutiques, renovated apartments, and converted loft spaces. In the late nineteenth century the area was outside the city gates and as I walked to my office built remains of a Jewish settlement were still visible. The street leading into the campus, Schönhauser Allee, had kiosks that mapped the Jewish historical sites in the district. Barely two blocks from my NYU office was the impressive and well-maintained Jewish cemetery at Senefelderplatz that opened in 1825. Nearby stood the neoromantic brick Rykestrasse Synagogue. Erected in 1903–1904 and seating 2,000, it remains the largest synagogue in Germany. Although I saw only a single mention of the synagogue in online advertisements for heritage tours of Jewish sites, the signage gave me hope that Berlin's tours might extend beyond the Holocaust, even if perhaps not beyond the conventional foci on cemeteries and synagogues.

Two other markers in the district reminded me both of Berlin's complicated past and that I was in the former Soviet sector. Schönhauser Allee began at a square named Rosa Luxemburg Platz, and a mile or two away a street named after the radical African America who had been shunned in Cold War America, Paul Robeson, crossed it. Both Rosa Luxemburg Platz and Paul Robeson

Strasse reflected the celebration of a radical (and for Luxemburg, Jewish) past in the GDR, though in a regime which had its own challenging racial and class agendas. Historical archeologist Reinhard Bernbeck, for example, notes how complicated politics of class and Jewish identity frame the treatments of Luxemburg: *Die Linke* (the Left), the contemporary democratic socialist political party, privileges Luxemburg as a communist revolutionary rather than a Jew, but Luxemburg's Jewishness constrains right-wing attacks on her as a communist lest they be seen as anti-Semitic.[2] Thus, for both Berlin gentrifiers and post-1991 politicians, such place names served as signifiers with multiple meanings. Embarking on my tourism, I recognized that streets named for radicals such as Luxembourg and Robeson had become part of the familiar, everyday experience and likely lost much of their oppositional meanings for many locals and visitors.

HISTORY

The history of the Jews of Berlin differs in significant ways from that of the history of the Jews in Poland and Ukraine, and the differences gave Berlin's Jewish tourism its own unique set of problems concerning Jewish identity. First, while Jews generally constituted one-quarter to one-third of the population of prewar Polish and Galician villages and cities, at their peak Jews were only 4.3 percent of the Berlin population (and less than 1 percent of the German [or earlier, Prussian] population). Second, most Jews in Berlin "Germanized," that is they spoke German, not Yiddish, and imagined themselves as Germans who were Jewish. Thus, the "assimilated Jew" and the "secular Jew" have both been central figures that have been incorporated into German Jewish history. As a result, the story of who is Jewish in Berlin tends to be remarkably inclusive. Tensions between religious and ethnic identities (and among the "assimilated" or "acculturated") and, in the first half of the twentieth century, between German Jews and *Ostjuden* (Eastern European Jews) in Berlin, remain relatively muted in German Jewish history. Third, as the capital of the Third Reich and the site of the Berlin Wall, both the Holocaust and Cold War cast long shadows over tourism to the city, and over Jewish heritage tourism in particular.

Such context could have constrained historians of Jewish Berlin, but instead they have laid out a richly textured history on which heritage tourism can draw. Jews have had a permanent settlement in Berlin since 1671, but had an uneasy and at times turbulent history in the city for nearly 400 years before then. Years of substantial settlement were punctuated by episodes of dramatic expulsion. The first account of Jews in Berlin dates from an order by the Wool Weavers' Guild in 1295 forbidding wool merchants from selling yarn to Jews. Nonetheless, Jews established a substantial community as early as the fourteenth century in the downtown area near the old City Hall. The settlement came to an abrupt end in 1349 when authorities blamed Jews for the Black Death and expelled them. They returned after five years only to confront repression a century and half later that echoed the Spanish Inquisition. In 1510, charged with "desecrating the host" and murdering Christian children, the Jewish community was expelled and thirty-eight Jews were burned at the stake.[3]

Ironically, Vienna's expulsion of its wealthy Jews after 1650 led to the return of the Berlin Jewish community. The Thirty Years' War (1618–1648) decimated the Berlin population and depressed its economy. To bolster the population and jump-start the economy, Berlin's leaders invited fifty prominent Viennese Jewish families into the city in 1671. In the next half century, this community, soon numbering over 1,000, established itself, building the Old Synagogue in 1714, a mikveh, and a cemetery.[4] By 1750, Berlin counted 2,190 Jews. Still less than 2 percent of the city's population of 113,000, the small Berlin Jewish community had a social profile that distinguished itself from that of the Jewish communities that would arise in Eastern Europe. It was, in the words of historian Claudia-Ann Flumenbaum, "a two-class Jewish society" with an unusually substantial affluent sector in which a wealthy top 15 percent were "under protection" of the state with status similar to that of Christian elite. Led by these wealthy Jews, the organized Jewish Community established a social network of hospitals, schools, and poor relief that attended to a broad "lower middle class" of Jews.[5]

With self-employed bourgeois entrepreneurs in a leading role, Berlin's Jews emerged in the second half of the eighteenth century as a modern social group. The Edict of 1812 abolished the requirement that Jews apply for "protection," and the newly unified Germany granted them full emancipation in 1871. Discrimination did not end, but led by its commercial and intellectual elite, Berlin's Jewish community made its mark in the city. Always the largest Jewish community in Germany (though tiny compared to those in Poland), the Berlin Jewish community was unusually successful. For example, Nathan Israel opened a business in 1815 that grew to be the Nathan Israel Department Store. Historian Christopher Friedricks notes the store, which eventually employed over 2,000 workers, became "one of the largest and most visible commercial enterprises in Berlin."[6] And Israel was not alone. In the next years a series of Jewish entrepreneurs opened stores in the Hausvogteoplatz neighborhood of Berlin, making the area a byword for ready-to-wear clothing: in 1836, Hermann Gerson opened a textile shop that expanded into a department store; Valentin Mannheimer established his ready-to-wear coat emporium in 1837; Rudolph Hertzog and David Leib Levin's department stores followed.[7]

Berlin's Jewish minority also played a disproportionately large role in the city's economy. In contrast to cities in Poland and Galicia, which had large Jewish proletariats, a majority (53.9%) of the 9,595 Jews in the city in 1849 worked in finance, commerce, transportation, industry, and the trades, and were overrepresented in each area. Another 20.8 percent worked in business, a category that presumably consisted of shopkeepers and manufacturers. Of the one in four others, some were "free professionals" (doctors, lawyers) and a small percentage subsisted as wage earners, domestic servants, or as paupers on relief.[8] Half a century later, the relatively high position of Jews in the Berlin economy remained fundamentally unchanged. At the beginning of the twentieth century, Jews, who were still only 4 percent of the city's population, paid 30 percent of its taxes. Moreover, twelve of the twenty most prosperous Berliners were Jewish.[9]

The prosperity of the Berlin's Jewish elite was one distinctive historical marker; equally significant was their identity by the late nineteenth century as German Jews—as both German and Jewish. The origins of this identity laid in the *Haskalah*, the Jewish Enlightenment, and the influence of the great Jewish philosopher Moses Mendelssohn (1729–1786). Mendelssohn understood Judaism as a religion of Reason (in contrast to Christianity, which he viewed as a religion of revelation) and he nurtured a reform of Judaism that at once reflected, stimulated, and coincided with the Germanization of Berlin's Jews. "Adopt the mores and constitution of the land in which you have settled," he wrote, "but keep the faith of your fathers."[10] Accordingly, at the same time as Mendelssohn translated the Bible into German, Berlin's wealthy Jews rejected Yiddish and adopted the dress and manners of their Christian neighbors. Some Jews, including Mendelssohn's youngest son Alexander, even converted, though the London examples of Benjamin Disraeli and Karl Marx's daughter Eleanor illustrate that one did not and could not change one's heritage. Both of Marx's grandfathers were rabbis and his father converted to Lutheranism to escape the constraints of anti-Jewish discrimination. Marx was baptized a Lutheran, but when his daughter Eleanor spoke in solidarity with the 100,000 striking tailors in London in 1890, she recognized his conversion did not obviate his Jewish heritage: "Dear comrade, I shall be very glad to speak at the meeting of 1 November [1890], the more glad that my father was a Jew."[11]

The Jewish Enlightenment and Germanization, then, created a unique hybrid version of Jewishness in Berlin that extended from religion to cultural and social life. The Enlightenment also informed the emergence of a Jewish bourgeoisie and a modern Jewish identity.[12] Elite Jewish women played a notable part in that identity formation, operating salons in which intellectual and social elite, Christians and Jews, mixed. Jewish women like Dorothea Veit-Mendelssohn, Henrietta Hertz, and Rahel Varnhagen hosted some of the most prominent salons in Berlin. The Enlightenment also most famously put its stamp on new Reform Judaism practices, which came to dominate the emerging middle-class Jewish Community over the course of the nineteenth century. The Society for Reform in Judaism organized in 1845 and moved into the Berlin Reform Temple in 1854. Another Reform synagogue, the New Synagogue, opened on Oranienburger Strasse in 1866. Incorporating the liturgical practices of the Reform movement, both Reform synagogues offered Germanized services that contrasted dramatically with traditional practices. Their services occurred on Sunday. Men and women sat together. Prayers were mostly in German, not Hebrew. And an organ accompanied a choir singing in German. However, while the Reform movement was dominant, a small but vocal group of Berlin's Jews opposed it and formed the Modern Orthodox community of Adass Jisroel in 1869.[13]

The boundaries of religious practice and Jewish identity more broadly were thus porous and, at times, elusive. Religion mattered to many even as they might disagree over liturgy: the Jewish Community newsletter in the fall of 1914 reported 42,441 seats were taken in the synagogues during the High Holidays. Yet this remarkable attendance figure does not count those who "only" attended on High Holidays, and it suggests that for a majority religion may not have been the central characteristic of their Jewish identity.[14] Some religious Jews patrolled the boundaries of Jewish identity, thinking the modernizing tendencies of acculturation or assimilation to be inimical to tradition. Rapid urban industrialization and political instabilities at the end of the nineteenth century led others to worry that radical ideologies could undermine German Jewish acceptance into Berlin society. Jewish elite, worrying that Zionist, socialist, anarchist, and communist ideologies undermined their status and the social order, directed their fears toward the "strange" (i.e., non German) Jews from Eastern Europe arriving with such ideas. So religion mattered, but it constituted one of many sources of identity that troubled German Jews. The historian Michael Brenner notes that the question that ultimately piqued Berlin's Jews then (and Jews everywhere since) boiled down to "Religious or Ethnic Community?"[15]

The hybrid identity of the German Jew was the answer for Berlin's turn-of-the-century Jews. And Berlin, moreover, was the center of German Jewry. Its Jewish community mushroomed in the last three decades of the nineteenth century: the Jewish population in the city almost tripled from 36,000 to 100,000. The period up to World War II was the heyday of Berlin's German Jewish community, and in the years before the outbreak of the Second World War, the Jewish population grew to number approximately 160,000.[16] A select few names give a sense of some of the extraordinarily accomplished men and women in prewar Berlin who excelled in the arts and sciences. Albert Einstein directed Berlin's Kaiser Wilhelm Institute for Physics between 1913 and 1933. The Berlin Committee for Psychoanalysis included Max Eitingon, Karl Abraham, Sigmund Freud, Hanns Sachs, Sandor Ferenczi, and Otto Rank (née Rosenfeld). A cultural Jewish Renaissance of the 1920s included the composers Arnold Schönberg (who converted back to Judaism in 1933) and Kurt Weill, the writer Walter Benjamin, and the impressionist painter Max Liebermann, who in 1920 was elected president of the Prussian Academy of Arts. And finally, in the making of "Berlin Chic," among others, was the fashion journalist Julie Elias and the milliner and designer Regina Friedländer.[17]

German Jewish businessmen and financiers also made their mark on the economy and culture of the city. For example, Moses Mendelssohn's sons Joseph and Abraham founded a bank, Mendelssohn & Co., at the end of the eighteenth century. It was but one of a handful of prominent Jewish-owned banks in Berlin until 1938, when the Nazis "aryanized" them. The fashion houses and the textile industry that provided the cloth were also decidedly Jewish. According to journalist Uwe Westphal's careful account, 49.8 percent of the *Konfektion* (ready-to-wear) businesses were Jewish-owned.[18] The fashion houses of Berlin Konfektion displayed ready-to-wear "chic" by Jewish designers alongside Parisian haute couture. And, as citadels to such fashion, the Israel, Mannheim, and Gersen department stores came to symbolize Berlin as a cosmopolitan center.[19]

Accounts acknowledge the achievements of Berlin's German Jews and the Jewish Renaissance of the 1920s, but too often they obscure the class character of this history. The development of the ready-to-wear industry, for example, coincided with the arrival of a group of Jews who moved into the German-Jewish realm from Eastern Europe during the last quarter of the nineteenth century: Eastern European Jews from the Congress of Poland (Russia) and the Austro-Hungarian Empire—the Ostjuden. At the turn of the century the Ostjuden numbered between 15 percent and 20 percent of Berlin's Jewish population, and congregated in the area known as the *Scheunenviertel* ("Barn Quarter"). The total number in Germany never constituted even a quarter of 1 percent of the country's population, but German Jews saw the poor Yiddish-speaking Polish and Galician Jews as "aliens," visible reminders to German Jews of their own origins and liminal status.[20]

Gender relations further complicated class relations of the garment industry and Jewish identity. Relatively little is known of Berlin's Jewish garment makers, and there is little evidence that large numbers were Jewish women. Some likely were though, and in any case, the harsh working conditions of the largely female labor force were integral to the history of the manufacturers—both Jews and non-Jews—and their financial success. For the making of clothes was a deeply gendered process. At the end of the nineteenth century, 155,000 women worked in the *Konfektionsindustrie,* a number that swelled to 200,000 in the 1920s. Some 80,000 businesses, typically run by men, employed these women. Most labored in the home where they worked under the supervision of more men—often their husbands. As historian David Clay Large notes, they worked under sweatshop conditions: "On average, they [the women] worked twelve hour days for about five or six marks per week," less than a quarter the wage of the average male factory worker.[21]

Finally, the traditional historical focus of Jewish history on the elite minimizes—if not obliterates—the story of Jewish political culture in Berlin, a history that often drew on the particular cultural interests and economic struggles faced by the poor newcomers. The exploitative labor in Berlin never produced the self-identified Jewish proletariat and labor movement that came to be associated with Yiddishkeit and the Bund in Eastern European cities. A vibrant Jewish political culture did materialize in different forms, however.

The histories of three institutions serve as examples. First, the Jewish Scientific Institute (YIVO, the center for the study of Yiddishkeit) was conceived of and founded in Berlin in 1924. In Brenner's words, German Jews "may have flinched" when they heard Yiddish spoken on the streets, but they flocked to Berlin's Yiddish Theatre "when they thought it represented avant-garde ideas."[22] Second, much to the chagrin of German Jews, the headquarters of the World Zionist Organization, which advocated Palestine as the Jewish homeland and Hebrew as its language (and not Berlin and German) was relocated to Berlin in 1911. A Berlin Jew, Otto Warburg, was elected its president.[23] Third, scions of Berlin Jewish families played major roles in the socialist Social Democratic Party (the Sozialdemokratische Partie Deutschlands or SPD), the party that advanced the interests of the Berlin working class. The SPD was organized by Ferdinand Lassalle, theorized by Eduard Bernstein, and in the aftermath of the Russian Revolution, its radical wing, the Communist Party of Germany (Kommunistische Partei Deutschlands), was led by two magnetic organizers, Karl Liebknecht and Rosa Luxemburg, the latter a naturalized German citizen of Polish Jewish descent. They were also the founders of the Communist Party of Germany. Ultimately, the ultra right-wing militia, Freikorps, murdered both in 1919.[24]

In contrast to the varied and colorful 650-year history of Berlin's German Jews and their accomplishments up to 1933, the National Socialist's unrelenting authoritarian regime of terror was monochromatic. Berlin's Jews had worked to meld into German society, but they had also established themselves as a community and individually. Still, as the class and gender divisions in the community illustrate, Jews differed among themselves. With the National Socialists' assumption of power in the years between 1933 and 1939, Berlin's Jews lost most of their rights and economic gains. Restrictive legal assaults on Jewish life became institutionalized violence on the night of November 9, 1938, when Nazi youth and authorities systematically vandalized and burned Jewish shops and institutions in what became known as Kristallnacht. In subsequent months Jewish men were arrested and sent to forced labor camps. By 1939, Berlin's Jewish population stood at only 75,000. Between 1941 and 1943, most remaining Jews were deported to camps across Europe, and the Nazi authorities declared Berlin "free of Jews" (*Judenrein*).[25]

The history of Berlin's Jews has a postwar coda. One-quarter of a million Jews living in and out of the displaced persons camps worked in the immediate aftermath of the war in Germany to negotiate the postwar chaos, but in 1990, about 28,000 Jews remained in the city.[26] Following the fall of the Berlin Wall, an influx of Jews from elsewhere started a new chapter in the history of Berlin

Jewry. As noted earlier, substantial numbers came from Russia and Israel, but as the presence of two of my cousins will show, the immigrants came from across the Jewish diaspora. In 2015, Berlin's Jewish community had grown to a number estimated at anywhere from 50,000 to 100,000. The religious community led a revitalization movement, establishing seven synagogues, several Jewish schools, and a number of kosher restaurants. Jewish Studies Programs have also flourished. The Freie Universität established an Institute for Jewish Studies in 1962, and the fall of the Wall encouraged other local and foreign universities to set up Jewish Studies programs in Berlin. One exemplary program among many others is the Leo Baeck Summer University in Jewish Studies, held since 2007 at the Humboldt-Universität in Berlin.[27] The well-publicized centerpiece of the Jewish revival is a ten-day festival called The Days of Jewish Culture. Launched in 1987 by the Berlin Jewish Community, the festival highlights theatrical performances, readings, discussion, film screenings, and klezmer concerts. The festival attracts an audience of Jews and non-Jewish Judeophiles. As noted earlier, critics worry that the program caricatures Jewish life, commodifying and reducing it to a pastiche of klezmer and knishes, both ironically associated with Eastern European Jewish food culture. For others, the Days of Jewish Culture are a modern reinvention of tradition and the cornerstone of a Jewish revival movement. Similar festivals are held throughout the Jewish diaspora, including in three cities that I visit in subsequent chapters and where I will revisit the debate about them—Kraków, Budapest, and Warsaw.[28]

∼ INTERLUDE ∼

Berlin was a strange place to find myself. Like many postwar Jews, growing up I identified Germans, Germany, and Berlin as headquarters of the Third Reich with Nazism and the genocide of the Jews. I had traveled extensively in Europe, but like my parents' promise to never set foot in fascist Spain, I studiously avoided Germany. Berlin was the proverbial belly of the beast, and to the best of my knowledge neither Bubbe Chaia nor Grandpa Max had ever been there.

Research for this book, however, and the reputation of the Berlin Jewish Museum, compelled a visit. My first cousin, Alex Berzin, with whom as a child I had been quite close, also lived in Berlin. Alex, whose travels with me to Mszczonów and Łódź in 2011 are described in chapter 2, had resided in Berlin since 1998. He had gone to Dharamsala, India, in 1969 as a Fulbright scholar to complete his doctoral dissertation at Harvard in Far Eastern Languages and Sanskrit and India Studies. Remaining there for twenty-nine years, he became a leading scholar, translator, and interpreter of Tibetan Buddhism. Alex had traveled the world translating for his own teacher, the assistant tutor to the Dalai Lama, and on occasion for the Dalai Lama himself. Deciding he needed a Western base from which to write, translate, and teach, he moved to Berlin. His fees from teaching classes on Buddhism and grants sustain him. Alex also developed a modest claim to fame as a JuBu—a Jewish Buddhist. In 1990, he served as the Western translator for a group of rabbis who had come to Dharamsala to initiate a dialogue with the Dalai Lama about Judaism and Buddhism. Their visit is described in a classic volume, *The Jew in the Lotus: A Poetic Rediscovery of Jewish Identity in Buddhist India*. In its seventeenth printing in 2015, the volume helped establish Alex as a voice for Tibetan Buddhism in the West and won him additional funding from Buddhist supporters.[29]

While conducting genealogical research, I was surprised to learn that Alex was not my only Berlin relative. The Walkowitzes, it will be recalled, had gone to Copenhagen from Łódź. I had visited some of my distant relatives there in 1965 in an early version of cultural heritage tourism. Zishe's sister, Laja, who had married and remained in Copenhagen, had a thirty-seven-year-old great-grandson, Adam Saks, my second cousin once removed, who now also lived in Berlin. An artist, the Danish-born Saks had trained and worked in Berlin since the beginning of the new millennium. Saks had also won something of a reputation in the Berlin art world, regularly exhibiting large canvasses that depict the grotesque and the horrors of plunder and colonialism in galleries and museums in the city.

Arriving in Berlin in 2011 and returning in 2013, I had few expectations for a heritage tour that would have personal resonance. I looked forward to a reunion with Alex and to meeting Adam, but had no evidence that my forbears had spent much if any time in the city. The passage of time, however, had softened my gut prejudices toward Germans and Germany and opened me up to hearing more than stories of a few "good" and many "bad" Germans. I had met German scholars over the decades with whom I felt simpatico. Moreover, my parents had been dead over thirty-five years and it had become easier not to see them looking over my shoulder; my daughter and ex-son-in-law, both literary scholars, had also visited Berlin and come back enthralled. In addition, iconic radical Polish Jews like Rosa Luxemburg had left their mark on the city, and I thought I had reason to hope to hear stories that resonated with my grandparents' past as labor radicals and Chaia's as a women activist.

~

HERITAGE

Holocaust Memoryscape

Cilly Kugelmann, the program director of the Jewish Museum Berlin, sees the Jewish Museum and Jewish tourism in Berlin as unique to the city. Jewish museums elsewhere in Germany focus on local histories and attract mostly local visitors. They are funded by localities and regional administrations. By contrast, the federal state funds Jewish Museum Berlin. Berlin and its historical venues also attract national and international tourists, the vast preponderance of whom are not Jewish. In exit interviews, less than 10 percent of the visitors to the museum identify themselves as Jewish.

Jews returning to Germany also engage a state with a particular historical relationship to Jews and the Holocaust. Their Eastern European brethren had perished or, if fortunate, had emigrated. For the most part German Jews had chosen not to emigrate; rather, many identified with Germany and fled when the Nazis rose to power. They returned as refugees, not emigrants. In addition, unlike Nazi-occupied lands in which locals can off-load blame to occupiers, the reunified German state has publicly had to accept its responsibility for the Holocaust. After several decades in denial, Germany embarked on a project of reconciliation in the 1980s and invited those forced to flee and their children to return. Thus, Kugelmann tells me, those Jews who visit and tour are typically individuals, children, and grandchildren of refugees who return to Berlin "to reconcile."

In "going back" the refugee background and the imperative to reconcile differently shapes the ambitions, agenda, and itinerary for German and Eastern European Jewish tourism. Kugelmann sees heritage tourism as "not so common in Germany. Germany is different. It is an Eastern European issue." For German Jews, the return focuses on coming to terms with the Holocaust and a German state that has publicly accepted its guilt. Tourists to Berlin see the Holocaust memorialized everywhere in concentration camp sites, memorials and museums, and on the street and in street furniture.[30]

To walk in Berlin is to engage in Holocaust tourism. The postwar and postreunification development of Berlin has made the city itself a museum. But unlike other cities scarred by the war, Berlin is also a museum to a second recent and politically fraught past: the city is also a museum of the Cold War. Remnants of the Berlin Wall snake through the city and citywide bus tours traverse it. Guides point out vestiges of Cold War Berlin, such as the classical monumental socialist boulevard and apartment blocks of Karl-Marx-Allee built by the GDR in the former East Berlin and Checkpoint Charlie in the former West Berlin.

Reminders of the Holocaust are embedded in the city anywhere tourists walk. Thousands of *Stolpersteine* (Stumbling Blocks), stones set in the cobblestone, have etched the tragedy into the urban fabric. The blocks are inscribed with reminders of a Jewish past brutally "disappeared." The creation of a Cologne sculptor named Gunter Demnig in 1990, around the same time as the Jewish Museum was being planned, the small stones (approximately four-inch cubes with a brass lettering) commemorate the diverse range of victims—Romany, homosexuals, communists, and others, but mostly Jews—whom Nazis deported to the concentration camps and murdered. Installing the stones in front of

Figure 15. Berlin Stumbling Blocks. "Here lies Alex Rosenberg, b. 1919, deported 1942, murdered in Auschwitz" (left). "Here lies Gertrud Rosenberg (née Brenner), b. 1879, deported 1942, murdered in Auschwitz" (right). Photo by the author.

their former homes, Demnig inscribed them with the words "here lived," with the name of the former residents along with their birthdates and dates of deportation to the camps following. Originally confined to Germany, by late 2015, Demnig had placed over 48,000 stones in over 1,000 German villages and cities and in 17 other European countries. Berlin has more than 5,500 of them.[31]

The ubiquitous presence of the stumbling blocks in Berlin are but one of a string of physical reminders of the Holocaust that are evident in dozens of memorials, monuments, and museums. Two memorials I found profoundly affective. The first, "Places of Remembrance: A Memorial in Berlin," is somewhat off the beaten track, but like the *Stolpersteine,* embeds the Holocaust experience in the landscape of the city. In 1993, two artists, Renata Stih and Frieder Schnock, inaugurated the installation of eighty brightly illustrated signs on lampposts throughout the Bavarian Quarter of the tree-lined middle-class Schöneberg district in Berlin. The Quarter once housed 16,000 Jews, including Hannah Arendt and Albert Einstein. Modest signs, perhaps no more than two by three feet, each list a law or regulations enacted by the Third Reich between 1933 and 1945 that constrained Jewish daily life. Each depicts in color a symbol of daily life, such as bread, while a brief black and white note in German on the reverse describes the restrictive rule. A bathing suit, for example, marks the December 1938 prohibition on Berlin's Jews from entering local bathhouses or swimming pools.[32] No one took much notice of me, nor of the signs as I walked on a cold early March afternoon. Neighbors once critical of them had evidently grown used to the signs, perhaps even appreciating how they brought tourists into the local shops. Blending naturally into the street architecture, they normalized

Figure 16. Front and back of a sign from Places of Remembrance, Bavarian Quarter, Berlin. The sign reproduces the 1938 prohibition on Jews using Berlin's swimming facilities. Photo by the author.

the horrific laws, much as I imagined it once had for non-Jews at the time. A strange compulsion drove me to find each new image.

Such signs of remembrance, whether on lampposts or on sidewalks, place the Holocaust front and center in Berlin, which undoubtedly suits the focus of those doing Holocaust tourism. A 2011 tourist brochure published by the citywide Permanent Conference of the Directors of National Socialist Memorial Sites in the Berlin area promotes a full menu of Holocaust museums and monuments to sate the appetite of the Holocaust tourist. The brochure directs tourists to fifteen "memorial sites, documentation centers and museums" that relate to the history of National Socialism in the city. Heritage itineraries described the two most well known and expansive sites, the Memorial (and museum) to the Murdered Jews of Europe and a newer museum called the Topography of Terror, as "must see" destinations.

The outdoor Memorial to the Murdered Jews in Europe designed by the architect Peter Eisenman is Berlin's official Holocaust memorial. Planning for the memorial had occasioned debates about whether the Holocaust could or should be represented at all, whether the place would degenerate into a site for ritualized political "wreath dropping."[33] Visitors have voiced few qualms though, and have come in droves to the Memorial since it opened in May 2006. I found it quite moving. The Memorial's 2,711 vertical concrete slabs of different heights form a disorienting maze. Pathways through 4.7 acres of sloping ground, evoke, in a powerfully symbolic experience, the anonymous gravestones of the millions murdered, their bodies burnt in mass cremations or tossed aside into unmarked mass graves.

The solemnity of the Memorial's stones left me unprepared for the powerful emotions generated by the exhibit in its adjoining underground museum. Deeply personal accounts of families on the road toward destruction, accounts made more dramatic in darkened rooms with illuminated panels, were over-whelming. It was not a reflective experience. Indeed, the exhibit worked on an emotional rather than intellectual level: it left no room to think or to imagine the history outside a narrative of anti-Semitism and genocide. It succeeded; I felt "the horror."[34]

The second major Holocaust museum, the Topography of Terror, fully opened in May 2010. It has since become one of Berlin's most widely attended museums, recording over 1 million visitors in 2014. Located on the former sites of the Gestapo and SS Headquarters and the Reich's Security Office, the museum exhaustingly documents the Third Reich's regime of terror. It especially tries to explain how German citizens came to support the populist appeals of the Nazis and the ideology of the *volksgemeinschaft* (Hitler's ideal of racially unified com-munity). The outline of the story repeated familiar tropes of Nazi perpetrators and Jewish victims, but the profiles of radical victims in a side room exhibit, *Berlin 1933*, offered hints of a different narrative based on a more complex social history. The exhibit depicted the men the Nazis imprisoned, brutalized, and murdered in 1933 (though some cheated the persecutors by taking their own life). But remembering the frequent characterization of Jews in Germany as bourgeois and respectable, the exhibit profiled a considerable number of victims as Jewish communists and trade unionists. Dramatic red panels with biograph-ical capsules describe approximately one hundred SPD leaders, predominantly male and most with "Jewish origins," who were the primary victims of repres-sion and the concentration camp prisoners prior to 1935. Again, the detail and emotional freight of the exhibit overwhelmed the intellect and the senses.

Holocaust tourists not yet sated could dine on additional smaller but no less interesting sites scattered about the city and its environs. I found some near the city center, which I subsequently found incorporated into Berlin Jewish walk-ing tours. One in particular, located on the outskirts of the city, merited a sepa-rate visit. A thirty-minute local train took me to the westernmost part of Berlin, the suburban locality on Lake Wannsee where generations of Berliners had trav-elled to visit the expansive public swimming beach. In January 1942, a lakeside industrialist's villa became the site of the Wannsee Conference at which fifteen high-ranking SS officers and National Socialist Party leaders planned the "Final Solution"—the deportation and murder of European Jewry (and other "unde-sirable" radicals, Romany and homosexuals). The villa now houses a museum in which fifteen rooms with an incongruously pleasing lake background describe the history of the house and National Socialism in text, film, and images. I tacked on to a docent's tour for a group of Mt. Washington College students from Virginia doing Holocaust/World War II tourism as part of a spring break mini course. The docent's elaborate description of Nazi stereotyping of Jews as animalistic and Aryans as wholesome elicited no questions from the students, who might well have thought of comparable stereotyping at home. They were attentive, if passive. Good Americans.

Just down the road from the House of the Wannsee Conference is a second site Kugelmann had encouraged me to see: the villa and famous gardens in which the premier impressionist painter Max Liebermann had lived and worked. The Liebermann Villa was easily overlooked, however, by anyone travelling exclusively for Holocaust heritage tourism and I had the place largely to myself. Liebermann's life illustrated the cultural accomplishments of Jews before the war and provided insight into how the war challenged notions of Jewish identity. Elected president of the Prussian Academy of Arts from 1920 to 1935 and made an Honorary Citizen of Berlin in 1927 at the age of eighty, Liebermann was ostracized by the Nazis in 1933 and forbidden to associate with non-Jews. Emphasizing the ephemeral and contested character of German Jewish identity, the exhibit explains that for the great Jewish painter, and for a generation of German Jews, the "dream" of assimilation was over. This observation, I thought, was the kind of question I hoped to hear engaged in Jewish heritage tourism. Holocaust tourism had not done so—or the subject had been buried like its Jewish victims. So, I turned to the city's two Jewish museums and walking tours, hoping to hear more of those questions and the stories behind them.

Berlin's Jewish Museums

Jewish Museum Berlin. Internationally acclaimed for its architecture, Jewish Museum Berlin is renowned as one of the leading museums of the Jewish experience in the world. Visitors come to it with high expectations. Mine, to hear of Jewish heritage, were immediately challenged in the underground entry into the museum. A maze of three intersecting and angled sloped corridors, an Axis of Exile, Axis of the Holocaust, and Axis of Continuity, enveloped visitors on the ground floor. At the juncture of the corridors, exhibits inside the walls housed poignant personal documents of Jewish life in those terrible years. The austere design and disorienting interiors were meant to create a visceral sense of the Holocaust experience.[35] They did. The simple bright lighting and simplicity of the displays, however, conveyed little of the dramatic power of the exhibit at the Memorial to the Murdered Jews of Europe.

Passing through the Holocaust gauntlet, visitors ascend the Axis of Continuity to view the historical exhibit. The museum offers one and half-hour guided tours with twelve different foci, though most include the Towers of the Holocaust and Exile. In his study of the museum's guides, Jackie Feldman finds most are graduate students, some in Jewish Studies. They receive training in a few workshops, and are then left to develop their own repertoire. In keeping with the founding curator's desire to create "a museum for everyone" and not for "nit-picking know-it-alls," Feldman notes that "the museum staff emphasizes communication skills and sees its role as edutainment: 'Wir sind spritzige [We are splashy] Guides.'"[36]

Touring without a guide, I began in a kiosk on the third floor where a half-hour video describes 2,000 years of Jewish history in Germany. The narration takes viewers from Roman soldiers raiding the Temple and sending Jews into exile in 70 AD to the eighteenth century. The museum continues the story in rooms that wind visitors around the usual stuff of museums—artifacts, images, and text. The exhibit's organization is chronological and any over-riding argument about the changing and contested past is lost in the dizzying amount of detail. To be fair, this problem is endemic to many large historical museums' permanent exhibitions: sensitive to visitors who all want to hear their particular story told, curators and directors are under pressure to touch all bases. As a result, in trying to cover everything they may leave the viewer remembering nothing. I plead guilty to creating such demands: I sought references to the political world my grandparents might have recognized. In walking through the exhibit, the one display that stayed with me was a line accompanying the extensive section on Moses Mendelssohn and the Jewish Enlightenment that noted "the concept of social justice is a crucial part of the Jewish tradition." The rest was a blur.

In her interview, the program director acknowledged the density of the information and overload in the museum, but explained the exhibit conveyed a larger message that could be appreciated in the detail and complexity. Kugelmann's larger take away for viewers was that Jews were both insiders and outsiders in German history. German Jewish history, she argued, spoke to the place of diversity in the national history and to the identity of the German Jew as integral to a collective national identity. In a contemporary world beset by fears of immigrants and antagonistic "others," the museum hoped to impart resonant messages of diversity and national identity for Jews and non-Jews, Germans, and international visitors.

Kugelmann did not dismiss the problem of overload. She saw the condition as both a strength and weakness of the museum. "[The exhibit is] so big everyone finds something to like." But, she acknowledged, "it's too big, too confusing . . . a bit like a theme park. . . . [B]ut visitors seem to like just that." In exit interviews, she noted that visitors report "they don't remember anything . . . , but what they do remember, and I think to me that is a success, is that it was a pleasant visit, and at the end, it is an emotional feel good moment."[37]

My own pleasure was more fleeting. There were nice moments, but they whetted my appetite for more. The museum exhibit was remarkably inclusive around Jewish identity, including secular, acculturated, and converted Jews. The place of Jewish socialists, communists, and radicals, however, was minimal. To be sure, some of my frustration was undoubtedly rooted in my unrealistic expectation. My frustrations also had a basis in the unusual history of labor in

Germany—the Bund and the Jewish labor movement were not major presences in Berlin. Still, as the Mendelssohn exhibit averred, social justice was central to the Jewish tradition and I missed its expression. Kugelmann acknowledged the absence of Jewish radicalism, attributing it to the lack of a Jewish proletariat in Germany, to "no left Jewish history" and only "a handful of Jews in the SPD." She explained the exhibit originally had no mention at all of Lassalle or Marx. The issue, she explained, was that "it was not clear to me what their contribution to Jewish life was."[38]

The fact that many Jews were leftists, who did not identify as Jews, complicated the curators' job in Berlin as it did in other Jewish museums. Some claim an essential Jewish identity whose characteristics can be checked off. Others understand people as identifying differently at different moments and under different circumstances. In this conception, Jewishness finds varied expressions within and across generations. This was how Kugelmann justified excluding Marx as non-Jewish: Marx's importance, she explained, was "as a Moses to lead Jewish workers out of their position" in the twentieth century long after he had died. In Germany, she claimed his life spoke more to "the story of anti-Semitism" than to German radicalism.[39] I thought it a remarkable but ambiguous statement. Was her appraisal a comment about Marx's writing about "The Jewish Question," essays thought by his critics to be anti-Semitic? Or was she thinking that Marx's centrality to the history of communism was responsible for twentieth-century anti-Semitism that identified Jews with support for Stalinism? In any case, the curators originally left Marx out of the story. In response to criticism from the left, they added mentions of both Lassalle and Marx, which Kugelmann characterized as minimal gestures. Indeed, I left the museum with no memory of Rosa Luxemburg or the many Jewish SPD members I had seen showcased in the Topography of Terror exhibit. Nor did I remember discussion of the Ostjuden.

The Jewish Museum Berlin exhibit did little to help me understand the history of Jewish socialism and any understanding of the urban milieu in which Jewish modernity was forged was lost in the detail. The museum whet my appetite for a fuller account of Jewish heritage in Berlin, but the architecture and power of its subterranean passages had embedded heritage again in service to Holocaust tourism, much as Libeskind intended. My visit to the much smaller museum of the Centrum Judiacum Foundation at the New Synagogue suggested other possibilities.

The New Synagogue. I deliberately arrived early for my interview with the Deputy Director Chana C. Schütz, in order to view the exhibitions there. A special exhibit on Moses Mendelssohn was, however, only open at night and an hour was more than enough time to walk through the permanent exhibit. The building, the historic home of Berlin's organized Jewish Community (JC), had been spared during Kristallnacht through the extraordinary intervention of a local police chief who insisted the fire brigade put out the fire before it destroyed the building. But the building did not escape the ravages of war. Allied bombs hit the synagogue's signature Moorish-style, fifty-meter high gilded dome in 1943. In 1988, at roughly the same time that Daniel Libeskind was winning the commission to rebuild the Jewish Museum, the GDR initiated renovation of the building as the prospective home of a Jewish museum for socialist East Germany. Schütz speculated that GDR founders' motives were not pure: she claimed that in hindsight, they saw "the handwriting [of the end of the Cold War] was already on the wall" and were reaching out to the United States and U.S. Jewry.[40]

In 1992, after the reunification of Germany, the property was returned to the organized Jewish Community and rebuilt. The permanent exhibit, *Open Ye the Gates*, debuted in 1995. The exhibit occupies an entry room and a good-sized back room from which visitors can view the footprint of the much larger original building through rear windows. In contrast to the full and busy (both with people and artifacts) Jewish Museum, this exhibit was simple and easy to follow. I suspected it told me little that I could not have found in the Jewish Museum, but who could remember!? *Open Ye the Gates*, like many smaller and specialized exhibits, was easier to recall. Its focus was also different: its exhibit was not dominated by intellectual and political history of great men or memory of the Holocaust. Rather, tracing its history and rebuilding, the exhibit focused on the social history of the people whose lives were connected to the synagogue. There was an open Torah. But this was not a religious exhibit. Preserved vestiges of the bombing and artifacts rescued from the bombed rummage provided visible evidence of the Holocaust experience. But this was also not a museum of the Holocaust. Rather, photographs and artifacts, with texts in German and English, illustrated the nineteenth and early-twentieth century voluntary societies, Jewish schools, asylums, hospitals, and orphanages established by wealthy German Jews. The subjects who inhabit these institutions were given no agency, and as elsewhere, the texts did not address the potentially uncomfortable issues of paternalism and class. There was also nothing on Jewish political affiliations in groups such as the SPD or on Jewish socialists.

Schütz's interview, however, surprised me with possibilities for elements of a heritage counter narrative. Socialist East Germany, she noted, reframed Jewish heritage somewhat more sympathetically to labor issues than had their West equivalents. A past and a potential future exhibit at the New Synagogue addressed political and social themes about women and democratic socialism in Jewish heritage. The SPD had proposed the New Synagogue mount a future exhibit on the Jewish workers who were "quite active in socialist politics" and who helped found and lead the Party. The possibility of SPD funding for such an exhibit made it plausible.

A second exhibit hosted by the New Synagogue in late 2012, *The Yellow Ticket: Traffic in Girls, 1860–1930*, integrated the history and daily struggles of working girls into the heritage narrative. Jointly sponsored by the German Emigration Center Bremerhaven, the exhibit documented the lives of poor Jewish girls in Galicia and the Russian Empire who turned to prostitution to survive. The "yellow ticket" was the colloquial term for the pass they carried in prerevolutionary Russia that allowed them to travel from Eastern Europe to the United States and Argentina. Notably, the exhibit focused on Eastern European Jewish women, not Berliners.

Although the four-month run of *The Yellow Ticket* drew the museum its most enthusiastic audience responses, Schütz voiced skepticism about the future of exhibits like it or the proposed one on the SPD. Opposition from the organized Jewish Community, she believed, would not sanction them. The JC, which typically consisted of traditional religious Jews, but in this case, possibly also of Russian immigrants, was small and relatively little engaged with the museum. Its view of *The Yellow Ticket* was not solicited, but Schütz thought the conservative impulse of current political passions inhibited the funding of such exhibits. She saw the JC as only wanting success stories that spoke positively about the Jewish past. Prostitution, which after all was a success story of mobility for poor girls, was not the traditional image of respectable Jewish womanhood. Similarly, an exhibit with any positive connection between Jews and socialism or communism, such as that proposed by the SPD, would also raise anxieties about "respectability." Acknowledging the more general absence of left Jews, Schütz, ruefully added, "It's really a problem."[41]

Walking Tours

Schütz's comments echoed with me as I embarked on walking tours of Jewish Berlin. The ubiquitous stumbling blocks meant I would never walk far from the presence of the Holocaust. But what more might I see and hear?

Before taking one of the typical advertised tours, I had the opportunity for an insider's tour. A NYU-Berlin faculty member, Ares Kalandides, offered a Jewish walking tour each semester, and I arranged to join it on a blustery March morning in 2013. I typically maintained anonymity on walking tours, only disclosing my interests after the tour in conversation with guides and other tourists. The NYU-Berlin director had apprised Kalandides about my project, however, so I came clean with him about my research agenda, and he made a special effort to address my historical interests. To this extent, Kalandides's tour was not a walk typical of those in mass tourism.

A month later I took a commercial Jewish walking tour, one of the many available to heritage tourists. Kalandides's walk served as a comparative referent. The commercial tour was one of nine walking tours run by Insider Tours.[42] The company's other trips were day excursions to Dresden and Potsdam and to the Sachsenhausen Concentration Camp. Titles of its various Berlin walking tours reflected the familiar mélange of history, fun and the fantastical: The Famous Insider walk, The Third Reich Berlin, Cold War Berlin, a Pub Crawl, Berlin Today, and Jewish Berlin.

The Jewish Berlin tour ran only on Mondays from April through October. My guide was Avigail Levy,[43] an Israeli-born journalist and playwright raised in Hong Kong. Levy, who had moved to Berlin in 2009, worked part-time as a guide to supplement her income. She was married to a Berliner who was not Jewish, but told me she attended one of the reform temples, at least on High Holidays. She looked to be in her mid-thirties and described herself as left wing.

The two tour leaders brought quite different training to their walks. Kalandides taught the foundational course in urban studies for NYU students on a semester abroad. An urban planner trained in cultural geography, he had completed his doctoral dissertation for the National Technical University of Athens on the various stories told by groups, including Jews, who historically identified with neighborhoods in Prenzlauer Berg. Levy, by contrast, was self-taught. Insider Tours did not require any course work or certification, but she had read widely and had the dramatist's ear for a good story well told. She had many anecdotes, and told them admirably. She also drew upon a loose-leaf book of historical photos. Most impressively, she had extraordinary command of names and dates. I could not remember a guide with her recall.

The few tourists that joined both walks were not a reliable sample, but their profile and comments about other tours confirmed Kugelmann's impression that gentiles dominated Berlin's heritage tourism. It was midterm exam week and the weather was brutally cold; only two students joined Kalandides's tour and neither was Jewish. The weather was no more inviting for Levy's walk and it attracted only one other student besides my wife and myself, a thirty-something American arts administrator visiting while on business in Vienna. She was also not Jewish. Levy observed, however, that English language Jewish walking tours were usually small (six to ten people would be a good group) and a mix of Jews and non-Jews.

Tours for Israelis were distinctly different. They were conducted in Hebrew and the groups were typically much larger. Many groups had to be divided into two. Many of the groups visited as school groups and came to Berlin with their own guides. They came primarily for Holocaust tourism, visiting camps and major Holocaust sites. Some undoubtedly learned much; I was a bit surprised, even chagrined, to hear curators and guides (in many cities) repeatedly speak dismissively of tourists who treated these trips as little more than photo ops.[44] To be fair, I suspect such criticisms could be levied against comparable school groups being force-fed heritage in many parts of the world. In any case, I witnessed a touring Israeli school group being herded before the Monument to the

Figure 17. The memorial to the 1943 German Jewish women's protest. The sculpture shows women protesting and the men behind bars. In the distance one can see remnants of the Old Synagogue wall. Photo by the author.

Ghetto Heroes in Warsaw (see Figure 23 in chapter 8) for a group photo replete with a large Israeli flag. In retrospect, it was easy to dismiss unruly children unhappy at being force-fed heritage, but I thought criticism of children might actually have been as much to the groups' patriotic, assertive self-representation and opposition to contentious Israeli politics.

In the end, the Kalandides's and Levy's tours differed surprisingly little. The guides, one trained as a historical geographer, the other as a journalist, brought different backgrounds to the walks, but the presence of the Holocaust dominated both tours. As I might have expected, Kalandides's presentation provided more of a historical frame. He began his tour in front of Marienkirche, Mary's Church on Karl Liebknecht Strasse near Central Berlin, with an account of Jewish settlement in Berlin from the thirteenth to eighteenth centuries. At the conclusion to his historical introduction, Kalandides walked around the corner to his first stop, a Holocaust memorial on the square at Rosenstrasse. This square was also an early stop for Insider Tours' walk. As a commercial enterprise, this tour had gathered at the confluence of mass transit stops at Hackescher Markt and walked the few blocks to the square. On the square, a small dramatic sculpted memorial erected in 1992 commemorated non-Jewish Berlin women who in 1943 protested the arrest and deportation of their Jewish or partially Jewish husbands and children whom the German state classified as Jewish. Behind the monument, the brick outline of the Old Synagogue, which was torn down in the Holocaust, could be seen. Kiosks nearby told the story of the protest, and the lobby of the adjacent hotel had a permanent photo exhibit of the area during the 1930s and 1940s. Although self-taught, Levy, like Kanidides, spoke knowledgably about recent scholarship that cast doubt on the extent of the husbands' plight (but not on the bravery of the wives).[45]

With a couple of interesting exceptions, the two tours made the same stops and the guides told much the same story. Both visited the Jewish cemetery on Grosse Hamburger Strasse, humorously translated for us as "Big Mac Street." As usual, the presence of the Holocaust experience was never far from the surface. The Nazis had destroyed the cemetery and a back wall contains a symbolic gravestone to Moses Mendelssohn. Mendelssohn is not actually buried there and the stone is easily mistaken for his grave.

Two themes framed the four or five other major sites on both tours. One focus, not surprisingly, was the Holocaust story of brutal Nazis and Jewish victims. A second major analytic thread, a Jewish success narrative, framed presentations of the Jewish prewar past and a Jewish future in Berlin. Guides may consider such perspectives appealing to Jewish visitors, but the guides' choice of these stops also reflects a traditional bias toward grand establishments, especially those with material remains. Guides pointed out mansions of German Jewish bankers and, in some cases, their wives who hosted famous salons at the end of eighteenth and early nineteenth centuries. Guides drew attention to the Jewish School built in 1862 that is adjacent to the cemetery, though it offered little visual attraction. Guides cited its revival as the Jewish High School as evidence of the renovation of Jewish life in contemporary Berlin.

More viscerally engaging than these sites was a monument on the plaza opposite to the entry to Humboldt University that commemorates the Nazi book burning on May 10, 1933. A small and poorly signed glass window in the pavement is easily missed, especially when covered by snow (as on my visits). Through the glass visitors see empty bookshelves symbolic of the thousands of books burned that day.[46]

Finally, both tours walked to view the spectacularly domed New Synagogue. Here the guides noted the building's importance as the institutional home of Berlin's JC, but never identified the particular traditional slice of the larger Jewish community this organization represents. The guides focused on the dramatic story of how the building was saved during Kristallnacht, then devastated by Allied bombs, and subsequently rebuilt. The site and the building's history served as a concluding symbol for the present and future reconstruction of the Berlin Jewish community.

Each tour had one additional stop that especially resonated with my personal interests. Early in her walk, Levy took her tour to three relatively small Holocaust sites that are grouped together on a courtyard on Rosenthaler Strasse, just off the Hackescher Markt. All were easy to see in an hour and were a welcome warm respite from the bitter cold on the day I visited. One, the Anne Frank Zentrium (a German partner institution to the Anne Frank House in Amsterdam), reprieved the well-known story of the young diarist in Amsterdam. The other two, however, reflected what Kugelmann described to me as the growing interest in German "helpers." Both opened after 2010 to memorialize Germans who worked to save Jews. The first, the museum of the brush maker Otto Weidt's Workshop for the Blind, relates the history of an institution that employed and then hid blind and deaf Jews up to and during the war. The second, the Silent Heroes Memorial Center commemorates Germans who protected Jews during the Nazi era. Even as, in Schütz's words, it remained "a challenge" to discuss collaboration at a German state institution like the Jewish Museum, these new museums offered psychic space for contemporary Germans in a memory landscape that relentlessly focuses on Nazi/German culpability in the Holocaust throughout Berlin.

In sum, dark sites and story of the Holocaust—each potentially problematic in their telling—dominated both tours, much as I found it embedded in the fabric of the memoryscape. The relatively limited discussion of pre-war Jewish heritage, as usual, privileged great men—bankers, rabbis, and intellectuals—and their wives and daughters who hosted salons and led charities. One heard little of the social history of work, labor, politics, and culture of ordinary Jews described in the New Jewish History. But one piece of Levy's tour, and a final stop on Kalandides's trip did make it clear to me that such history was there for the telling.

Walking around the corner from the three museums into other back courtyards off the Hackescher Markt, Levy entered the neighborhood where poor and working-class Jews lived in pre–World War I Berlin. She made no mention of Jewish political or cultural life, but spoke of how German Jews treated and mistreated their Polish brethren. Her emphasis was on charity and the tickets to the United States and UK that "saved them." She treated charity, like on the mainstream London tours, as beneficence. There was no discussion of the reception Polish Jews received abroad from German Jewish employers and benefactors, some of whom I had heard even raised money to send them back to Poland from London. Still, Levy brought a fuller range of Jews into a story enhanced with multiple Jewish voices.

The final stop on Kandidies's tour on Hausvogteiplatz did offer compelling hints of stories that would greatly benefit and enrich the typical Jewish heritage tour. On Hausvogteiplatz, a striking but simple modern memorial to the Berlin fashion industry and its many Jewish owners and workers reached tentatively to the sky. Three mirrors leaned toward one another, while small plaques below noted the once-robust fashion industry in the neighborhood. The monument was subtle, so much so that walking alone I might have missed it. Indeed, exiting from the U-Bahn station, Kalandides pointed to engravings on steps that I

Figure 18. Memorial Fashion
Centre Hausvogteiplatz.
Photo by Reinhard Berkbeck.
Courtesy of Reinhard
Bernbeck.

had also missed. Each bore the name and former address of the Jewish owners
of factories and workshops of the Berlin fashion industry. Kalandides spoke of
the Jewish workers in the industry. A website called Traces of War included this
labor history on its caption to a picture of the site, but the monument did not.
Plaques in German at the base of the mirrors spoke only in general terms of the
Jewish industry once there. The voices of the women who made the clothes,
working-class Eastern European Jews who lived and worked in Prenzlauer Berg
or the courtyards behind the Hackescher Markt, remained unheard.[47]

I spent a very enjoyable few hours with both Levy and Kalandides. Both were
lively, well-informed storytellers. The academic Kalandides was more the didact
and self-consciously provided a historical narrative. I do not think Kalandides's
insider knowledge of my interests fundamentally changed his itinerary or his
pitch. Ending with the Monument to the Fashion Industry, he did emphasize
that there was a history of working-class Jews to be heard in Berlin Jewish heritage tourism, though it might require taking the tour outside Central Berlin to
places like Prenzlauer Berg.[48]

Both guides focused on the Holocaust. Given Berlin's history and the
cityscape, that may be inevitable. But even so, the Holocaust was a greater focus

on Levy's walk. The two cemeteries and two synagogue sites she visited allowed for some historical perspective and a sense of the complexity of Jewish life, but the narration told little of the history of people with cultural and political commitments, of Jews who struggled among themselves as well as against oppressors.

It had become clear to me that the city of Berlin, with its signature Jewish Museum and a dozen other memorials and monuments, is itself a Holocaust museum. The thousands of stumbling stones and wartime fragments embed the Holocaust in the memoryscape of the place. Yet, Jewish Museum Berlin and the museum at the New Synagogue are memorable. The curators are articulate about curatorial possibilities and accomplishments, challenges and weaknesses. Both Kugelmann and Schütz are impressively thoughtful, progressive interlocutors with past and present political and curatorial dilemmas. Both interviewees spoke sympathetically of how curating a vast comprehensive exhibit in a state-run museum like the Jewish Museum provides challenges and constraints not faced by the independent and smaller museum.

However, the rise of the "helper" museums and some of the motives surrounding the state's commitment to reconciliation raised some disquieting concerns. They emphasize Germans who resisted Hitler, who were simply "caught up" in Nazi propaganda and military machines or "helped" Jews, and provide comfortable nationalist revisions to the Holocaust story.[49] Attention to the "good German" may complicate the view of the Nazi horrors as simply German, but it reproduces the tendency in Ukrainian and Polish tourism to shift responsibility or blame from local nationals to Nazis. Germany did not have the "other" to blame. But pressures to create something of a positive national narrative for German tourists is all too common in the politics of national heritage that encourages focus on a narrative about which a German tourist could feel good.[50]

―――――

I left Berlin feeling I had had a solid immersion in Holocaust tourism, but that Jewish heritage was better addressed elsewhere. I specifically missed hearing more of the stories of working-class Ostjuden and radical Jews, such as those suggested by *The Yellow Ticket* exhibit and the proposed exhibit on Jewish socialists in the German Social Democratic Party. In his study of "place identity" in Prenzlauer Berg, Kalandides had concluded that the reunified Germany stressed religious Jewish identity, blurring other alternative identities such as that of the communist or socialist Jew. He sees the GDR as having emphasized, probably even exaggerating, the place and role of the working class in the area. His insight led me to wonder if and how curators, guides, and museum professionals in other countries of the former Soviet bloc might incorporate the history of the working-class and socialist Jew into Jewish heritage tours. Opportunities to travel to three capital cities in Hungary, Serbia, and Romania—Budapest,

Belgrade, and Bucharest, respectively—provided opportunities to find out. These cities, though, were important to a second frame to my Jewish story, that of the Sephardim. In the midst of my travels, and much to my surprise, an online heritage research site's analysis of my DNA had identified nearly a quarter of my origins as Sephardic. So I headed off to Belgrade, Budapest, and Bucharest to hear the story of the Sephardim and renew my quest for the lost world of Jewish socialism.

CHAPTER 7

Budapest, Bucharest, and Belgrade

POSTWAR NATIONALISM AND SOCIALISM

Ashkenazi Jews were the dominant presence in the cities I visited in Ukraine, Poland, and Germany. I presumed visits to Hungary, Romania, and Serbia would counterbalance this lopsided picture with a look at how the Sephardim inflected the Jewish heritage story and the memoryscape. However, Chana Schütz's observation that support for exhibits on subjects such as the yellow ticket or German Socialist Party came from curators based in the former German Democratic Republic in East Berlin caused me to consider whether these cities' experience with state socialism might make them more receptive to stories of protean Jewish life and the role of Jewish radicals. How did the communist pasts of Budapest, Bucharest, and Belgrade shape the history of Jewish socialism? Did that past result in more sympathetic heritage accounts? Did their heritage sites and curators recuperate that past as part of struggles for justice? Or, conversely, did they incorporate Jewish communists into a story of Soviet totalitarianism, a past they worked to erase? It turned out that each place offered different answers. These cities exemplify the uneven development of Jewish heritage tourism in Eastern Europe, which depended on post-1991 political and economic conditions in each locale. More than other places, the Soviet-era legacy of socialism had some discernable impacts on Jewish heritage tourism in the present.

HISTORY

Until the mid-nineteenth century, the Jewish communities in Budapest, Bucharest, and Belgrade remained small.[1] In 1831, the mostly Sephardic Jewish population of Belgrade numbered 1,300; only 200 were Ashkenazi. A century later it would peak at approximately 12,000, constituting about 3 to 4 percent of the city's population. Bucharest's Jewish population was initially even smaller. In 1800, the city registered only 127 Jewish families. By 1860, the community had grown to 5,934, and by the end of the century it had burgeoned to 40,533, approximately 14.7 percent of the total population. In 1940, at the outset of World War II, the community counted 95,072 members. Of the three cities, Budapest had the most robust Jewish community. When Buda and Pest, on opposite sides of the Danube, merged to form modern Budapest in 1873, Jews in the city already numbered 45,000. By 1930, the Jewish population had grown to 200,000 and constituted about 5 percent of the city.[2]

The history of these three cities provides several themes for heritage tourism. To begin, while only Belgrade had a Sephardim majority, the population of all three was substantially more mixed than in the other cities I visited. In general terms, Ashkenazi Jews first settled the territory of all three cities in the Middle Ages and were joined in the late fifteenth and early sixteenth centuries by a larger number of Sephardic Jewish refugees from Spain and Portugal fleeing the wrath of the Inquisition. The Ottoman Turkish conquest of the area in the mid-sixteenth century inaugurated almost two centuries of relative stability for the Jews in these cities. Thus, when the Ottoman and Austrian Empires contested for control over the region across the sixteenth through eighteenth centuries, Jews tended to side with the Turks.

A second theme from the history is that regime change generally was not good for Jews in the past (or, necessarily, in the present). Of course, moments like the defeat of the Nazis were exceptions, and some regimes, such as that of Tito in Belgrade, were better for Jews than others. But on the whole, even Jewish support for "winners" did not insulate them from anti-Semitism. The story of the Jews in Buda is illustrative. Buda Jews supported the Turks in 1686, when Austria retook Buda. The Austrian army then ransacked the Jewish quarter and expelled the Jews. Jews were allowed to return three years later, but were expelled again in 1712, at which point they established Obuda, "Old Buda."

Belgrade and Bucharest Jews fared no better. Belgrade's location, at the confluence of the Sava and Danube rivers marked the boundary between the Austro-Hungarian and Ottoman empires and made it a flash point for conflict. In 1688, with the Austrians on their doorstep, Turkish infantry destroyed the Jewish quarter, capturing the city; the Austrian soldiers in turn killed Turks and Jews.[3] Finally, in power struggles between the Turks and Russians that regularly engulfed Bucharest, its Jews suffered. For example, in moments of disorder and upheaval during the Russo-Turkish Wars of 1768–1774 and 1806–1812, combatants and their masters found Jews easy targets to blame and Jews endured massacres and pillaging from soldiers.[4]

The geography of Jewish settlement in these cities constituted a third theme of the history and how it would be remembered in heritage tours. Like the Bałuty outside Łódź and Kazimierz outside Kraków, Obuda was a settlement in which local rulers allowed Jews to live outside the city proper. The distant location of Jewish settlement outside the commercial center of the city challenges contemporary walking tours' temporal and spatial constraints.

Jews in the Modernizing City

A hundred years prior to the Holocaust, Jews of all three cities engaged with cultural ideas of a new modern world, transforming these growing urban centers with new Jewish social and political institutions. Jewish encounter with the modern was distinctive in each locale, but the large size, relative wealth, and influence of Budapest's Jewish history merits first inspection.

Budapest. Expelled by the Hapsburg rulers from Buda and Pest in 1686, Jews settled in Obuda, an autonomous community in which Jews and Christians lived peacefully as neighbors.[5] By the early eighteenth century, Obuda had several substantial dye manufactures which became the base upon which a textile industry arose. By the mid-nineteenth century, Jews from Obuda had settled in Pest as well, establishing there the largest Jewish community in Hungary. They erected large synagogues and made Pest to the present the center of Jewish religious life in Hungary. Wealthy Jewish "burghers" such as Ferenc and Samuel Goldberger played a central and integral part in the Jewish community's growth and its citywide prominence. Goldberger & Sons, for instance, developed into one of the most significant enterprises in the entire Hungarian Empire. It developed new dye techniques, installed the first gas lamps, and employed over one hundred Jewish workers. Moreover, the paternalistic relationship between the Goldbergers replicated the pattern of benevolent paternalism seen elsewhere, including overseeing Jewish religious practice. According to one historian, "The boss [Goldberger] was a wholehearted supporter of the Jewish community of Obuda and especially its poorer members, *if* they strictly observed ritual law." Thus, "wholehearted support" did not extend to secular Jews.[6]

Goldberger's concern for Jewish spiritual observance reflected emerging religious and economic divisions within the Budapest Jewish community. Following the emancipation of the Jews in 1867, a General Jewish Congress that year established the legal equality of Jews within the state. Congress participants split dramatically over how to move forward as members of Budapest society. The Budapest Jewish community divided into three major groups. The largest group was made up of progressive Jews, the "Neologs." They were the adherents of the Jewish Enlightenment, the Haskalah, which reached Budapest earlier in the century and instituted changes in ritual and observance along German lines: the separate women's gallery was abolished, organs and a choir accompanied services, sermons once conducted in Yiddish were delivered in German or Hungarian, and so forth. As in Berlin, the Neologs tended to be urbane, bourgeois

Ashkenazi Jews of the city.[7] The remaining delegates, "Traditionalists," rejected all these changes, most walking out of the Congress in protest. Claiming the Torah and Bible as their only authorities, not the secular state, they wished to insulate the Jewish community from outside influence. A relatively smaller third group—"Status Quo Ante"—hoped to just keep Jewish life unchanged.[8]

Social and economic differences exacerbated religious schisms. The Budapest Jewish community was, again as in Berlin, a relatively cosmopolitan, affluent, well-educated minority. Jewish families owned or operated more than half of local businesses. Integrated (at least partially) into Hungarian society, these Jews were comfortable with a hybrid identity as Hungarian and Jewish. Originally from industrial cities in Germany, Austria, and Moravia, many were prominent Budapest tradesmen and professionals. Their success, however, contrasted with the experience of a second group of Budapest Jews who came from rural areas of the former Polish-Lithuanian Commonwealth and sought to preserve traditional village customs. Their urban, bourgeois brethren disparaged them as *polisi* (Polish) or dismissed them as "Sephardim of Pest," though they were actually Hasidim.[9]

Some of the institutions of Jewish communal life tried to bridge religious and social divisions, although Goldberg's requirement of "strict ritual practice" signifies how narrow that bridge was in practice. Still, a charitable network of burial societies, women's societies, and an orphanage, maternity hospital, soup kitchen, day-care center, and old-age home linked the Jewish community. A secular Jewish school opened in Obuda as early as 1784; in the next half century, a Jewish school, a second one for Girls, and a Teachers' College opened in Pest.

During the late nineteenth century, Jewish political and intellectual life also flourished, some of it outside the boundaries of "strict religious practice." Take the case of Jewish Scouts. At the end of the nineteenth century Neologs launched a strongly secular Jewish Scout program with the intent of instilling Zionism in Jewish youth. Pioneer skills would tame the "wilderness" and build a rural idyll on pristine land. A second example was Jewish socialism. According to Geza Komoroczy's coauthored 1995 history, *Jewish Budapest,* young Jewish intellectuals arrived in Budapest in the early twentieth century "influenced by the spirit of socialism. Although not all were observant, their main purpose was *not* to abandon Judaism." These young people struggled with the organized Jewish community, opposed the manufacturing and financial elite, and strove to advance modern ideas from Freud to socialism into the "mainstream of Hungarian intellectual life." In war-ravaged Hungary, some became Zionists, some social democrats, others communists.[10]

Bucharest. The century before World War II was hard on the small Bucharest Jewish community, especially in comparison with Budapest's community. The

Romanian ruler Alexandru Ioan Cuza, who took a leading role in the Revolutions of 1848 alongside "a number of Jewish intellectuals and craftsmen," granted native-born Jews suffrage in 1864. By 1866, however, illiberal forces ousted him and the German prince Charles von Hohenzollern, a strong-arm anti-Semite, ascended to the throne as Carol I of Romania. Anxious over the political instability, rioters targeted the Jews, destroyed the Choir Temple (it was rebuilt later that year) and plundered the Jewish quarter. The new regime instituted anti-Jewish policies. During the ensuing decades, statutes prohibited Jews from being lawyers, teachers, or traders of state-controlled products. New laws also decreed that only Christians could be citizens.[11]

International Jewish protest proved futile, as local dissidents faced persecution or expulsion. Following the 1866 riot, Sir Moses Montefiore traveled from England in an attempt to exert international pressure on Carol to stop the persecution. His effort was to no avail. Repeated interventions from Northern and Western European governments also fell on deaf ears; the Romanian government claimed this was an internal matter. In 1870, wealthy American Jews tried to intervene, too. The New York Jewish banking family, the Seligmans, convinced President Grant to appoint an American Sephardic Jew, Benjamin Franklin Peixotto, as the first American Consul to Romania. Peixotto failed to win Romanian Jews their independence but helped to create the Brotherhood of Zion, a forerunner of the B'nai B'rith, to help Jews adapt to modern Bucharest. In the end, he concluded that the best alternative for Bucharest Jews was mass emigration. In the late 1870s, large-scale immigration of Romanian Jews began to both the United States and Palestine. Data on emigration is sketchy, but one estimate of 1898 to 1904 puts the number at 70,000.[12]

However, many Bucharest Jews remained, and new immigrants kept arriving from small villages and rural settlements in search of work in the industrializing city. The Jewish population in the city swelled to over 40,000 by the turn of the century, a whopping increase of 673 percent in forty years. The Jewish community continued to struggle with state anti-Semitism, but was also riven by bitter internal conflicts: between immigrants, who were mostly Ashkenazi Jews, and the established Sephardim; between factions within the Ashkenazi community; and between the Orthodox and Reformers seeking to "modernize" religious practice. In the face of these squabbles, the Romanian government, disliking any hint of social disorder, dissolved the organized Ashkenazi Jewish Community in Bucharest in 1874.

During World War I, the postwar status of Bucharest Jews improved thanks to Jewish soldiers' service in defense of Romania. When the 1919 Treaty of Paris established Greater Romania, the state awarded Jews citizenship as a recognized minority. That same year, the Jewish community reorganized in Bucharest. Anti-Semitism remained strong, especially in reaction to Jewish Bolshevism.

Nonetheless, Bucharest's Jewish community flourished. It grew to about 70,000 (11% of the population) in 1930, and established more than three dozen synagogues, two cemeteries, and myriad educational and medical institutions.[13]

As in Budapest, during periods of stress, a rich array of Jewish voluntary societies and cultural activities in Bucharest bridged sectarian and ethnic differences. Yiddishkeit was a pillar of the emergent political culture. Some well-educated Jews learned Romanian with the development of modern Romanian literature at the end of the nineteenth century, but Yiddish remained the main language of the community. Yiddish was both the language of the Jewish street and home, and the expression of Jewish political culture. A society for research on the history of Romanian Jews organized in 1886 published Yiddish-language newspapers, journals, and scholarly books. The State Jewish Theatre in Bucharest, which dates to the late nineteenth century, remains the oldest operating Yiddish language theater in the world.[14]

Bucharest Jews also organized politically, and Zionism was a second pillar of the community's cultural politics. Peixotto, it will be recalled, had helped organize the Brotherhood of Zion in the 1870s to combat anti-Jewish policies and discrimination. In 1909, liberal Jews formed the Union of Native Jews (later, the Union of Romanian Jews) to the same end. Opponents from the Jewish right dismissed them as "assimilationists" and in 1931 organized a conservative Zionist alternative, The Jewish Party. In addition, almost a dozen journals and newspapers expressed pre-Zionist and Zionist principles.

Belgrade. Belgrade's Jewish community shared some characteristics with both Budapest and Bucharest. Belgrade's substantial Sephardic majority made its Jewish community unique, but like Bucharest, it was a small community constituting only 3.75 percent of the population. At the outset of World War II, between 10,000 and 12,000 Jews lived there, of which 80 percent were Ladino-speaking Sephardim. Like in Budapest, a relatively benign state in the late nineteenth and early twentieth centuries allowed Jews to flourish.

Belgrade's Jews thrived during the early nineteenth century under the ecumenical Prince Miloš. Their situation deteriorated, however, when in 1893 he relinquished his position to his son, Prince Mihailo. Under pressure from non-Jewish merchants, Mihailo restricted Jewish entry into professions and trades. The prohibition extended to tailoring, a staple occupation in the community. During the next fifty years, a series of anti-Jewish laws deprived Jews of basic citizenship rights. As with the Jews in the Bałuty outside Łódź, Serbian Jews were forced out of provincial villages into separate neighborhoods, typically outside the city or on its margins. In Belgrade, they settled in the lower part of the city, in the *Mahala* (Jewish quarter), the Dorcol neighborhood on the banks of the Danube.[15]

Jews gained full citizenship rights at the Congress of Berlin in 1887. For Belgrade's Jews the next forty years were a relative Golden Age, free of state restrictions and anti-Jewish policies. With their new freedom many Jews seized the opportunity to attend Belgrade's schools and universities. Some forsook Yiddish or Ladino for Serbian. A sizeable minority entered professions, finance or labored in the garment industry.

Belgrade's Jewish community was diverse and complicated, much like the communities in Budapest and Bucharest.[16] Jewish writers, intellectuals, and musicians created a rich cultural life of journals, bands, and orchestras. Sports clubs and work camps based on Zionist ideals attracted Jewish youth. Communism attracted many as well, and Belgrade communists fought against the anti-fascists in the Spanish Civil War. Jewish women created a Society of Jewish Women in 1875. And the Serbian-Jewish Singer Society formed in 1879. Renamed the Baruch Brothers Choir in 1950, it remains one of the oldest Jewish choirs in existence.[17] Yet the fraternal bonds forged in such clubs did not mask divisions. Separate neighborhoods for wealthier and poorer Jews, for instance, were visible cultural signifiers of different economic statuses. Wealthier Jews remained in the city and moved into its upper parts near the new Sephardic synagogue, Bet Yisrael (1907), while the largest number of Jews—and the poorest—lived in the Mahala.

The Holocaust and Postwar Era

Wartime. The Nazi army occupied all three cities during the war and decimated the Jewish communities, though Budapest's wartime and postwar history differed remarkably from that of Belgrade and Bucharest. Resenting its loss of territory in the World War I settlement, Hungary quickly aligned with Germany and Italy. As an ally, the Hungarian government deferred German occupation until March 1944. In the next fifty-six days, 437,000 Jews were deported from Hungary, about a quarter of them from Budapest. When the Red Army "liberated" the city on June 16, 1945, only about 80,000–90,000 of the 246,000 Jews residing there fifteen months earlier remained.[18]

The slaughter of Jews of the comparatively smaller Jewish communities of Belgrade and Bucharest began earlier in the war. In Belgrade, the destruction of the Jewish community was also more extensive, and by the spring of 1942 the Nazis had murdered almost the entire Jewish community. Bucharest's Jews also suffered throughout the war, but as in Budapest, a relatively substantial portion of the Jewish community survived. When Romania withdrew from the war in August 1944, Bucharest's prewar Jewish community of 102,018 in 1941 had shrunk to half its size. Most of the approximately 50,000 residents who remained were left destitute.[19]

A second feature of the war in these cities, the complicity of local groups in all three cities with the fascist invaders, especially complicates the presentation of the war experience in Jewish heritage tours that include non-Jewish local participants. Following the Nazi entry into Hungary, the Arrow Cross Party of Hungarian fascists who formed the new government killed between 10,000 and 15,000 Jews of the 100,000 that remained. Only the extraordinary intervention of Carl Lutz, the Swiss vice-consul, and Raoul Wallenberg, the secretary of the Swedish Ministry, prevented the slaughter of the rest; with the assistance of the Spanish and Portuguese legations, the ministry issued false international identity papers to protect them from deportation or murder. In Belgrade, when the Germans entered the city in April 1941, 20,000 ethnic German citizens of Belgrade proved to be willing collaborators. They assisted with the destruction of the Jewish community by identifying 10,000 to 12,000 Jews. And in Bucharest, many Romanian politicians also agreed to work with the advancing German army. King Carol was forced to abdicate in favor of the anti-Semitic Ion Antonéscu, and native fascists in the Iron Cross movement launched a three-day pogrom on January 21, 1941. Declaring a nationalist Legionnaire State, they instituted a five-month regime of ruthless anti-Semitic attacks on Jews and their institutions. Antonéscu finally succeeded in containing the Iron Cross's worse excesses; in 1943, under pressure from the Jewish underground, he partially succeeded in resisting German pressures to deport more Jews.[20]

The Postwar Era. In the aftermath of the war, Budapest and Bucharest were incorporated into the Soviet bloc, with its ideological commitment to communism; Belgrade (and Yugoslavia), under the leadership of the World War II partisan Josip Broz Tito, shared the commitment to communism but founded a Non-Aligned Movement that did not associate with either the Western capitalist or Eastern socialist bloc.

The distinct character and policies of communist leadership in each of the three cities differently shaped the experience of their Jewish communities from 1945 to the present. Jews who stayed or returned to Budapest after the war initially flourished in numbers and institutions, but languished under a renewed wave of anti-Semitism. Hungarians angry at the restrictions of communist rule on personal freedoms and national sovereignty revolted in the fall of 1956, but were ruthlessly repressed by the state. This repression resulted in a program of economic reforms under a new general secretary of the Party, János Kádár. Ruling from 1956 until his death in 1989, Kádár modulated restrictions and instituted what has been called "Goulash Communism" that brought a higher standard of living to Hungarians, including to the large "integrated" or acculturated Jewish community.

In contrast to Budapest, the Romanian dictator Nicolae Ceauçescu, who assumed power in 1965, ruled with an iron hand. Unlike Kádár, Ceauçescu humored himself with grandiose, self-indulgent economic and urban planning ventures (some that remain unfinished) and the country languished econom- ically behind its socialist neighbors. In the context of this repressive political environment, a second larger-than-life man, Romanian chief rabbi Moses Rosen, struck a devil's bargain with Ceauçescu on behalf of the Jewish community. In exchange for his political support for the corrupt and despotic regime, Rosen won some social and religious rights for Jews: in Bucharest, secular and religious Jewish artists and Yiddish writers and poets worked creatively in a relatively permissive environment. Rosen's "bargain" also included approval from the postwar Romanian government to continue to allow Jews to emigrate. Zionism was outlawed, but Ceauçescu refused to denounce Israel after the 1967 Six Day War and was the only country in the bloc not to break diplomatic relations. The World Jewish Congress tallied 428,312 Jews in Romania in 1947, but found fewer than 100,000 living there twenty years later. More than 200,000 had gone to Israel; the rest left for elsewhere, mostly the United States.[21]

As in Bucharest, a tiny Jewish Belgrade community numbering 2,271 survived the war. Many subsequently emigrated, but those who stayed lived in relative peace. Marshall Tito kept tight control over his citizens, but his well- publicized break from Moscow in 1948 translated into more political space for Jewish expression. Tito appreciated the support he had received from about 2,000 Jewish communist partisans who fought with him in the war against the Germans. The most prominent, Moša Pijade, was a painter and intellectual who went on to serve as one of Tito's four vice presidents. As a close confidant, Pijade facilitated immigration of some 3,000 Yugoslavian Jews to Israel after the war.[22] In Belgrade, the sole synagogue to survive the war reopened and Jewish com- munal life resumed. In keeping with the multiethnic socialist project, Tito's regime also recognized Judaism as a national identity. State authorities gave high priority to Jewish cultural institutions and exhibits in Zagreb and Belgrade. The Belgrade Jewish Community Center opened a kindergarten and youth club, housed its internationally famous choir, and in 1948, instituted a historical museum that included a research center on the history of Yugoslavian Jewry as both a national/ethnic and religious community.[23]

The Postcommunist Era. After the breakup of Yugoslavia in the decade follow- ing Tito's death in 1980, and with the fall of the Soviet Union, all three cities entered a post-Soviet, and more to the point, antisocialist and anticommunist era.[24] The rise of ultranationalist Slobodan Milošević to power in Serbia in 1989, and the brutal civil war that followed the breakup of Yugoslavia, led many Belgrade Jews to choose to emigrate, and in 2015, one synagogue and an active Jewish Community Center served the estimated 1,500 to 2,000 Jews who remained in the city.[25] Similarly, Jews continued to emigrate from Bucharest in the new mil- lennium. As the city's Jewish population shrunk to under 10,000, the international

Jewish Distribution Committee initiated modest efforts to rebuild Jewish identity in Romania with educational and cultural programs.[26] Ironically, though,
depressed economies may have had the greater impact on Jewish heritage tourism
in both Belgrade and Bucharest than repressive political climates. The political
chaos in Yugoslavia stripped the country of resources and friends and Belgrade's
tourist industry remained basic. Likewise, in Bucharest, a depressed economy
stunted the growth of tourism and Jewish heritage tourist sites did not receive the
infusion of funds that made possible new museums or exhibits.

By contrast, tourism boomed in Budapest and its Jews thrived as one of the
region's wealthiest, well-educated, and professionally accomplished Jewish communities. An estimated 80,000 Jews resided there in 2015 and they mounted a
robust communal life with twenty-six active synagogues, three Jewish schools,
kosher restaurants, a summer camp for children, a Jewish hospital, and a
biweekly newspaper. As home to the only active Jewish Theological Seminary
in the communist world, Budapest was also a hub of Eastern European Judaism. An estimated 80 percent of the Jews are Neologs (Reform and Conservative) and religious authorities do not deem the more secular younger generation
to be active in communal life.[27]

At the same time as the Budapest Jewish community continued to realize
considerable material success, the twenty-first-century election of Hungarian
president Victor Orbán instituted a full-throated reaction to communism,
accompanied by hyper-nationalism and state-sanctioned anti-Semitism. This
reaction included the monitoring of Jewish University students and efforts to
cleanse the Jewish heritage narrative of any suggestion of Hungarian culpability in the Holocaust.[28]

It remained to be seen how and if Budapest's right-wing political climate and
the strained economies of Belgrade and Bucharest would inform Jewish heritage
tourism. Would the heritage experience, as in the former East Berlin, reflect the
legacy of state socialism and include the history of Jewish socialism?

∼ INTERLUDE ∼

Of these three cities, Budapest had some relevance for my family story: the
image of Soviet tanks rolling through downtown Budapest in 1956 to suppress
the Hungarian Revolution led my parents to resign from the American Communist Party. They had moved only the year before into the split-level suburban
enclave in Cedar Grove, New Jersey, a town a couple of miles outside of Paterson. There they effectively became goulash communists, fighting for socialism
as suburban middle-class left-wing activists in the Peace and Freedom branch
of the local Democratic Party.

As far as I know none of my relatives had lived in or traveled to any of these
cities. Their migration paths took them northward. Chaia's brother Morris, for

example, traveled to the United States via Berlin and Paris. Other Walkowitz relatives traveled north from Łódź and sailed westward on steamers from North European ports. Max and other Margels migrating from the southern and eastern parts of Galicia might have passed through more southern parts of Europe. Max did tell me he had been in Vienna at some point after leaving Mostyska around 1902. He could have passed through Budapest, but such a visit never entered family lore. Still, while I had no ancestral link to these cities, I was anxious to hear any accounts of secular socialist Jews.

Recently I became cognizant of genealogical threads tying my family history to the region. The first came from the results of the aforementioned DNA test. Ancestry.com encouraged its members to test their DNA, promising to link participants with others who shared their genetic code. Offering a discounted home kit, I bought in. Within weeks I had my results, and as of November 2015 the company linked me with 1,333 "4th cousins or closer." Ancestry.com found, not surprisingly, that I was 95 percent "European Jewish." However, its report suggested familial origins over the past millennium from the Middle East and quite possible from the southern region of Europe: my DNA sample included 3 percent "Middle East" and 1 percent "Caucasus." Two years later, a refined analysis from an affiliated genealogical site, Family Tree DNA, raised my level of curiosity and expectations: it reported I was 16.9 percent Sephardic Jewish-North African, with another 5.4 percent Iberian.[29] Whatever the DNA test's reliability, it suggested the possibility that two of my great grandparents had come from the Iberian Peninsula or descended from ancestors who had lived there and settled in southern European cities such as these.

Communication with one of the many Margels researching our common ancestors led me to my kinship with a historical figure in Zagreb, another possible link to the region. Capital of an independent Croatia since 1991, Zagreb had earlier been an integral part of the former Yugoslavia whose capital was Belgrade. Pre-Holocaust Zagreb had a well-established Jewish community numbering 12,000. In 2007, the census counted only 232 Jews in the city, but the city had a major new institute to monitor and fight anti-Semitism: the Margelov Institut (Margel Institute). The Institute was named in memory of a prominent Zagreb citizen, educator and rabbi, the renowned Jewish scholar, Rabbi Dr. Moshe Margel. I have not been able to identify Moshe's relationship to Max, but the rabbi was born in Mostyska in 1875, only fifteen years before Grandpa Max. By the age of fifteen the precocious Moshe had published a poem in Hebrew in the Jewish magazine *Ha-Maggid* (The Narrator). With a PhD from the Rabbinical Theological Seminary in Vienna and Berlin, he became a leading authority on Hebrew literature. He founded a Hebrew language literary magazine in Kraków and made a "significant contribution" to *The Jewish Encyclopedia* published in New York. From 1903 until a couple of years before his death in 1939, he served as a rabbi in Croatia, the last of those years in Zagreb. At the outset of World War I, the Military Rabbinate in Zagreb appointed Margel the Royal Rabbi, and at the end of the war, the Austro-Hungarian emperor decorated him with the Golden Cross for Merit for, according to his official biography, "fearless engagement at the frontline on the river Soča and Liave."[30]

Both the DNA sample and the Margelov Institute offered the slim possibility that I possessed an ancestral connection to the large picture of Jewish heritage in these three cities. Still, they reminded me again of the diversity and reach of the Jewish diaspora, including of my own kin.

~

HERITAGE TOURISM

My tours of Jewish heritage sites in each of these cities followed well-trodden routes taken by many Jewish tourists on Grand Jewish Heritage Tours to cities where they themselves did not have ancestral homes. I had been invited to lecture in each city and took the opportunity to extend my stay to "do" Jewish heritage.

Budapest

In March 2013, my wife Judith and I both received invitations to speak later that month at the Central European University (CEU) in Budapest.[31] Before we arrived, I was advised that Budapest's large Jewish population and active Jewish heritage industry faced a hostile contemporary political environment. Eszter Gantner, a Hungarian Jew completing a dissertation comparing Jewish tourism in Berlin and Budapest, feeling the chilling effect of Hungarian xenophobia and nationalism on Jewish life, had moved her family to Berlin. Meeting for lunch in a Berlin café, she encouraged me to meet Katrina Pesci-Pollner, the curator of the Holocaust Memorial Center, during my Budapest visit. In response to my request for an interview, Pesci-Pollner wrote as to how she would be "pleased to meet" with me, but had not worked at the Center for a year and a half. Her explanation was disturbing. She wrote that in August 2011 she and "everyone in a leadership position (five people) were fired for political reasons. In the view of the current Hungarian government and the new director and president of the board of the Holocaust Memorial Foundation, there was NO Hungarian responsibility for the Holocaust in Hungary.... They needed collaborators who are willing to modify the narrative." She and her colleagues were not prepared to collaborate along those lines. She added that, ironically, the "exhibition has not changed yet, because the museum has no money for a new one" and encouraged me to speak with the new directors.[32] A day before departing for Budapest, Professor Gabriella Etmektsoglou, director of NYU-Berlin, lent credence to Pesci-Pollner's story. She had just returned from a conference where a Budapest representative ominously reported that the Student Union of Budapest had encouraged members to report on and take down the names of Jewish students in classes.[33] I wondered if I was going to Budapest to study representations of the anti-Semitic past or to relive it.

Walking Budapest. On the first morning of our visit, a generic Jewish walking tour provided a less fraught introduction to the city and its Jewish past. I had prebooked a Jewish Quarter tour scheduled to meet at the Dohany Street Synagogue, but the guide never appeared, perhaps to prepare for Passover, which began that evening. In any case, other tours met at the site and I simply asked another guide, Eszter Asher,[34] an animated, well-spoken Hungarian-Jewish woman in her mid-forties, if we could join her tour. The fact that my wife and I were in town to lecture at the CEU proved to be a good credential. According to Asher, her husband had recently lost his job due to the virulent anti-Semitism of the nationalist Hungarian government. She identified the CEU, a private university funded by the Budapest-born, Jewish-American philanthropist George Soros, as a beacon of intellectual freedom. We were welcome to join her tour.

The tour group consisted of twenty-six undergraduates from Northwestern University's Hillel. They were visiting on spring break for a noncredit week-long introduction to the Jewish history of Budapest. Most of them, though not all, were Jewish. Each had paid $600, plus airfare, for the trip. The fee included the tour, which might have cost as much as 6,500 forints (about $23). Cheaper daily alternatives were on offer from Free Budapest Tours (where travelers pay what they wish) and left from the tourist center.[35]

Asher structured her tour around the experience of the Holocaust, punctuated by a secondary narrative of contemporary anti-Semitism. The first half of the tour told the gripping, dramatic stories of Budapest's intense experience of the Holocaust and the heroic part played by Wallenberg, Lutz, and the Spanish diplomats in saving Jews. I had the sense that her focus on the Holocaust met the expectations of students. Asher's own perspective as a Jewish resident of Budapest, however, provided a fascinating critical edge. She expressed criticism of both Israel and the Hungarian state. She had already complained to me about the Hungarian state's treatment of her husband, but she added an edifying anecdote. While she was growing up, Hungary celebrated the date when the Russians victoriously entered the city as a Day of Liberation from the Nazis. However, in the postcommunist era, the conservative nationalist regime eliminated the holiday, denouncing it as the Day of Occupation by the Soviets.

When she came to the monument to the Swiss diplomat Carl Lutz, she voiced criticism of the Israeli memory industry as elitist. Yad Vashem in Israel anointed Lutz as a hero for saving Jews but had refused to acknowledge Rezso Kasztner. Negotiating with the Nazis, Kasztner had saved a trainload of 1,700 women and children rather than a prominent Jew. Yet of Kasztner's exploits, she complained, there was only silence both in Hungary and from Vad Vashem.[36] In Israel after the war, a prominent journalist accused Kasztner of being a Nazi collaborator for his negotiation. Kasztner sued for libel, and a court later absolved him of the accusation, but he became a virtual recluse for the remainder of his life. However, Asher's criticism echoed those of many public historians who complain that memory sites around the world celebrate and privilege the voices of the wealthy (often as "benefactors to the poor") and powerful, but ignore persons who make more subtle and challenging contributions. The narrative of the Holocaust and the history of anti-Semitism are unspeakable horrors that do not easily accommodate an assessment of class biases or recognition of subsets of Jewish heroes.[37]

Asher's presentation continued as a predominantly Holocaust tour. The ninety-minute walk was billed as the Jewish District Tour, but she spent more than half the time outside the Dohany Street Synagogue speaking of the Holocaust and postwar history of Jews in Budapest. She deviated from the focus on the Holocaust when we arrived at a monument to Theodore Herzl, the father of Zionism, who was born on Dohany Street. Other major monuments brought her narration back to the Holocaust: they included Raul Wallenberg Park with its Weeping Willow sculpture and memorial stone, and then across the street, the memorial sculpture for Carl Lutz. One brief sighting reminded us of the more mundane everyday life of the district now, and according to Asher, in the past, too: a busy sex shop operated across the street from the Lutz memorial.

The remaining part of the tour took us to a string of synagogues. The major exception was a brief visit to the Gozsdu Courtyard. The historic center of the Pest Jewish community, developers have revitalized the area with artisan shops, chic restaurants and cafés, and swinging nightclubs. But cold weather drove us to pass through the neighborhood and resume with synagogues. The group next walked to the former Rumbach Street Synagogue (1872), a Moorish-style synagogue that was now an art venue. We then moved on to the Kazinczy Street Synagogue, which now hosts the Chabad-Lubavitch movement. Finally, reflecting typical associations of the history of the Holocaust with support for Israel, the tour ended at the Israeli Cultural Institute.

The geographic limits of the tour did not allow us to visit one of the most well-known and moving local Holocaust memorials, the Shoes on the Danube Promenade. Hungarian Arrow Cross militia had ordered Jews to take off their shoes before being shot so their bodies would fall into the river and be carried off downstream. The memorial, a piece of conceptual art by the film director Can Togay and sculptor Gyula Pauer installed in 2005 along the river bank, consists of sculpted shoes that represent the shoes of the victims.

Museums. The Hungarian Jewish Museum, located inside the Dohany Synagogue, was another site requiring a separate visit. Temporary exhibits on Jewish art and culture reached back to the prewar era, but as in many Jewish museums, the permanent exhibit mostly consisted of old artifacts of Judaica. Possibly reflecting Director Szilvia Peremiczky's own professional expertise as a literary scholar, the thirty-six "highlights of the permanent exhibition" (with an excellent audio guide in English), were exclusively religious artifacts. The museum's website studiously avoided controversy and its main function as a memorial display led a Jewish curator to sarcastically deride the director to me as "a secret agent for the communist state."[38]

Under the supervision of the organized Jewish Community, the museum's prioritizing of religious life recapitulates interpretive limitations in much of Jewish heritage tourism. While claiming to represent the "Jewish Community," the organization restricts representation to the traditionalists who are only a minority of Budapest's Jewish population. A whole set of historical actors— secular Jews, Jewish politicians, Yiddish-cultural workers, the Hungarian Jewish working class that worked at the Goldbergers' factory, Jewish socialists, and communists—are dismissed as outside the Jewish legacy, as "assimilated." In 2013, I asked Director Peremiczky whether future exhibits on Jewish heritage would include discussions of experiences with socialism and Soviet communism, and if the museum's interpretation had changed since 1989. She candidly replied, "The current remit and operation of the Museum exclude consideration of the issues raised in these questions." She did hold out some hope for the future, acknowledging the museum has "been aware for a long time now of the need to renew the permanent exhibition" but lacked the funds to do so.[39] As of the summer of 2017, following the opening of the pathbreaking core exhibit in Warsaw's new Jewish museum, the Budapest Museum announced plans for the long-desired renovation of its exhibit.

The two major state museums, the Holocaust Memorial Center and the House of Terror, displayed the full state appropriation of the Holocaust as regime propaganda. The Memorial Center occupies a modern glass and steel building outside the Jewish Quarter, approximately a fifteen-minute walk from Dohany Street. Opened in 2004 under the auspices of the state, the site's choice helped preserve the synagogue to which it is attached. The museum is also not on walking tours as its site is too far from the main part of town for most foreign visitors. Most of its 30,000 annual visitors are Hungarian school children and Holocaust survivors. According to Pesci-Pollner, during the six-and-a-half years she served as the director of the Division of Educational and Cultural Programs, Hungarian adults tended to stay away as they regarded it as a testament to Jewish, not Hungarian, history.[40]

The permanent exhibit, titled *From Deprivation of Rights to Genocide*, divided the story of the Holocaust in Hungary into eight galleries. The exhibit used modern museological technologies to great effect in a moving and informative exhibit. It addressed the hot button issue of collaboration by balancing accounts of Arrow Cross attacks on Jews and the "thousands of Jews in Budapest [who] owed their lives to Gentiles." The end of the tour brings visitors to a modernized Synagogue, which celebrates 660 Hungarians named by Yad Vashem as "Righteous among the Nations." Gallery 7 might contain the only possible discordant note for local citizens: viewers are told "the increasingly influential right and extreme right" in wartime Hungary drowned out Gentile protests of anti-Semitism, so that by 1944–1945, "a majority of the [Hungarian] people looked on with indifference."[41] However, as Pesci-Pollner later pointed out to me, the Center's curators (an outside group of consultants) label antifascist intellectuals who resisted the right as "Christians," effectively sustaining the representation of Hungary as divided into Christians and Jews. In fact, many Budapest Jews, like the renowned composer Béla Bartók who fled to America in 1940, were atheists and part of an antifascist alliance that extended beyond religion.[42]

In contrast to the Holocaust Memorial Center, the House of Terror is a major tourist destination for both foreigners and Hungarians. It is located in a building that served as the headquarters of the Hungarian Arrow Cross Party and later as offices and prisons for the Soviet State Security. Presenting a seamless history of authoritarianism and terror in Budapest, the museum entwines the Holocaust and the Soviet eras, framing both stories around anticommunism and eliding any differences between the Nazis and Soviets.[43] There is no story of the Soviet "liberators" Asher mentioned; the museum renders the 1945 to 1989 era as marked only by Soviet totalitarianism. The exhibit also plays into young boys' fascination with weaponry: the centerpiece of the museum is a Soviet-era tank while much of the third floor is dedicated to rows of cabinets with military hardware. The Jewish past is folded into a Soviet-era nightmare, only now ended by the present Hungarian government. As the museum brochure reminds visitors, the House of Terror, the most popular tourist destination in the city, was built "with the support of Prime Minister Victor Orbán."[44]

Interviews with the Holocaust Center director Szaboles Szita, the Deputy Director Janos Botos, and then with Pesci-Pollner, highlighted the divisions among curators and officials over Jewish heritage. The interviews also provided context to my experience on the walking tour and at the museums. Their comments complicated the Budapest Jewish heritage story, but they also clarified why I had heard nothing of the world of Jewish socialism.

Szita, a well-published historian whose expertise is on the Holocaust, was appointed to direct the Center in 2011 by Prime Minister Orbán, the head of the right-wing conservative party Fidesz, which had come to power in 2010. Szita's 2001 book on the Holocaust had won first prize from the Education Department during Orbán's earlier term in office.[45] Szita's appointment coincided with rising anti-Semitism of the radically patriotic Christian Jobbik Party and Orbán's growing authoritarianism. One of Szita's first acts involved the firing of the five staff members, including Pesci-Pollner, and seemed to be a response to these political conditions. Newspaper reports on the firings drew heavily on Pesci-Pollner's account, warning, as one headlined, "They [nationalist politicians] want to rewrite history."[46] This institutional crisis was the context in which I (separately) interviewed Szita and Pesci-Pollner in March 2013.

In his interview, Szita spoke candidly about the challenges of working in a state institution. Indeed, Pesci-Pollner described Deputy Director Botos, who sat impassively in on the meeting, as a conservative Party functionary with a long history in the Hungarian right wing. According to Pesci-Pollner, Botos played a foundational role in the Association of Right-Wing Jews in the mid-1990s. (Szita was not Jewish.) Asked about constraints in the post-1989 Hungarian political environment of trying to represent the history of Jewish communists or Jewish partisans in prewar history, Szita acknowledged these as "hard questions," but felt he "has enough experience and patience to deal with these issues." Alternatively, he noted that working in a state institution had advantages: government funding met basic needs and alleviated some of the pressure to fundraise. On the question of state political pressure, Szita chose to emphasize the lack of local constraints, noting that the Center had not been defaced by Nazi or Arrow Cross graffiti. Any "cleansing" at the site he saw as a problem of modernist interventions, not the state. Previously the building had been shop-worn and used by Jews of modest means. Developers (presumably Jewish modernizers) had dressed up the synagogue as a "glossy" reconstructed space. Pointing with some pride to three new plaques at the entry that acknowledged the massacres of Jews in Hungary and offered a formal state apology for the role of Hungary in them, Szita presented State oversight as an antidote to distortions and censure, not a problem. In the end, when pressed further about content or changes, he acknowledged that all curatorial decisions had to be approved by the state.[47]

Pesci-Pollner's insights about her own Jewish identity helps explain the silences about a Jewish socialist and communist past in Budapest and the dim prospects for exhibiting it in the future. Echoing Joanna Olczak-Ronikier's memoir of the Mortkowicz family in Warsaw, Pesci-Pollner only learned of her own Jewish ancestry in the 1980s. At that time, her mother, aged and ill, confided that she and her husband had Jewish backgrounds. Her mother had been a Zionist in the mid-thirties, but under the influence of her more radical brother had rejected Judaism and Zionism, becoming an atheist and communist. Her father came from a more secular family. Both, however, ended up in Auschwitz during the war. Sent ostensibly as political prisoners—communists—they "arrived as Jews." Jewishness was an identity conferred on them by those who held power. Pesci-Pollner and her family now self-identified as Jewish. She had joined a synagogue and become a scholar of Jewish literature, feminism, and culture. Her brother's attitudes illuminated further the complex relationship between identity and history. He refused to visit the Holocaust Memorial

Center where she had worked for nearly seven years, insisting it had nothing to do with him.

Pesci-Pollner's mother's and brother's resistance to Jewish identity speaks both to the history of Budapest Jewish "assimilation" and how that conception continues to complicate questions of who is a Jew, who might be included in the story, and who is privileged to tell it. Before visiting Budapest, a well-regarded local historian advised me I would not hear of Jewish socialists as they are "all assimilated." Therefore, although I read accounts of such Jews in the scholarship, I arrived prepared to find them missing in tourist accounts of Jewish Budapest. But Pesci-Pollner's family story suggested alternative ways of thinking about the identity of the city's secular Jewish population. As acculturated or integrated Jews, these people expressed a hybrid form of partially conflicted Jewish identity. Their hybridized identity also helps explain the difference between data on the Jewish population of Budapest and the organized Jewish Community (JC) that oversees the Jewish Museum. In official city records Jews number between 80,000 and 90,000, but the JC estimates themselves as only between 10,000 and 12,000. After most Orthodox Jews left for Israel, JC members remaining overwhelmingly represented the Neolog Reform and Conservative Jews of an older generation.[48]

So where are the other Jews and how might their presence change the story? They are most evident in the streets, artisanal shops, "ruin pubs," and nightlife of Pest's Jewish Renaissance. Since 1999, the younger secular generation's hipster Judaism has also been yearly on display in the summer Jewish Festival, Budapest's version of Berlin's Days of Jewish Culture. With films, public prayer, cabarets, book fairs and concerts, and knishes, fun, fantasy, and food mix in a tasty, inebriating, and inventive Jewish cocktail.[49] Anecdotal evidence suggest that the festivals may even be beginning to include accounts of the long, diverse, and occasionally conflictual history of Budapest Jewish socialism, including the factory owner Goldberger and his workers.

But judging from my talks with Pesci-Pollner and an interesting recent study of Hungarian tourism, the dominant story of Budapest's Jewish history is unlikely to change in a fundamental way anytime soon. First, the Hungarian state and establishment Neolog old-timers in the JC are both invested in the present narrative. Second, development projects in Budapest like the renovation of the old Pest neighborhood, replicate many of the struggles seen in cities around the world, where local residents face developers who, in league with corrupt politicians, seek to commodify and prettify the past. Ironically, according to Pesci-Pollner, these developers are often Israeli. Thus, the development renaissance of Jewish Budapest finds Jews fighting Jews to create an "authentic" old Jewish neighborhood fit for tourist consumption. Third, according to an article by two of Budapest's professors of tourism studies, twenty years of marketing the postsocialist city have emphasized the "positive aspects of the city's history rather than more dissonant and dark elements."[50] Postcommunist branding by developers and state politicians erases any Hungarian complicity in the Holocaust, and likely precludes the history of Jewish socialist struggles for social justice as well.

In sum, Jewish heritage tourism in Budapest focused on the Holocaust while the government's branding of the past submerged that history into a narrative of relentless Soviet authoritarianism, as seen in the House of Terror. Daily accounts of state anti-Semitism at the time of my museum visit (and afterward) suggested the heavy hand of the Hungarian state, most evident in the House of Terror, constrained any changes to that interpretation in the state-run museums, including the Holocaust Center. The Day of Liberation, once important to Budapest Jews such as Asher, had been buried with Holocaust bodies. As important, Pesci-Pollner suggested that even the intervention by Jewish scholars was unlikely to change non-Jewish Hungarian attitudes about the Holocaust. The narrative at state institutions continued to advance the Soviet-era notion that all victims were Hungarians, leading non-Jews to see the Holocaust Memorial Center as a place that commemorates a past with no meaning for them. Most non-Jewish Hungarians went instead to the House of Terror, where the Holocaust was a backstory or was elided and where anticommunism was celebrated as the coin of the realm.

Bucharest and Belgrade

My expectation for Jewish heritage tourism in Bucharest and Belgrade was more modest than Budapest, yet they both turned out to be more promising for my particular quest. Both countries now have relatively small Jewish communities and lack human and financial resources. Ultimately, war, corruption, and weak economies in both countries prohibited development of their tourist industry and attracted relatively few Jewish tourists. In each city, my tourism consisted mostly of a walking tour that had to be privately arranged and a visit to an old Jewish museum whose infrastructure had not been upgraded. Yet these older establishments provided surprising hints of a world of Jewish socialism not totally lost.

Walking Bucharest. Three or four individuals offered Jewish heritage tours of Bucharest, but they were expensive and geared toward small groups. One agency, Jewish Tours, advertised a three-hour tour for two persons at $150; another, Unknown Bucharest, wanted €90 (about $110 in September 2013) for a small group of one to four people. I chose the latter, and my guide was Elena Funar,[51] the owner of the company. A colleague from the conference I was attending asked to join the tour and Funar met us both at our hotel. Since many sites were under repair and access was limited, Funar reduced our fee by one-quarter to €60 ($70) for the two-hour tour.

Funar was a former competitive chess player. Reading books published after 1989 piqued her interest in the Jewish history of Bucharest. What began as a hobby became a business. She did six to eight tours each month, mostly for tourists from ships docking on the Danube. Typically her customers were Americans, a few others might be Israeli. Her substantial fee likely compensated for her modest trade. Self-educated, she was well versed in Jewish history and in the sites we visited.

Funar provided a typical synagogue and Holocaust tour, but with the wonderful exception of a visit to the State Jewish Theatre. Jewish sites were especially limited because President Ceauçescu's grandiose and failed urban planning in the 1980s had destroyed whole blocks in the Jewish Quarter.[52] Funar focused on three synagogues. The first, the Great Polish Synagogue in the old Jewish Quarter, has since 1991 sheltered a small Museum of the Holocaust with an exhibit, *Memorial of Jewish Martyrs*, which consists of wall panels with pictures and documents. The second, the disused Holy Union Temple built by the Jewish Tailors' Guild in 1850, houses the History Museum of the Romanian Jews. The third was the Moorish-style Choral Temple built in 1864.

A visit to the Jewish State Theatre, known as the Baraseum Theater, dramatically broke the synagogue tour. The venue was closed at the time, but several of the actors came out in costume to greet assembled tourists with excerpts in Yiddish from the present production. The twenty-minute improvised performance, in song and verse, was one of the more memorable experiences in all my travels. Schmaltzy, romanticized and playful, in language and expressive gestures, it met my expectations of Yiddishkeit, albeit by a mixed troupe of Jewish and non-Jewish performers. Though the audience was largely unable to understand a word, pleasure radiated on their faces.

Geography and Funar's own interpretative framework limited her tour. It did not include sites that might have evoked daily life, labor, and politics in Jewish Bucharest. These imaginative limits may well have reflected her recent entry into the field. Limited tourist demand did not encourage her to expand her repertoire. She had not, for instance, included a visit to Filantropia, the Ashkenazi cemetery, because she had herself never been there and knew little about it. Otherwise, she was conscious of time and travel constraints: for instance, she apologized for not having taken us the Orthodox synagogue, explaining it was outside her route; it was in fact two blocks from the hotel where she had picked us up. Instead, the selection of sites reflected her conventional beliefs, shared in my experience by many guides, that most audiences want and need physical sights. Thus, in response to my questions about quotidian aspects of the Jewish past, Funar noted that she knew of many Jewish schools and community

Figure 19. The Jewish State Theater, Bucharest, September 2013. Photo by the author.

buildings, but they had been torn down so she did not discuss them. This need to have artifacts rather than to address spaces of memory resulted in a double erasure. Buildings and public sites of protest, celebration, and ritual were destroyed in the Holocaust and in the name of urban "development," but silences about them in heritage tourism constituted a second erasure of them from memory.

Walking Belgrade. If the visit to the Jewish State Theatre in Bucharest was a high point of my travels, my Jewish Belgrade Walking Tour was a low point. The director of Belgrade's Jewish museum highly recommended a woman she considered "the best such guide." Again, I had a companion for the walk: a Jewish curator and colleague from the Smithsonian Institution. The guide, Evica Babic,[53] seemed to be in her fifties. Stymied by a lack of work in education, she had become a guide. Her mother was the godmother to a Jewish child killed in the Holocaust and tales of the child had led her to Jewish tourism. She now slept on the child's birth pillow. Self-taught, she worked briefly with a tour company, but was now an independent state-certified guide listed on the city register. She attributed the paucity of Jewish heritage tours in town to the scarcity of tourists, and she promised us a special price on her next morning tour. She only asked that we not mention the bargain price to others. The cost of the three-hour walking tour for the two of us was the equivalent to $60. Joining the tour the next morning were two partially retired Jewish American couples from western

Massachusetts. The two couples were traveling together on a Jewish Heritage Tour of the Balkans. Belgrade was their first stop. Their itinerary included subsequent visits to Sarajevo, Dubrovnik, and Zagreb.[54]

I gained some background for the tour from formal meetings two days previously with a Belgrade historian, Professor Milan Rostovic, and a research scholar on Jewish history, Olga Manoljlovic Pindar. Unfortunately, they raised my expectations and probably spoiled me for my subsequent walking tour. Rostovic filled my head with facts and figures as well as interpretative trends in Jewish history that I would find woefully lacking in the tour. For her part, Pindar insightfully offered a nuanced history of postwar Serbia, emphasizing a problematic theme I had seen at the House of Terror in Budapest. Post-1989 Serbian/ Yugoslavian history, she argued, lumped Stalinism with the history of the Nazis. Her second point resonated with my interests in the history of socialism: Pindar argued that Serbian post-1990 anticommunism involved a complete rejection and denial of the history of self-management and nonalignment policies of Tito and any "distinctiveness of Socialist Yugoslavia."[55]

Rostovic and Pindar both also pointed out that Belgrade had some advantages as a Jewish heritage site. There was a secular history of Belgrade Jewry in the last hundred years, and unlike in Bucharest, the Jewish working-class settlement of Dorcal had not been destroyed. Jews were no longer much of a presence in the city, but visible reminders of Jewish daily life in the once working-class community remained. Unfortunately, the guide would the next day confirm Pindar's analysis of contemporary Serbian political amnesia and the role of anticommunism in it.

Babic's personal political views set the tone for the tour. Perhaps reading her audience as Americans who would be sympathetic to her perspective, she preceded the walk by explaining she came from a "strongly" anticommunist family that had been oppressed by the communist authorities. She warned us she was only offering her opinion, but added we would agree with her when we heard what she had to say. Communism had destroyed her families' and her own life and ruined Serbia. She then proceeded to deliver a nationalist history of the postwar era. The years between 1945 and 1990 were a seamless disaster without any redeeming qualities. She defended Milošević, who had led Serbia into ethnic wars during the past decades, as wrongly criticized; his wife was the problem. Even though Babic did not feel Jews were treated differently from Serbians, she proceeded to treat their histories as distinct. The other Americans on the tour took her interventions as an opportunity to learn about contemporary Serbia; I felt they distracted from attention to Jewish heritage.

Babic's anecdotes and data on Jewish Belgrade often conflicted with the account Professor Rostovic had provided, but unlike typical tours elsewhere, did not focus on synagogues. The tour began outside Dorcal at the handsome neoclassical Synagogue Sukat Shalom, the only active synagogue in Belgrade. Erected in 1925 for the Ashkenazi community, it now functioned as an Orthodox synagogue and provided community activities for its members. We visited during the Saturday morning service and the men on the tour sat in briefly before the group moved on to Dorcal for the rest of the walk.

Sadly, as in Bucharest the guide ignored the site of an important second synagogue with a remarkable sedimented history because it did not have a physical remain: the Fresco Museum built on the site of the former Synagogue Bet Israel. The text accompanying the 1997 Belgrade exhibit, *Jews of Dorcal: The Story of Our Neighbors Who Are No More*, demonstrated the significance of such sites for a social and cultural history of prewar daily life. The narrative contrasts the Old Synagogue we had visited as "the sign of traditionalism" with Bet Israel as the synagogue of "the more emancipated Jews with civil habits, European spirit, new professions and vocations." The choir of the Serb-Jewish Singing Society participated in its services, and members of the government and the Royal family visited it.[56]

Babic's tour did distinguish itself with visits to many sites at which visitors could imagine past daily life, and notably of ordinary working-class Jews. Walking downhill toward the river, we passed the Jewish communal building, home to the Jewish Historical Museum. She told us nothing of its history, ignored the museum and did not relate the unique and distinguished history of the Jewish Singing Society based there. However, proceeding to Jevrejska Ulica (Jewish Street), the Dorcal thoroughfare since the sixteenth century, she uncovered signs of benevolence, religiosity, and women's civic role in the old Jewish working-class neighborhood. The façade on the building of the Jewish Women's Society for the care of the aged, quoted Psalm 71: "Do not forsake me in my old age." Another building, once a lawyer's house, had a Star of David on its face. The walk concluded at a Holocaust memorial sculpture located near the river at the foot of the Dorcol area. The guide told the group that the large Sephardic and smaller Ashkenazi cemeteries were a taxi ride away if they were inclined to continue the trip.

In the end, Babic's narrative offered little insight on the spaces traversed, yet the walk had demonstrated that it was possible to see remnants of a complex and vibrant Jewish past in Belgrade. There were no visible signs of a world of Jewish socialism, but the tour of Dorcal proved to be a prelude to a visit to Belgrade's Jewish Museum, which brought that world to life.

Jewish Museums and the Socialist Past in Bucharest and Belgrade

The impoverished Serbian and Romanian states lacked funds to build new museums akin to those that have been opening across postsocialist Eastern and Central Europe since the 1990s. Instead, Belgrade and Bucharest museums retained exhibits from the state socialist era. In effect, economic constraints left unusually rich exhibits intact. Spared the political erasures of the post-1990 era, two museums in these cities retained signs of the history of secular Jewish culture and Jewish socialism. With my travels nearing their end, I found the world of Jewish socialism preserved in the most unlikely of places: in older, unmodernized Jewish museums of Bucharest and Belgrade.

Bucharest. The History Museum of the Romanian Jews opened in 1978. It is a small museum, consisting of a large ground floor room, a small backroom dedicated to the Holocaust and a first-floor balcony. It was renamed in 1997 after Rabbi Rosen, the city's longtime chief rabbi who had "bargained" with the totalitarian Ceauçescu. The exhibit was updated after 2000 to include a few additional documents on the Holocaust, but according to the long-time guide there, the content has not changed.[57]

A beautifully illustrated museum guide complements the collection. I was struck by its repeated reference to the collection as a history of Jews as an ethnic and not religious identity. According to the guide, the museum stands as the "sole museum of an ethnic minority" in Romania. It seeks to counter the "code of silence" over "Jews and ethnic minorities" imposed by the Communist Party and totalitarian Ceauçescu regime. The exhibit highlights six centuries in the "cultural and communal life of the Jews" in Romania and Bucharest. It depicts lives of the rich and powerful, including the financer Bercovitz and bankers Hillel and Leon Manoah, but also displays the banners and seals of the Jewish guilds to depict Jewish "diversity." "Not all Romanian Jews belonged to fashionable society," the text reminds viewers. "The community was actually quite polarized in terms of wealth and standing." Diversity extended to political life. Although the museum director insisted "we do not discuss politics in the museum," the exhibit explicitly does so. Drawing on photographs and documents, one panel displays the revolutionary manifestos of Jews who fought in the 1848 Revolution; another gives "particular emphasis" to the Jewish Enlightenment in the last half of the nineteenth century; a third depicts Romanian Jewry's involvement with Zionism in the early twentieth century; a fourth details Romanian Jewish engagement in the Romanian Unification War, 1916–1918. Judaica and the Holocaust receive their due, but so, too, do Hungarian Jewish contributions to science and culture, including literature, painting, fine arts, music, journalism, and theater.[58] This small museum managed in very little space to integrate the diversity and richness of Jewish identity as religious and secular, rich and poor, entrepreneurial and laboring.

Belgrade. As in Bucharest, the absence of a postsocialist modernizing project left visible socialist perspectives of the prewar and wartime eras in Belgrade's Jewish museum. Occupying the second floor of the Federation of Jewish

Communities of Serbia's six-story Communal Center, the museum had opened in May 1960. When I visited in the fall of 2012, the permanent exhibit dated from 1969. A new senior curator, Vojislavea Radovanovic, appointed by Federation in 2010, felt a new guide needed to make sense of an exhibit tracing the history of Jews that predated the dissolution of Yugoslavia. Drawing on her training in Ethnography Studies at the University of Belgrade, in 2010, well into the postsocialist era, Radovanovic prepared the comprehensive and ecumenical thirty-seven-page illustrated guide to the exhibit that honored the Jewish socialist past and both religious and ethnic identities.[59] The guide was new; the exhibit was only "subtly" redesigned. It had "not been possible to develop a new, differently designed museum exhibition," the guidebook explains, "due to the grave political and economic difficulty which, beginning in 1992, overwhelmed our country, Serbia." But thanks to a complex and subtly designed concept, it insisted that the aged permanent exhibition "does not bother anyone."

The exhibit, winding around one smallish room, packs a lot of history into a restricted space. An annotated map introduces visitors to centuries of Jewish settlement throughout the area of the former Yugoslavia, but Belgrade's large community gets special attention. A substantial early section of religious Judaica receives pride of place. The rest of the exhibit, however, organized chronologically, takes visitors through constructed corridors with photographs, documents, and official records of communal and associational life. Panels depict daily life in the Jewish quarters, on the streets, cemeteries, and synagogues where they lived, prayed, and were interred. The presentation consists of traditional "history on a wall," but is refreshingly attentive to daily life among prewar Yugoslavian Jews. Some photographs document the popular Jewish youth society, Hashomer Hatzair, and work camps at which Jewish youth prepared for life in Israel. Other photos of young men and women illustrate the history of vernacular Jewish culture in bands, concerts, and sports groups, and the social organization of communal life.

Although the exhibit fully incorporates a secular and socialist Jewish past into its history, its uncritical documenting of the romance of socialist Jewish proletarianism risks adding to what some local critics see as a growing "Yugo-nostalgia" and "Titonostalgia" in local tourism.[60] Dating from the Tito era, the museum exhibit's documentation of Jewish partisans and Tito's relatively cordial relations with Jews lends itself to such charges. But two images from the 1960s in the guidebook illustrate how the exhibit works in complex ways with Tito's legacy and a socialist past silenced elsewhere. One is a self-portrait by Moša Pijade, the painter and politician who led the partisans and became a Vicepresident under Tito; the other is a wooden sculpture by Slavko Bril entitled "Worker," a strong heroic image of masculine proletarianism in the tradition of Social Realism. Moving on, the museum also features a collection of

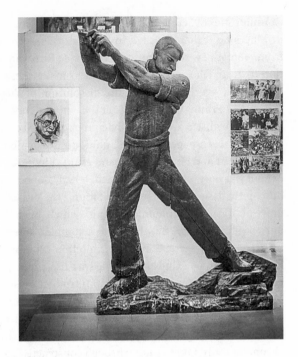

Figure 20. *Halutz*
(Worker), by Slavko Bril.
Belgrade Jewish Museum
Guide. Photo by Veselin
Milunović. Courtesy of
Jewish Historical Museum,
Belgrade.

photographs "dedicated to Yugoslav Jews, communists, and participants in the Spanish Civil War, 1936–1939," three identities all presented as a seamless whole. Further on, the exhibit describes "about 4,500" Jewish communists who joined the partisans during World War II. These positive representations run counter to the abiding anticommunist narrative that dominates most postsocialist Jewish museums. The guide praises the "basically humane, noble and protective idea of communism [which] attracted an increasing number of people, among them a relatively high number of Yugoslav Jews."[61]

––––––

The old Jewish museums of Bucharest and Belgrade managed to highlight the history of Jewish life muted or absent elsewhere. Much as the Holocaust erased bodies and buildings, other Jewish museums in the past two decades accomplished a second erasure of vernacular Jewish culture and the Jewish socialist past. What the future holds for the counternarratives in Bucharest and Belgrade remains unclear. The curator of the Belgrade museum, for example, told me they were looking to construct a modern museum within a new memorial center to be built on the site of the former concentration camp across the Danube in New Belgrade. Funding remained a problem. She believed the museum would continue to honor the general concept I had seen already, yet a site at the former concentration camp would cast a long Holocaust shadow over the exhibit. Curators also would have to worry about the triple pressures of marketing, branding, and postsocialist politics. In the breakup of Yugoslavia, the region had suffered through a troubling history of ethnic cleansing; time will tell if Belgrade's Jewish heritage tourism will manage to avoid historical cleansing.[62]

CHAPTER 8

Kraków and Warsaw

TROUBLING PARADIGMS

Kraków and Warsaw were historically among the most important Jewish settlements and today boost robust Jewish heritage tourist industries. Warsaw had by far the largest Jewish population of any city in Europe from the mid-nineteenth century until World War II. The 375,000 Jews living in the city at the beginning of the war constituted about one-third of the city's population, and their numbers swelled to half a million after the Nazis herded Jews from surrounding towns into the already crowded ghetto. Kraków's Jewish population was smaller, but significant. In 1939, the city's 60,000–65,000 Jews made up a quarter of that city's population.[1]

Almost four decades ago, in 1981, en route to a conference on industrial architecture and planning in Łódź, I visited Warsaw, Kraków, and the Auschwitz-Birkenau concentration and extermination camp created by the Germans. During the intervening years, Kraków, Warsaw, Gdansk, and Wrocław have emerged as Poland's most popular tourist cities. Kraków, followed by Warsaw, became a major destination for Polish and international Jewish heritage tourism.[2] According to Kraków officials, a record 10 million people visited the city in 2015, one-quarter of them from outside the country. Radio Poland reports the largest number, over 400,000 (15.76%), from Britain. In 2016, Auschwitz recorded 1.7 million visitors; in 2017 the number is expected to approach 2 million. The most visited tourist site in Kraków was the Main Market Square, one of UNESCO's first World Heritage sites (1978), followed closely by Wawel Castle and the Jewish Kazimierz District.[3]

Kraków's Jewish tourism is probably better known, but Warsaw's emergence as a cosmopolitan capital with a new world-class Jewish museum—POLIN Museum of the History of Polish Jews (*Polin* [Hebrew] and *poyln* [Yiddish] mean Poland)—is the future. According to MasterCard records, Warsaw's 1.38 million visitors ranked it eighth among the fastest growing cities in Europe in 2015 for international overnight stays. My decision to conclude with Warsaw is mostly tied to the promise for POLIN. I returned to Warsaw in March 2013, and even though the museum had not yet opened, I felt confident it would provide a fresh paradigm for the presentation of Jewish history, a model that would incorporate the history of Yiddishkeit, civic culture and Jewish socialism. My former colleague (and to be transparent, friend) Barbara Kirshenblatt-Gimblett, a folklorist by training and an authority on Eastern European Jewish life and Yiddishkeit, was chief curator for the core exhibit. The museum opened on September 13, 2013, and I returned in 2014 to view the core exhibit that debuted on October 28, 2014. Subsequently, the museum quickly became the most popular Jewish site in the city, though there was little competition. POLIN welcomed about 600,000 visitors in 2016, and received the 2016 European Museum of the Year Award and the 2016 European Museum Academy Prize, the first time any museum in Poland received awards of this order.[4]

World War II had dramatically different impacts on the urban fabric of the two cities and shaped the content and tone of its heritage tourism. Air raids and battles left Warsaw in ruins. The Nazis leveled the ghetto and eviscerated any remnants of Jewish life; damage from the 1944 Warsaw Uprising destroyed much of what remained. The communist government rebuilt the New City (Nowe Miasto) and the historic district, the Old Town (Stare Miasto), in the 1950s as Poland's first major urban development project, and Warsaw's emergence as a major Eastern European cosmopolitan capital occurred in the new millennium. Development centered on the "smartened" Old City, renovated with brightly painted buildings, new cobblestone, and a revived café life. Redevelopment extended to a revived downtown commercial district, and in an emerging museum culture. However, development of the Jewish quarter, a prewar tenement district to the west of the Old Town, languished. A few buildings from the prewar era and the marked footprint of the ghetto wall remained as relatively silent sentinels of a vanished past. Recently the urban revival of the last two decades has extended to Warsaw's Jewish quarter. POLIN Museum of the History of Polish Jews, located in the Muranów, the former Jewish neighborhood in the northern part of the city, represents a cornerstone of this cosmopolitan revival.

By contrast, World War II combatants left Kraków's urban fabric relatively untouched and its Jewish heritage tourism took a less somber tone. Allied and Nazi bombers respected Kraków's historic medieval architecture and left it relatively intact. Infantry and tanks also bypassed Kraków. The existence of the historic cityscape also created distinct content for Jewish heritage tourism in Kraków. Tourism took off in Kraków, in both the old historic market center and the Jewish district of Kazimierz. In contrast to the solemnity surrounding the Warsaw ghetto memorials and wall fragments, the commercialized folksiness of the postsocialist economic development of Kazimierz has struck visitors and scholars as a Disneyfied history. In 2002, journalist and travel scholar Ruth Ellen Gruber acknowledged Kazimierz's revival could be seen as a "debased folklore" and an "exploitative kitsch." But she also found evidence of "thoughtful reevaluations of [Jewish] history, culture and identity" that challenged such disparaging assessments.[5] A decade later, in her carefully nuanced 2013 ethnographic book on Kazimierz, Erica Lehrer defended the new voices and new spaces as providing a "surprising vibrancy" in the Jewish life in the city.[6]

Lehrer's 2013 study represents a landmark contribution to the New Jewish History, a corpus that led me to revisit these cities yet again. I came to realize a new generation of historians, ethnographers, and museum curators such as Lehrer, Meng, Ury, Wodziński, and Kirshenblatt-Gimblett, among others, were producing a social history on which a renovated heritage tourism in Eastern Europe might be established.[7] This new writing challenged conventions of "the Shoah business," of Jewish heritage as a unitary bleak narrative of anti-Semitism, persecution, and hatred. Whether "vibrant" or "kitsch," I wondered if and how such new research had been incorporated into heritage tourism. Returning to Warsaw and Kraków between 2015 and 2017, I arrived in search of signs of secular, activist, quotidian, socialist, and gendered history in a revitalized Jewish heritage narrative.

∾ INTERLUDE ∾

Given the size and prominence of the Jewish populations of prewar Kraków and Warsaw, it is likely that some members of my extended families lived in these cities at one time or another. I have found no record of Kraków relatives, but as the major western Galician city, it lays on a direct wagon and train line that stretches all the way to Lviv. Many of the towns and villages along this route had Margels in residence: traveling west, for example, Margels could be found in substantial numbers in Horodok, Mostyska (where Grandpa Max was born), and Łańcut, the birthplace of Max's mother Yettie. Continuing west from Łańcut about sixty miles one passed Tarnów, the town from which ancestors of my Grandmother Marian Tarnofsky's family may have come. It is easy to imagine that some relative, whether a trader to market or an aunt or uncle, arrived in Kraków at some point.

Records of family members exist in Warsaw, though the evidence is fragmentary and surprising. My maternal great-grandparents, Morris Tarnofsky and Gitla Freibaum, lived in Końskie, seventy-six miles south of Warsaw. Morris, like several generations of Tarnofsky men before him, trained and worked in Końskie as a doctor. The end of the century, however, found the family in Warsaw, where Marian was born on March 20, 1898. When her father died shortly thereafter, Marian, her siblings, and her widowed mother left Warsaw for New York. My wife Judith's family also had Warsaw roots, and provided a surprise link to my own genealogy: we were related.

Judith's maternal grandfather, Israel Geber, was born in Warsaw in 1884. The son of a builder, he attended the gymnasium, a secondary school that prepared children for higher education, and became a skilled dye master. When he immigrated to America in 1908, he became a wealthy dye house manufacturer in Rutherford, New Jersey. But Geber was an unusual name according to the genealogist at the Jewish Historical Institute in Warsaw, especially in comparison to Walkowitz, which I had learned "is like Smith" in the United States. Imagine my surprise when the genealogist found a Laja Geber married to Henoch Freibaum in 1860. Laja's place of birth in 1841 is not known, but the genealogist projected her to be Gitla Freibaum's mother, and my great-great-grandmother. In the context of Jewish insular community life, migration patterns, traditions of arranged marriage, including among cousins, and the desire to marry within the faith, the connection is not terribly surprising, but finding evidence of it was startling. A subsequent DNA test confirmed my wife as my fifth or distant cousin. Ironically, looking for socialist roots, I had uncovered a Warsaw link to a well-established, bourgeois family.

With a heightened appreciation of a more diverse ancestry, I remained focused on my quest for the Jewish socialist past. In truth, modest evidence of one-time family presence in these cities played a limited role in shaping my expectations for Jewish heritage tourism in Warsaw. Rather, the marked presence of the Polish Bund in the Warsaw 1905 Revolution made that city a particularly important site for Jewish socialism. But I begin in Kraków, a city renowned for its rich Polish-Jewish culture and robust contemporary Jewish tourism.

～

Kraków

History

Jews have a long history of settlement in Kraków. Most of them arrived from German lands in the early fourteenth century. In 1334, King Casimir III the Great granted them legal rights, including freedom of religion and the right to engage in trade and moneylending. Construction of what remains the only medieval synagogue in Poland, the Old Synagogue, began in 1407. (Two other former medieval synagogues in Silesia also exist, but the buildings have been reconsecrated as churches.) By the end of the fifteenth century, the Jewish community had established many of the basic institutions for communal life: a bathhouse, marketplace, cemetery, and Poland's first yeshiva. In 1485, however, Christian merchants forced an agreement eliminating Jews from commercial competition and limiting them to moneylending. A decade later, a fire racked the city and destroyed the Jewish quarter. Jews were relocated from Kraków to Kazimierz, a new royal town across the Vistula River on the outskirts of Kraków established by Casimir and named after him. From then on, Jewish settlement in Kraków was mostly concentrated in Kazimierz. By the end of the sixteenth century, the community, swelled by immigrants from Bohemia-Moravia, numbered over 2,000.[8]

Protected by the Polish king, Jewish culture flourished in Kraków from the mid-sixteenth to mid-seventeenth centuries. Six synagogues served Jewish congregants and the city became a center for Jewish learning. These good times ended, however, with the Swedish invasion and occupation of 1655–1657. Subsequent attacks on Jews revived accusations of blood libels—accusations that Jews murdered Christian children to use their blood for rituals. Plague in 1677 decimated the community, killing 1,000 of Kazimierz's Jews and compelling those remaining to flee. The community reestablished itself shortly thereafter, but as elsewhere in the Poland-Lithuania Commonwealth, Kraków's Jewish community was marked by great inequality and poverty in the seventeenth and eighteenth centuries. There was a small merchant class, but the vast majority remained poor.[9]

For much of the nineteenth century, Kraków was part of the Hapsburg Empire. After the third of the partitions of the Poland-Lithuanian Commonwealth at the end of the eighteenth century, Austria annexed Kraków in 1795. Then, after another Polish-Austrian War in 1809, Kraków was briefly annexed to the Duchy of Warsaw and ruled by Napoleon. With Napoleon's defeat in 1815, the Congress of Vienna created the Kingdom of Poland and the independent Free Republic of Kraków. At this time, Warsaw became the capital of the Congress of Poland under the dominion of the Russian czar. (The history of Jews in Warsaw under the Russian Empire is continued below.)[10] After a failed uprising in 1846, Kraków was absorbed into Galicia, as part of the Hapsburg Empire. In the nineteenth century, its Jewish community grew rapidly, sharing many of the social, political, and religious fissures that marked Jewish life elsewhere.

Kazimierz was incorporated into Kraków in 1802, and a spatial as well as a social and cultural divide characterized the Jews in the enlarged city. Although restrictions on Jewish life and labor continued, Jews won the right to settle in Kraków outside of Kazimierz, and many prosperous Jews took advantage of the right. Liberal Polish nationalism and the Jewish Enlightenment played an increasingly influential role among the Jewish elite. The elite, self-identified as "enlightened progressives," established the Tempel Synagogue in 1862. Meanwhile, the poor and growing Hasidic community and traditionalists lived in Kazimierz. Political power, however, adhered to those with economic, cultural, and social capital: after Jewish emancipation in 1867, three groups competed to control the Jewish community council, the Kahal, but only Polish speaking Jewish elite served on the City Council.[11]

By the end of the nineteenth century, Jews had established a vibrant, robust, and diverse cultural and political life in Kraków, now including Kazimierz. A secular public library opened in 1876, and the community sustained a network of Jewish schools with lessons in German, Polish, and Hebrew. Kraków did not have a Yiddish daily newspaper, even though many of the poor spoke Yiddish. But as a commercial city of craftsmen, shopkeepers, and professionals, rather than an industrial city like Łódź, Kraków attracted relatively fewer poor Yiddish-speaking Jews from the countryside. According to the 1931 census, only 41.4 percent of Kraków Jews declared Yiddish their mother tongue (in Warsaw an estimated 88.8 percent of Jews did). An almost equal percentage, 39.9 percent, spoke Hebrew, although many of them may have been Polish speaking Zionists making a political statement. Speaking Polish was, in fact, a status marker in Kraków. Though Kraków was in the orbit of the Hapsburg monarchy, after 1867 the city was under the political and cultural hegemony of Poles, and speaking Polish rather than German provided social currency. The percentage of Jews who spoke Polish as reported in the Census was only 18.7 percent, but that percentage was more than three times larger than the 5.4 percent in Warsaw, and historians believe the number to be considerably undercounted percent.[12] As a result, Jewish culture in Kraków was primarily conducted in Polish, although a cacophony of languages could be heard on the streets. Some Jews joined Polish struggles for an independent Poland; others espoused Zionism as a Jewish nationalist alternative. Others advanced socialism, especially the Polish Bund, which held its inaugural meeting in Lublin in 1917. These groups vied for support among Jews during the interwar years. Kraków, with its relatively small Yiddish-speaking working class, was not a leading Bund center, but Bund political culture and Yiddishkeit played important roles in forging modern Jewish identity, and in the face of rising anti-Semitism in the 1930s, Poland's Jews, including those in Kraków, increasingly turned to the Bund. In the municipal elections of December 1938 and January 1939, the Zionist-sponsored Representation of United Jewry was the decided victor with 58.8 percent of the Jewish vote, but the Bund won three seats and increased its share of the Jewish vote to 17.6 percent.[13]

Nine months after the municipal elections, on September 6, 1939, the Germans occupied Kraków. In March 1941, they established a ghetto south of Kazimierz in the Podgórze district. A year later they began to liquidate ghetto residents by deporting them to Auschwitz. Of the 65,000 Jews in prewar Kraków, only 2,000 survived the war. About 4,500 Jews who had escaped the war to Russia ultimately returned to Kraków, only to face postwar anti-Semitism and old fears of pogroms (and an actual pogrom in 1945). Few Jews remained long.[14] After a renewal of state-sponsored anti-Semitism in 1968, remaining Jews left.

In the 1980s, there were signs of a revitalizing Jewish life with the establishment of a Jewish Studies programs at the Jagiellonian University and at Warsaw
University. In the post-Soviet era, the 1993 release of the Hollywood blockbuster
film *Schindler's List* spurred tourist redevelopment of Kazimierz. In the new
century, cafés, gourmet restaurants, designer shops, and nightclubs established
the district as a tourist mecca and a bohemian hotspot for trendy Kraków youth
and international visitors. Jews and local Polish non-Jews, with the support of philanthropies such as American Jewish Joint Distribution Committee and the San
Francisco-based Taube Foundation, have made Jewish cultural life a core theme of
Kraków's Jewish renaissance. In 2015, although only 200 Jews participated in the
organized Jewish Community, an estimated 2,000 Jews resided in Kraków.

Heritage Tourism

Walking Kraków/Kazimierz. I booked a B&B in Kazimierz for my July 2014
visit. As elsewhere, the local version of the city guide *Kraków In Your Pocket*
introduced visitors to the sights and pleasures of the town. Nine pages adorned
with colorful pictures provided paragraph summaries of the history of Kazimierz and Podgórze, along with annotated lists of "What to See," "Museums," and
"Jewish Synagogues & Cemeteries." Two additional pages summarized the history of the Jewish Ghetto during World War II. Apart from dates of old synagogues, the historical summaries ignored the prewar lives of Jews.[15]

One did not have to walk far in Kazimierz to find guides ready to provide
more comprehensive tours. Everywhere electric carts with awnings advertised
"Old Town," "Jewish District Kazimierz," "Schindler's Factory." It cost 160 PLN
(Polish zloty, about $40 in 2014) to rent a cart for any one of the three tours,
each of which took about an hour. A guide, Kasia,[16] agreed to take me to both
the Kazimierz and Schindler's Factory tours for 200 PLN ($50). The latter, Kasia
explained, involved a tour of the former ghetto area in Podgórze.

Kasia worked with her husband for a company that operated 240 carts in
Kraków. They had purchased the cart from the company, complete with a certificate for tourism, so the cart represented an entrepreneurial franchise. Kasia's
husband had been conducting tours for four years; Kasia had been on the job
for just two months. They could work as long or as hard as they wished with no
guaranteed income. The business was also highly competitive. There were carts
festooned with the colorful banners everywhere, making it feel as if one were in
an amusement park.

Kasia was linguistically competent but not formally trained. She spoke
English, Russian, and Polish, and was able to respond to most questions from
visitors, the majority of whom were English (or English speaking), German, Italian, or Russian. She also turned on a canned narration, which visitors could
access in any of twelve languages via a headset plugged into an outlet at each
seat. The narration focused on remains of buildings, offering descriptions of

Figure 21. Typical electric tourist cart in Kraków. Photo by the author.

their architectural style, dates of origin and significance. Surprisingly, the Jewish District of Kazimierz tour began with stops at three Gothic Roman Catholic churches. It only afterwards proceeded to Jewish sites: many extant synagogues, a Talmud Torah school, and sites of the Gestapo prison and tram depot for deportations during the Holocaust. Apart from mention of the Jewish Community Center (JCC), which has become the focus of contemporary Jewish life, the Kazimierz tour centered Jewish heritage around Holocaust and religious sites with little attention to the rich and complex history of Jewish culture, politics, family life, work, and play in Kraków since the fourteenth century.

For the second tour, the cart traveled across the river to the historic site of the Jewish ghetto. In vignettes, this tour invoked images of daily life in the ghetto during the war. The narrator focused on privation and cruelty, speaking in solemn and respectful tones. Yet the message was unsettling in its omissions. While telling of the millions killed by the Nazis at Auschwitz, the narrator never spoke of Polish complicity, or even raised a question about it. Instead, the narrator praised two local Polish men as heroes who operated in the shadows of the ghetto, men Yad Vashem had declared "Righteous among the Nations": Tadeusz Pankiewicz, the Polish pharmacist who secretly provided food, medicine, and false papers to Jews in the ghetto; and Oskar Schindler, the Sudeten German factory owner who gained renown thanks to Hollywood. Jews were reduced to passive victims. Moreover, implying Jews were not Polish, the narrator reminded listeners that many Romany and Poles were also victims.

Kasia concluded her two tours with a contemporary look at Jewish street life on the central tourist square on Szeroka Street in Kazimierz. Busy restaurants and outdoor cafés lined the streets. The joyful wail of a Klezmer band clarinet and accordion could be heard at one of them. Walking the square, however, Kasia turned the focus back on the many religious sites that lined it. The Old Synagogue, which now housed a Jewish museum as a branch of the Museum of the History of the City of Kraków, was at number twenty-four. The beautifully restored Renaissance-style Remuh Synagogue (a Hebrew acronym for Rabbi Moses Isseries [1525–1572], after whom it was named) was at number forty. The Old Jewish Cemetery adjoined it. A third former synagogue, Popper's seventeenth-century Baroque synagogue (named for the merchant Wolf Popper) at number 16, now serves as a community art studio. Number 6, the former Mikvah (ritual bathhouse) had become part of the restaurant tourist scene, while number 14 Szeroka Street has the distinction of being the birthplace of the Jewish cosmetics pioneer, Helena Rubinstein.[17]

Free Walking Tours provided another chance to sample Jewish heritage. I hoped a walking tour would allow an opportunity to visit sights Kasia's cart had passed by, including some of the museums. It would also break out of the narrative cocoon of the cart's canned lecture. The company had become a Polish national urban tourist institution, offering walking tours in Warsaw, Kraków, Wrocław, and Gdańsk. The Kraków offerings were typical. A tourist could choose among Foods of Kraków, Kraków Macabre, Photo Tour, Street Art, the Old Town (both short and long walks), "special" tours with Polish or Kraków themes, and Jewish Kraków. The company offered most of these tours five or six times during the week, but English language tours of the Old Town and Jewish Kraków departed from the Main Market Square twice daily. The company also sustained two Spanish-language versions of Jewish Kraków daily.[18]

I joined one of the English-language morning tours. The leader, Karol,[19] met participants in front of St. Mary's Church across from the majestic Cloth Hall on Main Market Square. It was a warm June morning at the beginning of the prime tourist season. Judging from the size and character of the group, Jewish heritage tourism in Kraków was thriving. Most of the twenty-three participants on Karol's tour appeared to be between twenty and fifty years old. Two-thirds were women; half were Americans, five from the New York metropolitan area. A young woman standing in the back taking notes was a graduate student from England doing fieldwork for an MA thesis on the Free Walking Tours.

Karol told me the company had been in operation for eight years and he was in his third year as a tour guide with them. He read Hebrew and had done Jewish Studies in the pioneering department at Kraków's historic Jagiellonian University. To qualify to lead the tour, he completed an additional one-year course that culminated in a three-day exam. He passed it on his third try. There was no charge for the tour and Karol relied on tips at the end. The group put about 400 PLN (about $100) into the hat he passed around at the end of the tour. Karol lived on these contributions, and in winter when tourism declined, he filled his time with volunteer charity work. But Karol's future prospects from tourism seemed good. Increased demand had recently led the company to double the number of daily Jewish tours, and it was experimenting with a Polish language tour on Saturdays.

Karol was among the best-trained guides I encountered in my Eastern and Central Europe touring. He clearly benefitted from his training in Jewish Studies at the local university and spoke knowledgably about the long and diverse history of Jews in the city. On Main Market Square he pointed to the sites of early Jewish inhabitation in Kraków before Jewish resettlement in Kazimierz. Walking briskly to Kazimierz, he stopped on Szeroka Street in front of the Old Synagogue to give a mini-history lecture on the Ashkenazi origins of Kraków's Jews and the place of Yiddish language and culture in the community. He was lively, well spoken, and informative, but there were some key points absent in the tour that followed. Karol provided little sense of divisions within the Jewish community. Underscoring the double erasure of Yiddishkeit from the Holocaust and from memoryland, much as the Nazis were indifferent to Jewish multiplicity, his narrative tended to treat Jews as an undifferentiated category. He offered no insight into divisions between rich and poor, Orthodox and Reform, secular and religious. Visitors heard nothing of the political identities that animated the past: no mention was made of socialism, or the Bund, or Labor Zionism, and a discussion of communism only surfaced in the context of postwar history. Much as on Kasia's cart, Karol's walk through Kazimierz mostly focused on synagogues, cemeteries, and Holocaust memorials, with one notable difference: at numerous stops, Karol drew our attention to settings for *Schindler's List*. Building on the enormous popular appeal of the 1993 Hollywood blockbuster, heritage purveyors have memorialized the district as a film set for a melodramatic narrative of Kraków's Jewish past as a redemptive Holocaust tale.[20]

In keeping with this narrative line, Karol concluded his tour with a walk across the river to the site of the ghetto, ending at the Schindler Museum. The museum is actually not in Oskar Schindler's enamel factory; it is housed in the administration building in front of it. The factory is now occupied by a contemporary art museum. Karol encouraged participants to visit the museum, which I did on a subsequent visit in May 2017.

Museums. Both Karol and Kasia took participants to sites of the three major museums dedicated to the Jewish past, but neither tour provided time to visit. That required another occasion. The first of the three museums, the Jewish museum in the Old Synagogue, had a nominal 9 PLN ($2.25) admission fee. A visitor could move through it in an hour, and its focus on religion held little relevance for my quest. In the Main Hall, an exhibit mounted on the walls depicted the history of religious life and practice in the city. The side synagogue room, where the women traditionally sat, displayed ritual objects, photographs, and documents to convey a picture of the domestic side of religious practice and rites. Although the content was limited, the architectural grandeur of the synagogue was memorable.[21]

The second museum, the Schindler Museum, depicts a dramatic but narrow slice of Jewish history in Kraków. It is the best known and most popular of the city's Jewish-themed historical sites. For 23 PLN ($7 in 2017) each, an English-speaking guide spent an hour whisking our small group—my wife and two local anthropologist-curators—through the three floors of a high-tech, multimedia exhibition, replete with oral histories, documentary footage, and interactive touch kiosks. The pyrotechnics were no substitute for content, however, and the guide's schedule left no time to reflect on the meaning of many artifacts, panoramas, and exhibits.

The title of the core exhibit—*Kraków under the Nazi Occupation, 1939–1945*—describes the parameters of the exhibit. Recognizing that Polish visitors dominate Kraków tourism, the museum engages them with a story about the entwined lives of Polish and Jewish inhabitants of Kraków during the war. Physical replicas of the tiny rooms inhabited by five to seven people convey a sense of ghetto life during the war. Oskar Schindler's personal life and the nearly 1,000 Jews he saved, represented by his desk and the workspaces of the factory, give another human dimension to the story. The narrative acknowledges Schindler's complicated roles both as Nazi collaborator and as Jewish liberator. Finally, a sculptural installation, the *Hall of Choices,* visually raises the ethical choices people could and did make to resist, survive, serve, or be complicit with the enemy under dangerous conditions.[22]

While chock-a-block with artifacts, wall texts, and visual stimuli, unfortunately, neither the Schindler Museum nor our guide invited visitors to use their imagination. Visitors are effectively told, "this is what happened." When asked, our guide could provide no account of the role of Jewish socialists in interwar Kraków and during the ghetto resistance, nor did he show any interest in it. Nor did he show any interest in responding to questions. He did not want to be interrupted and his lecture was the equivalent of the canned lecture on the electric cart.

A particularly disquieting moment occurred near the end of the exhibit. There was an oversized depiction of Stalin. Much larger than any other person depicted in the exhibit, Stalin's demonic figure gestured toward a trope I had encountered in the Budapest House of Terror: the Nazi horror morphed seamlessly into the Stalinist era. Such a simplified compression of the past in postcommunist heritage sites reflects Eastern European resistance to exploring the legacy of a socialist past.

Kraków's third museum dedicated to the Jewish past, the Galicia Jewish Museum at 18 Dajwór Street in Kazimierz, is a Holocaust photography museum. It is the result of a twelve-year collaboration between the late British photojournalist Chris Schwarz and the anthropologist Jonathan Webber. Opened in 2004, the museum uses Schwarz's photos to document, interpret, and make visible traces of Jewish life and culture in Polish Galicia, the region south and east of Kraków. The book *Rediscovering Traces of Memory*, which Webber published two years after Schwartz's death in 2009, serves as the text for the museum's main exhibit, *Traces of Memory*.[23] The exhibit displays images of extant relics drawn from seventy-four handsome color photographs found in Schwarz and Webber's accompanying book. Images of remains of synagogues in easily forgotten Galician villages, of forest clearings where massacres of Jews took place, of cemetery fragments, and other traces of the Holocaust dominate the collection.

But the exhibit does occasionally step outside the frame of Holocaust and ceremonial life. One section, *Jewish Culture as It Once Was*, spotlights prewar Jewish life and culture. Many of the images are of synagogues, but one is of the Guild Hall of the Jewish artisans of Jaroslaw built in 1912; another shows the Jewish street in Tarnów; others depict prewar Jewish village life. While the preponderance of images in the collection is of synagogues, cemeteries, and relics of the Holocaust, Schwarz's focus on the lives of ordinary Jews (albeit without Jews any longer present to be photographed) makes the collection a distinctive look at the relics of the past. Photographed in color with careful framing of gritty urban and pastoral rural settings, the images aestheticize the traumatic past, but nonetheless leave a haunting memory.

Reflecting on my walks around Kazimierz and through its museums, I kept thinking of some provocative concluding observations Karol had made. Stepping outside the frame of his tour, he noted Kazimierz had changed over the past decade, thanks to the movement of students, restaurateurs, artists, and developers into the district. The transformation, he added, has challenged how Kazimierz can be remembered. Cafés, nightlife, and modern flats have turned a formerly rundown Old City into a fashionable, trendy place to live and play. One local sightseeing agency advertises the district as "Kraków's equivalent of London's Soho, Paris' Quartier Latin, and New York's [Greenwich] Village," noting the process has "recreated the [District's] Jewish past."[24] Karol did not speak explicitly of gentrification, but the subtext of his comments involved widespread presumptions of "authenticity" and an "essential" Jewishness. In that regard, my touring confirmed Erica Lehrer's observation that Kraków's heritage tourism obscured the complexities of Jewish life and identity.

But Lehrer also notes that when non-Jewish Poles and Jews from around the world visit Kazimierz, they find a place with the potential to stage a "complex" story of Jewishness in old, revived, and new spaces. Lehrer specifically identifies the Jewish bookstore, the JCC, and the annual ten-day Jewish Cultural Festival as spaces where these complexities can be experienced. The bookstore offers locals and visitors a rich and wide-range of original and translated scholarly and semi-scholarly publications on Jewish history and culture. All three venues provide ecumenical spaces to secular and religious Jews of any stripe. Finally, Lehrer points to the annual Jewish Cultural Festival held in Kraków at the end of June every year since 1988, which engages large crowds of Jews and non-Jews in Jewish history and culture. Over ten days, participants can attend workshops on Yiddish, dine at Shabbat dinners, hear concerts, take local walking tours, and attend lectures on the Jewish diaspora. (Of course, one has to be there on one of those specific days.)

These developments reveal a lively renaissance of Jewish life in contemporary Poland, but they are not unproblematic. It remains unclear, for example, how Jews and non-Jews differentially experience Jewish heritage presentations. Critics complain that Polish non-Jews who comprise most of the attendees at the Festival are "reinventing" Jewishness, "dressing up" as Jews in long coats and "dining" out on Jewishness through food culture. Others more sympathetic to the revival, such as Lehrer, defend the project of a "recreated Jewish past," as a contested work in progress always subject to invention and reinvention.

Figurines in shop windows offer one dramatic example of the contested nature of the past in the present. Figurines have a long history as folk art in Poland, much as they do elsewhere in the world. In the United States, for instance, folk artists routinely represented African Americans and Native Americans in woodcarvings. An image of Sambo or a statue of a "cigar store Indian," both draw on troubling racist stereotypes. In Poland, Jewish figurines also carry troublesome meanings. The most popular image since the 1990s is that of the Lucky Jew.[25] The Lucky Jew is carved with markers from a past, both real and imagined, to "look like a Jew." Sometimes he wears a long coat, or his face is adorned with *peyas* (sideburns worn by the ultra-Orthodox) or he has a hooked nose. The "Lucky Jew" is a good-luck charm, similar to an American child's rabbit foot, to be placed at the entrance to the home. However, this figurine, which draws on the stereotype of the Jew as avaricious and "good with money," of a Shylock, is only one of the several representations available. Others figurines depict Jewish musicians, or the "simple fool," Tevye the milkman, or draw on images from Chagall paintings and characters in *Fiddler on the Roof.*

Figure 22. Figurines in a Kazimierz shop window, June 2014. Photo by the author.

Carvers believe they are summoning up memories of a Jewish past that honor and refigure Jews in contemporary Poland. According to Lehrer, their work represents "the increasingly common efforts by non-Jewish Poles to grapple with Poland's Jewish history and their own responsibility towards it."[26]

But the producers and consumers of these figurines often invest them with different meanings, and an appendix to Lehrer's book, however, gives a more mixed assessment from Jewish consumers about the figurines. Comments left after seeing an exhibit of the figurines in Kraków show that only some appreciate the carvers' views and motives. An Israeli offered one positive reaction. He argues the figurines "convey the hidden and deep things that Judaism conceals. Through the figurines you get to know the nuances of the Jewish world—the norms and traditions, the role of the community, the way they are perceived in society." More typically, visitors left short bitter notes complaining that the figurines are "naïve," "repulsive," "ridiculous and anti-Semitic."[27]

Curators and guides as providers, and tourists as consumers might divide, but ultimately, Jewish heritage travelers to Kraków vote with their feet. Their preference continues to be for the canned and conventional walking and cart tours of heritage as Holocaust and Kazimierz as movie set. This paradigm defines Kraków's Jewish heritage tourism, and is likely to do so until expectations change and/or providers offer a more compelling alternative narrative.

May 2017: An Update. Visiting the Galician Jewish Museum in May 2017, I note new and recent displays that fall outside the dominant Jewish Holocaust heritage narrative. The museum hired a distinguished American photographer, Jason Francisco, to update the exhibit with new images. Francisco added 600 photos to the whole collection, and the public exhibit expanded from 104 to 144 photographs. In 2014, the core exhibit, *Traces of Memory*, was renamed *An Unfinished Memory: Jewish Heritage and the Holocaust in Eastern Galicia*. In this new exhibit Francisco's sixty new photographs supplement Schwarz's images. New images of former factories, empty town squares, and forgotten philanthropies evoke nonreligious dimensions of Galician Jewish life. It is true that by depicting Galicia without Jews, the museum still chooses to present visitors with images that are devoid of people, and the evocative relics of the past reference destruction rather than vitality.

Still, the exhibit's broadened perspective on Jewish heritage, while not a rejection of the dominant Holocaust narrative, creates an opening in it. The heritage focus ultimately, however, moves more forward toward the Jewish revival than back to the prewar past. A reorganized final section of the exhibit reflects this new double mission. The original final section, *People Making Memory*, has become *The Revival of Jewish Life*.

Webber's updated texts also suggest the social history and historical self-consciousness of the New Jewish History may slowly be making its presence felt in the heritage destinations. A new text linked to a Schwartz photograph of figurines is illustrative. The image, which is of tourist souvenirs common in Kraków stalls, features figurines, each about five inches tall, of five male Hasidic Jews dressed in traditional black garb. In a gesture to Lehrer's work, the caption tells viewers the figurines are "controversial" and, in doing so, invites them to reflect on multiple possible meanings. The text notes these figurines exist in shops alongside carvings of "similarly caricatured, overweight Polish peasants." Acknowledging that some Jews view the Hasidic figures as "post-Holocaust anti-Semitic caricatures," it adds that carvers and the merchants see them as "nostalgic recollections of a vanished past."

A second stop at the JCC confirmed the arrival of new intellectual energies in the heritage world of Kraków. The JCC does not operate commercial tours, but it serves as a meeting point for diverse communities of Jewish visitors. The organization holds Shabbat dinners and celebrates religious holidays, but it is not a synagogue. Rather, in coordination with the Galician Jewish Museum, Museum of the History of Polish Jews in Warsaw, and the annual Jewish Festival in June, the JCC invites any and all to participate in an expansive calendar of cultural and sporting events for children, families, and seniors. I did not expect to see programs on Jewish socialism or on the gendered politics of the Jewish family, and I did not find them on the calendar. Occasional programs introduced fractures of a broad cultural past, but their focus was on literature, painting, dance, and food culture, not political culture or points of tension and conflict within Jewry. Yet in the JCC I recognized a familiar inclusive space from my own days in Jewish theatre at the YMHA in Paterson, a space in which I thought it would be possible to build a renovated future of Jewish heritage.

WARSAW

History

At the outbreak of World War I, only New York City had a larger Jewish settlement than Warsaw. With 337,000 Jews in 1914 (38.1% of the city's population), Warsaw was home to the largest Jewish community in Europe, 50 percent more than Budapest, with just 215,512 Jewish residents.[28]

The Jewish settlement of Warsaw has a long history and rich diversity—a wealth of lived experiences that can be addressed in heritage tourism. Jews first settled on the west bank of the Vistula in present-day Warsaw during the second half of the thirteenth century. They had built a synagogue and cemetery on the site by the early fifteenth century, but they received little welcome from local authorities. From 1527 to 1795, Jews were allowed to enter Warsaw for restricted periods, and some prosperous Jews paid rent to live on noble properties in and around the city. But wherever they resided, they faced hostile attitudes and restrictions on their settlement. During the early modern era, much like the Jews of Buda, Warsaw's Jews developed a second settlement, Praga, across the river from the Old Town on the east bank of the Vistula. An independent city until the late eighteenth century, Praga would become a secondary but important industrial factory district that employed thousands of Jewish workers. The position of the Jews finally improved in Warsaw proper in 1796 under Prussian rule when the organized Jewish community, the Kehile, was recognized. The Warsaw Jewish community grew quickly, establishing a core settlement around the area to the west and north of the Old Town. (The Nazis established the Warsaw ghetto on this site in 1940.) In 1792, Jews in Warsaw numbered 6,750 and constituted 8.3 percent of the population (of 81,300); by 1810, the community had more than doubled to 14,600 (18%); and by 1864, expanded by more than five times that number to 72,800. As significant, one in three Warsaw residents was now Jewish (32.7%).

The Jewish community social structure and religious character vividly reflected the diversity and conflicts of nineteenth-century Jewish life. Non-Orthodox rabbinical opponents, though probably smaller in number than the Hasidim, formed a coalition with the integrationists to control the Kehile in the three decades after 1870. Fewer in number still was a small but growing Jewish bourgeoisie. Influenced by the Haskalah, this group of acculturated "progressive" Jews was sympathetic to more modern features of metropolitan life. They included large sections of the intelligentsia, teachers, authors, and state officials. In 1802, the "progressives" established the Daniłowiczowska Street synagogue, derided by the Orthodox as the "German Synagogue," even though it was not, in fact, German Reform. A haute bourgeoisie, a tightly knit, interlocking family network of about a dozen great banking families, constituted a subset of this group. Some converted to Christianity, but most were "integrationists," Poles of the Mosaic Faith, who consecrated the magnificent Great Synagogue on Tłomackie Street in 1878. The scale of the Great Synagogue reflected an ascendant social group within the Warsaw Jewish community.[29] While the vast majority of Warsaw's Jews (83.7%) spoke Yiddish and attended Orthodox synagogues, the Great Synagogue served Polonized Jews. Congregants listened to rabbis' sermons in Polish and to performances of an all-male choir singing arias from French, Italian, German, and Polish operas with compositions from classical composers.[30]

Industrialization and legalization of Jewish migration from the Pale after 1868 recharged and further transformed Jewish Warsaw. The Jewish presence made itself felt in the political, intellectual, and economic life of the city. Almost four of every ten residents (38.1%, or 337,000 of the 885,000 total) were Jewish. The Grand Rabbi of Warsaw's support for the Polish insurrection of 1863 reflected the engagement of Polish Jews with national identity and the politics of Polish culture. Jews also dominated textile and clothing industries and the tobacco trade. A majority of the city's artisans were Jewish, and as in Budapest, large numbers of Jews filled the liberal professions (lawyers, doctors, dentists, architects, accountants). A high birthrate accounted for some of the population increase, but new Jewish migrants from the Russian Pale called "Litvaks" (Jews with roots in modern-day Lithuania, Belarus, and Latvia), made up the largest number.[31]

Litvaks brought with them a range of new political ideologies such as Zionism and socialism that would later transform Jewish life. Ury's seminal study of the 1905 Revolution in Warsaw credits the defining role of the Jewish Labor Bund that originated in Vilnius in forging a self-conscious urban Jewish political culture in the first half of the twentieth century.[32] The Bund was popular among Warsaw's workers and helped promote Yiddish culture, Yiddishkeit, which flourished in Warsaw, especially in the years following the revolutionary upheaval of 1904–1907. As well as being the publishing capital for Hebrew books in Poland, Warsaw also became home to leading Yiddish writers such as Isaac Bashevis Singer, Shalom Asch, and I. L. Peretz. Plebian expressions of Yiddishkeit also materialized. Yiddish-speaking socialist workers organized unions in workplaces and forged cultural solidarities through singing groups such as the Grosser Choir of the Bund. By 1906, the Jewish community contained five Yiddish newspapers. By the early 1930s, their daily circulation grew to 170,000, dwarfing the sales of the three Hebrew and single Polish-Jewish papers. As state schools conducted classes in Polish, Warsaw Jews rapidly gained proficiency in Polish during the interwar years, and while a Polish newspaper circulated, Jews mostly got their news from the Yiddish dailies.[33]

Tłomackie Street, dominated by the imposing and polonized Great Synagogue, became the epicenter of Warsaw's Yiddish culture. The Association of Jewish Writers and Journalists was based at 13 Tłomackie Street and one of the Jewish choirs was based in the Great Synagogue. In Yiddish theaters, Jewish dramatic troupes such as the Warsaw Yiddish Art Theater (cofounded by Ida Kamińska and Zygmunt Turkow), performed classics of the Yiddish theater as well as Yiddish translations of standard British, American, and continental European repertoire. Yiddishkeit—expressed in art, cabaret, and music and interpreted by writers, journalists, publishers, and actors—transformed Warsaw into a cosmopolitan Jewish cultural city.

Jewish political culture was equally dynamic, with the Bund playing a major role. During the first half of the twentieth century, three rival ideologies—Zionism, Orthodoxy, and Socialism—struggled for control of the "Jewish street." As the British prevented Warsaw Jews from immigrating to Palestine in the mid-1930s, Zionists lost ground to the Bundists and communists. Unlike in Kraków, in the municipal elections of December 1938, Bundists dominated Jewish neighborhoods. The Bund captured 61.7 percent of the Jewish vote and won seventeen municipal seats. (Agudat Israel captured two seats, and the Democratic Zionists only one.)[34]

The Bund's success was tragically short-lived. The Nazis invaded Warsaw in September 1939, constructed the Warsaw ghetto on the sites of the major Jewish settlement, and sealed it on November 16, 1940. The Nazis herded almost half a million Jews from the city and surrounding countryside into the ghetto. In the winter of 1940/41, thousands died of disease, aggravated by malnutrition and starvation. There was a modicum of stability until the deportation of over 300,000 to the Treblinka extermination camp began in July 1942. Few who remained would survive the war.

Jewish political activists, including Bundists, organized a resistance movement in the ghetto and fought the Nazis, most famously in the Warsaw Ghetto Uprising. For four weeks in April and May 1943, 750 Jewish fighters heroically resisted over 2,000 heavily armed German troops. Both Gwardia Ludowa, the armed underground organization created by the communist Polish Workers Party in 1942, and the noncommunist Polish Home Army, offered support to the fighters by attacking German units, trying to blow up the ghetto wall, smuggling weapons, and so on. Polish resistance also helped fighters of the Jewish Combat Organizations and the Jewish Military Union to escape and find refuge outside the former ghetto area. Ultimately, fifty ghetto fighters joined the resistance.[35] Over 7,000 Jews died fighting in the ghetto, while the Nazis deported an estimated 7,000 to 13,000 more to the Treblinka killing center. On May 16, 1943, the Nazis destroyed the Great Synagogue and over the next three months liquidated the ghetto.[36]

After the war approximately 10,000 to 11,000 Jewish survivors returned to Warsaw.[37] Returning Jews made modest efforts to reestablish the Jewish community. Ida Kaminska reopened her Yiddish theater troupe, a new Yiddish language communist newspaper, *Folks-shtime*, appeared, and the Jewish Historical Institute was founded. The Kielce pogrom in 1946, however, led to a large Jewish exodus from Poland. In 1956–1957, yet another cohort of Jews from the former Soviet territories departed under the more liberal government of Władysław Gomułka. Emigration was strongest in Lower Silesia, the region with traditionally the largest Jewish settlement, but the drive to leave Poland spread elsewhere in 1956 as aggrieved Poles held Jews responsible for the hardships of Stalinism. Some left in the face of rising anti-Semitism, some because they were disappointed with communism, some because they were accused of Stalinist crimes, and many just because they had the opportunity to do so.

Events in 1967–1968 triggered the departure of the 13,000 Jews who had stayed. The Polish communist government's condemnation of Israel as Zionist "colonizers" for its part in the Six Day War fueled a new wave of anti-Semitism. In 1967, authorities targeted Jews, including those in important positions, as enemies of the state and society and had them removed. The next year, Warsaw students joined the international anti-Israel protest that erupted in spring 1968. After a particularly shameful student campaign and state-sponsored expulsion in 1968, only a handful of Jews remained in Warsaw.[38]

In the years following the breakup of the Soviet Union, as in Berlin, Budapest, Kraków, and elsewhere, Warsaw's Jewish community began to reorganize. In a post-1989 Jewish revival, about 500 Jews registered as members of Warsaw's organized Jewish Community, while scholars estimate that between 5,000 and 10,000 more residents identified as Jews. The Jewish revival's effect on heritage tourism was complicated. Developers converted formerly dilapidated factories in Praga, the old Jewish industrial district quarter across the river that was relatively untouched by German bombs, into trendy sites for art, loft living, and nightlife. Alternatively, POLIN provides a deeply historical and intellectual engagement with 1,000 continuous years of Jewish life in Poland. Navigating such diverse sites challenges heritage tourists with different senses of the lived experience of the Jewish past and present.[39]

Jewish Heritage Tourism

I briefly visited Warsaw en route to Łódź in 1981. Arriving in the glow of the Solidarity labor movement, I remember the city as gray but full of new possibilities. Beginning in mid-March 2013, I returned to the city for the first of three visits in twenty months to study Warsaw's Jewish heritage tourism. The grand new POLIN building was visible but not yet open. Online I found an extravagant tour scene: half a dozen companies offered Jewish heritage tours. Other than cost, little distinguished one from the other. Some agencies offered automobile tours. They varied from a nine-day group trip to Warsaw, Lublin, and Kraków for a group of at least eight travelers at a cost beginning at $2,495 to one-day visits for a fee of $150 to Treblinka. Tourists could also book a short visit to Praga as part of the Warsaw tour.[40]

Walking Warsaw: A Typical Tour. Walking tours in Warsaw, much as in most of the cities in Eastern and Central Europe I visited, focused on ghetto sites, local sites of the Holocaust and synagogues. Tours advertised by POLIN Tours, Free Walking Tours: Warsaw, and the Berlin-based agency Milk and Honey Tours, were typical. The core itinerary involved visits to the Ghetto, Nożyk Synagogue (Warsaw's only surviving synagogue), Remnants of the Ghetto Wall, The Ghetto Heroes Monument, *Umschlagplatz* (the deportation train station), the Jewish Cemetery, the Memorial of the Heroes of the Warsaw Ghetto, and the 18 Miła Street Bunker in which many of the resistance leaders of the Uprising died.[41] To quote Helise Lieberman, the director of the Taube Center for the Renewal of Jewish Life in Poland, like Berlin, Warsaw unfortunately all too often functions as "an outdoor Holocaust museum."[42]

Seeking a representative Jewish heritage tour, I chose a guide who was highly recommended on TripAdvisor. Szymon Nowicki met me at the tourist information booth in front of the Palace of Culture and Science. A stranger to the city, I was reassured by his plan to meet at the tallest building in the city. A licensed and self-taught tour guide, Nowicki describes himself on his website as inspired "by the multiculturalism of the city's past." Despite his strong TripAdvisor reviews, he was relatively new to the business, which may account for the conventional tour that followed. In any case, he collected 200 PLN ($50) from me for a two and a half-hour walking (and bus, tram, and subway) tour.[43]

It was a cold, snowy morning and I was the only person on the tour. Nowicki's tour could have been a personal chat rather than a lecture. He had his spiel though, and as we walked, he delivered a typical ghetto and Holocaust lecture. He began at the southern end of the ghetto, in order to view an existing fragment of the Ghetto wall. We then proceeded to all the usual ghetto/Holocaust sites. Advertised Ghetto wall markers embedded in the sidewalks all along the tour were constant reminders of the Holocaust. He concluded the first part of

Figure 23. A group of anonymous Israeli school children, accompanied by an armed guard off camera, pose with an Israeli flag before Natan Rapoport's 1948 Monument to the Ghetto Heroes to memorialize their visit and mark its meaning for the Israeli state. Photo by the author.

the tour with a walk along the Memorial Route to the Struggle and Martyrdom of the Jews, ending at Natan Rapoport's 1948 Monument to the Ghetto Heroes, which stood in front of the not yet open POLIN.

During the last part of his tour Nowicki broke his ghetto/Holocaust narrative to comment on prewar life and Jewish culture. A subway took us to the neighborhood of Grzybowski Square, historically a center of Jewish culture and intellectual life where Jewish theatre still operates. Briefly, he focused on two markers of the Jewish past and Warsaw's present future. On a street corner, pictures of poor early twentieth-century Jewish residents of the area, mostly women and children, adorned half of the windows on the façade of a boarded-up factory. Another one-time factory across from it had been renovated into a modern, pristine apartment house. The two buildings provided a parable on history and memory. The images depicted ordinary Jews who lived in the building before the war, although unlike the re-created living quarters in New York's Tenement Museum, the pictures could only hint at these people's lives. The renovated building symbolized how developers systematically layered over the past with a modern façade in the name of progress.

Figure 24. Former tenement (and factory workshop) adorned with photos of prewar residents, Grzybowski Square, Warsaw, north side. The building's renovated twin is partially visible on the right. Photo by the author.

Nowicki's tour spotlighted the devastation, heroics, and horror of the ghetto and Holocaust, but ended with an upbeat message about Jewish renewal in Warsaw. The renewal was intimately tied to institutionalized religion. Our final stop was to the canary yellow Nożyk Synagogue, home to the contemporary religious Jewish community and base for activities sponsored by the organized Jewish Community, including the annual Jewish Festival held on Grzybowska Square.

Nowicki did not speak much about the Bund, Jewish socialism, or Zionism; indeed, he mostly ignored the diversity and struggles of prewar Jews. But he pointed out various Jewish institutions that illuminated such matters but required separate visits. One, the Jewish cemetery, I visited later, and it reminded me that like synagogues, such sites can open up a broad panorama of the Jewish past. Located a few tram stops from the ghetto, the distance was not easily incorporated into the walking tour, but moving outside the bounds of the tour illuminated a world I sought: the cemetery was a social and historical text of Yiddishkeit. It was a cold, snowy day so I could not make an extensive tour of the site, but I looked for the burial place of many Bundists, including Marek Edelman, the last surviving leader of the Ghetto Uprising, and legends of

Jewish literature such as I. L. Peretz and S. Ansky. And I rejoiced to see the impressive headstone for the mother of the Yiddish theater, Ester Kaminska, prominently displayed.

The Jewish Historical Institute and Jewish Genealogical and Family Heritage Center. Among the other important sites for study of Warsaw's Jewish heritage, historians urged me to visit the Emanuel Ringelblum Jewish Historical Institute (JHI) at 3/5 Tłomackie Street. It was a solid stone building that commercial walking tour guides pointed to as they passed it by as adjacent to the site on which the Great Synagogue once stood. Directed by Paweł Śpiewak, a professor of sociology at the University of Warsaw, the Jewish archive housed in JHI provided researchers with seminars and publications and exhibits on Jewish history open to the public. The archive's strength in Jewish secular art and religious artifacts accounts for its selection of exhibit topics. Its most popular past exhibit consisted of powerful black and white photographs of the Warsaw ghetto, supplemented by forty minutes of original footage. During my 2013 visit, the exhibit consisted of a history of Polish rabbis.

When I returned to Warsaw in November 2014, I was able to view a dazzling exhibit at the JHI dedicated to artists from 1890 to 1943 that posed some thorny questions central to Jewish identity and heritage. While the art on display illustrated many modern styles, the collection of art by Jewish artists and its accompanying texts illuminated both prewar lived experiences and sensibilities and the horrors of life in the ghetto. Items included, for instance, poignant oil paintings by the artist Olga Zienkiewicz of her children, accompanied by a farewell letter to her "comrades and friends" that captured the physical and psychic horrors of the last days of the ghetto before its liquidation with deportation and mass executions. Postimpressionist, abstract, and social realist painters, among others, were showcased, and exhibition signage explicitly asked viewers to consider whether this was a collection of art by Jewish artists, or Jewish art? Jewish artists who organized the first exhibit of their art in the mid-1920s had addressed a similar dilemma, and their opinions diverged and shifted. The following note, for example, written in 1955 by Polish-Jewish abstract artist Henryk Berlewi appeared in a prominently placed text panel:

> When Ostrzega, Weintraub, Frydman, Minkowski and I organized the first Jewish exhibition in Warsaw almost thirty years ago, we had a long discussion about the name. Should it be an exhibition of Jewish art or of Jewish artists? We chose the first alternative. But later, when we founded the Association for Promotion of the Fine Arts, we deliberately avoided the term "Jewish art."[44]

The subjectivities of the artists demonstrated a long-standing and active engagement with questions of Jewish identity. Equally impressive, the exhibit provided depictions of daily life, but also diverse artistic modes of expressing it. Evocative languages of "comrade" and the engagement with social realism reflected socialist and communist doctrine, but the range of artistic expressions suggested broad modernist critiques and socialist sensibilities among self-identified Jewish artists.

Another resource for Jewish heritage, the Jewish Genealogical and Family Heritage Center, is located in a small ground floor office in the JHI. Two modest wooden desks with computers link the Center to JewishGen.org. Through these computers, Director Yale Reisner and his associate, Anna Przybyszewska, serve a worldwide network of Jewish genealogical researchers and visitors (preferably by appointment), providing data on birth, marriage, and death over generations. They remain a small operation with a big footprint in Jewish genealogical circles.

The Taube Center for the Renewal of Jewish Life. The Taube Center provides a third resource for Jewish heritage tourism beyond the walls of the Warsaw ghetto. Director Helise Lieberman summarized the work of the Center, and presented me with a copy of the Center's recent publication, *Field Guide to Jewish Warsaw and Kraków*, eight self-guided detailed walking tours. (In 2017, the Center announced plans to publish comparable tours of Łódź.) The Taube Center also offers guided day tours to Kraków and Łódź by appointment, as well as walking tours in Warsaw, and the itineraries in the *Field Guide* suggest they offer a different model than the commercial tours. The Center, Lieberman emphasized, is committed to the broad prewar and postwar history of Jewish life in Poland and the complexity of the Polish Jewish story, a history she believed would be amplified and detailed in POLIN when it opened.

The Center sees its second focus, a program committed to engaging and facilitating the rebirth of Jewish life in Poland, as integral to its heritage program. Mi Dor Le Dor (the Hebrew for "from generation to generation") trains Jewish educators to take an active role in the Jewish communal, educational, and cultural institutions. Both programs come together in the Center's self-guided walking tours, which often end at sites where the contemporary organized Jewish Community prays and holds its annual festivals: Grzybowski Square and the Nożyk Synagogue.

Having taken multiple tours in Berlin, London, and New York, I had come to recognize that most follow similar pathways. Nowicki, for instance, ended his tour at the same sites as the Taube Center tours. But my experience also led me to appreciate how much walking tours' interpretations of the same sites could differ. Chapter 4 on London illustrates this with comparisons of three tours. Similarly, the *Field Guide* walking tours expose the deficiencies of the commercial Kraków and Warsaw tours. Rather than clinging to the Holocaust narrative, several of the *Guide*'s self-guided Warsaw tours trace a complex prewar Jewish presence across the city in time and space. The accompanying text also raises provocative and knotty questions for the reader/walker about "authenticity" and Jewish identity. It invites viewers to think about what is remembered and preserved and how.

I took several of the tours and found Warsaw Tour One's integration of references to Jewish socialism into the walk exemplary. While taking me to the ghetto area where commercial tours had ended, the text provides an extended discussion of Yiddish culture and Bund politics. Turning onto Perec St., named after I. L. Peretz, paragraphs elaborate on the history of Yiddish culture, identifying famous Yiddish writers who lived and worked there, and positioning them in a broader discussion of Yiddish literature and culture tied to Bund political culture. At Grzybowski Square, the site with the boarded-up former factory, the text points to a memorial stone Nowicki had ignored. Signage on the stone memorializes the 1905 socialist uprising against the Czar and takes the opportunity to introduce visitors to the history of the Bund that year. The narrative also details the remarkable achievements and plight of a group barely addressed in Jewish heritage tourism: Jewish women. One passage mentions female celebrities such as Ester and Ida Kaminska and the Yiddish Theater where they both starred. A second passage notes that the square was Warsaw's red-light district and Jewish prostitutes worked there. The local sex trade provoked Bundist vigilantism: "The Bundists, whose socialism was based on a fundamental belief in human dignity, considered the situation outrageous and attacked the brothels to free the women and disrupt the trade." Because alternative sources of work for women that paid a living wage were few, it is not clear how Jewish sex workers felt about this paternalistic intervention. The text notes that pimps and their Jewish and Gentile "associates" fought back and a gun battle erupted.[45] Raising as many questions as it answers, the story nonetheless provides a rare glimpse into quotidian struggles in daily Jewish life, contests little found in tourist literature though heavily researched by historians.[46]

The *Guide*'s third Warsaw tour, of the Old City, illustrates a second major problem in conventional walking tours and offers a corrective: it demonstrates how Jewish heritage permeates the city and extends to districts that the commercial tours ignore. The text instructs readers to begin in the smartly renovated Old Town Square, where Jewish settlement began early in the fifteenth century. The *Guide*'s description establishes the intellectual arena for the tourist's experience: "A stroll through reconstructed lost times, some ancient and others quite recent, which raises questions about renewal, authenticity of place, and the importance of cultural icons and continuity."[47] Passing by government buildings and the University of Warsaw, the tour notes large numbers of Jewish students distinguished themselves, but omits mention of the Polish Jewish communist and socialist (and Bundist) student activists. Instead, the term "communists" becomes

W TYM MIEJSCU
DNIA 13 LISTOPADA 1904 R
ODBYŁA SIE
PIERWSZA NA ZIEMIACH POLSKICH
ZBROJNA DEMONSTRACJA ROBOTNICZA
ZORGANIZOWANA
PRZEZ POLSKĄ PARTIE SOCJALISTYCZNA
PAMIECI BOJOWNIKOW O WOLNOŚĆ SPRAWIEDLIWOŚĆ
I NIEPODLEGŁOSC KTÓRZY KREW SWĄ NA TYM PLACU
PRZELALI W WALCE Z CARSKIM NAJAZDEM
WARSZAWA 1992 R   W STULECIE PPS

Figure 25. The author stands before the memorial to the 1905 socialist uprising, Grzybowski Square, June 2014. Photo by the author.

a synonym for Stalinists as Luddites who "shave 'bourgeois' decorations off the remaining buildings to align them with the socialist vision" in reconstructing the Old Square.[48] There is no Yiddishkeit either; rather, the tour speaks of the Polish Jewish intelligentsia. But even with its occasional silences and conceptual choices, such walks in the Taube Center's *Field Guide* show the possibilities for an expansive and nuanced Jewish heritage tour in Warsaw.

Alas, the book has had little effect on Warsaw's mainstream commercial Jewish heritage tourism. The twenty-five guided tours led by the Taube Center in 2013 constituted only a drop in the proverbial tourist bucket. In addition, unlike the free copies of *Warsaw In Your Pocket* that every hotel and B&B provides its visitors, the center charges for the *Guide* and has been unable to distribute it to the public. I saw no copies of the *Field Guide* in the establishments I frequented. It would also take a particularly enterprising tourist to commit to a self-guided tour in a strange city.

History Museums and Jewish Heritage

I returned to Warsaw in early November 2014 shortly after the opening of the core exhibit for POLIN: The Museum of the History of Polish Jews. POLIN is now one of two ambitious and high-tech history museums to grace modern Warsaw. A decade earlier, the Museum of the Warsaw Uprising opened. Today the two museums compete for audience, cultural relevance, and historical legitimacy. Reviewing the Warsaw Rising Museum, the *Guardian* signaled these competing ambitions in its headline: "70 Years after WW2 Erupted, a new battle for history rages in Europe."[49] Tourists from abroad who visit Warsaw Rising could easily expect, as I did, to hear the story of the war in a city in which 375,000 Jews had lived. Some might have confused Warsaw Rising with the Warsaw Uprising, which outside of Poland tends to be better known. I learned the two events were quite distinct.

The Warsaw Rising Museum. With dynamic, hi-tech interactive displays, the Warsaw Rising Museum celebrates the sixty-three-day "suicidal rebellion" during August and September 1944 by the Polish Home Army. Anticommunist nationalists and anticommunist socialists in the Home Army wanted to liberate the city before the advance of the Russian army and, of course, kill brutal German occupiers. They were haunted by memories of the Russian czar's oppressive rule over Polish lands through 1918 and over Russia's conquering of East Polish territories throughout 1939–1941. The Red Army advance stalled, though, and the German army prevailed. At the rebellion's end, 200,000 Polish citizens lay dead and the city was in ruins, vindictively razed by the victorious Nazis. The exhibit concentrates on the nationalist impulses of the fighters; the museum website celebrates the fighters as "residents . . . who fought and died for independent Poland and its free capital."[50]

The museum provides a visceral experience. *Warsaw In Your Pocket* heralds Warsaw Rising as "one of Poland's best museums," and its "most popular." The exhibition builds on oral histories of survivors combined with a pastiche of wartime paraphernalia. Sounds of gunfire and bombs in a reconstructed documentary film that includes 3-D footage of a decimated Warsaw in 1945 echo through the space. It is a "high impact experience," according to the pocket guide. Several TripAdvisor respondents approvingly describe it as more of an "experience" than a museum.[51]

The power and appeal of Warsaw Rising poses a challenge to the Shoah's centrality in the memory landscape of wartime Warsaw. Located in a massive former tram power station, the museum's imposing structure and emotive displays enforce its claim to historical authority. As the *Guardian* headline suggests, the museum's exhibit represents one side in a "history war" where the Cold War and Soviet rule are primary targets, not the Holocaust and Nazi regime. Tellingly, a replica Allied B24 that dropped supplies for the beleaguered residents dominates the exhibit. Hanging from the ceiling in the center hall, Warsaw Rising's deployment of the plane with pride of place in the exhibit resembles the privileged position of the tank in Budapest's House of Terror Museum. Both oversize vehicles of wartime resistance imposingly symbolize postcommunist memorializations of a despised era. The House of Terror's exhibit reflects postcommunist nationalist politics of post-1989 Budapest; Warsaw Rising's focus is a product of post-1989 Warsaw, a story that many Poles felt unable to tell in Soviet-controlled Poland, and is now told under the banner of uncompromising nationalism. Notably, the museum ignores questions the Polish exile government raised about the devastating effect on the city and its noncombatants of a nationalist campaign in part targeted against Russia's allies.

Discussion of the Warsaw Ghetto Uprising of 1943 and the fate of the ghetto inhabitants is equally muted. The resistance of the Home Army takes place from 1939 to 1945, when the plight of Jews was also integral to the city's history (and resistance movements). An early section of the exhibit mentions some Jews who survived the ghetto and joined the Rising, and offers a brief description of the Ghetto Uprising. A small video kiosk also contains an oral history with Marek Edelman, the Bund leader who survived the Ghetto Uprising to join the 1944 struggle. This limited nod to the Ghetto Uprising is, however, easily lost in the cavernous, noisy exhibit. In two hours at the museum, I felt the exhibit failed to address the same questions that nagged the *Guardian* reporter. Could or should Jewish resistance be parsed as a separate non-Polish story? Does a nationalist and anti-Russian-tinged narrative that decenters Nazism (as genocide) and centers on Stalinism (as colonialism) in fact undermine the significance of the Holocaust?

POLIN History of the Museum of Polish Jews. In anticipation of the opening of the core exhibit, I returned to Warsaw in November 2014 to view POLIN's alternative version of the city's history. In prior interviews, I had gathered that curators and various scholars who had consulted or worked on the core exhibit were navigating complicated political landmines around the history on display. Not the least of them was how to deal with Polish neighbors' complicity in the destruction of Jewish communities in certain areas. For example, how would they represent Jan T. Gross's account of the complicitous role of Polish neighbors in the destruction of the Jewish community in Jedwabne?[52]

I toured the core exhibit less than two weeks after its formal opening. At the time, the infrastructure for POLIN's new core exhibit remained a work in progress. An advertised tour in English was unavailable. Eighteen months later regular guided tours were available in Polish or English, and by arrangement, in German, Hebrew, French, Russian, and Hungarian. In addition, POLIN was the first major museum to offer a guide in Yiddish. Audio self-guides were also available in all the languages of the guided tours, as well as in Italian, Spanish, and Polish sign language, with many more languages on the way. The audio guide in English helped chart a path through the at times overwhelming displays and artifacts. (POLIN also offers an online tour, hard copies of self-guided thematic tours, and downloadable PDFs.) However, audio guides come with their own baggage: they tend to impose a linear rather than multi-vocal narrative, and the authorial voice discourages reflection. Still, I thought the guide, rentable for 10 PLN ($2.50), was excellent and with a 25 PLN ($6.67) admission ticket in hand, I began to explore the museum's core exhibit of 1,000 years of Jewish life in Poland.

The exhibit was prodigious and stunning. Housed entirely below ground, it brings to life the history of Jews in Poland in seven galleries spread over 45,200 square feet: *First Encounters* (960–1500), *Paradisus Iudaeorum* [Jewish paradise] (1500–1648), *The Jewish Town* (1648–1772), *Encounters with Modernity* (1772–1914), *On the Jewish Street* (1918–1939), *Holocaust* (1939–1945), and *Postwar Years* (1945 to the present). Visitors begin with a walk through an introductory room, *Forest*, that contains wisps of trees emblematic of the area of early Poland as a presettlement resting place for travelers. *Forest* establishes a reflective, pensive tone for what follows.

Several interpretative moves distinguish POLIN from the other museums I had seen.[53]

- The exhibit traces Jewish life over 1,000 continuous years in Poland. The "critical period," writes Kirshenblatt-Gimblett, is not the Holocaust; it is a millennium.
- It tells the story of the Shoah in its own time. Its curators, in Kirshenblatt-Gimblett's words, "avoid the Holocaust as a teleological endpoint"; they do not see Polish history inevitably leading to genocide and mass hatred.
- It tells a history of Polish Jews as integral to the history of Poland. It counters the view of Polish nationalists that Polish history is Catholic history. Polish Jewish civilization is "categorically Jewish and distinctly Polish."
- Its multimedia narrative derives from and is driven by a story, not by objects, pointedly unlike walking tours organized around visible buildings and artifacts.
- Its history is multivocal, presenting the Jewish experience of all Jews, not just the elite. It details the story of patriarchs, mothers and children, who move from the synagogue to the home, tavern, cemetery, workshop, and onto the street. They conversed in Yiddish, Polish, and Hebrew; among many affiliations, they were secular and religious, Zionists, and Bundists.

- The exhibit eschews a dominant authorial voice in favor of a critical, open-ended presentation. Like the glass façade of the building, the curators seek a transparent, reflexive engagement with recurrent debates about the Jewish past and present. Repeatedly, exhibit text presents Jewish writers, political actors, rabbis, and others addressing vexing issues such as identity in different ways. Historical figures debate who is a Jew, what does it mean to be Jewish? Similarly, the exhibit addresses stereotypes such as Shylock (the money-grubber or the Lucky Jew) or the Commie Jew.
- The museum challenges the "object fetish" and dependence on the material to make "the hidden," "the lost," "the invisible" visible.
- POLIN recovers the history of Jewish socialism and seamlessly integrates it into the story of the making of Jewish modernity. In Gallery 5, *Encounters with Modernity*, I come full circle back to my visit to Łódź with which I had begun. A room addresses "the dark side of industrialization" and the rise of the Bałuty, the Jewish section where my grandparents lived. The exhibit challenges the heroic image of the manufacturer Izrael Poznański who had been lionized by the Manufaktura redevelopment project and in the Łódź History Museum. Documentary footage depicts the sweated working conditions in a typical early twentieth-century Bałuty Workshop and the coincident work of Bund organizers at the time to win better conditions.

POLIN still faces some challenges. As the curator of the Berlin Jewish Museum noted, core exhibits in large museums shoulder the unenviable and impossible task of telling "the whole story" and satisfying all visitors. POLIN bears witness to that burden, and a visitor can get lost in the details. During my initial visit, I was frustrated trying to find the objects the audio guide directed me to see. Since then, curators have had footsteps printed on the floor to guide walkers through the cavernous space and enormous number of artifacts and images.

Even as POLIN tries—and succeeds—to cover so much, some critics press for expanded treatment of certain topics, such as of the Holocaust. Others, like the historian Saul Friedlander, worry that its linear historical account moves inexorably past the messy ethical and legal issues embedded in this panorama of the past and defers them to a post-tour reflection.[54] As visitors walk through the exhibit, opportunities for reflection are only implicit. Viewers are provided with information, lots of it, and invited to make sense of it. At the time of my 2014 visit, however, POLIN had not yet created an explicit reflective space for visitors to think about memory, history and memory makers, about who was able to tell the story in the past, and who now dominates the narrative in the present.[55]

The museum did not cover everything, despite its volume, and I, too, had my critique. I would have appreciated greater attention to gender in the Jewish family and within the Jewish community. Women are actors in the narrative, but there was not much mention of the kind of patriarchal family that had sent my aunts to work in factories, kept their brothers in school, and then directed women into trade-union work. There was little insight as to why someone would have criticized Chaia, the Bundist, for "not being home to cook," and normalized Zishe as a "strict disciplinarian" cum child-beater. Anecdotes about Jewish crime, gambling, and prostitution appeared on many of my tours, sometimes as melodramatic tales of rogues, sometimes as ominous threats to Jewish respectability. They were voyeuristic tales told by outsiders. I missed more from the perspective of the people from the underside of Jewish life who navigated limited opportunities. I hoped such perspectives might also shed light on the world in which a young girl like Marian could be raped on the Jewish Lower East Side of New York and where many husbands, like Max, ran away from family responsibilities. POLIN shows multiple perspectives and identities challenging one another across history, but not all opinions and actors have equal resource to the political power to be authorized in policy and practice.

———

Despite my caveats, I left Warsaw heartened: POLIN had established a new paradigm for Jewish heritage. POLIN's curators understand and celebrate the museum's exhibit as an uncompleted story; they see it as depicting the history of a lived culture, resplendent in its contradictions, ironies, and multiplicities. Jewishness appears diverse, neither static nor uncontested. The exhibit gives voice to most of the burning internal debates among Jewish communities about Polish-Jewish identity, acculturation, orthodoxy, reform, secularism, and religious variation. It also confronts national and geopolitical questions about Polish wartime complicity and collaboration with the Nazis, both by Poles and Jews. Finally, in its focus on Jewish daily life, the exhibit, apart from its limited gender analysis, POLIN, in its new paradigm for Jewish heritage, demonstrates the analytic power of the new Jewish social history. Its narrative also had particular poignancy for my heritage quest: the exhibit's discussion of 1905 Łódź vividly integrated the socialist activism of Chaia and Zishe into the story of Jewish heritage. POLIN had helped me find the lost world of Jewish socialism.

Conclusion

I was raised in the Jewish tradition, taught never to marry a Gentile woman, shave on Saturday and, most especially, never to shave a Gentile woman on Saturday.

There are three things Jewish people worship—God, Chinese food and wall-to-wall carpeting.

—*Woody Allen*

Woody Allen's witticisms convey ephemeral cultural expressions of modern secular Jewish identity in America.[1] Such jokes, stock material of the Catskill's borscht belt and Jewish vaudeville, reflect the legacy of Yiddishkeit, which itself is part of the broader expressions of Jewishness and Jewish socialism I sought in my travels. However, my experiences confirm the critical observations of Jewish heritage scholars regarding the imaginative narrowness of Jewish heritage tourism. Historians such as Jack Kugelmass, Matthew Frye Jacobson, and Ken Waltzer all agree that "dark" Holocaust tourism has dominated Jewish heritage tourism since the mid-1990s.[2] Both Jewish tourists and package tour operators tend to conflate Jewish history with the short temporal moment of the Holocaust. The cityscapes of postwar Berlin and Warsaw remain Holocaust museums, but the Shoah also casts a long shadow over Jewish exhibitions in New York, Berlin, Lviv, and Kraków, and it dominates walking tours almost everywhere. The "typical" walks I took everywhere punctuated the Holocaust with an itinerary of synagogues and cemeteries that privileged religious identity and memories of the deceased, not of the vibrant cultural heritage. To be sure, there was always the occasional surprise. I was also chasing a moving target; the booming interest in Jewish heritage inspires museums to stage new exhibits and tour guides to create new walks all the time. My visits were time and place specific. Within that context, the sites I visited reflect a representative cross section of major Jewish heritage cities on offer between 2010 and 2017.

My research extended beyond the exhibitions and tour presentations. It was enriched by formal interviews with museum directors, curators and docents, and informal discussions with tour guides, who occasionally broke out of their canned Holocaust narratives with unexpected stories and analyses. Many museum professionals exhibited a double consciousness. On the one hand, they were often up-to-date with innovative historiography and aware of critiques of heritage tourism. On the other hand, they were sensitive to a set of local, national, and international constraints from groups with opposing interpretative agendas. Tour guides, constrained by prescribed preprogrammed itineraries and the need to meet consumer expectations, nonetheless interjected their own personal perspectives and knowledge, often with telling anecdotes. Some interjections detracted from the discussion on Jewish heritage, but most added insights. People both shaping and serving the heritage business provided perceptive historical experiences outside their formally prescribed role.

Despite these small formal deviations from a fixed script, the abiding logic of the Jewish heritage tourism on display remains "dark" tourism. The equation, Jewish Heritage = concentration camps = Israel, continues to burden Jewish heritage tourism with a nationalist agenda; it equates heritage with Holocaust touring and Israeli nationalism. March of the Living programs (MOTL) historically exemplifies such tourism. Since 1998 this not-for profit charity has conducted Poland-Israel tours for 220,000 students from fifty-two countries. Most of these students are Jewish, but the groups include non-Jews. Each year, during the two weeks following Passover, MOTL groups begin walking from the Auschwitz to the Birkenau concentration camp "to learn about the Holocaust." The tour then concludes in Israel as the state sanctuary from the Holocaust. People respond differently to the experience, but for many of the Israeli students studied by Feldman, the camps simply reinforce nationalist predilections.[3] My own limited experience with student groups in Berlin and Budapest was positive: they were respectful and generally interested in the subject matter. But museum curators and analysts in urban area sites concur with Feldman's findings. They report most tourist groups make a beeline for the concentration camps, with ritual stops at the Holocaust Museum. They find students touring the museums to be restless and impatient. Curators complain that students are absorbed with their smart phones and take selfies, perhaps marking time before a visit to a staple teenager tourist mecca in foreign quarters such as the Hard Rock Cafe.[4]

The guides and docents leading these tours are also important stakeholders in how the past is remembered. For some, being a tour guide is part-time work, but for others it is their principal livelihood. To keep their job, they need to attract visitors and obtain good recommendations from them (preferably online). Visitors-consumers' expectations and desires place enormous pressure on walking tour guides. One ethnographer praises their efforts to resist pressure to please them with "comfortable stories." Let me emphasize, however, that while tour guides are front-line content deliverers, they are not the main agents of the limitations of heritage tourism. Guides often position themselves against what they see as the crass materialism of commodified sites and offer idiosyncratic and often ironic perspectives that counter "official" memory narratives.[5] Still, while I similarly found guides stepping out of the fixed program with ironic insights, I also found they tended to counter the history of an uncomfortable past with comfortable stories of valiant Jewish defenders and local Heroes who saved Jews.

Limited access to the historical narratives constrains historical accounts offered by guides and docents. As each chapter demonstrates, historians have outlined a richly detailed, complicated past that is available to tourist service personnel. But tour guide certification programs, where they exist, often emphasize tour management and fact-driven history that is long on dates, names, and architectural styles and short on context and social history. Tour training programs mix education with entertainment. Often, however, guides are left to educate themselves. Of the walking tour companies, New York's Big Onion Tours is relatively unique in its employment of guides who are academically trained in history-related fields and schooled in public presentations. Many larger museums have instituted formal docent training programs, but to the extent the exhibit is limited to the Holocaust, so is the docent. Even in the best scenario, political constraints and the heritage impulse to commemorate events and certain figures undermine the presentation of dissident voices and heterogeneous perspectives.[6]

In mounting exhibits, museum curators also have to negotiate a world of local, state, and international funders, corporate sponsors, and academics with competing investments in the presentation. These groups can also disagree among themselves. For example, in interviews prominent museum curators and directors such as Cilly Kugelmann and Chana C. Schütz in Berlin, Barbara Kirshenblatt-Gimblett and Paweł Śpiewak in Warsaw, and Esther Brumberg in New York all described constraints and political pressures that frame their work. Schütz, for example, eloquently laid out the dilemma facing Berlin curators in the new millennium. History, she noted, is "messy," but people in the organized Jewish Community who support their programs are often social and political conservatives who only want a harmonious Jewish "success story," not exhibits such as the *Yellow Ticket* about Jewish prostitutes or other programs that might criticize Israel in any way.[7]

The panoramic format of the permanent core exhibit in the new large Jewish museums poses additional challenges. As national museums of Jewish history, these institutions operate with a mandated broad national scope. Visitors who want to find accounts of their own family stories put additional pressure on curators to cover "everything"—or at least the many variants of "my story." Of course, telling the whole story is never possible; space limitations require editorial decisions. Still, the drive to be inclusive ends up frustrating visitors who, according to exit interviews at the Berlin Jewish Museum, see so much that they remember nothing. My visits confirm this experience and suggest the need to rethink the immense scale of these exhibits: I personally remember more from the smaller and more focused temporary exhibits.

External pressures and institutional structures matter, but so do fundamental assumptions about Jewish identity and the centrality of certain Jewish actors/experiences to the heritage history. Such assumptions frame how curators, guides, and docents tell what they believe to be "the" heritage story. These interpreters address, reject, or ignore the "assimilated Jew." They face similar decisions about the inclusion of the Jewish socialist, and so forth. According to historian Holly Snyder, for example, the idea of the Jewish Community employs long-established mechanisms of social and cultural control and tends to dismiss the inclusion of the world of Jewish socialism. Snyder's insight certainly applies to the 12,000 members of the traditional and more religiously inclined organized Jewish Community of Budapest. It claims to represent the larger community of upwards to 100,000 Jews in the city and the perspective of its members guides the exhibit at the Hungarian Jewish Museum. Following Snyder, such people conflate "the synagogue with the Jewish Community" and create "a static system" that elides conflict, fracture and "much historical evidence that does not fit into the 'synagogue-community' framework."[8] A static system of this sort does not allow for multiple Jewish voices, nor does it encourage a range of ways to express Jewish identity. Ultimately, it also excludes the cultural and political institutions that generate Jewish socialism.

The history of the Holocaust remains the dominant narrative in Jewish heritage tourism in good part because powerful local and transnational Jewish groups concerned with the long history of anti-Semitism remain invested in highlighting that story. The recent rise of populist, right-wing governments in Poland and Hungary, and resurgent populist xenophobia and anti-Semitism in the United States, United Kingdom, and elsewhere certainly amplifies such concerns. Cemeteries and synagogues have good reason to remain critical sites for remembrance and observance. At the same time, though, the streets, homes, playing fields, theatres, and workplaces of Jews in Eastern and Central Europe also need to be heritage foci. Religious expression took many forms, but so too did communal life, political engagements, and cultural institutions.

SIGNS OF A COUNTERNARRATIVE

When I returned to various sites between 2015 and 2017, I found signs of a new storyline and interpretative approach making inroads in the dominant narrative. The impact of the New Jewish History, with its focus on the social history of everyday life, was palpable in several Central and Eastern European sites. The popular interest in the contemporary Jewish revival evidenced by the large crowds of Jews and non-Jews attending Jewish cultural festivals may have been one force propelling the heritage story forward from the Holocaust. To a lesser extent, the revival may also have propelled it backward to lived Jewish experiences before the war. Most of all, the celebrated opening of POLIN's core exhibit in late fall of 2014 jump-started a changing heritage landscape. In the wake of the extraordinarily positive reception of POLIN's core exhibit, Jewish museums in Berlin, Budapest, New York, and Bucharest have initiated plans to redevelop their exhibits. Even MOTL has expanded its itineraries to include POLIN, which brings some attention to the contemporary Jewish renewal in Poland.

New Museology

Innovations in museum design, practice, conception, and performance have also opened up the spaces of heritage to new ways of seeing and thinking. These changes draw on insights from social and cultural history that advance multiple perspectives of historical actors with unequal access to power. This history also foregrounds the subjective nature of historical knowledge, inviting reflection and tourist engagement with the tour narrative.

Jewish heritage programs could draw inspiration from some of the rich, inventive walking tours and museum practices around the world. A full exploration of these new best practices is beyond the remit for this study, but let me identify a few such projects to indicate what is possible.

Soundwalks, a New York-based group, layers sounds from the past and present on walking tours. On fourteen self-guided audio tours local experts narrate a history while field recordings of sounds from the area attune listeners to the aural environment of the city.[9]

Audio Walks, a joint project of Berlin-based visual and documentary artists Janet Cardiff and George Bures Miller, takes participants on walks during which they watch a 3-D video with multilayered sound tracks on an iPad of the same path on another occasion. The walking tour, combining the actual walk with a previous virtual trip, places participants in one place at two times and augments reality to reflect on the sedimented history of the streets.

Psychogeography, where the built environment "speaks" to individual emotions, informs a third innovative form of walking tour. Often associated with the Situationists, these tours compel participants to think about the logic of the walk. Why does the guide turn one way rather than another; what does the guide direct them to see, and what do s/he ignore? Participants are encouraged to "drift," following their own associative logic. "Discovering" sites themselves, their incidental or directed predilections destabilize the narrative authority of the organized tour.[10]

Online sites and downloadable apps also complement and expand museum offerings. The London Jewish Museum's collection of 310 oral histories with Jews from diverse sections of the Jewish community illustrates the enriched interpretative range of such material. POLIN's online multimedia Guide to Jewish Warsaw goes even further. It organizes new technologies for three virtual tours. One tour follows the life of a Jewish educator and doctor and is geared to middle school students (and contains suggestions to teachers for classroom use). A second tour for high school students introduces them to nine characters through a multimedia comic book. A third tour targeted to adults focuses on World War II and postwar Warsaw events and characters.[11]

Finally, innovations in museum practice, design, and exhibition technologies encourage temporal and conceptual expansion of the heritage narrative. Richard Rabinowitz's American History Workshop, which has pioneered interactive, multimedia, multi-vocal installations across the United States for almost forty years, is a prime example of such work. From the 1970s to the present, the New Social History strongly influenced his work, and in turn, his installations have been a model for museum design around the world. Rabinowitz's recent projects include his exemplary interpretative development of the *Slavery and Freedom* gallery at the acclaimed Smithsonian's National Museum of African America History and Culture, which opened in 2016.[12]

Models to Build Upon

Over the course of my travels I came across six practices and institutions that offer creative, thoughtful interpretative models for Jewish heritage in the new millennium. Five are innovative developments while one is a residual program. Although I raise questions about all of them in earlier chapters, I want to praise their strategies and conceptions as advancing a more inclusive, complex, open-ended Jewish heritage tourism, one where the world of Jewish socialism might be recuperated as part of a radical history of Jewishness.

1. The Lower East Side Tenement Museum in New York. This museum in a converted tenement demonstrates how quotidian daily life, including the experience of women and children, can excite audiences of all ages. The museum provides a comparative immigrant perspective over time: it has dedicated each room in the tenement to the history of an ethnic group that occupied an apartment at a period in the building's history. Any city could identify such a site and adapt it to its local history.

2. The Taube Center's *Field Guide to Jewish Warsaw and Kraków*. This colorfully illustrated volume of walking tours vividly counters the dreary, repetitive tendency of walking tours to address only those sites that have visible remains. The *Field Guide* provides a textured model for walking tours that brings to life a sense of place without extant artifacts. In Warsaw, a city largely destroyed in the war, the *Field Guide* tours recuperate the long history of Jewish life in the city, including Jewish

socialism. Urban space, not artifacts, become the object, places of life and struggle invoked by stories and imaginings of the past.

3. *Stolpersteine* (Stumbling Blocks) in Berlin and elsewhere. Many cities deploy memorial stones and historic markers to commemorate persons and events that meet criteria of significance. English Heritage blue plaques are typical of this genre. First inaugurated in 1866, the plaques mark houses where notable politicians, artists, writers, scientists, or reformers once lived. By contrast, the Stumbling Blocks inscribe the history of Jews (and others), both the average person and the more famous, living and working on a street. The blocks resurrect a past otherwise invisible in the urban environment. As important, they demonstrate what the urban geographer and public historian Delores Hayden calls *The Politics of Place*. In the ubiquity of the stumbling blocks, the entire city becomes an urban memoryscape. The blocks are a reminder that all spaces of daily life are inhabited and contested by people over time, not merely during the moment typically memorialized on a walk.[13]

4. Belgrade Jewish Historical Museum. A traditional exhibit lacking the bells and whistles of new high-tech Jewish museums, Belgrade's museum illustrates conceptual insights in older exhibits that face erasure in the name of modernization. With an exhibit dating from 1969 during the Tito era, Belgrade's Jewish museum documents (and romanticizes a bit) a history of Jewish socialism that could be lost in the postcommunist drive to erase uncomfortable elements of the past.

5. Annual Festivals of Jewish Culture in Kraków, Warsaw, Berlin, Budapest, and elsewhere. Commentators have both derided and lauded these festivals. Some critics object to the romanticized Judeophilism of non-Jews who make up the majority of the attendees. They decry these events as an "invented Jewishness." But this latter objection usefully reminds us that cultures constantly renovate and reinvent themselves. The festivals compel us to assess whether there is an essential Jewishness, a timeless checklist of proscriptions, prescriptions, rituals, and customs.[14]

6. POLIN Museum of the History of Polish Jews. POLIN is a highly capitalized project with substantial resources, and its exhibit provides a new conceptual paradigm for Jewish museums. The core exhibit respects but decenters the Holocaust to focus on the long thousand years of a lived Jewish past in Poland. It is not a history of Jews in Poland but a history of Polish Jews. Sensitive to ambiguities, ironies, and disputes in Jewish history, POLIN gives voice to the many different ways Jews (and Poles!) express their identity.

It remains unclear how Jewish tourists with conventional expectations of a redemptive Holocaust experience will respond to these shifts in Jewish heritage tourism. It also remains to be seen how local and national states, particularly those in Hungary and Poland which have taken ultra-nationalists turns, will respond to narratives that address a socialist past or the complicity of local non-Jewish neighbors with the Nazis. The Holocaust narrative, with its wide audience, seems likely to remain securely dominant. Still, I am impressed by the enormous good will, enthusiasm, and intellectual ambition of many curators and guides who seem dedicated to renovating Jewish heritage tourism for the future.

∼ INTERLUDE ∼

Eleven cities, two villages, eight countries. It has been a long trip. I was constantly surprised to find places that opened up the Jewish heritage tourism experience in rewarding ways. Radical women like Ida Walkowitz, my Bubbe Chaia, rarely bubbled up to the surface. But when I went on London's radical tour, or on the walking tours of immigrant New York, or when I visited museums as different as those in Belgrade and Warsaw, I saw manifestations of the otherwise lost world of Jewish socialism. I also discovered the broad cultural world of Yiddishkeit: Bucharest's Yiddish Theater, the Jewish Rialto on New York's Lower East Side, and statues and plaques commemorating Sholem Aleichem in Kiev and Lviv. POLIN moved the heritage story back and forward in time. In POLIN and other sites, I witnessed a new paradigm that began to make sense of the world of Ida (Chaia), Alexander (Zishe), Max, and Marian.

What in the end had I learned of Chaia, of Max, . . . of myself? I began my quest in search of signs of someone I identified as a secular Bundist/communist; I finished realizing these categories were deeply problematic. Even as a child I knew that there were profound differences within our extended radical family over what it meant to be a radical, a socialist and a communist. But in the McCarthy era and extended Cold War, it was easy to minimize internal differences in favor of a triumphalist familial and socialist narrative of parents and grandparents who "fought the good fight." As I pursued this family history and began to uncover oral histories and memoirs of family members, I came to realize that the grandparents in whose footsteps I had proudly imagined myself walking had human flaws that family lore masked. I could celebrate my parents' and ancestors' pasts. They created a rich and sustaining Yiddish culture, waged heroic struggles against poverty and rapacious bosses in the immigrant city, and stood up to federal witch hunters in the 1950s. At the same time, these people were not always as noble as I had imagined them. Lost in the lore are the place of irony, ambiguity, contradictions, and inglorious behavior that included stories of family desertion, battering, in-fighting, rape, and the psychic strains of just getting by.

Figure 26. Doppelganger: Danny Wolkowicz and Danny Walkowitz, Buenos Aires, December 2010. Photo by the author.

My own early genealogical research also alerted me to the great diversity in my family story. The diasporic reach of my family extended to Europe, the Middle East, South America, and across North America. I am sure had I pressed on, I would have found relatives in Asia and Australia, not to speak of South Africa. In the context of specific local Jewish cultures, branches of the same family with common roots developed quite diverse political and religious profiles. Within the same Walkowitz family, for instance, brothers and sisters took profoundly different paths. In Buenos Aires I met a doppelganger: Danny Wolkowicz, a second cousin my age and also a professor, with whom I bore a striking resemblance. Our grandfathers were brothers. Historical contingencies involving visas and war (or personal events) propelled one brother to America and another to Argentina (where perhaps the wife's relatives had settled). Still, we seemed to share values as well as high foreheads.

Yet relatively few members in the Walkowitz diaspora elsewhere had become Jewish socialists. Cousins from Denmark made different choices about their religiosity and secularism. In Berlin, I met Adam Saks, the son of a female second cousin in Denmark and a world-class artist. His branch of the family was deeply religious, an identity Adam explained partially as the family's effort to preserve its Jewishness in a country where Jews were a tiny minority. In London, I met Miriam Lipman, the great granddaughter of Reuben Walkowitz, the brother who remained in Copenhagen. Her family, too, were politically mainstream and practicing Jews. By contrast, the Lubertofskys, Bubbe Chaia's birth family, includes her brother David, whose branch ultimately settled in southern California and developed radical political profiles. In Paterson, Chaia's sister, my Tante Neche, and her cousin Joe Katz were socialist firebrands. Maybe the Bundist side of the family came through Bubbe and the Lubertofskys and not the Walkowitzes.

~

The uncovering of new family archival material and return visits to Eastern and Central Europe connected the research on my family with my research on Jewish heritage. The connection also reframed my understanding of my family history, the socialist narrative within it, and my tourism quest. To be sure, my travels to Jewish heritage sites offered me some views of radical Jewish culture, civic life, and Jewish socialism. The gender politics within the Jewish family was more occluded, but Jewish socialism peeked through fissures in the dominant Heritage narrative. But the lessons of the New Jewish History made me realize my quest was for more than the inclusion of socialism into the Jewish Heritage story; it was for changing the story itself. The Bund, Jewish culture, and Jewish socialism fundamentally shaped the formation of twentieth-century Jewish modern identity and exposed the limitations of both triumphalist heritage and family narratives. Rather than the inclusion of the "lost world" of Jewish radicals as a missing "piece," I came to realize that the quest for the future of a robust Jewish heritage tourism requires the radical reconceptualizing of the narrative itself.

Past examples suggested how openings could depend on the confluence of historically contingent political factors. Political forces could make change possible—or could impede it. Rabbi Rosen's "bargain" in communist Bucharest, for example, had opened doors for Jewish cultural expression; Tito's alliance with Jewish partisans had created space for Jewish socialists in the Belgrade Jewish Museum. But such spaces could close as quickly as they opened. Jewish celebrations of cultural revival were welcomed in postcommunist Warsaw, Berlin, Budapest, and Lviv even as reactionary political tides swept anti-Semitic leaders to power in Poland and Hungary.

I end then as I began, at once hopeful and wary. A fuller account of the lost world of Jewish socialism—and one that includes the history of Jewish women, and the Jewish family and gender relations—remains to be done, and its integration into the Jewish heritage narrative will likely remain contested. The history of Jewish socialism, while not "lost," was often at the margins, its story muted in the telling. The muted story also provides a sad final irony. I was committed to telling a story of my family's "secret life" in the 1950s that had been submerged and subterranean. Chaia and Zishe Walkowitz and their Bund comrades struggled to make their voices heard a half-century earlier in 1905–1907 Łódź, and then afterward in Paterson. In the twenty-first century, Jewish heritage tourism managed to silence these voices yet again.

Notes

PREFACE

1. In 1980 I helped found and direct at New York University one of the world's earliest major public history graduate programs. I subsequently integrated public presentations of history in film and museums into my work. I also coedited two volumes of essays on how museums, memorials, and public spaces around the world imagine and contest the relationship between history and memory. Daniel J. Walkowitz and Lisa Maya Knauer, eds., *Memory and the Impact of Political Transformation in Public Spaces* (Durham, NC: Duke University Press, 2004) and *Contested Histories in Public Space: Memory, Race, and Nation* (Durham, NC: Duke University Press, 2009).

INTRODUCTION

1. Marianne Hirsch, *The Generation of Postmemory: Writing and Visual Culture after the Holocaust* (New York: Columbia University Press, 2012).

2. Many have written of the impact of the Six Day War. See, for example, Jack Kugelmass, *Between Two Worlds: Ethnographic Essays on American Jewry* (Ithaca and London: Cornell University Press, 1988).

3. Matthew Rampley, "Heritage and/as the Construction of the Past: An Introduction," in *Heritage, Ideology, and Identity in Central and Eastern Europe: Contested Pasts, Contested Presents,* ed. Matthew Rampley (Woodbridge, Suffolk: Boydell Press, 2012), 14–16.

4. Jonathan Boyarin, *Storm from Paradise: The Politics of Jewish Memory* (Minneapolis: University of Minnesota Press, 1992).

5. I will often revert to Chaia or Ida rather than Bubbe. I knew my grandmother as Bubbe Chaia, but the term Bubbe has taken on clichéd connotations in contemporary popular culture as a stereotype domestic female stock figure.

PRELUDE

1. "Paterson Bans Red Flag," *New York Times,* April 30, 1934, 2. The incident is described as well in Robert Snyder, "The Paterson Jewish Folk Chorus: Ethnicity and Musical Culture," *American Jewish History* 74, no. 1 (September 1984): 27–44.

2. Lia Mandelbaum, "Go Down Moses: Finding Kinship between the Jewish and African American Slave Experience," *Jewish Journal* (May 14, 2013), http://www.jewishjournal.com/sacredintentions/item/go_down_moses_finding_kinship_between_the_jewish_and_african_slave_experience.

3. Joyce Antler, "Emma Lazarus Federation of Jewish Women's Clubs," *Encyclopedia*, Jewish Women's Archive, http://jwa.org/encyclopedia/article/emma-lazarus-federation-of-jewish-womens-clubs.

4. In Jewish mythology, a *dybbuk* (from the Hebrew verb meaning "adhere" or "cling") is a malicious possessing spirit believed to be the dislocated soul of a dead person.

5. Jane Wallerstein, *Voices from the Paterson Silk Mills* (Collingdale, PA: Diane Publishing, 2000.)

6. Vivian Gornick, *The Romance of American Communism* (New York: Basic Books, 1979).

CHAPTER 1 — THE JEWISH HERITAGE BUSINESS

1. The epigraph to this chapter is from Kenneth Waltzer, "Irving Howe's 'World of Our Fathers' Twenty Years Later," *Centennial Review* 41, no. 3 (Fall 1997): 571. Irving Howe, *World of Our Fathers: The Journey of the East European Jews to America and the Life They Found and Made* (New York: Harcourt, [1976] 1989). Ironically, Howe engages in his own act of exclusion and his world notably minimizes religious Jews. The central place afforded "fathers" is another exclusion. Women are present but made secondary and readers do not get a gendered history of patriarchy. Howe's book, its significance and its blind spots on gender and religion is celebrated in a special issue of *American Jewish History* 88, no. 4 (December 2000).

2. See Alisa Solomon, *Wonder of Wonders: A Cultural History of 'Fiddler on the Roof'* (New York: Metropolitan Books, 2013). See also Solomon, "How Fiddler Became Folklore," *Jewish Daily Forward*, September 1, 2006, and Robert Brustein, "Fiddle Shtick," *New York Review of Books* 61, no. 20 (December 18, 2014): 82–83. These article references are drawn from https://en.wikipedia.org/wiki/Fiddler_on_the_Roof.

3. Yohanen Petrovsky-Shtern, *The Golden Age of the Shtetl: A New History of Jewish Life in East Europe* (Princeton: Princeton University Press, 2014), 2.

4. *Time*, May 26, 2008, 51, as cited in Andrea Most, *Theatrical Liberalism: Jews and Popular Entertainment in America* (New York: New York University Press, 2013), 153.

5. Elizabeth Becker, *Overbooked: The Exploding Business of Travel and Tourism* (New York: Simon & Schuster, 2013), 17; and Donald E. Lundberg, M. Krishnamoorthy, and Mink H. Stavenga, *Tourism Economics* (New York: John Wiley, 1995), 8.

6. Brenda Sprague, as cited in Ellen Brennen, "Going Abroad? How the State Department Can Help," *New York Times*, January 30, 2013, 2. To be sure, the Patriot Act required that travelers to Mexico and Canada produce a passport and that contributed to some of this increase. Adventure travel for an expanded middle-class market undoubtedly accounted for another share.

7. Barbara Kirshenblatt-Gimblett, *Destination Culture: Tourism, Museums and Heritage* (Berkeley: University of California, 1998).

8. Hasia R. Diner, *A Time for Gathering: The Second Migration, 1820–1880*, volume 2 in *The Jewish People in America*, Henry Feingold, ed. (Baltimore: Johns Hopkins University Press, 1992).

9. Jacob Glatstein, *The Glatstein Chronicles*, trans. Maier Deshell and Norbert Guterman, edited with an introduction by Ruth Wisse (New Haven: Yale University Press, 2010).

10. An example is Gustave Eisner, the travel agent described by Daniel Soyer, "The Immigrant Travel Agent as Broker between Old World and New: The Case of Gustave Eisner," *YIVO Annual* 21 (1993): 345-368. Thanks, too, to Daniel Stone, email remarks to the author, July 19, 2015.

11. Suzanne Rachel Wasserman, *The Good Old Days of Poverty: The Battle over the Fate of New York City's Lower East Side during the Depression* (PhD diss., New York University, 1990); Hasia R. Diner, *The Lower East Side Memories: The Jewish Place in America* (Princeton: Princeton University Press, 2000); Deborah Dash Moore, *At Home in America: Second Generation New York Jews* (New York: Columbia University Press, 1981).

12. See Daniel Soyer, "Revisiting the Old World: American Jewish Tourists in Interwar Eastern Europe," in *Forging Modern Jewish Identities*, ed. Michael Berkowitz, Susan Tananbaum, and Sam Bloom (London: Valentine-Mitchell, 2003). See also Daniel Soyer, "Transnationalism and Americanization in East European Jewish Immigrant Public Life," in *Imagining the American Jewish Community*, ed. Jack Wertheimer (Waltham, MA Brandeis University Press, published by University Press of New England, 2007); Daniel Soyer, "Soviet Travel and the Making of an American Jewish Communist: Moissaye Olgin's Trip to Russia, 1920-1921," *American Communist History* 4, no. 1 (June 2005); "Abraham Cahan's Travels in Jewish Homelands: Palestine in 1925 and the Soviet Union in 1927," in *Yiddish and the Left: Papers of the Third Mendel Friedman International Conference*, ed. Gennady Estraikh and Mikhail Krutikov, Studies in Yiddish 3 (Oxford: Legenda, 2001); and, Daniel Soyer, "Back to the Future: American Jews Visit the Soviet Union in the 1920s and 1930s," *Jewish Social Studies* 6 (Spring–Summer 2000). See also the special issue of *YIVO Annual* 21 (1993), "Going Home." On the invention of tradition, the classic work is Eric Hobsbawm and Terrence Ranger, eds., *The Invention of Tradition* (Cambridge: Cambridge University Press, 1983), and Michael Kammen, *Mystic Chords of Memory: The Transformation of Tradition in American Culture* (New York: Knopf, 1991).

13. Michael Meng, *Shattered Spaces: Encountering Jewish Ruins in Postwar Germany and Poland* (Cambridge, MA: Harvard University Press, 2011).

14. "Cemetery," in *Encyclopedia Judaica*, 271-75, cited in Samuel D. Gruber et al., *Jewish Cemeteries, Synagogues and Mass Grave Sites in Ukraine* (Washington, DC: United States Commission for the Preservation of America's Heritage, 2005), 31.

15. Gruber et al., *Jewish Cemeteries*, 68-71.

16. Ibid., 5-8.

17. See Sharon Macdonald, *Memoryland: Heritage and Identity in Europe Today* (London: Routledge, 2013), chap. 8. A special issue of *East European Jewish Affairs* 45, nos. 2-3 (August–December 2015), "New Jewish Museums in Post-Communist Europe," Barbara Kirshenblatt-Gimblett and Olga Gershenson, eds., reviews new Jewish museums, large and small that are transforming Jewish heritage in the region. I especially recommend Gershenson's essay critiquing the grand new Moscow museum, which I do not visit for this book. Gershenson suggests how the working relationship between leaders of the Jewish community and Vladimir Putin, the authoritarian postcommunist Russian leader, shapes the exhibit's celebratory history and general silence on Russian anti-Semitism.

18. MacDonald, *Memoryland,* and Kirschenblatt-Gimblett and Gershenson, eds., "New Jewish Museums."

19. Hasia Diner, *We Remember with Reverence and Love: American Jews and the Myth of Silence after the Holocaust, 1945–1962* (New York: New York University Press, 2010); Peter Novack, *The Holocaust in American Life* (New York: Mariner Books, 2000).

20. Erica Lehrer, *Jewish Poland Revisited: Heritage Tourism in Unquiet Places* (Bloomington: Indiana University Press, 2103), 3.

21. Jack Kugelmass, ed., *Between Two Worlds: Ethnographic Essays on American Jewry* (Ithaca: Cornell University Press, 1988); Jack Kugelmass, "The Rites of the Tribe: The Meaning of Poland for American Jewish Tourists," in *Going Home, YIVO Annual* 21 (Evanston, IL: Northwestern University Press, 1993); and Jackie Feldman, *Above the Death Pits, Beneath the Flag: Youth Voyages to Poland and the Performance of Israeli National Identity* (New York: Berghahn Books, 2008).

22. Joanna Olczak-Ronikier, *In the Garden of Memory: A Memoir* (London: Weidenfeld & Nicolson, [2001] 2004).

23. Zvi Gitelman, *A Century of Ambivalence: The Jews of Russia and the Soviet Union, 1881 to the Present,* 2nd ed. (Bloomington: Indiana University Press, 2001); also, Daniel Stone, email comments to the author, August 10, 2015.

24. Vladimir Bilovitsky, "Institute of Jewish Proletarian Culture," *YIVO Encyclopedia of Jews in Eastern Europe,* http://www.yivoencyclopedia.org/article.aspx/Institute_of_Jewish_Proletarian_Culture. For the earlier period, see Natan M. Meir, *Kiev: Jewish Metropolis: A History, 1859–1914* (Bloomington: Indiana University Press, 2010).

25. Daniel Stone, comments to the author, August 10, 2015. See Tony Judt, *Postwar: A History of Europe since 1945* (New York: Penguin Press, 2005), 434–435; Barbara Kirshenblatt-Gimblett, "Historical Space and Critical Methodologies: Museum of the History of Polish Jews," in *From Museum Critique to Critical Museum,* ed. Katarzyna Murawska-Muthesius and Piotr Piotrowski (London: Routledge, 2015).

26. The impact of regime change was on display in 2017 Poland when a new right-wing nationalist government intervened to close a new museum on World War II it saw as insufficiently nationalist. This is a familiar story though; see Daniel J. Walkowitz and Lisa Maya Knauer, eds., *Memory and the Impact of Political Transformations in Public Space* (Durham: Duke University Press, 2004).

27. Conversations with Stuart Hall over many dinners. See also Stuart Hall, "Gramsci and Us," *Marxism Today* (June 1987), http://www.hegemonics.co.uk/docs/Gramsci-and-us.pdf.

28. Daniel Mendelsohn, *The Lost: A Search for Six of Six Million* (New York: Harper-Perennial, 2006): Marianne Hirsch and Leo Spitzer, *Ghosts of Home: The Afterlife of Czernowitz in Jewish Memory* (Berkeley: University of California Press, 2011); David G. Roskies, *Yiddishlands* (Detroit: Wayne State University Press, 2008).

29. Israel Joshua Singer, *The Brothers Ashkenazi,* trans. Joseph Singer (New York: Scribner, [1936] 1980); Andrzej Wajda, *The Promised Land* (Poland, 1975). The film is based on Władisław Reymont's book of the same title.

30. Tamar Katriel, *Performing the Past: A Study of Israeli Settlement Museums* (Mahwah NJ: Lawrence Erlbaum Associates, 1997), 2–8, 33.

31. Chaim Noy, *A Narrative Community: Voices of Jewish Backpackers* (Detroit: Wayne State University Press, 2007), 16, 200.

32. James Young, *The Texture of Memory: Holocaust Memorials and Meaning* (New Haven: Yale University Press, 1994), x–xiii, 2–3.

33. Macdonald, *Memorylands*, 65–84.

34. Ibid., 46–64.

35. Lehrer, *Jewish Poland Revisited*; Meng, *Shattered Spaces*; Erica Lehrer and Michael Meng, eds., *Jewish Space in Contemporary Poland* (Bloomington: Indiana University Press, 2015); Scott Ury, *Barricades and Banners: The Revolution of 1905 and the Transformation of Warsaw Jewry* (Stanford: Stanford University Press, 2012); Tony Michels, *A Fire in their Hearts: Yiddish Socialists in New York* (Cambridge, MA: Harvard University Press: 2005); Daniel Katz, *All Together Different: Yiddish Socialist, Garment Workers, and the Roots of Multiculturalism* (New York: New York University Press, 2011).

36. Macdonald, *Memorylands*, 199.

37. Macdonald nicely summarizes all these developments in *Memorylands*.

38. Michels, "Introduction," *A Fire in their Hearts*.

39. A. L. Patkin, *Origins of the Russian-Jewish Labour Movement* (Melbourne: Cheshire, 1947), 109; Katz, *All Together Different*, 23.

40. Thanks to David Feldman, in conversation with the author, for these distinctions.

41. Gitelman, *A Century of Ambivalence*, 2; Katz, *All Together Different*, 22.

42. Jack Jacobs, ed., *Bundist Counterculture in Interwar Poland* (Syracuse, NY: Syracuse University Press, 2009); and Jack Jacobs, ed., *Jewish Politics in Eastern Europe: The Bund at 100* (New York: New York University Press, 2001). See also Ury, *Barricades and Banners*, 4–6; Michels, *A Fire in their Heart*, 19–20; and Tony Michels, "Socialisms with a Jewish Face: The Origins of the Yiddish-Speaking Communist Movement in the United States, 1907–1923," in *Yiddish and the Left*, ed. Gennady Estriakh and Mikhail Krutikov (Oxford, UK: European Humanities Research Centre, 2001), 24–55; Moss, 198; Patkin, *Origins of the Russian-Jewish Labour Movement* 109.

43. Michels, 27.

44. Karen Brodkin, *How Jews Became White Folks and What That Says about Race in America* (New Brunswick, NJ: Rutgers University Press, 1998), 107.

45. Ibid. See also Annelise Orleck, *Common Sense and a Little Fire: Women and Working-Class Politics in the United States, 1900–1965* (Chapel Hill: University of North Carolina Press, 1995).

46. Although his wife was pregnant, Zishe was anxious to avoid conscription into the czar's army, so he emigrated with his daughter Belle in 1913. His wife gave birth a few months later to my aunt Rose. Chaia, accompanied by her aunt, Lea Klapersak, then joined her husband in Denmark, baby Rose in tow.

Recent scholarship (Yohanan Petrovsky-Shtern, *Jews in the Russian Army, 1827–1917: Drafted into Modernity* [Cambridge: Cambridge University Press, 2009]) challenges the collective memory of fear regarding conscription. Societal anti-Semitism existed, of course, as did discriminatory military policy, but many Jewish soldiers in the Russian army got release time for Jewish holidays and received kosher food. Quite a few garrison synagogues also had army chaplains/rabbis and Russian military commanders reported that Jewish soldiers served well, often as enthusiastic patriots. None of this precludes individuals preferring not to serve in any military.

47. Many good historians could be cited. Among them, see Marion A. Kaplan, *The Making of a Jewish Middle Class: Women, Family, and Identity in Imperial Germany* (New York: Oxford University Press, 1994); Hasia R. Diner and Beryl Benderly, *Her*

Works Praise Her: A History of Jewish Women in America from Colonial Times to the Present (New York: Basic Books, 2002).

48. Henry Tobias, quoted in Gitelman, *A Century of Ambivalence*, 6-9.

49. Ury, *Barricades and Banners*, 1-28, 268-270; Katz, *All Together Different*; Michels, *A Fire in their Hearts*.

50. Jan T. Gross, *Neighbors: The Destruction of the Jewish Community in Jedwabne, Poland* (Princeton: Princeton University Press, 2001). The number murdered is hotly disputed and the actual number will probably never be known though that hardly diminishes the horror of the story. For the nuances of the debate and contested bits of evidence, see Alisse Waterston, *My Father's Wars: Migration, Memory, and the Violence of a Century* (New York: Routledge: 2014), 90.

51. Pawel Pawlikowski, dir., *Ida* (Poland, 2013).

52. Annie Polland, "'May a Freethinker Help a Pious Man': The Shared World of the 'Religious' and the 'Secular' Among Eastern European Jewish Immigrants to America," *American Jewish History* 93, no. 4 (December 2007): 375-407. Seth Kamil, president of Big Onion Tours, was impressed by the more secular character of the Jewish community. Seth Kamil, interview with the author, Tannersville, New York, August 2, 2013.

53. Harvey E. Goldberg, M. Cohen, and Ezra Kopelowitz, eds., *Dynamic Belonging: Contemporary Jewish Collective Identities* (New York : Berghahn Books, 2012), 3-13.

54. Jonathan Boyarin, *Jewish Families* (New Brunswick, NJ: Rutgers University Press, 2013), 112, 156; and his *Storm from Paradise*, 128.

55. See, for example, S. Levenberg, "Dreamers and Fighters" (March 1966, reprinted in "100 Years of Jewish Labour Movement in Britain") (Poale Zion Labour Zionist Movement, January, 1967), 4.

56. Todd M. Endelmann, *The Jews of Britain, 1656-2000* (Berkeley: University of California, 2002), 137.

57. Raphael Samuel, "The Lost World of British Communists," *New Left Review* 154 (1985): 50. See also Stephen M. Cullen, "'Jewish Communists' or 'Communist Jews'? The Communist Party of Great Britain and British Jews in the 1930s," *Socialist History* 12, no. 41 (1912): 22-42.

58. Daniel J. Walkowitz, *City Folk: The Transatlantic Politics of the Folk in Modern America* (New York: New York University Press, 2010).

59. Olczak-Ronikier, *In the Garden of Memory*.

60. Ibid., 143-160. The Soviet secret police arrested him as subversive in 1937 and, shortly after, he was executed.

61. Olczak-Ronikier, *In the Garden of Memory*, 9.

62. Ibid., 267.

63. Daniel Stone, email to the author, August 10, 2015.

64. Ibid., 309.

65. A friend, Deborah Holmes, turned out to be Joanna Olczak-Ronikier's cousin, and updated the family story to me in various discussions between 2014 and 2017. See Katarzyna Zimmerer, *Kronika Zamorowanego Świata: Żylzi w Krakowie w czasie okupacji niemieckiej* [The Chronicle of a murdered world: Jews in Kraków during the occupation] (Kraków: Wydawnictwo Literackie, 2017).

66. Boyarin, *Storm from Paradise*, 82-83.

67. The major exception was evident at the core exhibit at POLIN Museum of the History of Polish Jews, which opened in late October 2014. It has a prominent display

on the acculturation of Jews who were subjects of the former Polish-Lithuanian Commonwealth.

68. David Feldman, *Englishman and Jews: Social Relation and Political Culture, 1840–1914* (New Haven: Yale University Press, 1994); Marcin Wodziński, "Good Maskilim and Bad Assimilationists, or Toward a New Historiography of the Haskalah in Poland," trans. Sarah Cozens, *Jewish Social Studies* 10, no. 3 (2004): 87–122; Marcin Wodziński, "Language, Ideology, and the Beginnings of the Integrationist Movement in the Kingdom of Poland in the 1860s," *East European Jewish Affairs* 34, no. 2 (2004) L 21–40; and Antony Polansky, *The Jews in Poland and Russia*, pt. 2 (Liverpool: University of Liverpool Press, 2009), introduction, 182–189.

69. Jonathan R. Wynn, *The Tour Guide: Walking and Talking New York* (Chicago: The University of Chicago Press, 2011).

70. Lehrer, *Jewish Poland Revisited*, 23–24, 93–99.

71. Ruth Ellen Gruber, "A Virtual Jewish World," lecture delivered at the Central European University, http://web.ceu.hu/jewishstudies/pdf/o2_gruber.pdf and *Virtually Jewish: Reinventing Jewish Culture in Europe* (Berkeley: University of California Press, 2002). See also Jonathan Webber, *Rediscovering Traces of Memory: The Jewish Heritage of Polish Galicia* (Bloomington: Indiana University Press, 2009), with photographs by Chris Schwarz.

72. Lehrer, *Jewish Poland Revisited*, 203–209, 215.

73. Macdonald, *Memorylands*, 100–106; Lehrer, *Jewish Poland Revisited*, 199; Meng, *Shattered Spaces*, 11–13.

74. Lehrer, *Jewish Poland Revisited*, 208.

75. Boyarin, *Storm from Paradise*; see also books by Ury, Moss, Michels, and Katz.

76. "A Portrait of Jewish Americans," Pew Research: Religion & Public Life Project, October 1, 2013, http://www.pewforum.org/2103/10/01/Jewish-american-beliefs-attitudes -culture-survey/.

77. For the development and character of the Israel Visit or Birthright Israel tourism in the last two decades, see Lilach Lev Ari and David Mittelberg, "Between Authenticity and Ethnicity: Heritage Tourism and Re-Ethnification among Diaspora Jewish Youth," *Journal of Heritage Tourism* 3, no. 2 (2008): 79–103. For the rich engagement with Jewish heritage tourism in Poland, see Lehrer, *Jewish Poland Revisited*.

INTERLUDE

1. Elissa Bemporad, *Becoming Soviet Jews: The Bolshevik Experiment in Minsk* (Bloomington: Indiana University Press, 2013), 8–10.

2. Belle Walkowitz Bernstein, interview with Robert Snyder, October 9, 1980, Fair Lawn, New Jersey, Jewish Historical Society of North Jersey archive; Joseph Walkowitz, interviewed by Randy Freeman and Jerry Nathan, April 6, 1980, Wayne, New Jersey, Jewish Historical Society of North Jersey archive.

3. Snyder, "Paterson Jewish Folk Chorus," 27–44.

4. "Historical/Biographical Note," *Guide to the Tamiment Library and Robert F. Wagner Labor Archives Printed Ephemera Collection on the Socialist Party (U.S.),* http://dlib.nyu.edu/findingaids/html/tamwag/pe_032/bioghist.html.

5. Ruthie Lubert Sacks, emails to the author, October 14, 15, 17, 2011 and April 13, 2017; Charlotte Berzin Tambor, email to the author, March 21, 2017; and Paul C. Mishler,

Raising Reds: The Young Pioneers, Radical Summer Camps, and Communist Political Culture in the United States (New York: Columbia University Press, 1999).

6. William E. Mitchell, *Mishpokhe: A Study of New York City Jewish Family Circles* (The Hague: Mouton Publishers, 1978); Daniel Soyer, *Jewish Immigrant Associations and American Identity in New York, 1880–1939* (Cambridge, MA: Harvard University Press, 1997).

CHAPTER 2 — MSZCZONÓW AND ŁÓDŹ

1. "Mszczonow: Jewish Community Before 1989," *Virtual Shtetl,* http://www.sztetl.org .pl/en/article/mszczonow/5,history/.

2. *25th Anniversary: Amshenover Independent Benevolent Society, 1916–1941,* New York, May 11, 1941.

3. Ela Bauer, "Industry," in *The YIVO Encyclopedia of Eastern Europe.* http://www .yivoencyclopedia.org/article.aspx/Industry.

4. There were textile mills in nearby towns and, while Jews may have even owned one, most Jewish workers were compelled to work at home or in family workshops. See, for example, Israel Joshua Singer's novel of Jewish life in industrial Łódź, *The Brothers Ashkenazi,* trans. Maurice Samuel (New York: Knopf, 1936). The story focuses on a textile factory complex, presumably like that owned by the wealthy Jewish manufacturer, Izrael Poznański, whose skilled German weavers kept Jews from taking work that they wanted for other Germans. Limiting alternative labor was also a way of increasing the value of their own labor.

5. Harry Koyfman, "From a Stormy Time," in *Pincus Zyrardow, Amshinov un Viskit,* ed. M. W. Bernstein (Buenos Aires: Association of Former Residents in the USA, Israel, France and Argentina, 1991).

6. The spelling among relatives has varied with Polish, Yiddish, and American variants, and Wolkowicz may be closest to the original.

7. "Błonie," Virtual Shtetl, http://www.sztetl.org.pl/en/article/blonie/6.demography/.

8. *American Jewish Yearbook* (1906, 47), cited by Ezra Mendelsohn, *Class Struggle in the Pale: The Formative Years of the Jewish Workers' Movement in Tsarist Russia* (Cambridge: Cambridge University Press, 1970). See also Wallerstein, *Voices from the Paterson Silk Mills,* 14.

9. Hershel Gunther's daughter tells how revolutionary weavers like her father relied on the underground network for the risky flight out of Łódź: Wallerstein, *Voices from the Paterson Silk Mills,* 21.

10. Vladimir Levin, "The Jewish Socialist Parties in Russia in the period of Reaction," in *Revolution of 1905 and Russia's Jews,* ed. Stefani Hoffman and Ezra Mendelsohn (Philadelphia: University of Pennsylvania Press, 2008), 119.

11. Omer Bartov, *Erased: Vanishing Traces of Jewish Galicia in Present-Day Ukraine* (Princeton: Princeton University Press, 2007); and Webber, *Rediscovering Traces of Memory.*

12. Mauricio Olsztajn, "The Beginnings of Jewish Settlement in Łódź"; and "Łódź," in *Encyclopedia of Jewish Communities, Poland,* trans. Morris Gradel (Jerusalem: Yad Vashem, 1976), 1:1–41, http://www.jewishgen.org/Yizkor/pinkas_poland/pol1_00001.html; Antony Polansky, *POLIN Studies in Polish Jewry,* vol. 6: *Jews in Lodz, 1820–1939* (Liverpool: Liverpool University Press, 2005).

13. Olsztajn, pt. II, section a (n.p.).

14. Ibid., pt. III, sections b and c (n.p.).

15. Ibid., pt. III, section c. (n.p.).

16. Ibid., pt. III, sections c and d.(n.p.) and dispatches from Poland, "Riotous Strikers Arrested: Lodz, in Poland, in the Hands of the Police," *New York Times*, May 11, 1892, 2; and, "Polish Rioters Punished: Long Term in Jail for the Leaders at Lodz, *New York Times*, May 12, 1892, 2.

17. Leo Greenbaum and Marek Web, curators, *The Story of the Jewish Labor Bund, 1897–1997: A Centennial Exhibition* (New York: YIVO, 1998); "The Beginnings of Jewish Settlement," part III, section d (n.p.).

18. Ibid.

19. Ibid.

20. See, for instance, "Lodz 4 Cultures Festival," http://culture.pl/en/place/lodz-4 -cultures-festival; for advertised tours, see, http://www.toursbylocals.com/JewishŁódźTour.

21. Paulina Zatorska, interview with the author, Łódź, Poland, June 19, 2014.

22. *In Your Pocket* (Łódź: In Your Pocket, 1999–2011). The guide is now available online, too: https://www.inyourpocket.com/lodz.

CHAPTER 3 — MOSTYSKA, LVIV, AND KIEV

1. Israel Bartal, *The Jews of Eastern Europe, 1772–1881* (Philadelphia: University of Pennsylvania Press, 2005); Larry Wolff, *The Idea of Galicia: History and Fantasy in Hapsburg Political Culture* (Stanford: Stanford University Press, 2010).

2. Webber, *Rediscovering Traces of Memory*, chap. 2; Endelmann, *The Jews of Britain*, 123–130; Daniel Stone, email comments to the author, August 18, 2015.

3. Wolff, *The Idea of Galicia*.

4. "Mosciska," Mosciska—Family Crossroads, http://sites.google.com/site/familyxroads /mosciska (as of August 2011).

5. B. Wasiutyński, *Ludność żydowska w Polsce* (1930), 96, 107, 116, cited in www .jewishvirtuallibrary.org/jsource/judaica/ejud_0002_0014_0_14307.html. The data is confirmed by the entry for Mościska at http://www.sztetl.org.pl/en/city/mosciska/.

6. See Margelov Institut website, at http://www.margel-institute.hr/aboutm.html.

7. Vladimir is a pseudonym.

8. Bartov, *Erased*.

9. "Establishment of Monument at Destroyed Jewish Cemetery after Trip to Czernowitz" (blog post), http://ehpes.com/blog1/?p=2657.

10. See Wolff, *The Idea of Galicia*; Petrovsky-Shtern, *The Golden Age Shtetl*; Eva Hoffman, *Shtetl: the Life and Death of a Small Town and the World of Polish Jews* (New York: Houghton Mifflin, 2007); and, Joseph T. Katz, ed., *The Shtetl: New Evaluations* (New York: New York University Press, 2009).

11. Yohanen Petrovsky-Shtern, *Anti-Imperial Choice: The Making of the Ukrainian Jew* (New Haven: Yale University Press, 2009); Piotr Wrobel, "The Jews of Galicia under Austrian-Polish Rule, 1867–1918," http://easteurotopo.org/articles/wrobel/wrobel .pdf; Education Program on Yiddish Culture (EPYC), Political Life, "Eastern European Jewish Political Life before and during World War I," http://epyc.yivo.org/main .php?uid=3.

12. See Meir, *Kiev*; Michael F. Hamm, *Kiev: A Portrait, 1800–1917* (Princeton: Princeton University Press, 1996); Jerzy Mazur, "Lviv in the Eyes of Jewish Historians in the Late 19th and Early 20th Centuries," lecture delivered at the Center for Urban History,

Lviv, January 17, 2011; John Czaplicka, ed., *Lviv: A City in the Crosscurrents of History* (Cambridge, MA: Harvard Ukrainian Research Institute, 2005).

13. Hamm, *Kiev*; Meir, *Kiev*; "Kiev," in *YIVO*.

14. Samuel Gruber et al., *Jewish Cemeteries*, 13–16.

15. Ibid.; see also Gitelman, *A Century of Ambivalence*; "Bund," in *YIVO*.

16. Gitelman, *A Century of Ambivalence*; Mendelsohn, *Class Struggle in the Pale*; Henry Abramson, "Zionist Movement," in *Internet Encyclopedia of Ukraine*, vol. 5, 1993, 3–5, http://www.encyclopediaofukraine.com/display.asp?linkpath=pages%5CZ%5CI%5CZionistmovement.htm.

17. UNESCO, quoted in The Jewish Traveler: Lvov, a reprint from an essay in *Hadassah Magazine* (April 2008), http://www.hadassahmagazine.org/2008/04/02/jewish-traveler-lvov/.

18. Ibid. A good description of some of the sites on my tour led by the same guide appears in an essay in the April 2008 issue of *Hadassah Magazine*. Jewish tourists post photographic essays on these sites and new postings appear regularly. One excellent site is http://www.pbase.com/nuthatch/ua_jewish_lviv.

19. "International Design Competition for Sites of Jewish Heritage in Lviv," Center for Urban History of East Central Europe, http://www.lvivcenter.org/en/conferences/competitionjewishsites/. Thanks to Olga Linkiewicz for this cite.

20. Michael Goldfarb, "How about Some Anti-Semitism with That Dish?" *Global Post*, April 2, 2012, http://www.globalpost.com/dispatch/news/regions/europe/120329/golden-rose-lviv-ukraine-anti-semitism-with-dish-echoes-hitler-pt-3. Forty-five customers had submitted evaluations as of November 2014, of which only six rated it "terrible" or "poor," http://www.tripadvisor.co.uk/Restaurant_Review-g295377-d2164473-Reviews-At_the_Golden_Rose-Lviv_Lviv_Oblast.html.

21. Goldfarb, "How about Some Anti-Semitism"; Daniel Estrin, "Slideshow: Ukraine's Controversial Theme Restaurants," *Vox Tablet*, February 6, 2012), www.tabletmag.com/podcasts/90161/cheap-eats.

22. On Sheykhet, see http://samgrubersjewishartmonuments.blogspot.co.uk/2011/09/ukraine-golden-rose-synagogue-ruins-not.html.

23. "Jewish Museum Lviv (Ukraine)," http://www.tripadvisor.com/Attraction_Review-g295377-d3460309-Reviews-Jewish_Museum_Lviv-Lviv_Lviv_Oblast.html.

24. "The Space of Synagogues: Jewish History, Common Heritage and Responsibility," Center of Jewish History, http://www.lvivcenter.org/en/space-of-synagogues.

25. Meir; "Kiev" in *YIVO*.

26. A distinguished scholar with an honorary doctorate from a local Research Institute on architecture and urban planning, Kalnytskyi had recently published a pamphlet on objects and structures of Jewish life in nineteenth- and twentieth-century Kiev, *Jewish Addresses in Kiev, a Guide Book* (Kiev: Dukh I Litera, 2012).

27. Gruber, *Jewish Heritage Travel*. Among the more interesting web-advertised tours, see, http://www.getyourguide.co.uk/kiev-l185/kiev-jewish-heritage-3-hour-tour-t20851/ and, http://www.albatros.travel/en/JewishTour/.

28. Ibid., 223–228.

29. Meir, *Kiev*, 216.

30. Ibid., 34, 237–245, 258; Hamm, *Kiev*, 131. Meir's excellent history also does not discuss the gendered nature of philanthropy.

31. Gruber, *Jewish Heritage Travel*, 104.

32. Solomon, *Wonder of Wonders;* Jeremy Dauber, *The Worlds of Sholem Aleichem: The Remarkable Life and Afterlife of the Man Who Created Tevye* (New York: Schocken Books, 2013).

CHAPTER 4 — LONDON

1. "Census 2100," http://www.boardofdeputies.org.uk/page,php/Census2011/397/1/13.

2. Geoffrey Alderman, *Modern British Jewry* (Oxford: Oxford University Press, 1992); Feldman, *Englishmen and Jews;* David S. Katz, *The Jews in the History of England, 1485–1850* (Oxford: Oxford University Press, 1994); Endelmann, *The Jews of Britain;* Stephen M. Cullen, "'Jewish Communists' or 'Communist Jews'? The Communist Party of Great Britain and British Jews in the 1930s," *Socialist History* 12, no. 41 (1912): 22–42; and Geoffrey Alderman, ed., *New Directions in Anglo-Jewish History* (Boston: Academic Studies Press, 2010).

3. Ernst Krausz, "Postwar Period," and Anne J. Kershen, "Later Developments," both in *Encyclopedia Judaica: London, England,* http://www.jewishvirtuallibrary.org/jsource /judaica/ejud_0002_0013_0_12735.html.

4. Feldman, *Englishmen and Jews.*

5. W. Gilbert, "The London Jews," in *Good Words V* (1864), quoted in James Appell, "The Jews of Leeds: Immigrant Identity in the Provinces, 1880-1920," 3, in Alderman, *New Directions.*

6. Feldman, *Englishmen and Jews*, 329; Sara Abosh, "'Good Jews and Civilized, Self-Reliant Englishmen': Crafting Anglo-Jewish Education in the 19th Century," in Alderman, *New Directions,* 49; and Arie M. Dubnov, "'True Art Makes for the Integration of the Race': Israel Zangwell and the Varieties of the Jewish Normalization Discourse in *fin de siècle* Britain," in Alderman, *New Directions,* 101–134; and Appell, "The Jews of Leeds," 31.

7. Alderman, *Modern British Jewry,* quoted by Appell, "The Jews of Leeds," 27.

8. David Graham and Daniel Vulkan, "Synagogue Membership in the United Kingdom, 2010," The Board of Deputies of British Jews, London, May 2010.

9. S. Levenberg, "Dreamers and Fighters," reprinted in "100 Years if the Jewish Labour Movement in Britain," Poale Zion Labour Zionist Movement (January 1967), 1–2; Endelmann, *The Jews of Britain,* 137–139.

10. Feldman, *Englishmen and Jews.*

11. Endelmann, *The Jews of Britain,* 207; Cullen, "'Jewish Communists' or 'Communist Jews.'"

12. A small 2015 exhibit at the London Jewish Museum, opened to coincide with the British national elections, told the story of the British Jewish suffragettes. See Anne Joseph, "Jewish Sister Suffragettes on Display in New UK Exhibition," *Times of London,* May 6, 1915, http://www.timesofisrael.com/jewish-sister-suffragettes-on-display-in -new-uk-exhibition/; Judith R. Walkowitz, *Nights Out: Life in Cosmopolitan London* (London: Yale University Press, 2012), especially chaps. 5 and 6, "Schleppers and Shoppers" and "A Jewish Night Out."

13. Walkowitz, *Nights Out.*

14. Endelmann, *The Jews of Britain,* 229–256.

15. "Jewish Socialists' Group," http://www.jewishsocialist.org.uk.

16. Appell, "The Jews of Leeds," 25–48.

17. Inbound tourism to the UK, http://www.visitbritain.org/insightsandstatistics
/inboundtourismfacts/.

18. The Museum Association of Britain cites data from monthly reports by VisitBritain. See http://www.museumsassociation.org/download?id=128002.

19. "History of the Museum," www.jewishmuseum.org.uk/history-of-the-museum-new; Jill Lawless, "London Jewish Museum Reopens after Major Facelift," AP wire service, reprinted at http://www.jewishmuseum.org.uk.

20. "Plan Your Visit to the Jewish Military Museum," www.thejmm.org.uk/plan-your-visit.

21. Thanks to Barbara Kirshenblatt-Gimblett for this history of the collection. Letter to the author, February 7, 2017.

22. Jerry White, *London in the Eighteenth Century* (London: Bodley Head, 2012); *London in the Nineteenth Century* (London: Jonathan Cape, 2007); *London in the Twentieth Century* (London: Viking, 2001); *Rothschild Buildings: Life in an East-End Tenement Block, 1887–1920*, rev. ed. (London: Pimlico, [1980] 2003).

23. Elizabeth Selby, Curator of Social History and Collections Manager, London Jewish Museum, Questionnaire response to the author, August 2013.

24. *Fodor's Great Britain*, as listed on the London Walks website but *Fodor's London* is where the travel company discusses walking tours. http://www.walks.com/London_Walks_Home/What_They_Say/default.aspx.

25. "Guide Training: Introduction," Guild of Registered Tourist Guides. http://www.britainsbestguides.org/training-introduction/.

26. Anonymous Blue Guide, conversation with the author, London, November 13, 2014.

27. Mike is a pseudonym.

28. Wynn, *The Tour Guide*.

29. The David Mocatta fountain was erected in memory of the financier's philanthropic efforts on behalf of East End Jews. The site speaks to the presence of early Sephardic Jews in London. Jewry Street is the site of the medieval and early modern Jewish settlements and the John Cass Foundation, educational mission to Aldgate children founded in the eighteenth century. These early sites provide historical context of pre-1656 settlement of Marranos and prosecution.

30. Bevis Marks Synagogue leaders employed an English architect to mask the Jewish presence and he designed the exterior to resemble a Norman church. The interior has seven original candelabras still used on holidays and for weddings. The benches are all original, and one seat is roped off in front. It was Moses Montefiore's seat, the synagogue and community benefactor. The lecture focuses initially on the financier Montefiore's good works. Visitors are not encouraged to think about the sources of his wealth and its relation to poverty, or about charity or paternalism. The rest of the lecture focuses on Benjamin Disraeli, another one-time congregant. Disraeli, who always acknowledged his Jewish heritage, was baptized and converted at age twelve to Anglicanism, and is buried in a churchyard.

31. The Jamme Masjid Mosque at 59 Brick Lane was erected in 1742 as a Huguenot Protestant Church; in 1898 it became the Spitalfields Great (Orthodox) Synagogue at which Jewish anarchists in 1904 had thrown ham sandwiches. It became a mosque in 1976 with fragmentary evidence of its Jewish past. See WORLDwrites' alternative online tour of Brick Lane and Whitechapel, "London behind the Scenes," http://www.worldwrite.org.uk/londonbehindthescenes/bricklane/jammemasjidmosque.html.

32. See Delores Hayden, *The Power of Place: Urban Landscapes as Public History* (Cambridge: MIT Press, 1997).

33. Judith R. Walkowitz, *Prostitution and Victorian Society: Women, Class and the State* (New York: Cambridge University Press, 1980).

CHAPTER 5 — NEW YORK

1. Debra Rubin, "New Study: New York Jewish Population Rising, Increasing in Diversity," *Jewish Telegraphic Agency* (June 12, 2013), www.jta.org/2102/06/12/life -religion/new-study-new-york-jewish-population-rising-increasing-in-diversity; Derek Kravitz, "New York City Area's Jewish Population Rises," *Wall Street Journal,* October 1, 2013, http://online.wsj.com/articles/SB10001424052702304373104579109671 933282670.

2. The bloodiest and most well-known riots were in Chicago, Washington, DC, and Ealine, Arkansas. See *William* Tuttle, *Race Riot: Chicago in the Red Summer of 1919* (Urbana: University of Illinois Press, 1970); and, Femi Lewis, "The Red Summer of 1919," http://afroamhistory.about.com/od/segregation/p/The-Red-Summer-Of-1919.htm. Goldstein dates Jewish "whiteness" to the late nineteenth century with roots, for instance, in early interactions where Jews hired black women as their "schwartzas." See Eric L. Goldstein, *The Price of Whiteness: Jews, Race, and American Identity* (Princeton: Princeton University Press, 2008).

3. A detailed bibliography of work preceding Howe's book can be found in the notes and bibliographical essay of Howe, *World of Our Fathers.*

4. Notable, among many other fine books are Moses Rischin, *The Promised City: New York's Jews, 1870–1914* (Cambridge, MA: Harvard University Press, 1978); Arthur A. Goren, *New York Jews and the Quest for Community the Kehilla Experiment, 1908–1922* (New York: Columbia University Press, 1978); Ronald Sanders, *The Downtown Jews: Portraits of an Immigrant Generation* (New York: Dover Publications, 1969); Michael Gold, *Jews Without Money* (New York: Horace Liveright, 1930); Harry Rogoff, *An East Side Epic: The Life and Times of Meyer London* (New York: Vantage Press, 1930); Abraham Cahan, *The Education of Abraham Cahan*, ed. Leon Stein (Philadelphia: Jewish Publication Society of America, 1969).

5. Michels, *A Fire in Their Hearts.*

6. Howe, *World of Our Fathers*; Rischin, *The Promised City*; Diner, *A Time for Gathering* and *Lower East Side Memories: A Jewish Place in America* (Princeton: Princeton University Press, 2002); Deborah Dash Moore, *At Home in America: Second Generation New York Jews* (New York: Columbia University Press, 1981); Susan Glenn, *Daughters of the Shtetl: Life and Labor in the Immigrant Generation* (Ithaca: Cornell University Press, 1991); Jonathan D. Sarna, *American Judaism: A History* (New Haven: Yale University Press, 2005); Daniel Soyer, *Jewish Immigrant Associations and American Identity in New York, 1880–1939* (Cambridge, MA: Harvard University Press, 1997); Deborah Dash Moore, *B'nai B'rith and the Challenge of Ethnic Leadership* (Albany: State University of New York Press, 1981); Dustin M. Wax, "'Brother, Friend, Comrade': The Workmen's Circle and Jewish Culture, 1900–1930," www.dwax.org/2000/07/28/brother_friend .comrade_the_workmens_circle_and_jewish_culture_1900-1930/. Most recently, Deborah Dash Moore has edited a prize-winning three-volume history, *A History of the Jews of New York*: Howard B. Rock, *Haven of Liberty*; Annie Polland and Daniel Soyer, *Emerging Metropolis: New York Jews in the Age of Immigration, 1840–1920*; Jeffrey S. Gurock,

Jews in Gotham: New York Jews in a Changing Story, 1920–2010 (New York: New York University Press, 2012).

7. See Daniel J. Walkowitz, *Working with Class: Social Workers and the Politics of Middle-Class Identity* (Chapel Hill: University of North Carolina Press, 1999).

8. Feldman notes the weakness of the Jewish labor movement in the decades following the 1899 Tailors Strike. British Jews could join a self-consciously socialist Labour Party; for American Jews seeking a socialist movement, the alternatives were the Socialist and later the Communist parties.

9. Richard Greenwald, *The Triangle Fire: The Protocols of Peace and Industrial Democracy in Progressive Era New York City* (Philadelphia: Temple University Press, 2005). See also the website of the Kheel Center at Cornell University for the papers of the garment workers union and a documentary history of the fire: http://trianglefire.ilr .cornell.edu/index.html.

10. There is a substantial literature on the garment industry; less on department store labor. See, for example, Daniel Opler, *For All White-Collar Workers: The Possibilities of Radicalism in New York City's Department Store Unions, 1934–1953* (Columbus: Ohio State University Press, 2007); Greenwald, *The Triangle Fire.*

11. Walkowitz, *Working with Class.*

12. Opler, *For All White-Collar Workers*; Walkowitz, *Working with Class.*

13. Thanks to Daniel Soyer for clarifying in personal communications the complexity of the Jewish political life among Eastern European and German Jews. See also Polland and Soyer, *Emerging Metropolis,* especially chap. 6.

14. A cynical account of the Promised Land stories is told by the renowned Jewish novelist, playwright and essayist Israel Zangwell in his 1899 short story, "The Land of Promise," in *Ghetto Tragedies* (Philadelphia: Jewish Publication Society of America, [1899] 1938, 12–1-55), as discussed in Hannah Ewence, "Between Daydreams and Nightmares: Fin de Siècle Journeys and the British Imagination," in *New Directions in Anglo-Jewish History,* ed. G. Alderman, 1–24. Feldman, *Englishmen and Jews,* 162–165, notes how the reality of privation in London often did not meet the ambitions and dreams immigrants brought with them.

15. Bernstein interview, October 9, 1980.

16. Ruthie Lubert Sacks, email to the author, October 14, 2011.

17. Ibid.

18. Belle Bernstein, quoted in Joe H. Roach, "Women in the Communist Party and How Their Party Activities Affected Them as Wives and Mothers" (PhD diss., New York University, 2000), 19.

19. Sholem Aleichem, quoted by Bernstein in an interview, October 9, 1989.

20. Bernstein, interview; Roach, "Women in the Communist Party," 22–23; Joseph Walkowitz, interview, April 6, 1980.

21. Wallerstein, 11–14, 88–96.

22. Joseph Walkowitz, quoted in Jane Wallerstein, *Voices from the Paterson Silk Mills* (Collingdale, PA: Diane Publishing Co., 2000), 13, 97.

23. Belle Bernstein, quoted in Roach, "Women in the Communist Party," 23; Joseph Walkowitz, interview with Randy Freeman and Jerry Nathans, April 6, 1980, the Jewish Historical Society of North Jersey, Tape 320; Ruth Sacks, email to the author, March 21, 2017.

24. Belle Bernstein, quoted in Roach, "Women in the Communist Party," 46–47.

25. Ibid., 20, 24.

26. Joseph Walkowitz, interview with Jane Wallerstein, ca. 1992, quoted in Waller-stein, *Voices from the Paterson Silk Mills*, 112–113.

27. "America's 30 Most Jewish Cities, from New York to Miami to Los Angeles," December 1, 2010, http://www.thedailybeast.com/articles/2010/12/01/americas-30-most -jewish-cities-from-new-york-to-miami-to-los-angeles.html.

28. Yiddishisms in English are many. A sample list is available at https://www.wordnik .com/lists/yiddishisms.

29. Seth Kamil, "Tripping Down Memory Lane: Walking Tours on the Jewish Lower East Side," in *Remembering the Lower East Side: American Jewish Reflections,* ed. Hasia R. Diner, Jeffrey Shandler, Beth S. Wenger (Bloomington: Indiana University Press, 2000), 226–240. Full disclosure, as a resident who has lived in lower Manhattan since the mid-1970s and teaches the history of New York City, I have known, admired, and in some cases, trained, some of those who have helped develop this living archive.

30. Jeffrey Shandler and Jack Kugelmass, "Going Home: How American Jews Invent the Old World," exhibition catalogue, YIVO institute for Jewish Research, New York, 1989, 22.

31. For a taste of what a self-directed Jewish food tour might be like, see, Will Hawkes, "New York Food: A Tour of the Jewish Lower East Side," *Independent,* October 22, 2014, www.independent.co.uk/travel/americas/new-york-food-a-tour-of-the-jewish -lower=eas-side-9809185.html. See also the Jewish immigrant and food tour, "Immigrants and Noshes," offered by Levy's Unique Tours, www.levyuniqueny.com.

32. Allon Schoener, *Portal to America: The Lower East Side, 1870–1925* (New York: Holt, Rinehart and Winston, 1967).

33. I visited the Rubenstein exhibit in November 2014. See also http://thejewish museum.org.

34. The Center, located only a block from my home, is a frequent base for my own research. The American Jewish History Society exhibits are described at http://www .ajhs.org/exhibitions.

35. See http://yivoexhitions.com/index.php/past and http://www.yivoinstitute.org.

36. "New York, NY—Museum Officials Divided over Museum of Jewish Heritage Struggles," CedarhusrstNewYork.com, November 11, 2015, http://www.cedarhurstnewyork .com/new-york-ny-museum-officials-divided-over-museum-of-jewish-heritage -struggles/.

37. Esther Brumberg, interview with the author, New York, July 1, 2013.

38. Beth S. Wenger, "Memory as Identity: The Invention of the Lower East Side," *American Jewish History* 85 (March 1997): 4. This theme is developed more fully in the collection of essays that came out of a 1998 conference: Diner et al., eds., *Remembering the Lower East Side.*

39. Suzanne Wasserman, "Re-Creating Recreations on the Lower East Side: Restaurants, Cabarets, Cafes and Coffeehouses in the 1930s," in Diner et al, *Remembering the Lower East Side,* 170.

40. Diner, *Lower East Side Memories*; Paul Berman, "Tell Me What Street Compares with Mott Street," *New York Times,* November 12, 2002.

41. Jack Kugelmass, "Turfing the Slum: New York City's Tenement Museum and the Politics of Heritage," in Diner et al., *Remembering the Lower East Side,* 179–211.

42. Ibid., 182.

43. Ibid., 201.

44. "Tenement Museum Leadership Changes," *New York Times*, April 15, 2008. I have known Vogel during this time to be a smart, productive, and engaging social historian.

45. Kamil, "Tripping Down Memory Lane."

46. Phillip E. Schoenberg, interview with the author, July 9, 2013, New York City. See also newyorktalksandwalks.com/about.html.

47. See the video of the tour on the Chassidic Discovery Center website, jewishtours.com.

48. The museum at Eldridge Street website describes its history, early membership, and calendar of events, http://www.eldridgestreet.org/events/. The 92nd Street Y advertises its program in semiannual bulletins and online. The fall 2013 schedule of Tours and Excursions is on pages 83–84.

49. The Lower East Side Jewish Conservancy, "Public Tours and Events," http://www .lesjc.org/calendar.htm; David Kayton, *Radical Walking Tours of New York City* (New York: Seven Sisters Press, 2003).

50. Joyce Gold's tours and her own biography are available at http://joycegoldhistorytours .com/tour-descriptions.html,

51. Seth Kamil, interview with the author, August 2, 2013. See also http://www .bigonion.com/tours/.

52. See http://levysuniqueny.com/tours.

53. A brief history of Congregation Emanu-El is available at http://www.nycago.org /organs/nyc/html/EmanuEl.html.

54. Adam Chandler, "Buried," *Tablet Magazine*, August 26, 2011, htpp://tabletmag .com/jewish-news-and-politics/76248/buried.

55. Opler, *For All White-Collar Workers*.

56. Sven Beckert, The *Monied Metropolis: New York City and the Consolidation of the American Bourgeoisie, 1850–1896* (New York: Cambridge University Press, 2003).

57. Hirsch, *Postmemory*.

58. Kamil interview.

59. Kamil, "Tripping Down Memory Lane."

60. Elizabeth Tietjen, evening events associate, Lower East Side Tenement Museum, email to the author, November 20, 2014.

61. Norval White and Elliot Willensky, *AIA Guide to New York City*, 4th ed. (New York: Three Rivers Press, 2000); Federal Writers Project, *The WPA Guide to New York City* (New York: New Press, 1995); Seth Kamil and Eric Wakin, *The Big Onion Guide to New York City: Ten Historic Tours* (New York: New York University Press, 2002).

62. See "Emma Lazarus: Poet of Exiles," Museum of Jewish Heritage. The actress Julianna Margulies narrates the walking tour, "Walk in Emma's Footsteps," http://www .newyorkholocaustmuseum.com/emma/newyork.html.

63. Jack Kugelmass, "The Rites of the Tribes: The Meaning of Poland for American Jewish Tourists," in "Going Home," *YIVO Annual 2*, ed. Jack Kugelmass (Evanston, IL Northwestern University Press, 1993), 417.

CHAPTER 6 — BERLIN

1. David Shyovitz, "The Virtual Jewish History Tour," Jewish Virtual Library, http:// www.jewishvirtuallibrary.org/jsource/vjw/berlin.html; Toby Axelrod, "Berlin Offers Jewish Tourists More Than Holocaust History," *Jewish Telegraph Agency*, December 21,

2012, http://www.jta.org'2012/12/21/news-opinion/world/berlin-offers-jewsih-tourists -more-than-holocaust-history.

2. Thanks to Reinhard Bernbeck for this observation.

3. The literature is vast but the most accessible comprehensive book is Andreas Nachama, Julius H. Schoeps, and Hermann Simon, eds., *Jews In Berlin*, trans. Michael S. Cullen and Allison Brown (Berlin: Henschel, [2001] 2002). More general is David Clay Large, *Berlin* (New York: Basic Books, 2000). Notes below suggest more specific readings.

4. Shyovitz, "The Virtual Jewish History Tour."

5. Claudia-Ann Flumenbaum, "From the Beginnings until 1789," in Nachama et al., eds., *Jews in Berlin*, 36–37.

6. Christopher R. Friedricks, "Rags to Riches—Jews as Producers and Purveyors of Fashion," in *Broken Threads: The Destruction of the Jewish Fashion Industry in Germany and Austria,* ed. Roberta S. Kremer (Oxford: Berg, 2007), 24.

7. Ingrid Loschek, "The Contribution of Jewish Fashion Designers in Berlin," in Kremer, ed., *Broken Threads,* 51–52.

8. Julius H. Schoeps, "The Process of Adaptation (1790–1870)," in Nachama et al., eds., *Jews in Berlin*, 64.

9. Chana C. Schütz, "The Imperial Era (1871–1918)," in Nachama et al., eds., *Jews in Berlin*, 97.

10. Moses Mendelssohn, *Jerusalem*, quoted by Flumenbaum in Nachama et al., eds., *Jews in Berlin*, 45.

11. John Rose, "Eleanor Marx," *Socialist Worker,* December 10, 2005, http://www .socialistworker.co.uk/art.php?id=7941.

12. Marion A. Kaplan, *The Making of a Jewish Middle Class: Women, Family, and Identity in Imperial Germany* (New York: Oxford University Press, 1994).

13. Julius H. Shoeps, "The Process of Adaptation (1790–1870)," in Nachama et al., *Jews in Berlin*, 61, and Schütz, "The Imperial Era," 102. See also Shyovitz, "The Virtual Jewish History Tour: Berlin."

14. Schütz, "The Imperial Era," 98.

15. Michael Brenner, "The Weimar Years (1919–1932)," in Nachama et al., eds., *Jews in Berlin*, 142.

16. Ibid., 96; also citing *Jews in Berlin,* http://www.jg-berlin.org/en/about-us/history .html.

17. Brenner, "The Weimar Years," 137–180; Kerry Wallach, "Weimar Fashion Chic: Jewish Women and Fashion in 1920s Germany," in *Fashioning Jews: Clothing, Culture, and Commerce, Studies in Jewish Civilization,* no. 24 (October 2011): 114–120.

18. Uwe Westphal, *Berlin Konfektion und Mode: Der Zerstörung einer Tradition, 1836–1939* (Berlin: Edition Hentrich Berlin, 1986), cited in Katrina Sark, "Tracing the Locations of Berliner Chic: Then and Now," http://suitesculture;;es.wordpress.com/2011 /11/14/tracing-the-locations-of-berliner-chic-then-and-now/. See also Susan Ingram and Katrina Sark, *Berliner Chic: A Locational History of Berlin Fashion* (Chicago: University of Chicago Press, 2011); Roberta Kremer, ed., *Broken Threads: The Destruction of the Jewish Fashion Industry in Germany and Austria* (Oxford: Berg, 2007); and Leonard J. Greenspan, ed., "Fashioning Jews: Clothing, Culture, and Commerce," Special issue of *Studies in Jewish Civilization* 24 (October 2011).

19. Loschek, "The Contribution of Jewish Fashion Designers," 49–67.

20. Jack Wertheimer, *Unwelcome Strangers: East European Jews in Imperial Germany* (New York: Oxford University Press, 1987), 18–19, 80, and table 1; Schütz, "The Imperial Era," 120–122.

21. Large, *Berlin*, 100, and Wertheimer, *Unwelcome Strangers*, 86–102.

22. Brenner, "The Weimar Years," 154–155.

23. Schütz, "The Imperial Era," 128.

24. See Geoff Eley, *Forging Democracy: The History of the Left in Europe, 1850-2000* (New York: Oxford University Press, 2002); Richard J. Evans, *Proletarians and Politics: Socialism, Protest, and the Working Class in Germany Before the First World War* (New York: St. Martin's Press, Inc., 1990).

25. "Virtual Jewish World: Berlin, Germany," Jewish Virtual Library, http://www.jewishvirtuallibrary.org/jsource/vjw/berlin.html. This article is a version of the essay by Shyovitz, "The Virtual Jewish History Tour."

26. Atina Grossmann, *Jews, Germans, and Allies: Close Encounters in Occupied Germany* (Princeton: Princeton University Press, 2006). In oral interviews conducted just before the fall of the Berlin Wall, some Jews hint at how they and their brethren in East Berlin expressed their Judaism and socialism: see Robin Ostow, *Jews in Contemporary East Germany: The Children of Moses in the Land of Marx* (New York: Palgrave Macmillan, 1989).

27. "Leo Baeck Summer University in Jewish Studies," http://www.projekte.hu-berlin.de/en/lbsu. For the Freie University program, see, "Institute of Jewish Studies," http://www.fu-berlin.de/en/einrichtungen/fachbereiche/fb/gesch-kultur/jda/.

28. Magdalena Waligórska, *Klezmer's Afterlife: An Ethnography of the Jewish Music Revival in Poland and Germany* (New York: Oxford University Press, 2013); "Berlin Revival: Jewish, Secular, Anti-Fascist Community Salon Project," http://berlinrevival.blogspot.com; "Judische Kulturtage Berlin / Days of Jewish Culture," Jewish Community of Berlin, http://www.jg-berlin.org/en/institutions/culture/juedische-kulturtage.html.

29. Rodger Kamenetz, *The Jew and the Lotus: A Poetic Rediscovery of Jewish Identity in Buddhist India* (New York: Harper Collins, 1994). Alex Berzin's work in Berlin has focused on a comprehensive international website of Tibetan Buddhism, http://www.berzinarchives.com/web/en/about/author/short_biography_alex_beriin.html. Alex's role in the meeting is described by Bhikshuni Thubten Chodron, "The Origin of 'The Jew in the Lotus,'" http://thubtenchodron.org/2011/06/interfaith-jewish-buddhist/.

30. Cilly Kugelmann, interview with the author, March 5, 2013, Berlin, Germany.

31. See Gunter Demnig's homepage, http://www.stolpersteine.eu. See also Christopher Alessi, "'Stumbling Blocks': Cobblestone Memorials to Murdered Jews in Berlin," *Forward*, April 30, 2014, http://forward.com/news/breaking-news/197383/stumbling-blocks-cobblestone-memorials-to-murdered/. Not all Jews are happy about these stones. Some feel walking on the stones desecrates the dead. But Reinhard Bernbeck suggests creating a discomfort for viewers may encourage awareness and be part of the artist's intention. Bernbeck, comment to the author, November 17, 2015.

32. Stacy Perman, "The Right Questions: German Conceptual Artists Find Provocative Ways to Confront the Holocaust," *Tablet: Visual Art & Design* (July 25, 2007), http://www.tabletmag.com/jewish-arts-and-culture/719/the-right-questions. See also the author's website: http://www.stih-schnock.de/remembrance.html.

33. Bernbeck, comment to the author, November 14, 2015.

34. The journalist Edward Rothstein captured the mood I felt seeing the memorial and its museum in his "In Berlin, Teaching Germany's Jewish History," *New York Times,* May 1, 2009.

35. Xanthi Tsiftsi, "A Jewish Museum in the Post-Conflict Terrain of Berlin: A Building Evolved For and Evoking a Painful History," paper presented at the Conference on Museums and Their Publics at Sites of Conflicted History, POLIN Museum of the History of Polish Jews, Warsaw, March 13–15, 2017.

36. Jackie Feldman, "Holocaust Museums as Agents of Citizenship: Between Historical Knowledge, Commemoration and Identity Politics," paper presented at the International Conference, "Museums and Their Publics at Sites of Contested History," POLIN Museum of the History of Polish Jews, Warsaw, March 13–15, 2017.

37. Kugelmann interview.

38. Ibid.

39. Ibid.

40. Chana Schütz interview with the author, March 8, 2013, Berlin, Germany.

41. Ibid.

42. See http://www.insidertour.com/tours.php/cat/27/id/73/title/Tourdetails.

43. Avigail Levy is a pseudonym.

44. J. Feldman, *Above the Death Pits.* The historian Mary Nolan notes having heard of this criticism at Sachsenhausen and other such sites. Communication with the author, May 20, 2016.

45. Wolf Gruner, "The Factory Action and the Events at the Rosenstrasse in Berlin. Facts and Fictions about 27 February 1943—Sixty Years Later," *Central European History* 36 (2003): 178–208.

46. Ironically, in one of the books burned, the German Jewish poet Heinrich Heine, had written a prophetic poem on the Christians conquering Grenada and burning the Koran: "Wherever they burn books, they will in the end also burn human beings." Heinrich Heine, quoted by Bernbeck, comment to the author, November 14, 2105.

47. "Memorial Fashion Center Hausvogteiplatz," https://www.tracesofwar.com /sights/5310/Memorial-Fashion-Centre-Hausvogteiplatz.htm.

48. Kalandides's dissertation argues that the GDR's focus on the working-class and Jewish identity in Prenzlauer Berg reflected its own privileging of a story it probably exaggerated. See Ares Kalandides, "Place Identities: Multiple Narratives from Prenzlauer Berg" (PhD diss., National Technical University of Athens, 2011).

49. Schütz interview; Kugelmann interview.

50. See Andrea Riedle, ed., *Sites of Remembrance, 1933–1945* (Berlin: n.p., 2011). I toured these sites in 2014. For an example of the politics of heritage tourism, see, Melanie Smith and László Puezko, "Out with the Old, in with the New? Twenty Years of Post Socialist Marketing in Budapest," *Journal of Town & City Management* 3 (2010): 288–299, and, "Budapest: From Socialist Heritage to Cultural Capital?" *Current Issues in Tourism* 15, nos. 1–2 (2012): 107–119.

CHAPTER 7 — BUDAPEST, BUCHAREST, AND BELGRADE

1. For short summary histories of Jews in the three cities, see Ruth Ellen Gruber, *Jewish Heritage Travel: A Guide to Eastern Europe* (Washington, DC: National Geographic Society, 2007), 211–217, 249–253, 305–308. For more extended history of Budapest, see Geza

Komoroczy, ed., *Jewish Budapest: Monuments, Rites, History* (Budapest: Central European University Press, [1995] 1999). See also Mendelsohn, *The Jews of East Central Europe*, chap. 2; and "Jewish Budapest," http://visitbudapest.travel/guide/jewish-budapest/.

2. Mendelsohn, *The Jews*, chaps. 2 and 4; Eli Valley, *The Great Jewish Cities of Central and Eastern Europe* (Northvale, NJ: Jason Aronson, 1999); William O. McCagg, *A History of Hapsburg Jews, 1670-1918* (Bloomington: Indiana University Press, 1992).

3. Jews became further implicated in these struggles and paid the price when they aligned themselves with the losing side. For instance, after Jews provided weapons to the Serbs in 1804, they met violent Turk retaliation; Serbs, however, had limited memory or appreciation of the Jewish support and periodically enacted new anti-Jewish restrictions, including expelling them from the city in 1807. Jennie Lebel, *Until the "Final Solution": The Jews in Belgrade, 1521-1942,* trans. Paul Münch (New Haven, CT: Avotaynu, 2007).

4. Non-Jewish locals, put in a frenzy by Romanian Orthodox Church assertions of Jewish ritual blood murders, forced Jewish children to be baptized and drove Jews from their homes, robbed them, or worse. See Lebel, *Until the "Final Solution"* and Mendelsohn, *The Jews*, chap. 4. See also Hary Kuller and Lya Benjamin, *The History Museum of the Romanian Jews: Chief-Rabbi Dr. Moses Rosen* (Bucharest: Hasefer Publishing House, 2012).

5. Yehuda Aharon Horovitz, "Münz, Mosheh," in *YIVO Encyclopedia* http://www .yivoencyclopedia.org/article.aspx/Munz_Mosheh.

6. *Jewish Budapest*, 52-54, 67 (emphasis added).

7. Ibid., 121-123; Michael K. Silber, "The Historical Experience of German Jewry and Its Impact on Haskalah and Reform in Hungary," in *Toward Modernity: The European Jewish Model*, ed. Jacob Katz (New Brunswick, NJ: Transaction Books, 1987), 107-157.

8. Michael K. Silber, "The Emergence of Ultra-Orthodoxy: The Invention of Tradition," in *The Uses of Tradition: Jewish Continuity since Emancipation*, ed. Jack Wertheimer (New York: Jewish Theological Seminary of America, 1992), 23-84.

9. *Jewish Budapest*, 125.

10. Ibid., 271-273 (emphasis added).

11. *The History Museum*, 61; E. Mendelsohn, *The Jews*, chap. 4.

12. Ibid. See also J. L. Blau and S. W. Baron, *Jews of the United States, 1790-1840* (New York: Columbia University Press, 1963), 2: 336-339.

13. "Bucharest, Romania," in *Encyclopedia Judaica*; Mendelsohn, *The Jews*, chap. 4.

14. Mendelsohn, *The Jews*, chap. 4; Costel Safirman, "Romanian State Yiddish Theater," in *YIVO Encyclopedia*, trans. Anca Mircea, http://www.yivoencyclopedia.org /article.aspx/Romanian_State_Yiddish_Theater.

15. Gruber, *Jewish Heritage Travel*, 305-308; "Belgrade, Serbia," in *Encyclopedia Judaica*.

16. Harriet Bass Friedenreich, *The Jews of Yugoslavia: A Quest for Community* (Philadelphia: Jewish Publication Society of America, 1979).

17. Vojislave Radovanovic, *The Jewish Historical Museum in Belgrade* (Belgrade: Federation of Jewish Communities of Serbia, 2010); Lebel, *Until the "Final Solution."*

18. Gruber, *Jewish Heritage Travel*, 212-214. How June 16 and its aftermath is remembered in Budapest frames the politics of its history sites. It was a Day of Liberation for the surviving Jews and others oppressed by the Nazis and their collaborators. But Soviet propaganda's enshrinement of the term complicates its post-Soviet era usage, and the

atrocities and rapes of the "liberators" and the subsequent Soviet authoritarian regime told a different story.

19. Lebel, *Until the "Final Solution,"* 281–339; Gruber, *Jewish Heritage Travel,* 255, 307.

20. Ibid.

21. On Rabbi Rosen's "bargain," see Ioanid Eadu, *The Ransom of the Jews: The Story of the Extraordinary Secret Bargain between Romania and Israel* (Lanham, MD: Ivan R. Dee, 2005).

22. "Pijade, Mosa," Jewish Virtual Life, https://www.jewishvirtuallibrary.org/jsource /judaica/ejud_0002_0016_0_15763.html.

23. Ruth Ellen Gruber, "Post-Trauma 'Precious Legacies': Jewish Museums in Eastern Europe after the Holocaust and before the Fall of Communism," in *Visualizing and Exhibiting Jewish Space and History,* ed. Richard I. Cohen (New York: Oxford University Press, 2012). According to the historian Cvi Rotem, "religious life was only part, and not necessarily the outstanding part, of Jewish community life." Cvi Rotem, "Contemporary Period," in "Jewish History of Yugoslavia," ed. Nenad Porges, http://www .porges.net/JewishHistoryOfYugoslavia.html.

24. My discussion of the postwar era draws substantially on Ruth Ellen Gruber, "Post-trauma 'Precious Legacies': Jewish Museums in Eastern Europe after the Holocaust and before the fall of Communism." In *Visualizing and Exhibiting Jewish Space and History.* Richard I Cohen, ed. (New York: Oxford University Press, 2012), 113–132.

25. Porges, "Jewish History of Yugoslavia"; "Encyclopedia Judaica: Belgrade, Serbia."

26. Ruth Ellen Gruber, "Post-trauma."

27. "Virtual Jewish World: Budapest, Hungary."

28. Gruber, "Post-Trauma," quotes Zsuzsanna Toronyi, the current head of the Hungarian Jewish Archives, on Ilona Benoschofsky, who served as museum director from 1963 to 1994.

29. Ancestry.com DNA FAQ, http://dna.ancestry.com/legal/faq#about-1.

30. Margelov Institut, "About Margel," http://www.margel-institute.hr/aboutm.html.

31. I was invited to Budapest's Central European University to show one of my documentary films and discuss the presentation of the past to public audiences. I was in Belgrade with a colleague from the Smithsonian Center for Folklife and Cultural Heritage to premiere a screening of the documentary, *City Folk,* at the Belgrade International Ethnographic Film Festival. In Bucharest, I delivered a keynote lecture on Edith Wharton at a conference of European American Studies scholars.

32. Eszter Gantner, emails to the author, January 14, 2013, March 4, 2013; Katalina Pesci-Polliner, email to the author, March 9, 2015.

33. See, for instance, Marton Dunai, "Hungary's Jews Face Down New Extremism," Reuters, December 16, 2012, http://www.reuters.com/article/us-hungary-jews-idUSBR E8BF0HI20121216#wE6Me6rVzSxukP3L.97; Robert Myles, "Hungary: A New Synagogue for Budapest but Anti-Semitism on Rise," *Politics,* February 9, 2013, reprinted in *DIGITAL JOURNAL,* http://www.digitaljournal.com/article/343168.

34. Eszter Asher is a pseudonym.

35. "Free Walking Tours: Jewish District Walk," http://www.triptobudapest.hu/v2/tours /jewish-district-tour/; "The STANDARD Jewish Walking Tour," and "The EXTENDED Jewish Walking Tour," http://www.greatsynagogue.hu/jewishquartertours.html.

36. Daniel Stone, in correspondence with me, notes, "Kasztner was very controversial from the beginning," both from his choice of beneficiaries and allegations he collaborated

with the Nazis because he had negotiated with Eichmann for the release of the train. "He was condemned by an Israeli court (later reversed posthumously) and assassinated in 1957 [in Tel Aviv] by a Lehi hit squad." A recent defender is Anna Porter, *Kasztner's Train: the True Story of an Unknown Hero of the Holocaust* (New York: Walker Books, 2009).

37. Agi Asher, walking tour, oral tape in the author's possession, March 25, 2013. This story of the "controversial" Kasztner Group is told in Gallery 7 of the Holocaust Memorial Center exhibit. For the more general critique of elitist foci in public history, see Hayden, *The Power of Place*.

38. "Hungarian Jewish Museum and Archives: Highlights of the Permanent Exhibition with Audioguide," http://enmilev.weebly.com/museum_permanent_audio.html.

39. Szilvia Peremiczky, questionnaire response to the author, email, March 24, 2013.

40. Szaboles Szita, interview with the author, with translator and Janos Botos, Budapest, March 26, 2015, oral tape in the author's possession; Katalin Pesci-Pollner, interview with the author, Budapest, March 27, 2015, oral tape in the author's possession.

41. Holocaust Memorial Center, exhibit, Galleries 7 and 8, Budapest, Hungary, March 26, 2015.

42. Pesci-Pollner interview.

43. In his meticulous account of totalitarian murder of civilians in Eastern Europe between 1933 and 1989, the historian Timothy Snyder, *Bloodlands* (New York: Basic Books, 2010), provides ammunition for accounts emphasizing, as he does, similarities between the Nazi and Soviet regimes. The book received many favorable reviews but also has its critics who complain, among other things, of Snyder's "moral equivalence" between the two regimes. See Richard J. Evans, "Who Remembers the Poles," *London Review of Books* 32, no. 21 (2010): 21–22.

44. "House of Terror," museum brochure (Budapest, 2002).

45. András Levante Gál, "The Budapest Holocaust Memorial Publishes Its 'Professional Communiqué,'" *Hungarian Spectrum,* February 10, 2014, http://hungarianspectrum.org/tag/szabolcs-szita/.

46. Ingrid Heinisch, "Sie wollen die Geschichte umschreiben" [They want to rewrite history], *New Germany,* July 9, 2012, http://www.ag-friedensforschung.de/regionen/Ungarn/antisem.html; Dunai, "Hungary's Jews Face Down New Extremism"; and Myles, "Hungary."

47. Szita interview; Pesci-Pollner interview.

48. Pesci-Pollner interview.

49. "FEATURE: Alternative Jewish Center Makes a Bridge in Budapest," http://artsculturebeat.tumblr.com/post/114186558244/feature-alternative-jewish-center-makes-a-bridge.

50. Smith and Puczko, "Out with the Old, in with the New?"

51. Elena Funar is a pseudonym.

52. "Ceaușima," Wikipedia, https://en.wikipedia.org/wiki/Ceaușima.

53. Evica Babic is a pseudonym.

54. I was an "accidental tourist" to Belgrade (and Serbia) and my conference obligations and need to focus on Belgrade's Jewish history did not permit my visits to these other cities. Once part of Yugoslavia, Sarajevo was now in Bosnia-Herzegovina, and Zagreb and Dubrovnik were in Croatia. Sarajevo's and Dubrovnik's Jewish communities

traced their origins to Sephardic refugees from the Spanish Inquisition; Zagreb's Jewish community was mostly Ashkenazi.

55. Milan Rostovic, interview with the author, October 12, 2012, Belgrade; Olga Manolijlovic Pindar, interview with the author, October 14, 2012, Belgrade.

56. *Jews of Dorcol: The Story of Our Neighbors Who Are No More*, Exhibition Guide, Belgrade, 1997, http://rexpro.b92.net/rexold/jewsdet.htm.

57. Hilda Grunberg, curator questionnaire submitted to the author, January 2014; Mariana Net, email to the author, January 14, 2014.

58. Ibid.; and Kuller and Benjamin, *The History* Museum *of the Romanian Jews.*

59. *The Jewish Historical Museum in Belgrade, the Guide* (Belgrade: The Federation of Jewish Communities of Serbia, 2010) is available as a booklet and at http://www .jimbeograd.org/en/wp-content/uploads/2013/12/publication_of_jim_eng.pdf.

60. Mitja Velikonja, "Titonostalgia: A Study of Nostalgia for Josip Broz" (Ljubljana: Peace Institute, 2008), cited in a paper abstract submitted to the *Radical History Review* by Ivona Jovanovic et al., "Tourism, Identity and Socialist Cultural Heritage: Montenegro after the Dissolution of Tito's Yugoslavia."

61. Ibid.

62. Vojislava Rodovanovic, interview with the author, October 12, 2012.

CHAPTER 8 — KRAKÓW AND WARSAW

1. Antony Polonsky, "Warsaw," in *YIVO Encyclopedia*, http://www.yivoencyclopedia .org/article.aspx/Warsaw; "Kraków, Poland," Jewish Virtual Library http://www .jewishvirtuallibrary.org/jsource/vjw/Cracow.html.

2. Kraków tops all lists as a tourist destination in Poland. TripAdvisor's list is typical, see https://www.tripadvisor.com/Travelers-Choice-Destinations-Top-g274723.

3. Radio Poland, "Over Ten Million Tourists Visited Kraków in 2015," http://www .thenews.pl/1/12/Artykul/231460,Over-10-million-tourists-visited-Kraków-in-2015; Kraków Convention Bureau, "Record Year for Kraków's Tourist Business," http://www .Kraków.pl/ccb_en/hot/196351.251.komunikat.record_year_for_Kraków_s_tourist _business.html.

4. MasterCard, Global Destination Cities Index, "Europe's Fastest Growing Destination Cities for International Overnight Visitors (2009–15)," Table 6, 2015, https://newsroom .mastercard.com/wp-content/uploads/2015/06/MasterCard-GDCI-2015-Final-Report1 .pdf. For attendance at POLIN, see Barbara Kirshenblatt-Gimblett, "Jewish Museums in the 21st Century," Center for Jewish History, New York, January 10, 2016.

5. Gruber, *Virtually Jewish*, 5–11; Lehrer and Meng, *Jewish Space*, "Introduction."

6. Lehrer, *Jewish Poland*, 8, 200.

7. Ury, *Barricades and Banners*; Lehrer and Meng, *Jewish Space*; Lehrer, *Jewish Poland.* The New Social History of the 1960s and 1970s influenced history museums in the United States and Western Europe (i.e., the Tenement Museum is an obvious example), but had less impact on Eastern Europe historiography.

8. Heidemarie Petersen, "Kraków before 1795," in *YIVO Encyclopedia*. http:// yivoencyclopedia.org/article.aspx/Krakow/Krakow_before_1795.

9. Ibid.

10. The 1863 revolt against the Russian Empire was the third such uprising; the first was the Kosciuszko Uprising of 1794, with some participation of peasants and other underprivileged groups; the second was in 1830–1831.

11. Sean Martin, "Kraków," in *YIVO Encyclopedia,* http://www.yivoencyclopedia.org /article.aspx/Krakow/Krakow_after_1795,

12. "Polish Census of 1931." Hebrew and Polish speakers in Warsaw were 5.6 percent and 5.4 percent respectively; Kraków percentages were 39.9 percent and 18.7 percent. See https://www.revolvy.com/main/index.php?s=Polish%20census%20of%201931. Thanks to Ola Linkiewicz for this reference. On the undercount of Polish speakers, see Marcin Wodziński, "Languages of the Jewish Community in Polish Silesia (1922–1939)," *Jewish History* 16, no. 2 (2002): 131–160.

13. Daniel Blatman, "Bund," in *YIVO Encyclopedia,* http://www.yivoencyclopedia .org/article.aspx/Bund. Thanks, too, to Antony Polonsky, email to the author, October 21, 2017. On the use of Polish and Hebrew, thanks to Samuel D. Kassow, email to the author, June 17, 2017.

14. Jan T. Gross, "After Auschwitz: The Reality and Meaning of Postwar Anti-Semitism in Poland," in *Dark Times, Dire Decisions, Jews and Communism,* ed. Jonathan Frankel (New York: Oxford University Press. 2004), 214.

15. *Kraków In Your Pocket* 88 (Kraków: IYP City Guides, June–July 2014), 86–95.

16. Kasia is a pseudonym.

17. "The Great Mikveh (6 Szeroka Street)," Virtual Shtetl, http://www.sztetl.org.pl/en /article/Kraków/11,synagogues-prayer-houses-and-others/3779,the-great-mikveh-6 -szeroka-street-/#footnote_2.

18. FreeWalkingTour.com, http://freewalkingtour.com/Kraków/tours/calendar-Kraków/.

19. Karol is a pseudonym.

20. See Robert Pfaller, "The Work of Art That Observes Itself. Eleven Steps towards an Aesthetics of Interpassivity," in *Presencias en el espacio publico contemporaneo,* ed. *Centro de studios por la scultura publica ambiental* (Barcelona, 1998), 229–240 and Paco Barragán, "Push to Flush: Culture of Impassivity," *ArtPulse,* June 6, 2013, 1, http:// artpulsemagazine.com/push-to-flush-culture-of-interpassivity. Thanks to Reinhard Bernbeck for the references.

21. For a summary and view of the collection, see http://www.mhk.pl/exhibitions/the -history-and-culture-of-jews-in-Kraków.

22. For more detail, see the website of the Enamel Factory of Oskar Schindler Museum, http://www.mhk.pl/branches/oskar-schindlers-factory.

23. Webber, *Rediscovering Traces of Memory.*

24. "Kraków: Poland's Foremost City," Kraków-Info, http://www.Kraków-info.com.

25. Erica T. Lehrer, *Lucky Jews: Poland's Jewish Figurines* (Kraków: Korporacja Halart, 2014).

26. Erica Lehrer, "Seeing the Unnoticed," in *Field Guide to Jewish Warsaw and Kraków,* ed. Edyta Gawron et al. (San Francisco: Taube Foundation, 2012), sidebar, 95.

27. Lehrer, *Lucky Jews,* 166, and 157–174.

28. "Warsaw," in *YIVO Encyclopedia,* http://www.yivoencyclopedia.org/article.aspx /Warsaw; "Encyclopedia Judaica: New York City," http://www.jewishvirtuallibrary.org /newyorkcity; "Budapest," in *YIVO Encyclopedia,* http://www.yivoencyclopedia.org /article.aspx/budapest.

29. Misnagdim," in *YIVO Encyclopedia,* http://www.yivoencyclopedia.org/article .aspx/misnagdim; "Haskalah," in *YIVO Encyclopedia,* http://www.yivoencyclopedia .org/article.aspx/haskalah.

30. "Warsaw," in *YIVO Encyclopedia*.

31. Allan Nadler, "Litvak," in *YIVO Encyclopedia*, http://www.yivoencyclopedia.org /article.aspx/Litvak.

32. Ury, *Barricades and Banners*.

33. Michael C. Steinlauf, "The Polish-Jewish Daily Press," *POLIN* 2 (1987): 219–245.

34. Ibid.; Ury, *Barricades and Banners*.

35. Barbara Engelking and Jacek Leociak, *The Warsaw Ghetto: A Guide to the Perished City* (New Haven: Yale University Press, 2009).

36. "Warsaw," in *Holocaust Encyclopedia*, https://www.ushmm.org/wlc/en/article .php?ModuleId=10005069.

37. Karen Auerbach, *The House at Ujazdowski 16: Jewish Families in Warsaw after the Holocaust* (Bloomington: Indiana University Press, 2013).

38. Dariusz Stola, "Fighting against the Shadows: The Anti-Zionist Campaign of 1968," in *Antisemitism and Its Opponents in Modern Poland*, ed. Robert Blobaum (Ithaca: Cornell University Press, 2005), 284–300.

39. Ibid.

40. "Poland Jewish Heritage Tour," http://www.polandjewishheritagetours.com /Poland_Tour.php.

41. Leaflet, "Free Walking Tour: Warsaw," advertises a "Jewish Warsaw" tour at 4 pm every day from April to October; "Discover Jewish Europe; Discover Jewish Warsaw," Milk and Honey Tours, http://www.milkandhoneytours.com/en/jewish_tours/warsaw/.

42. Helise Lieberman, interview with the author, March 11, 2013, Warsaw, Poland.

43. "Warsaw for You," TripAdvisor, https://www.tripadvisor.com/Attraction_Review -g274856-d2208940-Reviews-Warsaw_For_You_Warsaw_Mazovia_Province_Central _Poland.html. Szymon Nowicki, a pseudonym, worked as a guide starting in October 2012, http://www.yourdest.com/UK/PAGE_Guide.awp?Guide=267. By 2016 he had created his own company, Walking Tour of Warsaw, @ Warsaw4U.com, http://www .warsaw4u.com/contact/.

For an excellent critical look at Warsaw's Free Walking Tours, see Sabine Stach, "Narrating Jewish History in Free Walking Tours: Warsaw as a Case Study," *Kultura Popularna* 51, no. 1 (2017): 77–91.

44. Henryk Berlewi, "'The Winding Paths of Jewish Art,' 1955," text accompanying *18901939* exhibit, Jewish Historical Institute, Warsaw, November 2015.

45. Ibid., 25.

46. Two landmark books by Judith R. Walkowitz, *Prostitution and Victorian Society*, and *Nights Out* are good introductions to the substantial literature on the history of prostitution.

47. *Field Guide*, 50.

48. Ibid., 53.

49. "70 Years after WW2 Erupted, A New Battle for History Rages in Europe," *Guardian*, November 11, 2009. Warsaw's Poles did not face death camps, and the Home Army's decision against overwhelming odds, which resulted in the decimation of the city's remaining civilian population, has been variously seen as heroic and suicidal.

50. My diary of my visit records seeing this on the website then. The new interactive website in 2016 does not use the quote, as best I can determine.

51. *Warsaw In Your Pocket.*

52. Kirshenblatt-Gimblett interview; Gross, *Neighbors.*

53. The program director of the Core Exhibit presents her view of the exhibit's guiding principles, Barbara Kirshenblatt-Gimblett, "A Theatre of History: 12 Principles," *TDR: The Drama Review* 59, no. 3 (Fall 2015): 49–50. See also her "Historical Space and Critical Museologies" and "Museum of the History of Polish Jews: Postwar, Post-Holocaust, Post-Communist Story," in *Jewish Space,* chap. 12.

54. In conversation with the author Kirshenblatt-Gimblett described some pushback POLIN'S curators received from some scholars (and politicians) wanting to soften the exhibit's comments on Polish anti-Semitism and from some Jewish critics who want the treatment of the Holocaust expanded. See also Saul Friedlander, *The Years of Extermination, 1939–1945* (New York: HarperCollins, 2007).

55. Returning to POLIN for an international conference in spring 2017, visitors were invited to write notes with their impressions, questions and recommendations. It was a modest start to what curators more widely acknowledge to be a thorny challenge for museums.

CONCLUSION

1. Ruth A. Wisse, *No Jokes: Making Jewish Humor* (Princeton: Princeton University Press, 2013).

2. Kugelmass, "The Rites of the Tribe," 417; Kamil interview; Matthew Frye Jacobson, *Special Sorrow: The Diasporic Imagination of Irish, Polish, and Jewish Immigrants to the United States* (Cambridge, MA: Harvard University Press, 1995), 243–239.

3. International March of the Living, http://motl.org; Feldman, *Above the Death Pits.*

4. Kugelmass, "The Rites of the Tribe," 402.

5. Wynn, *The Tour Guide.*

6. Ibid.

7. Schütz interview.

8. Holly Snyder, "Rethinking the Definition of 'Community' for a Migratory Age, 1654–1830," in *The Imagining of the American Jewish Community,* ed. Jack Kugelmass (Waltham, MA: Brandeis University Press, 2007), 3–17.

9. *Soundwalks* is available at https://www.timeout.com/newyork/things-to-do/listen-up-sound-walks-in-nyc.

10. See, for example, Elihu Rubin, "Catch My Drift: Situationist Derivé and Urban Pedagogy," 114 *RHR* 2012 (Fall): 175–190.

11. The online guide is available at http://warsze.polin.pl/en/.

12. Rabinowitz summarizes his career of work in public history across the United States in a recent book: Richard Rabinowitz, *Curating America: Journeys through Storyscapes of the American Past* (Chapel Hill: University of North Carolina Press, 2016).

13. Delores Hayden, *The Politics of Place: Urban Landscapes as Public History* (Cambridge: MIT Press, 1997).

14. Katka Reszke, *Return of the Jew: Identity Narratives of the Third Post-Holocaust Generation of Jews in Poland* (Boston: Academic Studies Press, 2013). Reszke's book is based on her oral histories collected from 2001 through 2011 with Poles discovering or "inventing" themselves as Jews in Poland. See also the authors' introduction in Lehrer and Meng, *Jewish Space in Contemporary Poland;* Lehrer's essay on Kazimierz in

Lucky Jews, 170–192; and Kirshenblatt-Gimblett "*Inside the Museum*: Curating between hope and despair; POLIN Museum of the History of Polish Jews," in Kirshenblatt-Gimlett and Gershenson, eds., "New Jewish Museums," and Kirshenblatt-Gimblett, "A Theatre of History: 12 Principles," *TDR: The Drama Review* 59, no. 3 (Fall 2015): 49–59.

Bibliography

INTERVIEWS WITH THE AUTHOR

Brumberg, Esther. July 1, 2013. New York City.

Kamil, Seth. August 2, 2013. Tannersville, NY.

Kirscenblatt-Gimblett, Barbara. March 13, 2013. Warsaw.

Kugelmann, Cilly. March 5, 2013, Berlin.

Pesci-Pollner, Katalin. March 27, 2015. Budapest.

Pindar, Olga Manolijlovic. October 14, 2012. Belgrade.

Rostovic, Milan. October 12, 2012. Belgrade.

Schoenberg, Phillip E. July 9, 2013, New York City.

Schütz, Chana. March 8, 2013. Berlin.

Śpewak, Paweł. March 11, 2013. Warsaw.

Szita, Szaboles, and Janos Botos. March 26, 2015. In Hungarian with an English translator.

Zatorska, Paulina. June 19, 2014. Łódź, Poland.

ORAL HISTORIES

Bernstein, Belle Walkowitz. October 9 and November 1980. Interviewed by Robert Snyder. Fairlawn, NJ. Jewish Historical Society of North Jersey. Fairlawn, NJ.

Walkowitz, Joseph. April 6, 1980. Interviewed by Randy Freeman and Jerry Nathans. Wayne, NJ. Jewish Historical Society of North Jersey. Fairlawn, NJ.

Walkowitz, Joseph. October 8, 1980. Interviewed by Robert Snyder. Fairlawn, NJ. Jewish Historical Society of North Jersey. Fairlawn, NJ.

GENERAL REFERENCE WORKS

Virtual Shtetl. POLIN Museum of the History of Polish Jews. Warsaw. http://www.sztetl .org.pl/en/.

The YIVO Encyclopedia of Jews in Eastern Europe. YIVO Institute for Jewish Research. New York. http://www.yivoencyclopedia.org.

SECONDARY SOURCES

Abramsky, Chimen, Maciej Jachimczk, and Antony Polonsly, eds. 1986, *The Jews in Poland*. Oxford: Basil Blackwell.

Alderman, Geoffrey. 1992. *Modern British Jewry*. Oxford: Oxford University Press.

Alderman, Geoffrey, ed. 2010. *New Directions in Anglo-Jewish History*. Boston: Academic Studies Press.

Anderson, Benedict. 1991. *Imagined Communities: Reflections on the Rise of Nationalism*. London: Verso.

Atkinson, David. "Heritage." In *Cultural Geography: A Critical Dictionary of Key Ideas*, edited by David Sibley et al., 141–148. London: I.B. Tauris, 2005.

Auberbach, Karen. 2013. *The House at Ujazdowski 16: Jewish Families in Warsaw after the Holocaust*. Bloomington: Indiana University Press.

Barragán, Paco. 2013. "Push to Flush: Culture of Impassivity." *ArtPulse: ArtPulse,* June 6, 2013, 1. http://artpulsemagazine.com/push-to-flush-culture-of-interpassivity.

Bartal, Israel. 2005. *The Jews of Eastern Europe, 1772–1881*. Trans. Chaya Naor. Philadelphia: University of Pennsylvania Press.

Bartov, Omer. 2007. *Erased: Vanishing Traces of Jewish Galicia in Present-Day Ukraine*. Princeton: Princeton University Press.

Becker, Elizabeth. 2013. *Overbooked: The Exploding Business of Travel and Tourism*. New York: Simon & Schuster.

Beckert, Sven. 2003. *The Monied Metropolis: New York City and the Consolidation of the American Bourgeoisie, 1850–1896*. New York: Cambridge University Press.

Bemporad, Elissa. 2013. *Becoming Soviet Jews: The Bolshevik Experiment in Minsk*. Bloomington: Indiana University Press.

Bilovitsky, Vladimir. 2010. "Institute of Jewish Proletarian Culture." In *YIVO Encyclopedia of Jews in Eastern Europe*. http://www.yivoencyclopedia.org/article.aspx/Institute _of_Jewish_Proletarian_Culture.

Bodnar, John. 1992. *Remaking America: Public Memory, Commemoration, and Patriotism in the Twentieth Century*. Princeton: Princeton University Press.

Boyarin, Jonathan. 2013. *Jewish Families*. New Brunswick: Rutgers University Press.

Boyarin, Jonathan. 1992. *Storm from Paradise: The Politics of Jewish Memory*. Minneapolis: University of Minnesota Press.

Brodkin, Karen. 1998. *How Jews Became White Folks and What That Says about Race in America*. New Brunswick: Rutgers University Press.

Butwin, Francis, and Joseph Butwin. 1977. *Sholem Aleichem*. Boston: G.H. Hall, 1977.

Cahan, Abraham. 1969. *The Education of Abraham Cahan*. Edited by Leon Stein. Philadelphia: Jewish Publication Society of America.

Cullen, Stephen M. 1912. "'Jewish Communists' or 'Communist Jews'? The Communist Party of great Britain and British Jews in the 1930s." *Socialist History* 12, no. 41: 22–42.

Czaplicka, John, ed. 2005. *Lviv: A City in the Crosscurrents of History*. Cambridge, MA: Harvard Ukrainian Research Institute.

Dauber, Jeremy. 2013. *The Worlds of Sholem Aleichem: The Remarkable Life and Afterlife of the Man Who Created Tevye*. New York: Schocken Books.

Diner, Hasia R. 1992. *A Time for Gathering: The Second Migration, 1820–1880*. Vol. 2 in *The Jewish People in America*. Edited by Henry Feingold. Baltimore: Johns Hopkins University Press.

Diner, Hasia R. 2000. *Lower East Side Memories: A Jewish Place in America.* Princeton: Princeton University Press.

Diner, Hasia R. 2002. *Lower East Side Memories: A Jewish Place in America.* 3rd ed. Princeton: Princeton University Press.

Diner, Hasia R. 2010. *We Remember with Reverence and Love: American Jews and the Myth of Silence after the Holocaust, 1945–1962.* New York: New York University Press.

Diner, Hasia R., and Beryl Benderly. 2002. *Her Works Praise Her: A History of Jewish Women in America from Colonial Times to the Present.* New York: Basic Books.

Diner, Hasia R., Jeffrey Shandler, and Beth S. Wenger, eds. 2000. *Remembering the Lower East Side: American Jewish Reflections.* Bloomington: Indiana University Press, 2000

Dyak, Sofia. 2011, October. *International Design Competition for Sites of Jewish History in Lviv/Ukraine: Documentation.* Lviv: City of Lviv.

Eley, Geoff. 2002. *Forging Democracy: The History of the Left in Europe, 1850–2000.* New York: Oxford University Press,

Endelmann, Todd M. 2002. *The Jews of Britain, 1656–2000.* Berkeley: University of California.

Engelking, Barbara, and Jacek Leociak. 2009. *The Warsaw Ghetto: A Guide to the Perished City.* New Haven: Yale University Press.

Estraikh, Gennady, and Mikhai Krutikov, eds. 2001. *Yiddish and the Left.* Oxford: European Humanities Research Centre.

Evans, Richard J. 1990. *Proletarians and Politics: Socialism, Protest, and the Working Class in Germany Before the First World War.* New York: St. Martin's Press.

Evans, Richard J. 2010. "Who Remembers the Poles." *London Review of Books* 32, no. 21: 21–22.

Feldman, David. 1994. *Englishman and Jews: Social Relation and Political Culture, 1840–1914.* New Haven: Yale University Press.

Feldman, Jackie. 2008. *Above the Death Pits, Beneath the Flag: Youth Voyages to Poland and the Performance of Israeli National Identity.* New York: Berghahn Books.

Frankel, Jonathan. 1981. *Prophecy and Politics: Socialism, Nationalism, and the Russian Jews, 1862–1917.* Cambridge: Cambridge University Press.

Friedenreich, Harriet Bass. 1979. *The Jews of Yugoslavia: A Quest for Community.* Philadelphia: Jewish Publication Society of America.

Friedlander, Saul. 2007. *The Years of Extermination, 1939–1945.* New York: HarperCollins.

Gillis, John R. 1996. *Commemorations: The Politics of National Identity.* Princeton: Princeton University Press.

Gitelman, Zvi. 2001. *A Century of Ambivalence: The Jews of Russia and the Soviet Union, 1881 to the Present.* Rev. 2nd ed. Bloomington: Indiana University Press.

Gitelman, Zvi. 2003. *The Emergence of Modern Jewish Politics: Bundism and Zionism in Eastern Europe.* Pittsburgh: University of Pittsburgh Press.

Glatstein, Jacob. 2010. *The Glatstein Chronicles.* Edited with an introduction by Ruth Wisse. Trans. Maier Deshell and Norbert Guterman. New Haven: Yale University Press.

Glenn, Susan. 1991. *Daughters of the Shtetl: Life and Labor in the Immigrant Generation.* Ithaca: Cornell University Press.

Gmelch, Sharon Bohn. 2004. *Tourists and Tourism: A Reader.* Long Grove, IL: Waveland Press.

Gold, Michel. 1930. *Jews without Money.* New York: Horace Liveright.

Goldberg, Harvey E., Steven M. Cohen, and Ezra Kopelowitz, eds. 2012. *Dynamic Belonging: Contemporary Jewish Collective Identities*. New York: Berghahn Books.

Goldstein, Eric I. 2008. *The Price of Whiteness: Jews, Race, and American Identity*. Princeton: Princeton University Press.

Goren, Arthur A. 1978. *New York Jews and the Quest for Community: The Kehilla Experiment, 1908–1922*. New York: Columbia University Press.

Gornick, Vivian. 1979. *The Romance of American Communism*. New York: Basic Books.

Graham, Brian, and Peter Howard, eds. 2008. *The Aldgate Companion to Heritage and Identity*. Aldershot: Aldgate.

Greenbaum, Leo, and Marek Web, curators. 1998. *The Story of the Jewish Labor Bund, 1897–1997: A Centennial Exhibition*. New York: YIVO.

Greenspan, Leonard J., ed. 2011. *Fashioning Jews: Clothing, Culture, and Commerce*. Special issue of *Studies in Jewish Civilization* 24 (October).

Greenwald, Richard. 2005. *The Triangle Fire: The Protocols of Peace and Industrial Democracy in Progressive Era New York City*. Philadelphia: Temple University Press.

Gross, Jan T. 2004. "After Auschwitz: The Reality and Meaning of Postwar Anti-Semitism in Poland." In *Dark times, Dire Decisions, Jews and Communism*, edited by Jonathan Frankel, 199–226. New York: Oxford University Press.

Gross, Jan T. 2001. *Neighbors: The Destruction of the Jewish Community in Jedwabne, Poland*. Princeton: Princeton University Press.

Grossmann, Atina. 2006. *Jews, Germans, and Allies: Close Encounters in Occupied Germany*. Princeton: Princeton University Press.

Gruber, Ruth Ellen. 2007. *Jewish Heritage Travel: A Guide to Eastern Europe*. Washington, DC: National Geographic Society.

Gruber, Ruth Ellen. 2012. "Post-Trauma 'Precious Legacies': Jewish Museums in Eastern Europe after the Holocaust and before the Fall of Communism." In *Visualizing and Exhibiting Jewish Space and History*, edited by Richard I Cohen, 113–132. New York: Oxford University Press.

Gruber, Ruth Ellen. n.d. "A Virtual Jewish World." Lecture delivered at the Central European University. http://web.ceu.hu/jewishstudies/pdf/02_gruber.pdf.

Gruber, Ruth Ellen. 2002. *Virtually Jewish: Reinventing Jewish Culture in Europe*. Berkeley: University of California Press.

Gruber, Samuel D., et al. 2005. *Jewish Cemeteries, Synagogues and Mass Grave Sites in Ukraine*. Washington, DC: United States Commission for the Preservation of America's Heritage.

Gruner, Wolf. 2003. "The Factory Action and the Events at the Rosenstrasse in Berlin. Facts and Fictions about 27 February 1943—Sixty Years Later." *Central European History* 36: 178–208.

Gurock, Jeffrey S. 2012. *Jews in Gotham: New York Jews in a Changing Story, 1920–2010*. New York: New York University Press.

Halbwachs, Maurice. [1925] 1980. *On Collective Memory*. Trans. Francis H. Ditter, Jr., and Vida Yazdi Ditter. New York: Harper & Row.

Hall, Stuart. 1987. "Gramsci and Us." *Marxism Today*, June. http://www.hegemonics.co.uk/docs/Gramsci-and-us.pdf..

Hamm, Michael F. 1996. *Kiev: A Portrait, 1800–1917*. Princeton: Princeton University Press.

Harvey, D. C. 2008. *The History of Heritage.* In the Aldgate Companion to *Heritage and Identity,* edited by B. Graham and P. Howard, 19–36. Aldershot: Aldgate.

Hayden, Delores. 1997. *The Power of Place: Urban Landscapes as Public History.* Cambridge: MIT Press.

Hirsch, Marianne. 2012. *The Generation of Postmemory: Writing and Visual Culture after the Holocaust.* New York: Columbia University Press.

Hirsch, Marianne, and Leo Spitzer. 2011. *Ghosts of Home: The Afterlife of Czernowitz in Jewish Memory.* Berkeley: University of California Press.

Hobsbawm, Eric, and Terrence T. Ranger, eds. *The Invention of Tradition.* Cambridge: Cambridge University Press.

Hoffman, Eva. 2007. *Shtetl: The Life and Death of a Small Town and the World of Polish Jews.* New York: Houghton Mifflin.

Hoffman, Stefani, and Ezra Mendelsohn, eds. 2008. *The Revolution of 1905 and Russia's Jews.* Philadelphia: University of Pennsylvania Press.

Howe, Irving. [1976] 1989. *World of Our Fathers: The Journey of the East European Jews to America and the Life They Found and Made.* New York: Harcourt.

Ingram, Susan, and Katrina Sark. 2011. *Berliner Chic: A Locational History of Berlin Fashion.* Chicago: University of Chicago.

Jacobs, Jack, ed. 2009. *Bundist Counterculture in Interwar Poland.* Syracuse: Syracuse University Press.

Jacobs, Jack, ed. 2001. *Jewish Politics in Eastern Europe: the Bund at 100.* New York: New York University Press.

Jacobson, Matthew Frye. 1995. *Special Sorrow: The Diasporic Imagination of Irish, Polish, and Jewish Immigrants to the United States.* Cambridge, MA: Harvard University Press.

Jews of Dorcol: The Story of Our Neighbors Who Are No More. 1997. Exhibition Guide. Belgrade. http://rexpro.b92.net/rexold/jewsdet.htm.

Judt, Tony. 2005. *Postwar: A History of Europe since 1945.* New York: Penguin Press.

Kalandides, Ares. 2011. "Place Identities: Multiple Narratives from Prenzlauer Berg." PhD diss., National Technical University of Athens.

Kalnytskyi, Mykhailo. 2012. *Jewish Addresses in Kiev, a Guide Book.* Kiev: Dukh I Litera.

Kamenetz, Rodger. 1994. *The Jew and the Lotus: A Poetic Rediscovery of Jewish Identity in Buddhist India.* New York: HarperCollins.

Kamil, Seth, and Eric Wakin, 2003. *The Big Onion Guide to New York City: Ten Historic Tours.* New York: New York University Press.

Kammen, Michael. 1991. *Mystic Chords of Memory: The Transformation of Tradition in American Culture; The Transformation of Tradition in American Culture.* New York: Knopf.

Kaplan, Marion A. 1994. *The Making of a Jewish Middle Class: Women, Family, and Identity in Imperial Germany.* New York: Oxford University Press.

Kassow, Samuel D. 2001. "The Left Poale Zion in Inter-War Poland." In *Yiddish and the Left,* edited by Gennady Estriakh and Mikhail Krutikov, 109–128. Oxford: European Humanities Research Centre.

Kassow, Samuel D. 2007. *Who Will Write Our History? Emanuel Ringelblum, the Warsaw Ghetto, and the Oyneg Shabes Archive.* Bloomington: Indiana University Press.

Katriel, Tamar. 1997. *Performing the Past: A Study of Israeli Settlement Museums.* Mahwah, NJ: Lawrence Erlbaum Associates.

Katz, Daniel. 2011. *All Together Different: Yiddish Socialist, Garment Workers, and the Roots of Multiculturalism*. New York: New York University Press.

Katz, David S. 1994. *The Jews in the History of England, 1485–1850*. Oxford: Oxford University Press.

Katz, Joseph T., ed. *The Shtetl: New Evaluations*. New York: New York University Press.

Kayton, David. 2003. *Radical Walking Tours of New York City*. New York: Seven Sisters Press.

Kirshenblatt-Gimblett, Barbara. 1998. *Destination Culture: Tourism, Museums and Heritage*. Berkeley: University of California.

Kirshenblatt-Gimblett, Barbara. 2015. "Historical Space and Critical Methodologies: Museum of the History of Polish Jews." In *From Museum Critique to Critical Museum*, edited by Katarzyna Murawska-Muthesius and Piotr Piotrowski. London: Ashgate.

Kirshenblatt-Gimblett, Barbara. 2015. "A Theatre of History: 12 Principles." *TDR: The Drama Review* 59, no. 3 (Fall): 49–59.

Kirshenblatt-Gimblett, Barbara, and Olga Gershenson, eds. 2015. "New Jewish Museums in Post-Communist Europe." Special issue of *East European Jewish Affairs* 45, nos. 2–3 (August–December).

Komoroczy, Geza, ed. [1995] 1999. *Jewish Budapest: Monuments, Rites, History*. Budapest: Budapest Central European University Press.

Koyfman, Harry. 1991. "From a Stormy Time." In *Pincus Zyrardow, Amshinov un Viskit*. Buenos Aires.

Kremer, Roberta S., ed. 2007. *Broken Threads: the Destruction of the Jewish Fashion Industry in Germany and Austria*. Oxford: Berg.

Kugelmass, Jack, ed. 1988. *Between Two Worlds: Ethnographic Essays on American Jewry*. Ithaca: Cornell University Press.

Kugelmass, Jack, ed. 1993. "Going Home." *YIVO Annual* 2. Evanston, IL: Northwestern University Press.

Kugelmass, Jack, ed. 2007. *The Imagining of the American Jewish Community*. Waltham, MA: Brandeis University Press.

Kuller, Hary, and Lya Benjamin. 2012. *The History Museum of the Romanian Jews: Chief-Rabbi Dr. Moses Rosen*. Bucharest: Hasefer Publishing House.

Large, David Clay. 2000. *Berlin*. New York: Basic Books.

Lebel, Jennie. 2007. *Until the "Final Solution": The Jews in Belgrade, 1521–1942*. Trans. Paul Münch. New Haven, CT: Avotaynu.

Lehrer, Erica. 2013. *Jewish Poland Revisited: Unquiet Tourism in Unquiet Places*. Bloomington: Indiana University Press.

Lehrer, Erica. 2014. *Lucky Jews: Poland's Jewish Figurines*. Kraków: Korporacja Halart.

Lehrer, Erica, and Michael Meng, eds. 2015. *Jewish Space in Contemporary Poland*. Bloomington: Indiana University Press.

Lev Ari, Lilach, and David Mittelberg. 2008. "Between Authenticity and Ethnicity: Heritage Tourism and Re-Ethnification among Diaspora Jewish youth." *Journal of Heritage Tourism* 3, no. 2: 79–103.

Levenberg, S. Mar. 1966. "Dreamers and Fighters." Reprinted in "100 Years of Jewish Labour Movement in Britain." *Poale Zion Labour Zionist Movement*, January 1967.

Lowenthal, David. 1985. *The Past Is a Foreign Country*. Cambridge: Cambridge University Press.

Lundberg, Donald E., M. Krishnamoorthy, and Mink H. Stavenga. 1995. *Tourism Economics*. New York: John Wiley.

Macdonald, Sharon. 2013. *Memorylands: Heritage and Identity in Europe Today*. London: Routledge.

McCagg, William O. 1992. *A History of Hapsburg Jews, 1670–1918*. Bloomington: Indiana University Press.

Meir, Natan M. 2010. *Kiev: Jewish Metropolis: A History, 1859–1914*. Bloomington: Indiana University Press.

Mendelsohn, Daniel. 2006. *The Lost: A Search for Six of Six Million*. New York: HarperPerennial.

Mendelsohn, Ezra. 1970, *Class Struggle in the Pale: The Formative Years of the Jewish Workers' Movement in Tsarist Russia*. Cambridge: Cambridge University Press.

Mendelsohn, Ezra. 1987. *The Jews of East Central Europe between the World Wars*. Bloomington: Indiana University Press.

Mendelsohn, Ezra. 1993. *On Modern Jewish Politics*. New York: Oxford University Press.

Meng, Michael. 2011. *Shattered Spaces: Encountering Jewish Ruins in Postwar German and Poland*. Cambridge, MA: Harvard University Press.

Michels, Tony. 2005. *A Fire in Their Hearts: Yiddish Socialists in New York*. Cambridge, MA: Harvard University Press.

Michels, Tony. 2001. "Socialisms with a Jewish Face: The Origins of the Yiddish-Speaking Communist Movement in the United States, 1907–1923." In *Yiddish and the Left*, edited by Gennady Estriakh and Mikhail Krutikov, 24–55. Oxford: European Humanities Research Centre.

Mishler, Paul C. 1999. *Raising Reds: The Young Pioneers, Radical Summer Camps, and Communist Political Culture in the United States*. New York: Columbia University Press.

Mitchell, William E. 1978. *Mishpokhe: A Study of New York City Jewish Family Circles*. The Hague: Mouton.

Moore, Deborah Dash. 1981. *At Home in America: Second Generation New York Jews*. New York: Columbia University Press.

Moore, Deborah Dash. 1981. *B'nai B'rith and the Challenge of Ethnic Leadership*. Albany: State University of New York Press.

Moss, Kenneth B. 2008. "1905 as a Jewish Cultural Revolution? Revolutionary and Evolutionary Dynamics in the East European Jewish Cultural Sphere, 1900–1914." In *The Revolution of 1905 and Russia's Jews*, edited by Stafani Hoffman and Ezra Mendelsohn, 185–198. Philadelphia: University of Pennsylvania Press.

Nachama, Andreas, Julius H. Schoeps, and Hermann Simon, eds. [2001] 2002. *Jews in Berlin*. Trans. Michael S. Cullen and Allison Brown. Berlin: Henschel.

Nora, Pierre. 1996–1998. *Realms of Memory: Construction of the French Past*. 3 vols. Trans. Arthur Goldhammer. New York: Columbia University Press.

Novack, Peter. 2000. *The Holocaust in American Life*. New York: Mariner Books.

Noy, Chaim. 2007. *A Narrative Community: Voices of Jewish Backpackers*. Detroit: Wayne State University Press.

Olczak-Ronikier, Joanna. [2001] 2004. *In the Garden of Memory: A Memoir*. London: Weidenfeld & Nicolson.

Olsztajn, Mauricio. 1976. "The Beginnings of Jewish Settlement in Łódź." In *"Łódź"— Encyclopedia of Jewish Communities in Poland*. Vol. 1. Trans. Morris Gradel. Jerusalem: Yad Vashem.

Opler, Daniel. *For All White-Collar Workers: The Possibilities of Radicalism in New York City's Department Store Unions, 1934–1953*. Columbus: Ohio State University Press.

Ostow, Robin. 1989. *Jews in Contemporary East Germany: The Children of Moses in the Land of Marx.* New York: Palgrave Macmillan.

Patkin, A. L. 1947. *Origins of the Russian-Jewish Labour Movement.* Melbourne: Cheshire.

Pawlikowski, Pawel, dir. 2013. *Ida.* 82 min. Poland.

Perman, Stacy. July 25, 2007. "The Right Questions: German Conceptual Artists Find Provocative Ways to Confront the Holocaust." *Tablet: Visual Art & Design,* July 25. http://www.tabletmag.com/jewish-arts-and-culture/719/the-right-questions.

Petrovsky-Shtern, Yohanen. 2009. *Anti-Imperial Choice: The Making of the Ukrainian Jew.* New Haven: Yale University Press.

Petrovsky-Shtern, Yohanen. 2014. *The Golden Age of the Shtetl: A New History of Jewish Life in East Europe.* Princeton: Princeton University Press.

Pew Research Center. October 1, 2013. "A Portrait of Jewish Americans." Religion & Public Life Project. http://www.jewishdatabank.org/studies/details.cfm?StudyID=715.

Pfaller, Robert. 1998. "The Work of Art That Observes Itself. Eleven Steps towards an Aesthetics of Interpassivity." In *Presencias en el espacio publico contemporaneo,* edited by Centro de studios por la scultura publica ambiental, 229–240. Barcelona.

Polonsky, Antony. [1993] 2011. *From Shtetl to Socialism: Studies from POLIN.* Oxford: Littman Library of Jewish Civilization. http://hdl.handle.net/2027/heb.31317.0001 .001.

Polonsky, Antony. 2009. *The Jews in Poland and Russia.* 3 vols. Liverpool: University of Liverpool Press.

Polonsky, Antony. 2005. *POLIN Studies in Polish Jewry.* Vol. 6: *Jews in Lodz, 1820–1939.* Liverpool: Liverpool University Press.

Polland, Annie. Dec. 2007. "'May a Freethinker Help a Pious Man': The Shared World of the 'Religious' and the 'Secular' among Eastern European Jewish Immigrants to America." *American Jewish History* 93, no. 4: 375–407.

Polland, Annie, and Daniel Soyer. *Emerging Metropolis: New York Jews in the Age of Immigration, 1840–1920.* New York: New York University Press.

Porter, Anna. 2009. *Kasztner's Train: The True Story of an Unknown Hero of the Holocaust.* New York: Walker Books.

Rabinowitz, Richard. 2016. *Curating America: Journeys through Storyscapes of the American Past.* Chapel Hill: University of North Carolina Press.

Radovanovic, Vojislave. 2010. *The Jewish Historical Museum in Belgrade.* Belgrade: Federation of Jewish Communities of Serbia.

Radu, Ioanid. 2005. *The Ransom of the Jews: The Story of the Extraordinary Secret Bargain between Romania and Israel.* Lanham, MD: Ivan R. Dee.

Rampley, Matthew, ed. 2012. *Heritage, Ideology, and Identity in Central and Eastern Europe: Contested Pasts, Contested Presents.* Woodbridge, Suffolk: Boydell Press.

Reszke, Katka. 2013. *Return of the Jew: Identity Narratives of the Third Post-Holocaust Generation of Jews in Poland.* Boston: Academic Studies Press.

Riedle, Andrea, ed. 2011. *Sites of Remembrance, 1933–1945.* Berlin: n.p.

Rischin, Moses. 1978. *The Promised City: New York's Jews, 1870–1914.* Cambridge, MA: Harvard University Press.

Roach, Joe H. 2000. "Women in the American Communist Party and How Their Party Activities Affected Them as Wives and Mothers." PhD diss., New York University.

Rock, Howard B. 2012. *Haven of Liberty*. New York: New York University Press.

Rogoff, Harry. 1930. *An East Side Epic: The Life and Times of Meyer London*. New York: Vantage Press.

Roskies, David G. 2008. *Yiddishlands*. Detroit: Wayne State University Press.

Samuel, Raphael. 1985. "The Lost World of British Communists." *New Left Review* 154 (November–December). https://newleftreview.org/I/154/raphael-samuel-the-lost-world -of-british-communism.

Samuel, Raphael. 1994. *Theatres of Memory: Past and Present in Contemporary Culture*. London: Verso.

Sanders, Ronald. 1969. *The Downtown Jews: Portraits of an Immigrant Generation*. New York: Dover Publications.

Sarna, Jonathan D. *American Judaism: A History*. New Haven: Yale University Press.

Shandler, Jeffrey. 2006. *Adventures in Yiddishand: Postvernacular Language and Culture*. Berkeley: University of California Press.

Shandler, Jeffrey. 2014. *Shtetl: A Vernacular Intellectual History*. New Brunswick: Rutgers University Press.

Shandler Jeffrey, and Jack Kugelmass. 1989. "Going Home: How American Jews Invent the Old World." Exhibition catalogue. New York: YIVO institute for Jewish Research.

Silber, Michael K. 1987. "The Historical Experience of German Jewry and Its Impact on Haskalah and Reform in Hungary." In *Toward Modernity: The European Jewish Model*, edited by Jacob Katz, 107–157. New Brunswick: Transaction Books.

Silber, Michael K. 1992. "The Emergence of Ultra-Orthodoxy: The Invention of Tradition." In: *The Uses of Tradition: Jewish Continuity since Emancipation*, edited by Jack Wertheimer, 23–84. New York: Jewish Theological Seminary:.

Singer, Israel Joshua. [1936] 1980. *The Brothers Ashkenazi*. Trans. Joseph Singer. New York: Scribner.

Smith, Melanie, and László Puezko. 2010. "Out with the Old, in with the New? Twenty Years of Post Socialist Marketing in Budapest," *Journal of Town & City Management* 3: 288–299.

Smith, Melanie, and László Puezko. 2012. "Budapest: From Socialist Heritage to Cultural Capital?" *Current Issues in Tourism* 15, nos. 1–2: 107–119.

Snyder, Holly. 2007. "Rethinking the Definition of 'Community' for a Migratory Age: 1654–1830." In *Imagining the American Jewish Community*, edited by Jack Wertheimer, 2–17. Waltham, MA: Brandeis University Press.

Snyder, Robert. 1984. "The Paterson Jewish Folk Chorus: Politics, Ethnicity and Musical Culture." *American Jewish History* 75, no. 1: 27–44.

Snyder, Timothy. 2010. *Bloodlands*. New York: Basic Books.

Solomon, Alisa. 2013. *Wonder of Wonders: A Cultural History of Fiddler on the Roof*. New York: Henry Holt.

Soyer, Daniel. 1993. "The Immigrant Travel Agent as Broker between Old World and New: The Case of Gustave Eisner." In *YIVO Annual* 21: 345–368.

Soyer, Daniel. 1997. *Jewish Immigrant Associations and American Identity in New York, 1880–1939*. Cambridge, MA: Harvard University Press.

Soyer, Daniel. 2000. "Back to the Future: American Jews Visit the Soviet Union in the 1920s and 1930s." *Jewish Social Studies* (Spring–Summer): 124–159.

Soyer, Daniel. 2001. "Abraham Cahan's Travels to Jewish Homelands: Palestine in 1925 and the Soviet Union in 1927." In *Yiddish and the Left*, edited by Gennady Estriakh and Mikhail Krutikov, 56–79. Oxford: European Humanities Research Centre.

Soyer, Daniel. 2003. "Revisiting the Old World: American Jewish Tourists in Interwar Eastern Europe." In *Forging Modern Jewish Identities*, edited by Michael Berkowitz, Susan Tananbaum, and Sam Bloom. London: Valentine-Mitchell.

Soyer, Daniel. 2005. "Soviet Travel and the Making of an American Jewish Communist: Moissaye Olgin's Trip to Russia, 1920–1921." *American Communist History* 4, no. 1 (June): 1–20.

Soyer, Daniel. 2007. "Transnationalism and Americanization in East European Jewish Immigrant Public Life." In *Imagining the American Jewish Community*, edited by Jack Wertheimer. Waltham, MA: Brandeis University Press published by University Press of New England.

Srebrnik, Henry. 2001. "Diaspora, Ethnicity and Dreams of Nationhood: American Jewish Communism and the Birobidzhan Project." In *Yiddish and the Left*, edited by Gennady Estriakh and Mikhail Krutikov, 80–108. Oxford: European Humanities Research Centre.

Steinlauf, Michael C. 1997. *Bondage to the Dead: Poland and the Memory of the Holocaust*. Syracuse: Syracuse University Press.

Steinlauf, Michael C. 1987. "The Polish-Jewish Daily Press." *POLIN* 2: 219–245.

Stola, Dariusz. 2005. "Fighting against the Shadows: The Anti-Zionist Campaign of 1968." In *Antisemitism and Its Opponents in Modern Poland*. edited by Robert Blobaum, 284–300. Ithaca: Cornell University Press.

Tuttle, William M. 1970. *Race Riot: Chicago in the Red Summer of 1919*. Urbana: Illinois University Press.

Ury, Scott. 2012. *Barricades and Banners: The Revolution of 1905 and the Transformation of Warsaw Jewry*. Stanford: Stanford University Press.

Valley, Eli. 1999. *The Great Jewish Cities of Central and Eastern Europe*. Northvale, NJ: Jason Aronson.

Wajda, Andrzej, dir. 1975. *The Promised Land*. 179 minutes. Poland.

Waligórska, Magdalena. 2013. *Klezmer's Afterlife: An Ethnography of the Jewish Music Revival in Poland and Germany*. New York: Oxford University Press.

Walkowitz, Daniel J. [2010] 2014. *City Folk: The Transatlantic Politics of the Folk in Modern America*. New York: New York University Press.

Walkowitz, Daniel J. 1999. *Working with Class: Social Workers and the Politics of Middle-Class Identity*. Chapel Hill: University of North Carolina Press.

Walkowitz, Daniel J., and Lisa Maya Knauer, eds. 2004. *Memory and the Impact of Political Transformation in Public Space*. Durham: Duke University Press.

Walkowitz, Judith R. 2012. *Nights Out: Life in Cosmopolitan London*. London: Yale University Press.

Walkowitz, Judith R. 1980. *Prostitution and Victorian Society: Women, Class and the State*. New York: Cambridge University Press.

Wallach, Kerry. 2010. "Weimar Fashion Chic: Jewish Women and Fashion in 1920s Germany." *Fashioning Jews: Clothing, Culture, and Commerce*. Special issue of *Studies in Jewish Civilization* 24 (October): 114–120.

Wallerstein, Jane. 2000. *Voices from the Paterson Silk Mills*. Collingdale, PA: Diane Publishing.

Wasserman, Suzanne Rachel. 1990. "The Good Old Days of Poverty: The Battle over the Fate of New York City's Lower East Side during the Depression." PhD diss., New York University.

Waterston, Alisse. 2014. *My Father's Wars: Migration, Memory, and the Violence of a Century.* New York: Routledge.

Webber, Jonathan. 2009. *Rediscovering Traces of Memory: The Jewish Heritage of Polish Galicia.* Bloomington: Indiana University Press.

Wenger, Beth S. 1997. "Memory as Identity: The Invention of the Lower East Side." *American Jewish History* 85, no. 1: 3–27.

Wertheimer, Jack. 1987. *Unwelcome Strangers: East European Jews in Imperial Germany.* New York: Oxford University Press.

Westphal, Uwe. 1986. *Berlin Konfektion und Mode: Der Zerstörung einer Tradition, 1836–1939.* Berlin: Edition Hentrich.

White, Jerry. 2012. *London in the Eighteenth Century.* London: Bodley Head.

White, Jerry. 2007. *London in the Nineteenth Century.* London: Jonathan Cape.

White, Jerry. 2001. *London in the Twentieth Century.* London: Viking.

White, Jerry. [1980] 2003. *Rothschild Buildings: Life in an East-End Tenement Block, 1887–1920.* Rev. ed. London: Pimlico.

White, Norval, and Elliot Willensky. 2004. *AIA Guide to New York City.* 4th ed. New York: Three Rivers Press, 2000.

Wisse, Ruth A. 2013. *No Jokes: Making Jewish Humor.* Princeton: Princeton University Press.

Wodziński, Marcin. 2004. "Good Maskilim and Bad Assimilationists, or Toward a New Historiography of the Haskalah in Poland." Trans. Sarah Cozens. *Jewish Social Studies* 10, no. 3: 87–122.

Wodziński, Marcin, 2004. "Language, Ideology, and the Beginnings of the Integrationist Movement in the Kingdom of Poland in the 1860s." *East European Jewish Affairs* 34, no. 2: 21–40.

Wodziński, Marcin. 2002. "Languages of the Jewish Community in Polish Silesia (1922–1939)." *Jewish History* 16, no. 2 (2002): 131–160.

Wolff, Larry. 2010. *The Idea of Galicia: History and Fantasy in Hapsburg Political Culture.* Stanford: Stanford University Press.

Wynn, Jonathan R. 2011. *The Tour Guide: Walking and Talking New York.* Chicago: University of Chicago Press.

Yiddish Lodz; A Yizkor Book. 1974. Trans. Yocheved Klausner. Melbourne: Lodzer Center.

Young, James, ed. 1994. *The Texture of Memory: Holocaust Memorials and Meaning.* New Haven: Yale University Press.

Katarzyna Zimmerer, Katarzya. 2017. *Kronika Zamorowanego Świata: Żylzi w Krakowie w czasie okupacji niemieckiej* [The Chronicle of a murdered world: Jews in Kraków during the occupation]. Kraków: Wydawnictwo Literackie.

Index

About the Author

Daniel J. Walkowitz is emeritus professor of history and emeritus professor of social and cultural analysis at New York University, where he founded and codirected the graduate program in public history (1980–1989), directed the metropolitan studies program (1989–2003), and served as inaugural director of the program in college honors (2003–2006) and director of experiential education (2006–2009). A labor and urban historian associated with the development of both the new social history and public history in the 1970s, he is the author or editor of ten books and four films for public television. His books include *Worker City, Company Town: Protest among Troy Iron Workers and Cohoes Iron Workers, 1955–84* (1978), *Working with Class: Social Workers and the Politics of Middle-Cass Identity in America* (1998); *City Folk: English Country Dance and the Politics of the Folk in America* (2010).